AFRICAN CINEMAS

AFRICAN CINEMAS

DECOLONIZING THE GAZE

OLIVIER BARLET

Translated by Chris Turner

LIBRARY
FRANKLIN PIERCE COLLEGE
RINDGE, NH 03461

ZED BOOKS
London & New York

African Cinemas: Decolonizing the Gaze was first published in French
under the title *Les Cinémas d'Afrique noire* in 1996 by L'Harmattan, Paris

This English translation was first published in 2000 by
Zed Books Ltd, 7 Cynthia Street, London N1 9JF, UK,
and Room 400, 175 Fifth Avenue, New York, NY 10010, USA

Distributed in the USA exclusively by St Martin's Press, Inc.,
175 Fifth Avenue, New York, NY 10010, USA

Copyright © Olivier Barlet 1996
Translation copyright © Chris Turner 2000

Translation made possible by the Fondation Charles Léopold Mayer
pour le Progrès de l'Homme
Ouvrage publié avec le concours du Ministère français charge de la Culture
– Centre nationale du livre

The rights of Olivier Barlet to be identified as the author of this
work has been asserted by him in accordance with the Copyright,
Designs and Patents Act, 1988

Designed and typeset in Monotype Garamond
by Illuminati, Grosmont.
Cover designed by Andrew Corbett
Printed and bound in the United Kingdom by Bookcraft (Bath) Ltd

All rights reserved

A catalogue record for this book is available from the British Library

Library of Congress Cataloging-in-Publication Data applied for

ISBN 1 85649 742 9 (Hb)
ISBN 1 85649 743 7 (Pb)

PN
1993.5
.A35
B3713
2000

CONTENTS

PART III **BLACK PROSPECTS?**

PREFACE

You lie when you assert that we are the same.
I call on this people to bear witness before history
We are not what we are!

Francis Bebey, 'Concert pour un vieux masque'

This book has been a trap.

My initial intention was purely journalistic. The aim was simply to take a phenomenon and describe it, hoping thereby to connect my two passions – Africa and cinema. But the complexity and diversity of the subject rapidly overtook me. If I was confronting the Western view of African cinema, I could not remain at a simplistic level without running the risk of lapsing into what I was seeking to condemn: platitude and pretence.

I was, however, intent on avoiding hermeticism and jargon, since this book is intended, first and foremost, as an *invitation to a voyage*. To a voyage to another continent, of course, but also to an inner journey. Opening oneself up to a different kind of cinema is not a neutral act, since what is at stake is a questioning of one's own way of looking. This requires courage, for it involves confronting one's own origins. But the detour is a profitable one, since it is one of the ways of not remaining stuck in those origins and hence escaping stupidity: the stupidity of complacency and universal truth.

Africa is plural and so is its cinema. Hence the reference to African cinema*s*. There is, however, also a great unity to Black Africa – in a continent which was for many years isolated from the rest of the world, but has seen so many teeming migrations. Black African civilizations are multiple, but these influxes of different populations have established a community of culture which does not end with polygamy or hereditary monarchy. The search for consensual decision-making in assemblies, the primacy of kinship relations, an integrative upbringing, the pursuit of harmony in social relations and the value accorded to the vital force of the individual are common features, overarched by a sense of meaning sought in life itself, and not in some transcendent realm. The respect for ancestors does not prevent the Senegalese director Moussa Sene Absa from writing on a wall in his film *Yalla Yaana* (1995): 'Life is just a stage. Everyone plays his role and disappears.'

The absence of indigenous cinema industries prevents African cinema from achieving a sense of individual national identities. How many people know a particular director's origins? As far as most are concerned, he or she is just an African! Yet many 'African filmmakers' feel cramped by that label, which hangs restrictively around their necks, connecting them, among other things, with the imperfections of others, but most importantly subjecting them to the scornful or paternalistic vision of the Western viewer. Like so many non-Western practitioners, they argue that they are not making 'African' films: they are artists; they are making films.

My approach is thematic in the first part, narrative in the second and economic in the third. But the subject is the same throughout: our view of the Other and of other countries. Rather than seeking out purported truths, I have tried to give in to disorientation: how is it that this return to origins, in which Black African cinemas engage in their quest for identity, affects me so deeply? How do fictions, images, language and sound come to convey this questing, and what is its cultural basis? How can people remain creative in the face of the constant problems of raising money and finding an audience? My conclusion will be that African cinema invites us in to a genuine process of learning how to look. I have set aside all chronology, and rejected documentary rigour to embrace diversity. I have tried to let the filmmakers speak as much as possible, and been playful about my section headings so as to leave a degree of uncertainty, in order to focus on films as they come to mind and take the reader with me on a journey in which we don't always know what lies around the next corner...

This is an invitation to a voyage, then. But it is a short one, given the limitations of a book and the limitations of writing in general where images are concerned. There is a Yoruba proverb which says: 'Even when there are lots of them, words don't fill up a basket.' But it is an adventure in which complexity may bring forth some simple ideas, for Africa, better than anyone or anything else, teaches us that everything is connected, and to isolate things would yet again be reductive.

I have settled on one *parti pris*, which some may regard as questionable. I am never negative about the form of a film. This has nothing to do with that widely shared paternalism which implies that African films are 'slightly flawed, but very attractive all the same'. My concern, rather, was not to consign a film to oblivion with one stroke of the pen with snap judgements which leave no time for analysis. The reader will easily see which films I like, but that is not central to my concerns here. The aim, rather, is to appreciate the advantages of another way of seeing. This book will not engage in the eternal business of comparison with our own cinema.

'Why is he putting his hand in a shirt that is not his own?' some will ask.[1] As Amadou Hampâté Bâ has said: 'When the goat's there, you don't have to do the bleating for it!'[2] I believe I have understood that there is no point speaking for others. This book in no way aspires to write the history of African cinema in the Africans' stead. My concern is with my own way of looking. Africa and its cinema – that is to say, the way that continent looks at itself and at the world – help me to root out from my own looking an aspect which was unwittingly concealed within it: that terrible way of referring everything back to oneself, of believing one is universal – which leads to destroying the Other and, ultimately, destroying oneself – and that aestheticiz-ation of the world which leads us to look for seductiveness rather than understanding in the image of the Other. But do not expect to find traces of some sort of guilt here. What there is is simply the desire that this book should be, as Kafka put it, 'the axe which breaks the sea frozen inside us'.

Africa and its cinema have helped me to understand that the weariness I often feel when I look at images produced here in the West has a meaning. In a word, there is hope. There is another way of looking, even if it is painful – and contradictory. And this way of looking awakens within me that element which speaks to me of my belonging to humanity. And there is much to discover, much to understand. With this one pleasant certainty: that questioning brings the beginnings of an answer. As the filmmaker from Guinea-Bissau Flora Gomes told me: 'Asking oneself the question is the beginning of understanding something.'

Amadou Hampâté Bâ also explained that a human life contains nine stages of seven years each. Between the ages of one and seven, the child is taught by his mother, then between seven and fourteen he is taught at school, though he also checks with his mother that what he is told is true. Between fourteen and twenty-one he reasons and may possibly confront his mother. Over the next twenty-one years he comes to a deeper understanding of these initiatory stages and proceeds to add a phase of practice to them. At forty-two he is entitled to speak on his own account and he has twenty-one years to teach – that is to say, to convey to others what he himself has learnt – before reaching the age of sixty-three, from which time he may continue to give of himself, but nothing more will be asked of him. I find this wisdom comforting and moving, for I am not long arrived at the age of speaking myself. However, I know that my thinking is only just beginning. I should be grateful, then, if the reader would accept this book as a stage in that thinking, for, as Amadou Hampâté Bâ also said, 'You have to know that you don't know, for if you know you don't know, you will know; but if you don't know that you don't know, you won't know.'

I have been concerned to provide plentiful notes on my sources. It is as well to be clear about these things. All creation is somewhat vampiric, as Manu Dibango said. A book is simply the branch of a tree: it changes only slightly the central trunk or core of our knowledge.

Where the illustrations are concerned, I have tried to give a sense of atmosphere. Rather than reproducing what are often reductive stills from films, I have preferred to show shots of the filming. I have also tried to convey a sense of how African cinema presents itself to its public, by including posters, film music sleeves, cinema buildings, and so on.

I wish to thank all those who have talked with me while I was producing this work, and have given often more than an hour of their time – in Abidjan, Cannes, London, Manosque, Milan, Montreal, New York, Ouagadougou and Paris – to speak to me in interviews which I tried to make as non-directive as possible. They are the filmmakers of Africa, but also those who support that filmmaking. I hope I have not left anyone out.

Actors and directors: John Akomfrah, David Achkar, Sidiki Bakaba, Balufu Bakupa-Kanyinda, Ola Balogun, Timité Bassori, Jean-Pierre Bekolo, Joseph Bitamba, Ferid Boughedir, Mohamed Camara, Mamo Cissé, Larry Clark, Issa Serge Coelo, Mustapha Dao, Idriss Diabaté, Yemané Démissié, Ahmadou Diallo, Cheik Doukouré, Adama Drabo, Henri Duparc, Safi Faye, Gahité Fofana, Anne-Laure Folly, Flora Gomes, Mahamet Saleh Haroun, Med Hondo, Imunga Ivanga, Gaston Kaboré, Maurice Kaboré, Daniel Kamwa, Wanjiru Kynianjui, Abdoulaye Komboudri, Jean-Marie Koula, Dani Kouyaté, Sotigui Kouyaté, Fadika Kramo-Lanciné, José Laplaine, Djingarey Maïga, Sarah Maldoror, Gnoan Roger M'Bala, Ngangura Mweze, Fanta Nacro, Samba Félix Ndiaye, Lionel Ngakane, Funmi Osoba, Idrissa Ouedraogo, Raymond Rajaonarivelo, Joseph Gaye Ramaka, Ousmane Sembène, Moussa Sene Absa, Bouna Medoune Sèye, Menelik Shabazz, Abderrahmane Sissako, Cheikh Oumar Sissoko, Ramadan Suleman, Jean-Marie Teno, Drissa Touré, Kitia Touré, Jacques Trabi, Salif Traoré, Melvin van Peebles, Mansour Sora Wade, Were Were Liking, François Woukoache and Pierre Yameogo.[3]

Critics and writers: Jean-Servais Bakyono, Françoise Balogun, Marie-Christine Peyrière and Clément Tapsoba.

Producers: Jacques Bidou (France), Maria-Cecilia Fonseca (Guinea-Bissau), Joel Phiri (Zimbabwe), Alain Rozanes (France) and Ben Zulu (Zimbabwe).

And also: Jacqueline Ada (CNC), Patrice Bauchy (Canal Plus), Frédéric Bontems and Michel Brunet (Ministry of Co-operation, France), Andrée Davanture (Atria), Pascal Diekebre ('Les Studios' cinema, Abidjan), Katharina von Flotow ('Black Movie' festival, Geneva), Georges Goldenstern (La Sept–Arte), Alain Jalladeau ('Festival des Trois Continents', Nantes), Michel Janin (French cultural centre, Abidjan), Robert Lombaerts (Agence de la Francophonie), Sanvi Panou ('Images d'ailleurs' cinema, Paris), Lucien Patry (manager of the technical unit of the French Ministry of Co-operation 1962–87), Marc Silvera (former director of Écrans du Sud), Justin K. Kagambega (Sonacib, Ouagadougou), Keith Shiri (Harare Festival) and Dominique Wallon (former director of the CNC).

Thanks are also due for their hospitality and assistance to Claude Le Gallou and Annabel Thomas (Atria), Jeanick Le Naour (Audecam), and to the team at the Médiathèque des Trois Mondes.

Thanks also to Michel Sauquet of the Charles Léopold Mayer Foundation for the Progress of Humankind, who has shown faith in this work and supported it.

I would also like to thank the photographers Maya Bracher, Françoise Huguier and Félix von Muralt for the illustrations of filming, and cinematographers Gérard Payen and Marc Salomon for making their photographic treasures available to me – not forgetting Katharina von Flotow (Black Movie Festival, Geneva), Gahité Fofana, Djingarey Maïga, André Valio (Argos Films) and Ashley Woods (Agence Lookat, Zurich) – and Alessandra Speciale and the Centro Orientamento Educativo of Milan for the posters, and Wolfgang Bender, head of the African music archive at the University of Mainz, Germany, for the film music sleeves and video magazine covers.

Lastly, thanks are due to the others – all the others – whom discretion prevents me from mentioning, but whom I have not forgotten.

NOTES

1. Proverb quoted in *Wariko* (Fadika Kramo-Lanciné, Ivory Coast, 1993).
2. In *Amadou Hampâté Bâ*, an interview filmed by Ange Casta and Enrico Fulchigioni (1969).
3. The complete text of all these interviews can be read at website www.africultures.com, together with reviews of all the recent films.

PART I

THE ORIGIN, AKIN TO A PASSAGE

ONE

HUMAN BEINGS, NOT ANTS!

I shall rip down the laughing Banania faces from all the walls of France.

Léopold Sédar Senghor[1]

From Independence onwards, black African cinema cultures sought to assert themselves politically in order to reconquer a territory, a way of thinking and of self-perception that was opposed to the ethnological perspective. This was not without its contradictions.

BLACK IS BLACK

The rejection of the Black goes back to the Middle Ages, and forms the basis of the current dual Western mode of seeing. Before the great fifteenth-century voyages of discovery, Europe regarded itself as the centre of the world. On its southern fringes, in Africa, Ethiopia [or Aethiopia] was the general name given to the land of the 'men with burnt faces'. Some medieval encyclopaedists described them as men of justice and wisdom. The great majority, however, associated them with darkness and evil, with the forces of night and the underworld. The requisite imagery for enslaving Blacks was in place. The first travellers were to draw on it unabashed. Later, black men of the Nilotic type left a considerable impression on Christians when they faced them in the Muslim armies. The crusade argument was used as justification for the seizure of the black Africans' lands, and this led on to the slave trade and colonialism.[2]

It was only when they were integrated, and therefore less threatening, that black people were able to acquire a more familiar image: they gradually came to be regarded as a decorative element of folklore. In the nineteenth century, while passionate debate raged on the unity of the human race and the notion of race was being developed and becoming generally accepted, Stanley fascinated his contemporaries by wandering 'through the dark continent', penetrating into 'darkest Africa'.

This left the white man, endowed with the power of reason, with a real burden: the duty to civilize. The notions of race and civilization contributed to forming imperialist ideology in the sense in which Hannah Arendt understood it: as a vision of the world and the key to history.

In search of the sources of the Nile, Speke in 1861 and Stanley in 1876 described Rwanda as a mythic land.[3] In 1994, television stations celebrated the modernity of a West that was capable, through humanitarian aid, of rescuing a country sinking into genocide. Motivated as much by fear as by compassion for those facing hunger, violence and chaos, civilized man went to the aid of savages and barbarians.

With no camera to film it, suffering does not become a media phenomenon. It does not exist. Yet an excess of footage which is too painful to watch in the end breeds indifference. Upon what image, what gaze, is solidarity to be established? If the Other is wretched, troubling or exotic, he remains external to me – alien. If not, indeed, inferior. The great 'melting pot' of the media and the 'united colours' of advertising in fact rank cultures hierarchically on the basis of the values of Western civilization, which are declared to be universal. However, in order for solidarity to be able to assert itself, writes Claude Liauzu, 'not only do you have to recognize part of yourself in the Other, but you have to recognize a part of the Other in yourself'.[4]

For the Mauritanian filmmaker Abderrahmane Sissako, this is what is fundamental in the cineaste's gaze: 'When I approach the people I want to film, I have in me a confusion which is gradually cleared up: what I lack I find in the Other, and I take it. I also recognize myself in him and accept myself the more.' Sissako's film *La Vie sur terre* (1998) is, he says, 'a hymn to justice, love, sharing and respect, understood as a – not especially African – philosophy of life, a life on earth possible even in a place where it is difficult to have contact with the earth.'[5] And in what are often humorous anecdotes, without great ostentation, he goes on to describe the very simple life of the inhabitants of Sokolo, so that nothing seems ossified in that village where time appears to stand still...

Over thirty-five years the filmmakers of Africa have appropriated cinema, that discovery of the age of Pierre Loti and Jules Verne – travellers of the imagination who sang the praises of the exotic and of technical modernity. For thirty-five years African filmmakers have rejected the dual Western gaze with its opposing components of abject poverty and exoticism.

COLONIAL PROJECTIONS

The Malian director Souleymane Cissé told Rithy Pahn from Cambodia:

> Those who came to film us never showed the people here as human beings. They came to show us to their audiences as though we were animals. They saw us with their eyes. They filmed us any old how. We know the camera can give a positive image of human beings. This White cinema shows Africans as not belonging to the human community. They film wild animals with more respect![6]

Has the approach not really changed at all, then? Often unwittingly, the Westerner blithely reproduces the old colonial schemata...

Only now are researchers analysing the colonial image from this point of view.[7] Colonial cinema fed the European audience's appetite for fantasy, escape and exoticism with picturesque, sensational material. An exotic approach is inevitably superior and reductive. Africa is merely a backdrop and the African is an animal. 'A lion pounces on a native and tears him to pieces... We are sure everyone will enjoy this film', comments a critic of the time on *L'Afrique vous parle*![8] In the cinema and in advertising the African is kin to the ape, a figure which Josephine Baker personifies to the point of caricature in *La Sirène des Tropiques*.[9]

The image of the Black does not, however, limit itself to the simple 'gollywog' figure: the rhetoric of colonial cinema conforms to a truly Manichaean code. Shooting from behind shows 'animal force' and occludes the face, the symbol of the thinking being. The naked native, the 'state of nature', contrasts with the clothed colonial, the 'state of culture'. The African is shown in the right-hand half of the frame, in the negative part of the image, or on the ground to express his 'animality'.[10]

Today the colonial image of the black man continues to characterize white mental projections, revealing a profoundly racist unconscious. In a montage of extracts from colonial films and current advertisements, *Le Noir des Blancs* (1995), Youssef El Ftouh sketches the main features of that ideology: the Blacks are overgrown children; they live like animals; they have natural rhythm; they are inferior to the Whites. The opposition between the savage or dirty Black and the civilized White has subsequently been taken over in advertisements – with the use, for example, of symbolic contrasts between white and black cats – or in Michael Jackson videos. The damage is universal. Like Josephine Baker singing 'Je veux être blanche', many black women have ruined their skins following the fashion for skin-bleaching personified by that singer.

Both in advertising and in cinema, washing powder washes away the black.[11] Hollywood's black American actors seldom have very black skins.

Many colonial representations still persist. So we see the 'Monsieur Propre' figure of the French household cleaning fluid[12] depicted as a black man with a shaven head and a ring in his ear. Today, black characters in some adverts for chocolate or washing powder have been replaced by monkeys, while the monkey in Disney's *The Lion King* has a voice which is supposed to sound African.[13]

THE ETHNOGRAPHIC GAZE:
INVOLVEMENT OR CONTEMPT?

When, after the Second World War, the efforts of Marcel Griaule led to film becoming an instrument of ethnographic research, the approach changed. These films saw themselves as respectful of human beings, but sought above all to document a tradition, a disappearing world, a past. The purpose was to build up a fund of information that could be used in teaching. Although they cannot be exhaustively described with the written word, the movements of a dance can be captured on film. But the use of film also makes it possible to have the participants react to their own rituals, their own cultures.[14]

The context here is one of anti-colonial struggle. While René Vautier was being thrown into prison for recounting in his film *Afrique 50* the bloody repression of popular risings in Dimbokro, Ivory Coast, some ethnologists were attempting a new approach. Taking his inspiration from Dziga Vertov's kino-eye (or camera-eye) and Flaherty's 'participant-camera', Jean Rouch, his 16 mm handheld camera slung over his shoulder, was innovative in camera technique, developing his method through trial and error: cine-trance, a choreography of shooting on the move. When 'the American', the lion in *La Chasse au lion à l'arc* (1965), who has to be killed not simply because he is a lion, but for his dangerous behaviour, attacks one of the hunters pursuing him, we are far removed from *L'Afrique vous parle*. Although sensationalism is still present, the emotion grows, rather, out of respect and involvement. Rouch's is an attentive gaze, in which the spectator/filmmaker participates in what he is observing: 'When in 1954, in an Accra seething with excitement, Damouré, Lam and I filmed Kwame Nkrumah inventing African independence with such seriousness and joy, we completely shared that sense of gravity and that laughter.'[15] This was a gaze, then, which Miguel Benasayag encapsulates well in his fine book on happiness with a play on the French word *regarder*. It was not a question of looking [*regarder*], but of saying 'Ça me regarde!': 'That's my business!'[16]

Rouch often goes beyond ethnographic cinema to make what he himself terms 'ethnofiction', in which the fiction is based on long ethnographic

Oumarou Ganda on the set of *Le Wazzou polygame*,
Niamey, 29 November 1969 © Gérard Payen.

research. *Moi, un Noir* (1957) was hailed by Jean-Luc Godard as a 'cinematic revolution', the 'Open Sesame of poetry'.[17] In that film, Oumarou Ganda and his compatriots from Niger, working as dockers in the port of Abidjan, are given an opportunity to talk about their lives in the working-class district of Treichville. It would seem, therefore, to be their own subjectivity which comes across to us on the screen, describing the reality of their lives. However, Oumarou Ganda, the central protagonist, remains critical: 'I felt that the realization of what I was thinking had to be different because in reality I was also to some small extent the co-director of that film. I made my contribution on a daily basis: we worked together, then Rouch did the editing.'[18]

There was to be fierce debate on the question of Rouch's practice, given how easy it is for involvement to serve as an alibi for manipulation. Whereas French critics saw the film as the first example of a collaboration between the filmed and the filmmakers, 'the Africans', writes the Senegalese Paulin Soumanou Vieyra, 'merely saw it as a distortion which was the more dangerous for having all the outward trappings of authenticity.'

Med Hondo speaks with abhorrence of Rouch's cinema of contempt: 'In all his films he brings out an alleged African cultural specificity which makes us appear ridiculous. He is a man who has always regarded us, deep down, as insects.'[19] The comparison with insects was one the doyen of African filmmakers, the Senegalese Sembène Ousmane, had made before.[20]

Rouch, with the experience of Antonin Artaud's 'theatre of cruelty' behind him, sought to disturb and unsettle his audience.[21] Using images from 'other lands', which were at times cruel, he was combating the colonial mind-set inside every European head. Thus *Les Maîtres fous* (1958) describes the very disturbing spirit possession trances experienced by members of the Haouka cult, the 'masters of madness.' Some Africans have, however, condemned the ambiguity of a partial, external and residually exotic approach. This criticism is backed up by European critics like Gaston Heustrate, who see in Rouch merely a 'paternalistic "scientist"'.[22] This is no doubt an overhasty verdict, but it stresses the external nature of Rouch's approach: he has never stepped over the line and relinquished control; he has never gone over to the other side of the camera and let himself be carried along in the destabilizing rituals he was filming.

AFRICAN RESPONSES

In the face of the superiority, paternalism and exteriority of the Western gaze, the first act of African filmmakers would be to assert the authenticity of their perception of their own reality. If Rouch particularly comes under fire, this is because, in allowing the participants to speak while retaining directorial control, his work has an aspect of ambiguity about it. 'Taking perceptions of people for those people's perceptions is the most tenacious cinematic illusion', writes Paulin Soumanou Vieyra.[23]

What response were African filmmakers to make? '*Yeelen* was in part made in opposition to European ethnographic films', Souleymane Cissé told *Cahiers du Cinéma* in 1987. 'I wanted to make a response to an external perception, a perception by white technicians and academics, an alien perception.'[24] It was a question of substituting an inner world, culturally anchored in tradition, for the external gaze of the ethnologist – of establishing an approach directed at the present, not the past.

The problem was not whether the ethnologist was white or black: 'The question of the ethnographic gaze', says the Senegalese Joseph Gaye Ramaka, is not who is doing the looking, but the content of ethnography itself. You have to know what you want to see before you know how to look at it: is it to be the Other as what he is and whom I am going to dissect or, alternatively, the Other in so far as I feel an affinity with him and he with me. The documentaries I have made have no value other than their subjective expression.[25]

Archive-building gave way, then, to testimony, to attending to the local people themselves: 'I was an observer, I merely listened to them. I didn't move and I filmed everything as though I was the one they were talking to', said Safi Faye of her *Kaddu beykat/Letter from My Village* (1975), the first full-length film made by an African woman.[26] However, her slow description of the daily goings-on in a Serer village, which demonstrates in the end that it is impossible for a young peasant to live in an area of groundnut mono-culture, is an insider's view. 'You are going to spend a while with me in my home', announces the commentary. 'I've had some criticism from my parents. They say the people who watch this are going to laugh at us because we're badly dressed, because we're always working.' At the end, she thanks them: 'The letter is from me. All the rest is from my farming parents.' The film is dedicated to her grandfather, who died eleven days after the end of filming and whose face, which fills the entire screen, etches itself into our memories.

When it comes to reacting against the ethnic conflicts which arose out of the colonial period, there has been a healthy reaction. In Burundi, as in Rwanda, after the 1994 genocide and the massacres which are continuing even today, artists of all disciplines united in their efforts to oppose the language of ethnicity. Oppositions between the different factions mean nothing to the street children Joseph Bitamba filmed in *Le Métis* (1996). The camera fluidly captures their daily efforts to get by, their joys and the tensions between them. Eric and his gang live out that tolerance and sense of community which the adults find so difficult to achieve. 'Whereas everyone talks of antagonism between the two ethnic groups', says the director, 'the film shows, through the character of Eric, that they can have a common future. There's no difference in my eyes between Hutus and Tutsis. That difference was promoted only for power-political ends.'[27]

Even when exploration of traditions is the aim, the theme is often not the pure description of customs and mores. Very often it is a quest, an attempt by the filmmakers to go back to their roots in their region of origin. This is what Ngangura Mweze does in *Le Roi, la vache et le bananier* (1994), an hour-long film made among the Bashi of Zaïre, for whom the numbers of cattle owned and the size of the banana plantation are the two traditional marks of wealth. The description of the traditional authority – the king – who still largely governs the lives of the peasants enables the film to show that democratic forms which already existed before colonization have persisted up to the present: 'It is the people which is the chief of the Mwami.'[28] This return to roots makes it possible to ask how things stand in the here and now: what part is this authority to play in contemporary Africa? The 'backward-looking' values seen here, such as belief in traditional medicine or ancestral faiths, are often rejected as an obstacle to progress. The film shows us, however, the degree to which they are 'closely bound up with solid common sense'.

BEING ON THE SAME WAVELENGTH

It is easier for locally born filmmakers to listen to their people and understand their roots. To do so is an aid to understanding their own original identity before making the break from it: filmmakers often begin their careers with a film about their family or their village. As a member of the community, with a rootedness in it and a direct perception of their society and culture, the local will have a better understanding than an outsider of comments and behaviour which often have a double meaning. As Maurice Kaboré from Burkina Faso remarks, 'In Mossi country, you don't tell everything to someone you don't know.'[29] Because he has the power of the image, the filmmaker then becomes responsible for transmitting language and rites, and hence for the perpetuation of values. The films which have come out of Africa teem with scenes documenting initiation rites, traditional dances and ancestral skills, all at great length.

However, the rituals are chosen more to evoke the tradition and values of the village community than to document a disappearing past. At the risk of interrupting the narrative and releasing the tension, they remind us of the cosmic dimension of the order of things. This is the case, for example, with the initiation of the young boys in Drissa Touré's *Laada* (Burkina Faso, 1991):

> Do not fear the earth, for the earth will possess you.
> Remain on the earth and you will possess the heavens.
> Remain in the heavens and you will possess the earth.
> In the light, you will know what is in the dark.
> In the dark, you will know what happens in the light.

While Sina prefers to stay in the village to be initiated into the principles and secrets of *laada*, the customary law, Do and Demba go off to the city to seek out other values which might be of advantage to the village. There they make their fortunes by dishonest means. On their return to the village, they end up taking opposing courses of action. While Do carries on with banditry, Demba becomes reintegrated into the community, taking part in the teaching of literacy. The moral of the story is given by Baï, a farmer who is open to modern ways: 'Nowadays, our traditions have to be properly understood before we can be committed to them. Writing reveals the world to us better. This must not dehumanize us. Do has disrupted the order of the village; do not disrupt the order of the world.'

There is no conservatism in this. It is not because the ravages of modernity disrupt the ancient order that the filmmaker is concerned with them, but because they disrupt the order of the world. The tone becomes serious. 'We are going to disappear', observes Mangala, a Babinga pygmoid, sadly, in David Pierre Fila's *Le Dernier des Babingas* (Congo, 1990). Since the Société Centrafricaine de Déroulage has intensified its forest clearance efforts, the little men have been forced to leave the forest, whose 'guardians' they had always been. Pygmy encampments have increased along the sides of the roads. The gazelles and the game have fled; the mushrooms and medicinal plants have disappeared, and with them the store of memory of the traditional healers.[30] Documentary observation gives voice to the need, as a question of survival, for another practice of modernity.

THE POLITICS OF EVERYDAY LIFE

It is the good fortune of current cinema that it is freed from the obligation to convey an ideological message. A simple activity such as beating jerry-cans into trunks – as in *Les Malles* (1989), a film by the Senegalese filmmaker Samba Félix Ndiaye – may be recognized in its political dimension as the affirmation of a different economy, the economy of the informal sector – a monetarily deprived culture and, as such, a possible model for a different society.[31]

This has not always been the case: the didacticism of the 1970s marked the films of Africa as it did those of Europe, but ideology often informed the debates around cinema more than it permeated the images. The apprehension of reality gave politics back its pragmatism, with the view of the people which was generated merging with the people's own views. In *Kaddu beykat/ Letter from My Village* (1975), a man comes to read a newspaper beneath the 'talking tree'. He opens the 'politics' page, and people ask him to read it. Each of the men present responds in his turn to this caricature of political life:

'My politics is that for six months of the year I eat once a day.'
  'My politics is that I can't make sacrifices any more.'
  'My politics is that my father killed an ox for my wedding and I won't be able to do the same for my son.'

Safi Faye on the set of *Kaddu beykat,* Fad'jal 1974. © Maya Bracher

Safi Faye's militant vision consists in asserting a politics of the everyday without leaving economic issues out of account. Beneath the 'talking tree', the villagers discuss the problems raised by groundnut monoculture. Can they trust the Whites of the European Development Fund?

The response lies in affirming one's culture. Confronted with a West which does not believe Africa is able to resolve contemporary problems, a West which is not even aware of the existence of African thinkers, the filmmaker wishes to show that 'Africa is', as Anne-Laure Folly from Togo puts it, 'equipped, in its thinking and its writing, for the twenty-first century and its modernity.'[32] Documentary is a good way of asserting this. 'We are all living on the same earth at the same time', she adds. 'The difference is merely one of décor. We all ask the same questions about democracy, human rights, freedom, and the need not to develop a culture of warfare.' In *Femmes du Niger, entre intégrisme et démocratie* (1993) or *Femmes aux yeux ouverts* (1994),[33] 'the women ask the same questions as an intelligent and aware Western woman would do, even though they are taken at random from the villages. They have the same questions – and suffer the same exploitation.'

Thus reversing the approach means shifting from the ethnological gaze to attend to essential values. 'The first task of African filmmakers is to affirm that the people here are human beings and to make known those of our values which could be of use to others', says Souleymane Cissé.[34] Nandi, the central character in his film *Waati* [Time] (1995), studies not ethnology but civilizations: 'If you study African civilizations, you observe that enlightenment has gone out from Africa to other civilizations.'[35]

FOUNDING FIGURES

Cissé's career path is eloquent in itself: 'The cinema I make was born in violence, both physical and economic. I must emphasize this point: I continue to suffer from that violence.' In the programme on Cissé in Rithy Pahn's *Cinéastes de notre temps* series, there are images of the arrest and humiliation of Patrice-Eméry Lumumba. 'I was overcome with emotion. I cried. I was convinced cinema was of crucial importance and I decided to make it my career.' Lumumba, who was assassinated by the new political authorities at the behest of the forces of neo-colonialism six months after Congo (Kinshasa) gained its independence, remains in the African imagination the one who most clearly asserted the demand for freedom. Linking his personal history – memories of his mother – to historical facts, to history, the Haitian Raoul Peck shows in *Lumumba, la mort d'un prophète* (1992, the forerunner to his new film, *Lumumba, 2000*) the place the murdered leader occupies in African collective memory. Peck is concerned not so much with the man as such and his biography as with the historical figure. Rather than recounting Lumumba's life, Peck stresses the prophetic aspect of his ideal.[36] Punctuating his account with phrases such as 'My mother tells how...', he offers a sensitive, personal perception of an individual destiny. Contrary to Judaeo-Christian culture, which privileges identification with paternal models ('the imitation of Christ'), African initiation leaves each person free to define their modernity within the framework of collective universal values. Each person can define the contents they will assume. Here, then, it is not so much the man as model which is to the fore, but the demand for freedom he personifies.

It is the same with the other figures in the African collective memory. Kwame Nkrumah remains the promoter of the grand idea of pan-Africanism despite all that might be said about the man and his methods of government. Barthélemy Boganda, the father of the Central African nation, remains, for his part, the advocate of the regional integration of African political and economic spaces which could have made Independence a reality.

One might equally list the errors made by the revolution guided by Thomas Sankara in Burkina Faso between 1983 and 1987. There remains of the man and his actions the endeavour to bring his people prosperity with dignity. In reading occasional extracts from the book which gives his film its title – *Thomas Sankara, l'espoir assassiné* (1991) – Balufu Bakupa-Kanyinda does not try to produce a meaningful biography of the charismatic leader but, rather, to apply his maxim: 'I think there are three ways to be: the way others perceive you, the way you perceive yourself, and the truth, which is somewhere between these two views of a single individual.'[37] He explains the genesis of his film: 'Sankara was in power for four years, and today his parents are poor people. That fact alone deserves the respect of the whole of Africa!'

Le Damier (1997) provides a fictional illustration of the clash between the government and the people. Shot/reverse-shot and high-angle/low-angle are used here to express relations of domination. In order to pass a night of insomnia, the father-of-the-nation/president-for-life plays draughts against an ordinary citizen, a local champion. 'The draughts player rails against the president the way they talk about him on the streets', explains Balufu Bakupa-Kanyinda.

> Power is a hallucinogen. To be on the same level as the dictator the draughts champion wants to smoke a joint. The dictator is happy to agree to this. However, when the draughts champion says he is hungry, the president feels he is being accused of starving his people... You can't just show African poverty. I wanted to show where it is produced.[38]

CLASS STRUGGLE WITHOUT PLACARDS

Class struggle is no more presented as an absolute model than are the great politicians. When the immigrant in Med Hondo's *Soleil ô* (1969) is contemplating political struggle in the forest to which he runs to utter his cry of despair in the face of his rejection by (and the decadence of) French society, he sees the portrait of Lumumba in a fiery vision, together with that of Che Guevara. Similarly, when the soldiers of *Cry Freedom* (Ola Balogun, Nigeria, 1981) attack to cries of 'Our people will be free!', a series of portraits of African leaders, Lumumba foremost among them, appear superimposed one on another. It is without doubt class struggle, not merely an identity-based pursuit of African values, which is envisaged here as Africa's road to liberation. But – unlike their leaders, who, as is well documented, fell into the trap of mimicking the West – the filmmakers do not advocate some imported pattern of action. In *Jom ou l'histoire d'un peuple* (1981), the Senegalese

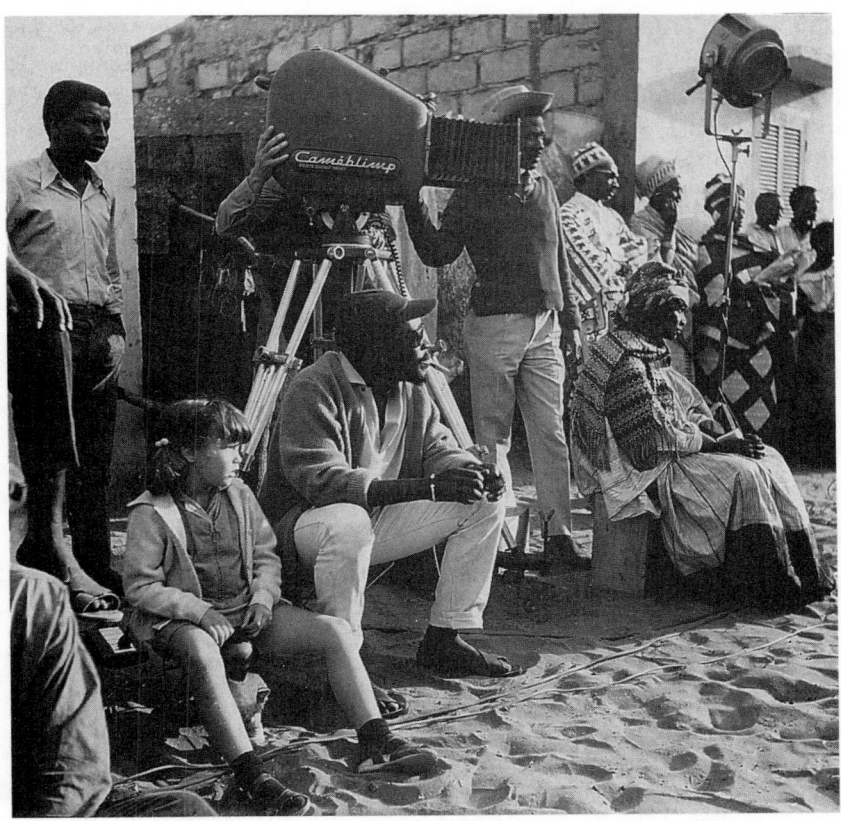

Sembène Ousmane on the set of *Mandabi/The Money Order*,
Dakar, 1968. © Maya Bracher.

filmmaker Ababacar Samb Makharam, working with a scenario written by
the Marxist sociologist Babacar Sine, links political ideology effectively to
African cultural values. The oppression of subject people by colonialist, of
servant by master, and of worker by boss is presented each in its turn by a
griot who stresses throughout the African concept of *jom*, which means
honour, dignity, courage and respect. Man exists for himself and asserts
himself as such.[39]

To describe his country's situation some years after independence, the
Senegalese Sembène Ousmane, in his 1968 film *Mandabi/The Money Order*,
takes as his hero Ibrahima, a practising Muslim with two wives, seven children
and a nephew working in Paris. The latter informs him that he is to receive

a money order for a substantial sum. Ibrahima's wives are getting into debt with the grocer and his friends are asking for assistance, but administrative wranglings will prevent him from cashing the money order and in the end an unscrupulous relative cashes it in his stead. So, argues Sembène, 'it is not the hero's misfortunes alone that are the true subject of the film, but the emergence of an African bourgeoisie. There are no longer Whites and Blacks; the problem lies at the level of social class.'[40]

Sembène, who was a *tirailleur sénégalais* during the war, became a docker in the port of Marseille in 1949 and joined the French Communist Party the following year, remaining a member until Senegalese independence in 1960. He first came to prominence as a self-taught writer. *Le Docker Noir*[41] is a protest against the suspicion which surrounds a writer because he is black. The hero will not accept a role as *nègre*, the French term for a ghostwriter. He kills the French woman who misappropriates his manuscript, and publishes it in her own name. With *God's Bits of Wood*,[42] his third novel, the prophetic account of a strike, Sembène was to find international success. Conscious, however, of how little impact literature makes in Africa, when Senegal achieved its independence he turned to film, and he still asserts this precedence of film over literature: 'What books can do is limited by purchasing power. I go into schools, colleges and cinemas and meet people and I find that the image affects them directly, which a book cannot do.'[43] But this does not mean film can do everything: 'It is a means of political action. But I must add that I don't intend to produce a sloganizing cinema and I don't think it's possible to change a given situation with just one film... I like Brecht and I'm trying to take inspiration from his example.'[44]

This Brechtian inspiration characterizes Sembène's films more than it does his literary output. There is a difference between book and film, as we can see in *Xala* (1974). Whereas Sembène's novel draws the reader in through the powerful psychological portrayal of the character of El Hadji, the film invites the spectator to distance himself from this character to become an attentive, critical observer. In a manner typical of an elite as keen to profit from the West as to copy it, El Hadji lives beyond his means, taking a third wife. His contempt for beggars and for those who are in any way disabled echoes his rejection of tradition. They succeed in casting a spell on him, the *xala*, which makes him impotent. Both in business and in polygamy, El Hadji loses the virility which seemed so natural to him. The marabout of his driver's village releases him from the spell, but El Hadji pays him with a bouncing cheque. Rendered impotent once more, he comes to understand that virility is not the product of a will to power, but requires respect for its own values. He will manage to regain it by rejecting his alienation and allowing the outcasts, in an extraordinary expiatory scene, to cover him with their spit.

THE NOVELISTIC PATH

'Who and what are we? An admirable question', said Aimé Césaire. Africa's filmmakers were going to 'hold up a mirror to their people',[45] seeking to engage them, to involve them. 'My ambition is for my cinema to reflect a reality in which I participate and which I contribute to shaping', writes Gaston Kaboré from Burkina Faso, the president of the Pan-African Federation of Filmmakers (FEPACI).[46] African cinema is, he says, 'an *auteur* cinema, an urgent cinema which finds its true legitimacy only in a kind of deep explanation of contemporary reality rather than in added artistic value. Reality is always the body and heart of the films.'[47] Similarly, when June Givanni asked the Senegalese filmmaker Djibril Diop Mambety where he got the inspiration for his first film, *Badou Boy* (1970), he replied: 'If one follows a character from morning to evening, one has a script. And if one observes a town day after day over the years one has an inexhaustible décor. The only motor, to turn these into a film, is the interest in doing so.'[48]

Garbage Boys/Nyamanton ou la leçon des ordures (Cheikh Oumar Sissoko, 1986) was made on such a small budget that it leaves something to be desired technically, but it is such a touching film that it gained an international audience.[49] In a district of Bamako (Mali), Khalifa and Fanta are excluded from school because they don't have the desks they need for attending lessons. Their parents borrow money to buy one for them, but the children themselves also have to work to help: Khalifa collects refuse and Fanta sells oranges in the street. However, the money needed for their schooling is often spent on the urgent necessities of a life of poverty. One can see the political project of social realism here in Sissoko's conception of militant cinema: 'I mean by this a cinema which works to dispel social inequalities, forms of domination which merely reduce our people to poverty.'[50] However, the film quite often reaches greater heights: the characters' emotions overturn the argument and take it on to another – novelistic – plane, and it is this which gives it its power.

It is on this plane that cinema can achieve a prophetic dimension. Just as Jean-Luc Godard, by putting the imagination in charge in *Weekend* (1967), prefigured the events of May 1968, so, by linking tradition and daily realities, Malian filmmaker Souleymane Cissé foreshadowed the riots of March 1991 which were to overthrow the Malian dictator Moussa Traoré in his film *Finye* [The Wind] (1982). When the old blacksmith Kansayé implores the help and

Poster for
Nyamanton/
The Garbage Boys
(Cheikh Oumar
Sissoko, Mali, 1986).

protection of his ancestors to get his grandson Bâ out of prison, the message he receives brings him back to present reality: 'Act according to your own intuition and on your own initiative.'[51] He will join the students, who are rejecting the established order and demonstrating against the existing authorities.

Even before this film, Cissé had denounced the collusion between the economic and political spheres in *Baara* [Work] (1978). An engineer with new ideas pays the price of that collusion, his dead body being carried in procession by the workers, their bare torsos indicating their determination and new-found political awareness. The film represents a new departure in so far as it takes on the question of trade-union action in an urban milieu.

Poster for *Baara*
(Souleymane Cissé,
Mali, 1978).

Its strength, however, is that it goes beyond stereotypes and does not stop
at the social message: the exchanges between the young peasant who has
become a blue-collar worker and the professional engineer add substance to
the argument; the relations between men and women – particularly the
touching figure of the boss's wife, Djénéba, who meets her death as a result
of revealing too many of his failings – open the door to emotion and
representation.

In the Portuguese-speaking countries which were fighting Portuguese
colonial power in the 1960s, there arose a cinema of anti-colonial propaganda, based on the ideas of African revolution developed by Frantz Fanon

and Amilcar Cabral.[52] However, it was Sarah Maldoror, a French-born Guadeloupean and the partner of an Angolan nationalist, who made the film with the greatest impact. *Sambizanga* (1972), filmed in the Congo with a French crew and non-professional actors affiliated to the Popular Movement for the Liberation of Angola (MPLA) and the African Party for the Independence of Guinea and Cape Verde (PAIGC), describes the atrocities of Portuguese repression and offers a picture of the Angolan resistance. The revolutionary activist Domingo is tortured to death because he will not betray his companions, while his wife, who knows nothing of his activities, sets out to look for him. Her long march will be the discovery of another reason to live: the fight for freedom. The film was criticized for overemphasizing the personal development of this particular woman to the detriment of the liberation struggle in general, but here again, it is precisely this novelistic emphasis which makes the impact. 'In *Sambizanga*', explained Sarah Maldoror, 'I wanted above all to express ... the time you spend walking.'[53]

It was when African films, in all their social realism, took a novelistic turn that they began to gain recognition in the latter half of the 1980s and an international audience developed for a cinema culture which had previously been confined to a small band of devotees. Thus, for example, European film critics confronted with Idrissa Ouedraogo's first full-length feature, *Yam Daabo* [The Choice] (1986), saw an economic and political subject 'treated in terms of emotion and sensuality'.[54] The choice in question is whether a family from a village in the Sahel should continue to wait for international food aid or move out to seek a better life in the South. Although there are to be many ordeals and sacrifices on the way, they will in the end recover their *joie de vivre* and their love. Such a summary cannot do justice to the emotional impact of the film. Yet it is there, generated by a visual reserve which merely hints at reality rather than showing it, not from any diffidence, but out of respect – as exemplified in the off-camera death of Ali, the family's little boy, knocked down by a car in a city street.

The critics seized eagerly on the opposition between the 'political' and 'ideological' tendencies of early African cinema and new internationally oriented 'cultural' films, often presenting a timeless Africa and based on fables of a universal kind. These latter films they rewarded with prizes at the Cannes Film Festival.[55] Whereas Souleymane Cissé's *Finye* [The Wind] received only the 'Un Certain Regard' award in 1983, his *Yeelen* [Brightness] won the 'Prix du Jury' in 1987; in that same year *Yam Daabo* won a prize at the Semaine de la Critique. Idrissa Ouedraogo's new films, *Yaaba* and *Tilaï*, won the 'Prix de la Critique' of 1989 and the 'Grand Prix du Jury' in 1990, respectively.[56]

AFRICA FIRST

If, from the very beginning, black African cinema cultures wove a whole host of fictional responses upon a realist canvas, Western recognition did not come (specialist festivals apart) until sociological realism was transcended by drawing on the novelistic dimension and a certain sensuality. But enough of European opinions. The filmmakers laid claim to their own vision, and until recently they have mostly addressed themselves unambiguously, with a collusive nod and a wink, to an African audience: 'I'm talking to you about yourself.' It has been a cinema of affirmation in which the specatator has been invited to recognize his own experience, and take a different angle on it. Europe is secondary here. 'I have first of all to have my films accepted by my people, then by the whole African continent. Only after that can I begin to think about Europe and about the possible access of non-African spectators to African films made for Africans', declared Cissé in 1986.[57]

There is a permanent commitment to contributing to changing the social order. This means a new 'take' on African reality. The audience have to recognize themselves in the films, to feel involved and ask themselves the questions the filmmaker wants to raise, though on occasion the directors are not above spelling out the moral of the film themselves, as Sembène Ousmane does at the end of *Mandabi/The Money Order* (1968):

'Honesty is a crime among our people!' remarks Ibrahima bitterly.
  'We'll change all that!' replies the postman.
  'Who?'
  'You!'
  'Me?'
  'We'll change all that. You, your wives, your children, me!'

With some rare exceptions, 'ambivalence and ambiguity were generally shunned' until the 1980s.[58] Should we see the influence of a specific training or a particular school in this? Did not Sarah Maldoror and Sembène Ousmane earn filmmaking at the All-Soviet State Cinematography Institute under Gerassimov and Donskoi? Yet a large number of directors were trained in the Paris schools. They may, admittedly, have been influenced there by a certain French-style realism which emphasized the mid-shot and a use of depth of field and sequence shots, contributing to a certain naturalness of narration. Director Inoussa Ousseini from Niger stressed the influence of Italian neo-realism,[59] and it is true that in many African films one finds an aesthetic close to news footage (documentary images, rejection of effects, unsophisticated editing), non-professional actors, the use of natural settings and a degree of improvisation. As a result, Africans, brought up on American action films, often have the impression that their filmmakers 'don't know how to make films yet'![60]

The cineastes of Black Africa have not developed an aesthetic form as distinctive as that of, say, the Brazilian *cinema novo* of the early 1960s, the metaphorical style of which stands in total opposition to Western cinema. Yet their realism is a response to colonial deculturation. It is a new approach to, and a reclaiming of, African reality and African space – a thumbing of the nose at films like *La France est un empire* (1939), which mythified the close ties between France and its colonies (a banner at a 'native' gathering in the film bears the slogan 'France is our mother').

Yet, to begin with a paradox, the first African film was called *Afrique sur Seine* (1955)! Paulin Soumanou Vieyra, the first black African to attend IDHEC, and his friends in the 'Groupe africain du cinéma' had not been granted authorization to film in Africa. Since the Laval decree of 1934, no one could film in the colonies without first seeking approval: the scenario and the people involved were all vetted. The decree was not often applied, except to ban *Afrique 50* (Robert Vautier, 1950) – for its condemnation of colonial exactions – and *Les Statues meurent aussi* (Chris Marker and Alain Resnais, 1955), that admirable *jeu de lumières* in black and white which committed the offence of showing how colonial business was killing native art. But the decree did at the very least exert a pressure which delayed the birth of African film.[61] *Afrique sur Seine*, made under the patronage of the French Committee for Ethnographic Film, showed 'some aspects of the life of Africans in Paris.'[62] A number of films made in subsequent years were also inspired, wrote Victor Bachy later, 'by that distant Europe which they had reached as independent citizens and which fascinated and at the same time disappointed them.'[63] He is thinking, among others, of *Concerto pour un exil* and *A nous deux, France* (Désiré Ecaré, 1968 and 1970) and *Paris, c'est joli* (Inoussa Ousseini, 1974).

Following the French example, the Belgians had also passed a law in 1936 forbidding unauthorized filming in Congo–Rwanda–Urundi. The only films to be made there were educational ones aimed at those who at the time were referred to as 'backward peoples' or 'natives'. However, whereas the films produced under the control of the Belgian Ministry of Information were naive and paternalistic, those made *in situ* by the missionaries of the Congolese Centre for Catholic Action through Cinema (CCACC) speak a 'simple, direct language, that was received, understood, appreciated and requested again and again'.[64] Let us have no illusions about this, however: the missionaries still had a blatantly colonial agenda.[65] The Mobutu regime, which inherited the structures and equipment of colonial cinema, passed these over to its national television station, 'The Voice of Zaïre', without attempting to develop a Congolese cinema.

ENGLISH-SPEAKING AFRICA:
EDUCATIONAL CINEMA AND THE HOLLYWOOD DREAM

The success of the 'Bantu Educational Cinema Experiment', set up in 1935, which, with the help of the Africans themselves, produced thirty-five films in two years with commentaries in local languages, prompted the British in 1939 to found the Colonial Film Unit and this had a presence in every country. According to Jean Rouch, the central aim was to make propaganda films that would promote African involvement in the Second World War. Once the war was over, however, these organizations produced and distributed a host of educational films, peddled around the outlying areas by projection vans, which reached an audience estimated at 16 million a year!

The habit was formed. Pierre Haffner writes:

> After independence the English-speaking countries continued to produce a basic educational output long before they made feature films. They also introduced television ahead of most of the French-speaking states, as though the small screen were the natural successor to the mobile unit.[66]

Many countries, however, espousing the narrowly pragmatic spirit of their former colonial masters, were to neglect the potential of that documentary school, and allow the potential of the Africans who had been trained as technicians and directors to be wasted. Giving priority to the more concrete problems of development, they closed their film units. It was in Southern Africa, particularly in Portuguese-speaking Mozambique, that the documentary tradition was to survive best. The countries which achieved independence late needed propaganda and information films, and set up the appropriate structures to provide them.

In Ghana, however, the Nkrumah regime nationalized distribution and production, and developed that production by equipping itself with technically advanced laboratories for 16 and 35 mm. When Nkrumah was overthrown in 1966, the documentaries, newsreels and propaganda films produced since 1957 were seized: they were criticized for encouraging the Nkrumah personality cult. At this point Sam Aryetey was put in charge of the Ghana Film Corporation; he attempted to develop co-productions with Europe.[67] For this he engaged foreign directors, but the project hit severe financial setbacks.[68] The first person to achieve international success was

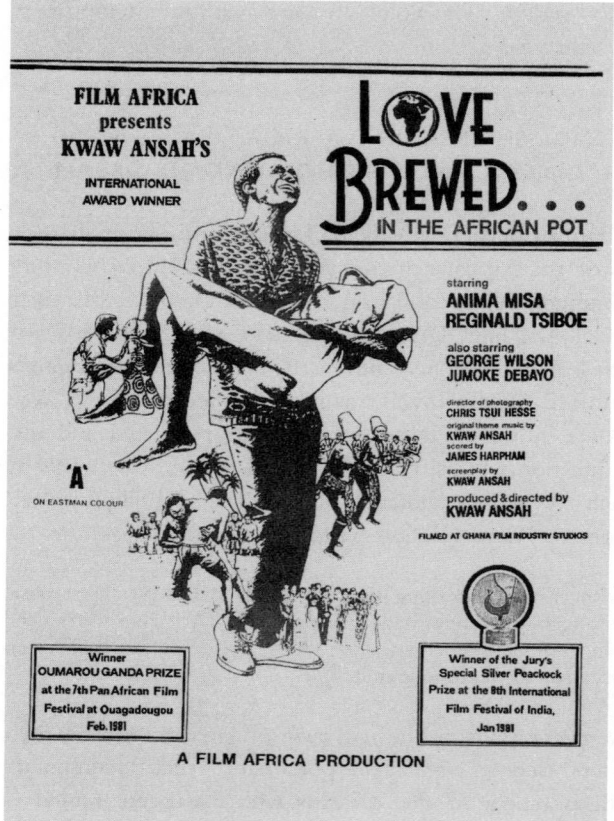

Poster for *Love
Brewed in the
African Pot*
(Kwaw Ansah,
Ghana, 1981).

Kwaw Ansah, with a satire on the ruling class through a story of love between two young people from different social classes. That film, entitled *Love Brewed in the African Pot* (1981), used Ghanaian facilities and technicians.

Nigeria also embraced the Hollywood style with the films of Francis Oladele, who adapted work by Nigerian dramatists for the screen, but these, too, were directed by foreigners. *Kongi's Harvest* (1971), directed by the black American Ossie Davies, was based on the play by Wole Soyinka, who also acted in the film; *Bullfrog in the Sun*, directed by the West German Hans Jürgen Pohland, was based on two stories by Chinua Achebe. The Nigerian Film Corporation, established in 1979, set out to build a veritable African Hollywood on a 300-hectare site on the Shere hills near Jos. But this turned out to be a white elephant, the structure 'not being designed to create a cinema industry, but being built purely as a "business venture"'.[69] As a result, the successes remained confined to the Nigerian market (100 million inhabitants): by drawing on the tradition of Yoruba theatre, Ola Balogun succeeded in making popular films with a message.

Travelling Yoruba theatre in fact possessed 'a forty-year-long tradition, a loyal audience, and tried-and-tested formulas for success.'[70] With *Ajani-Ogun* (1976), the story of a young hunter who attacks a dissolute, corrupt politician, Balogun pulled off a masterstroke: an immense popular success for a film denouncing corruption.

FRENCH GUARDIAN ANGELS

In French-speaking Africa, there was no Hollywood dream. The French government, with its assimilationist colonial traditions, gave support, after independence, to the emergence of a French-speaking African cinema as an economic and cultural link to its old colonies. Since it had not developed local cinema units, as the British had done, aid was centralized in Paris. In 1961, the Consortium Audiovisuel International (CAI), in which Les Actualités françaises, Éclair-Journal, Gaumont Actualités and Pathé-Actualités combined, was created to enable the production of newsreels and documentaries which could replace the French news in African cinemas. In 1963, the former head of IDHEC (Institut des Hautes Études Cinématographiques), Jean-René Debrix, was given a post in the cinema bureau of the French Ministère de la Coopération.[71] He managed to convince his superiors that cinema might be the best way of helping Africans to regain their cultural identity. Jean Rouch had laid the ground for this in the 1950s and two of his actor-assistants, Oumarou Ganda and Mustapha Alassane, both from Niger, were to become successful directors in their own right. To provide support for the emergence of these varied cinema cultures, the French Ministry of Co-operation became what it still is today: the main producer of African cinema.

In Debrix's view, African cinema could save film culture by restoring the 'enchantment, magic and poetry' the West had lost. As Louis Malle put it: 'Any African filmmaker who thought he "had a film in him" could quite freely obtain the wherewithal to make it from the Bureau du Cinéma.'[72] Lucien Patry, who also came from IDHEC and was the mainstay of the technical unit at the Bureau du Cinéma between 1962 and 1987, says:

> The rue de la Boétie was the meeting point for all the filmmakers who came to France. We were their technical guardian angels. Filming in Africa with no laboratories meant that you couldn't view the rushes. We developed Cissé's as he sent them to us when he was making *Baara*. He telephoned from the French cultural

centre every two days to ask what they were like. I could point out where there was shadow or a speck of dust in a particular reel or shot... I often had to dash off frantically to Africa because a cameraman couldn't stand the climate or to take a new camera...[73]

The French cultural centres thus provided logistical back-up for a great many African films. Some were able to provide the first filmmakers with facilities. 'I went there [to the French Cultural Centre in Dakar] with my script', says Djibril Diop Mambety.

The centre's director, Michel Letellier, gave me a cameraman and we began to shoot the film. This was in spite of the fact that it was the first time they were presented with someone who was convinced he was already a filmmaker, and was asking for technical help! So this was how the first *Badou Boy* was made, when I was twenty-one. I remade it four years later [1970] in colour.[74]

In many cases, the cultural centres were also the only places where audiences could see these films. But they also made their contribution in educating people in cinema, if not indeed introducing them to it. One can, for example, imagine the feelings of the Tuaregs from the Aïr region of Niger as they gathered one dark, Saharan evening to watch the creatures of Jacques-Yves Cousteau and Louis Malle's *Silent World* (1956) moving about under the sea thanks to the magic of cinema.[75]

REVOLUTIONARY FILMMAKERS?

In 1970, not long after the death of Debrix, France froze its aid temporarily.[76] In Manthia Diawara's view, this was done for political reasons. Filmmakers were beginning to seem troublesome to certain African governments who put pressure on France, which they criticized for manufacturing revolutionaries. It is difficult to verify whether this kind of intervention actually took place. The editor Andrée Davanture reports that a letter was received from the Ambassador of Cameroon asking them not to help with the film *The Price of Freedom/Le Prix de la Liberté* (Jean-Pierre Dikongué Pipa, 1978): 'As a result we weren't able to go ahead with the editing, though we had made a commitment to do it. It was only after an exchange between the embassies that we were able to start work again.' Similarly, the government of Mali criticized the French Ministry of Co-operation for helping to make *Den Muso* [The Young Girl] (Souleymane Cissé, 1975), a film denouncing the condition of African women, and 'Malians came to Paris to retrieve the material, which prevented us from carrying on working on it.'[77]

Such intervention remained external. Andrée Davanture is adamant that the Ministry of Co-operation never tried to interfere with the content of a film: 'We were asked, just once, to take out a French flag in the film *La Chapelle*.[78] We had a laugh about it and left it in!'

Admittedly, the filmmakers who came together in Algiers in 1969 to form the Fédération Panafricaine des Cinéastes (FEPACI) were 'for the most part leftists and idealists who were committed to the notion of Pan-Africanism'. They believed it was 'their prophetic mission … to unite and to use film as a tool for the liberation of the colonized countries and as a step towards the total unity of Africa.'[79] The goal was to create a new aesthetics: semi-documentaries denouncing colonialism where it still existed, and fictions to combat the economic and cultural alienation of the independent countries in respect of the West. Tahar Cheriaa writes of 'an initial period of fanatical activism and general dynamism, very much bearing the stamp of the outstanding personality of the first general secretary of FEPACI, the Senegalese filmmaker Ababacar Samb Makharam'.[80] In 1975, FEPACI again met at Algiers, where they rejected all forms of commercial cinema: the way forward was to unite with the progressive filmmakers of other countries to fight neo-colonialism and imperialism. There were no further meetings until 1982, when FEPACI assembled at Niamey. There a manifesto was drawn up with the emphasis more on the construction of a cinema industry than on anti-imperialist struggle. The notion of 'economic operator' appears at this point, the reference being to the businesspeople who would have to invest in African film if it was to develop.

At the 1981 Ouagadougou pan-African festival, a group of young filmmakers seceded from FEPACI. This was the 'L'Oeil Vert' collective, which attempted to restore the lost dynamism and find a rapid solution to the thorny question of African production through inter-African organization. The move came to nothing; nonetheless, it had the merit of focusing debate on the still active contradiction within African cinema of the dependence on the West for the means of production. Although he praises FEPACI for the advances it made, Manthia Diawara stresses the lack of trained African technicians. These increased in number proportionately more slowly than directors, which means that African filmmakers have generally been forced to call on Western technicians.

Moreover, Diawara is amazed that someone like Sembène Ousmane should have continued filming in 35 mm when 16 mm would have reduced his costs considerably. 'The important thing is the film's content', says Andrée Davanture. '*Finye* was shot in 16 mm, then blown up to 35. Who realized this had happened?'[81] Filming with amateurs increases the number of takes; 35 mm, which is often advocated by cinematographers – who are afraid of losing depth of field when they move up from 16 to 35 mm, and also fear graininess – is too expensive to allow that freedom. Things are changing today. Video – in particular digital Beta SP 16/9, which restores cinema format with excellent quality at a cost appreciably below that of 35 mm film – opens up previously undreamt-of possibilities, and is obliging enough to be less sensitive to dust and heat. Furthermore, it has the enormous advantage that one can view the rushes immediately without damaging them.[82] For a long time, however, the use of 35 mm was the prerogative of an elite; it corresponded to the image a filmmaker worthy of the name wanted to project.

Jean Rouch and Jean-Luc Godard ran up against this kind of contradiction in Mozambique. Samora Machel's government – prompted by Ruy Guerra, one of the masters of Brazilian *cinema novo* and head of the National Film Institute – had invited them there to undertake specific projects. In 1978, Rouch led a 'super-8' workshop at Maputo University, and Godard had a two-year contract to study the video needs of the new national television station. Rouch, an opponent of heavy Hollywood-style equipment, used 'super-8' as one uses a Biro, for writing a 'postcard'. His students filmed in the morning, and could show the results in the evening to the people they had been filming. The problem was one of preserving the images, since the originals wore out quickly when projected. For this reason, his group ended up joining forces with Godard's video people. Both groups criticized the Cinema Institute, which gave priority to heavy equipment, such as 16 and 35 mm. A cinema for independence should be made with simple tools, they argued, so that it could be within everyone's reach and able to keep up with technological advances. Such films could be used by the embryonic television station. Guerra did not take kindly to these criticisms; he also accused Rouch's *cinéma vérité* of downplaying the importance of the *mise en scène*. According to Manthia Diawara, by teaching everyone how to make a film, Rouch and Godard 'were breaking the monopoly hold of African filmmakers on that form of knowledge'.[83] Rouch was asked to leave the country, while Godard and Anne-Marie Mieville cut short their stay.

Not so very far away, in South Africa, two workshops of the Association Varan financially aided by the French Ministry of Foreign Affairs explored 'direct' cinema in the Jean Rouch style from 1984 onwards, producing chronicles of everyday life.[84] In the view of some of the black participants, the constraints of *le direct* and the determination not to compromise limited the critical dimension of some of these realist films. The video collectives, which, from the 1980s onwards, were innovative players in the struggle for what Keyan Tomaselli calls a 'culture of resistance', were to adopt a clear perspective of political commitment.[85] White teachers and students, together with cinema professionals, made films with church and trade-union activists, which the latter disseminated through their own networks.

Collectives in which Whites and Blacks work together to 'reject the negative portrayal of black people' have taken stock of the changes within South African society, and borne poignant witness to them. The Johannesburg-based Varan studios has produced some exciting illustrations of the South African experience, such as *Chroniques sud-africaines* (1988), a series of portraits on the mind-sets of various different groups within that society. The 1994 elections were also documented, with great respect for people expressing their emotions, by filmmakers trained at the Varan 'Direct Cinema Workshop' (Julie Henderson, Thulani Mokoena and Donne Rundle), in *My Vote is My Secret*. The title of the film strikes a sardonic note, as the woman who uses the phrase leaves no doubt as to which way she is going to vote.

The political strategy of the early days of black African cinema still makes its indelible mark on a number of films made today. However, filmmakers are looking for – and gradually working towards – a modern response to the worldwide invasion of screens by the Hollywood film industry, and the logic it is able to impose in terms of plot. That response is not specifically African. This, no doubt, is why a considerable number of young directors, abandoning the example of those who stay rooted in Africa in order to resist, through a militant cinema, those 'rubbishy films which merely bring in the negative values of other civilizations',[86] reject the 'African filmmaker' label, which seems to confine them narrowly to the options chosen by their elders. They refuse to be regarded – to use an expression coined by the Guinean David Achkar – as 'the compulsory spokespeople for, and ethnologists of, their own culture', whose function will be to explain to Westerners how things are in Africa.[87] In much the same way as Sony Labou Tansi wrote 'To those who are looking for a politically "engaged" author, I respond by offering an engaging man',[88] they assert themselves as independent creative artists, attempting to break through to recognition. The cineaste is a creative artist and cinema an art.

This response, however, cannot conceal a deep cultural specificity among the filmmakers of Black Africa, as there is among those in the rest of the world. This is rooted as much in the familial and social culture as in the recent history of the continent and the developments of the African imagination. Far from being a 'ghetto cinema', African films show their originality, the originality of their cultural diversity, in a context in which the world is being Westernized. It is in the face of the standardization of plot-lines that the filmmaker must assert his status as artist, in order to exist as a creative thinker. It is the domination of the American industry which makes him want to free himself from economic constraints and, consequently, prompts him to call for state aid. It is as an African at the crossroads of two cultures that he shapes his approach to the questions of modernity and his otherness.

NOTES

1. 'Hosties noires, Poème liminaire' (1940), in *Oeuvre poétique*, Le Seuil, Paris, 1990, p. 55.
2. François de Medeiros, *L'Occident et l'Afrique (XIIème–XVème siècle)*, Karthala, Paris, 1985, p. 268.
3. Gudrun Honke, *Als die Weissen kamen – Ruanda und die Deutschen, 1885–1919*, Peter Hammer Verlag, Wuppertal, 1990, p. 81.
4. Claude Liauzu, *Race et civilisation: L'autre dans la culture occidentale. Anthologie critique*, Syros, Paris, 1992, p. 456; also pp. 163 ff., 288.
5. Interview with Abderrahmane Sissako, *Africultures* 10, L'Harmattan, Paris, 1998; and on www.africultures.com.
6. In Rithy Pahn's film *Cinéastes de notre temps: Souleymane Cissé* (1991). Rithy Pahn is the director of *Les Gens de la rizière* (1994).
7. The 'Association 21 bis, cinéma et histoire', 46 rue Saint-Sébastien, 75011 Paris, is a group of researchers working on this topic.
8. Yrzoala Jean Claude Meda, 'Le Cinéma colonial: les conditions de son développement', *Écrans d'Afrique* 9–10, 1994, p. 89.
9. H. Etiévan and M. Nalpas, 1927.
10. The exhibition 'L'Afrique au regard du cinéma colonial', presented at the Institute of the Arab World in 1994 and at Fespaco (The Ouagadougou Pan-African Festival of Cinema and Television) in 1995, which was mounted by the '21 bis cinéma et histoire' group, presented stills systematically classified by the following criteria: in the right of the frame, seen from behind, seen in profile, exposed on the ground, close-up black face, large/small, one/multiple, naked/dressed, dressed in plain or striped clothing, accessories such as earrings or knives, visible/invisible.
11. See A.C. Lelieur, M.C. Peyrière, R. Bacholllet and J.B. Debost, *Negripub: l'image des noirs dans la publicité*, Éditions d'art, Somogy, Paris 1992 (second edition, 1994).
12. This is the French version of 'Mr Clean' [*Trans.*].
13. Youssef El Ftouh, 'L'Afrique dans les images coloniales', *Écrans d'Afrique* 9–10, 1994, p. 85.
14. Germaine Dieterlen, 'A propos de Marcel Griaule et du cinéma ethnographique', in C.W. Thompson (ed.), *L'Autre et le sacré – surréalisme, cinéma, ethnologie*, L'Harmattan, Paris, 1995, pp. 434, 440.
15. Jean Rouch, 'Cartes postales', *Cinémaction* 26 ('Cinémas noirs d'Afrique'), undated, p. 11.
16. Miguel Benasayag and Edith Charlton, *Critique du Bonheur*, La Découverte, Paris, 1989, p. 178.
17. Alain Bergala, *Jean-Luc Godard par Jean-Luc Godard*, Cahiers du Cinéma/Éditions de l'Étoile, Paris, 1985, p. 178.
18. These words are from Oumarou Ganda's last interview on 16 November 1980 with Pierre Haffner, first published in *Sahel* 2078, p. 7, and quoted by Maïzama

Issa, *Un regard du dedans: Oumarou Ganda, cinéaste nigérien*, Editions Enda, Dakar, 1991.

19. Ibrahima Signaté, *Med Hondo, un cinéaste rebelle*, Présence Africaine, Paris, 1994, p. 40.

20. Pierre Haffner, 'Jean Rouch jugé par six cinéastes d'Afrique noire', *Cinémaction* 17 ('Jean Rouch, un griot gaulois'), 1982, p. 77.

21. See Reda Bensmaïa, 'Jean Rouch ou le cinéma de la cruauté', *Cinémaction* 17, 1982; Paul Stoller, 'Artaud, Rouch et le cinéma de la cruauté', in Thompson, *L'Autre et le sacré*, together with Rouch's comments in that same work, p. 408.

22. Gaston Heustrate, *Le Guide du cinéma*, vol. 2, Syros, Paris, 1984, p. 102.

23. Paulin Soumanou Vieyra, *Sembène Ousmane cinéaste*, Présence Africaine, Paris, 1972, p. 195.

24. *Cahiers du Cinéma* 402, December 1987, p. 29.

25. Interview with Joseph Gaye Ramaka, Paris, 1996. He is the author of two ethnographic documentaries on Senegalese rain-making rituals: *Baw-Naan* (1984) and *Nitt... Ndoxx* [The Rainmakers] (1988).

26. Guy Hennebelle and Catherine Ruelle, *Cinémaction* 3 ('Cinéastes d'Afrique noire'), p. 65.

27. Interview with Joseph Bitamba, *Africultures* 7 ('Les grands lacs et après'), L'Harmattan, Paris, 1998, and on www.africultures.com.

28. 'Rencontre avec Ngangura Mweze', *Le Film Africain* 13, November 1993, p. 10.

29. Interview with Maurice Kaboré, Paris, 1995.

30. *Le Film Africain* 2, May 1991, p. 7.

31. Serge Latouche, *La Planète des naufragés, essai sur l'après-développement*, La Découverte, Paris, 1991.

32. Interview with Anne-Laure Folly, Paris, 1995.

33. In Burkina Faso there is a poem which says that a sensible woman must not have her eyes open. In her film, Anne-Laure Folly shows that they have their eyes wide open to the particular themes of forced marriage, female circumcision, AIDS, and the economic role and political struggle of women.

34. In Rithy Pahn's 1991 film *Cinéastes de notre temps: Souleymane Cissé*.

35. Interview with Souleymane Cissé, *Cahiers du Cinéma* 492, June 1995, p. 58.

36. Séverin Akando from Benin had recounted Lumumba's life in *Histoire d'une vie* (1984), but 'where is the truth of that portrait, and where the lie, when the sites of memory no longer bear any trace of the dead man?' (Marie-Christine Peyrière, 'Visages volés, cachés, recomposés', in Fédération Panafricaine des Cinéastes (FEPACI), *L'Afrique et le centenaire du cinéma*, Présence Africaine, Paris, 1995, p. 360).

37. Valère D. Somé, *Thomas Sankara, l'espoir assassiné*, L'Harmattan, Paris, 1990.

38. Interview with Balufu Bakupa-Kanyinda, *Africa International* 308, October 1997.

39. Ababacar Samb Makharam, interviewed by Pierre Haeffner, in *Kino in Schwarzafrika*, CICM, Munich, 1989, p. 128.

40. Sembène Ousmane, *Le Film Africain* 14, February 1994, p. 9.

41. Editions Debresse, Paris, 1957.

42. Heinemann Educational, London, 1970.

43. Interview with Sembène Ousmane, *Africa International* 311, February 1998.

44. Quoted by Antoine Kakou, 'Sembène Ousmane', *Cinémaction* 34, 1985, p. 17.

45. Sembène Ousmane, quoted by Balufu Bakupa-Kanyinda in Fédération Panafricaine des Cinéastes [FEPACI], *L'Afrique et le centenaire du cinéma*, p. 25.

46. Gaston Kaboré, 'Mon rapport au cinéma', in ibid., p. 374.

47. Conversation with Gaston Kaboré, Ouagadougou, 1995.

48. June Givanni, 'African Conversations', *Sight and Sound*, vol. 5, no. 9, September 1995, p. 31.

49. 'Nyamanton' means 'heap of rubbish'. It is the name the Bambara often give to their eldest child, in accordance with the proverb: 'Everything is hidden under the rubbish heap, but the rubbish heap isn't hidden under anything', which indicates that the eldest child is responsible for the whole brood.

50. Interview by Emmanuel Saba, *Sidwaya* 2012, 5 May 1992, Ouagadougou.

51. Jean-Marie Gibbal, 'Si jeunesse pouvait, si vieillesse savait…', *Positif* 264 February 1983, p. 82.

52. See Nwachukwu Frank Ukadike, *Black African Cinema*, University of California Press, 1994, pp. 231 ff., and Manthia Diawara, *African Cinema: Politics and Culture*, Indiana University Press, Bloomington, 1992, pp. 88–103.

53. Sarah Maldoror, *Le Monde*, 27 April 1973, p. 15. Quoted by Michel Larouche, 'Le Temps que l'on met à marcher', in M. Larouche (ed.), *Films d'Afrique*, Guernica Press, Montréal/Québec, 1991, p. 27.

54. Joël Magny, 'Le Sens des gestes', *Cahiers du Cinéma* 404, February 1988, p. 53.

55. Sembène Ousmane had already received an award for *Mandabi/The Money Order* at the 1968 Venice Film Festival. *Le Vent des Aurès* by the Algerian director Lakhdar Hamina had received an award at Cannes in 1967 and, in the following years, *Concerto pour un exil* (Désiré Ecaré, Ivory Coast, 1967) and *Cabascabo* (Oumarou Ganda, Niger 1969) had been presented there. Mohammed Lakhdar Hamina was to receive the Palme d'Or in 1975 for his *Chronicle of the Year of Embers*.

56. Before this, black African films were almost totally absent from the screens of Cannes. The panel of judges of the 'Un Certain Regard' prize had shortlisted *Fad'jal* (Safi Faye, Senegal) in 1979 and a Senegalese short, *Le Certificat d'indigence* (Moussa Yoro Bathily), in 1983.

57. Cited by Antoine de Baeque and Stéphane Braunschweig, 'Pionnier en son pays', *Journal des Cahiers du Cinéma* 381, March 1986, p. VI.

58. André Gardies, *Cinéma d'Afrique noire francophone, l'espace miroir*, L'Harmattan, Paris, 1989, p. 164. The exceptions mentioned by Gardies are *Touki-Bouki* (Djibril Diop Mambety, Senegal, 1975), *Fad'jal* (Safi Faye, Senegal, 1979), and *Nelisita* (Ruy Duarte de Carvalho, Angola, 1983).

59. *Cinémaction* 3, p. 103.

60. Pierre Haeffner, 'L'Esthétique des films', *Cinémaction* 26, 1981, p. 61.

61. Diawara, *African Cinema*, pp. 22 ff.

62. Paulin Soumanou Vieyra, *Le Cinéma africain des origines à 1973*, Présence Africaine, Paris, 1975, p. 156. The film has a failing 'in terms of both its conception and its realization' in that, as a result of the collective nature of the project, no one managed to impose a style upon it.

63. Victor Bachy, *Pour une histoire du cinéma africain*, OCIC, Brussels, 1987, p. 19.

64. Ibid., p. 12. Jean Rouch was an admirer of this work, and he wrote in the catalogue of *Ethnographic Films in Black Africa* (UNESCO, 1967): 'I do not know what missionary cinema would have produced if it had been able to continue its activity.'

65. Pierre Haffner, 'Stratégies du ciné-mobile, une note pour une histoire parallèle du cinéma et de l'Afrique noire', in Fédération Panafricaine des Cinéastes (FEPACI), *L'Afrique et le centenaire du cinéma*, p. 88.

66. Ibid., p. 87.

67. Aryetey was the director of the first Ghanaian feature film, *No Tears for Ananse*, based on a traditional folk tale and made in a style akin to filmed theatre.

68. *Contact* (1976), directed by the Italian Giorgio Bontempi; *The Visitor* (1983) by Mike Fleetwood.

69. Interview with Françoise Balogun, 1995.

70. Françoise Balogun, *Le Cinéma au Nigeria*, OCIC/L'Harmattan, Paris, 1984, p. 23.

71. The French equivalent of VSO. [Trans.]

72. Jean-René Debrix, 'Dix ans de coopération franco-africaine ont permis la naissance du jeune cinéma d'Afrique noire', *Sentiers* 1, 1970, quoted by Diawara, *African Cinema*, p. 26. See also the interview with Debrix in *Cinémaction* 3 ('Cinéastes d'Afrique noire'), 1978, pp. 153–8.

73. Interview with Lucien Patry, Paris, 1995.

74. Givanni, 'African Conversations', p. 31.

75. Interview with Michel Janin, director of the French Cultural Centre, Abidjan.

76. Safi Faye dedicated the film *Fad'jal*, which came out in the same year, to Debrix, who died of a heart attack.

77. Interview with Andrée Davanture, Paris, 1995.

78. Jean-Michel Tchissoukou, Congo, 1979.

79. Diawara, *African Cinema*, p. 39.

80. Tahar Cheriaa, 'La FEPACI et nous', in Fédération Panafricaine des Cinéastes (FEPACI), *L'Afrique et le centenaire du Cinéma*, p. 253.

81. Interview with Andrée Davanture, Paris, 1995.

82. Sarah Thaouss Maton, 'Interview with Jean-Pierre Garcia and Mathieu Krim', *Le Film Africain* 22, November 1995, p. 17.

83. Diawara, *African Cinema*, p. 102.

84. John van Zyl, 'Une expérience: le Centre du Cinéma Direct', *Cinémaction* 39 ('Le Cinéma sud-africain est-il tombé sur la tête?'), 1986, p. 84.

85. Keyan Tomaselli. 'Le Cinéma et la vidéo d'opposition', *Cinémaction* 39, 1986, p. 79.

86. Cheikh Oumar Sissoko, interviewed by Emmanuel Sama in the Burkina Faso newspaper *Sidwaya* 2012, 5 May 1992, Ouagadougou.

87. Interview with David Achkar, Paris 1995.

88. Foreword to *La Vie et demie*, Seuil, Paris, 1979.

TWO

DECOLONIZING THOUGHT

Though this child is not of noble birth, may Allah make him become noble and be so by his conduct. From the children the new will be born.

Sembène Ousmane, *Niaye*, Senegal, 1965

Reflecting reality in African film initially meant denouncing the corruption of the elites and their mimicking of Western ways. The aim was to revive the African cultural heritage, with films here echoing an ethic which draws on notions of authenticity. However, a critique of the shortcomings of tradition also became necessary, and this produced a new social vision in which the collective retained its determining force, but did so without opposing individualization. In this way, the cinema cultures of Black Africa have moved away from their initial ideological legitimation (reflecting reality in order to reclaim it) and have come, in the end, to assert the primacy of culture in social change.

AFRICA BETRAYED

I lived in a world of revolutionaries. Africa was not independent at the time, and we lived in a utopian world. If someone had told us that Africa was going to be what it is today, we would never have believed them. The start it has made has been worse than bad! We were convinced that Africa would carve out a place for itself in the world. When General de Gaulle said, 'If you want independence, take it', only one country dared to. There were worrying signs already.[1]

As Sarah Maldoror indicates here, cinema was for many African filmmakers a tool of revolution, a means of political education to be used for transforming consciousness. African film was part of an emerging Third World cinema, the aim of which was to decolonize thought in order to promote radical change in society. Hence the objective was to work out a new cinematic

Poster for
Nuages noirs
(Djingarey Maïga,
Niger, 1980).

language, aimed at '[developing] the cultural ethos of a people';[2] to study the psychological dimensions of oppression and underdevelopment, and express this in cultural terms in the cinema to advance the liberation struggle in contemporary Africa.

In a context of political impotence, where neither economic nor cultural independence had been achieved, such a cinema could exist only as a result of the determination of a number of individuals with strong personalities who did not hesitate to attack the established regimes. The films in question contain a great many attacks on corruption. In *Nuages noirs* (Djingarey Maïga, Niger, 1980), for example, Bonzei, head of Customs and Excise at Niamey – a post given to him, a former politician, as a reward for party loyalty – does not hesitate to corrupt a police superintendent, a magistrate and a midwife. He accuses Boubacar, a capable young manager who seems to be in line to replace him, of raping his fourteen-year-old daughter. The girl, forced to lie by her father and herself in danger of being convicted for this, commits suicide. In a dramatic scene, Boubacar goes to see Bonzei and, to his face, declares: 'You are responsible, you and your party!' In the end, an investigation conducted by a new magistrate of Boubacar's generation, a serious, upright young man, establishes his innocence for all to see.

UNSPOILT AFRICA

Fostering the emergence of new nations which were not mere carbon copies of the old colonial states meant reviving the African cultural heritage. The new heads of state were criticized for not having kept the promises made at Independence, and for not putting the values of precolonial society into practice and building a new Africa. It is with images of what awaits them, images of contemporary protest movements destabilizing the puppet states – from May 1968 in Paris to the riots in Salisbury (present-day Harare) – that Oumarou Ganda from Niger begins his film *L'Exilé/The Exiled* (1980). An African former ambassador, whose friends ask him why he had to go into exile, tells a traditional story on the theme of giving one's word and failing to keep it: 'Long ago, Africa was unspoilt. It was alone with itself and knew no outside influences. It worshipped living gods. One's word was sacred.' There is a king who has absolute power. Out walking one day, he overhears two young men who say they would be prepared to be beheaded if only they could spend a night with one of the king's daughters. He takes them at their word, and gives them his daughters' hands in marriage. A year later, he reminds them of the commitment they made. One of the sons acquiesces, and allows himself to be beheaded. The other takes his wife and runs off with her. This is the beginning of a long adventure, which will lead to his becoming, in turn, the king of a distant land. When his people are threatened by a terrible famine, he sacrifices himself to spare them that misfortune.

By the use of slow panning shots sensually embracing the bush and the village huts, by sparing use of a dialogue which maintains a sense of his characters' humanity, and drawing on a traditional folktale introduced with modern images, Oumarou Ganda, the former Abidjan and Marseille docker and actor-assistant on *Moi, un Noir*, elucidates that independence which Africans experienced both as dream and as nightmare: the elites in power had not kept their word, and they used the language of African authenticity as a veil with which to conceal their continuing mental attachment to the old colonial ways. Revolt is stirring, however, both in Paris and in Africa.

The need for an independence that is experienced as a return to traditional values was to leave a deep imprint on the first two decades of African creative art in general, and on its cinema in particular. 'It is assumed that the reference to African tradition is the seal of authenticity', writes Fabien Eboussi-Boulaga. 'Any future cultural project needs the warrant of that tradition. Every *Muntu* thinker must refer to it, must at least pay occasional lip service to it, or be suspected of treason and irremediable alienation.'[3] The *Muntu* – which, in all the languages of the Bantu group, means human being – was culturally destroyed by colonization: decolonization will often mean taking inspiration from the supposed 'golden age' of precolonial times. Not to make reference to those times would be to betray one's culture.

To decolonize thought means, in the first instance, to change one's vocabulary. In the later editions of his novels, Sembène Ousmane amends those expressions which seem too European: in *Xala*, melting 'like snow in the sun' becomes 'like shea butter in the sun'; a smile that is 'bittersweet' becomes a 'sweet potato–chilli pepper' smile; while in the French original of *God's Bits of Wood*, the expression 'un sourire mi-figue, mi-raisin' (a wry smile; literally, half-fig, half-grape), becomes 'mi-mangue, mi-goyave' (half-mango, half-guava)![4] Even today, Sembène declares: 'What interests me is to find the language that will enable me to reach the peasant of the Limpopo when I'm on the banks of the Senegal river!' And although he works on the book and the screenplay in tandem, a distance is emerging between literature and screen writing.

> I work on the book and the film at the same time, which is difficult. They act on each other. For example, I've been working for a week on a little scene. On the literary level, I've got it right. But on the cinematic level, I'm still working on it, because it's difficult: I still have a few seconds to find. There it's not a question of emotion any more: it's a mathematical framework to arrive at saying things. While remembering that I'm addressing the peasant of Senegal as well as the one on the Limpopo![5]

Similarly, the use of proverbs often gives films an aura of authenticity, though Sembène avoids any descent into ethnocentrism. Indeed, he has the griot in *Niaye* (Senegal, 1965) say: 'The blood of truth is always noble, whatever its source.'

POINTING THE FINGER

It is striking how much the political change to which these films aspire is ethical in nature. The commentary to *Niaye* poses the question: 'If we are in fact mere shades here below, if everything is decided, written before we are born, why do we need morality? Why good and evil? Why beauty and ugliness?' And it goes on: 'Everyone assumes some false attribute in order to swindle their neighbour. Our country is dying of lies and false morality.' Who defines good and evil? The return to cultural sources takes us back to a tribal society where chance does not exist, to a language in which there is no word for the absence of causality. In the absence of absurdity, there is always an explanation for misfortune and suffering, and the person who plays the role of sorcerer – that is to say, the one who is expert in things of the night and the unseen, the possessor of knowledge – will be responsible for finding it. He names the cause of the misfortune – generally, another protagonist: 'no one is immune from the accusation of playing the role of malign external influence: to put it plainly, everyone is a potential incarnation of evil.'[6]

As a cultural sorcerer, the moralist filmmaker points the finger at those who arrogate power to themselves, but also at his or her contemporaries who accept alienation at the hands of elites they have not chosen. At the end of a film in which corruption, incest, suicide and parricide follow one upon the other and in which, at the end, power is seized from a council of elders which has become a mere assembly of puppets, willing to cover up any crime to retain their privileges, the griot of *Niaye* decides to leave his village:

> I can't live in a place where dignity is not respected. You don't have to be a griot to tell the truth. I'm going into exile, but they are exiled within themselves! What has become of the men of yesteryear whose praises my father sang? Our inability to discern the truth comes not from our minds, but from the excessive respect we pay to birth and wealth!

Independence calls for a return to traditional values, but also for a critical reassessment of those values.

'Our community is breaking down!' Before reversing his decision and returning to the village – where he will, in the end, see the new headman driven away by the elders – the griot announces that the new must be constructed by developing tradition while at the same time respecting it: 'The new can be born only out of the old as it decays.' The new does not replace the old; it comes out of it. They go together, interlock, combine. There is no hint here of the idea of sweeping everything away and creating a *tabula rasa*, such as has long underlain the Western conception of revolution.

One would search in vain, then, in black African film for a call for the proletariat or the people to seize power, such as one finds in Glauber Rocha's Guevarist films, Youssef Chahine's Nasserite works, or American 'Black Power' cinema. Among the ideologues and leaders of Africa in the period

of Independence, one similarly finds that despite the Marxist inspiration of
many of the movements, the idea of class struggle as the motor of history
was rejected. From Amilcar Cabral, who advocated a revolution entirely
without class war,[7] to Julius Nyerere's 'African socialism' or *Ujamaa*, as
practised in Tanzania (the term is a Swahili one denoting membership of a
family), 'the negation of the class struggle was elevated', writes the Burundian
Melchior Mbonimpa, 'to the status of a prior condition for African socialism'.[8] By contrast, every time a model as clearly European as Marxism–
Leninism was applied (in the Congo, Benin, Angola, Mozambique and
Ethiopia), it was more as a result of political and diplomatic decisions made
by an elite steeped in Western culture than from an analysis of real social
relations.[9] The independent figures who were the first African filmmakers
never really subscribed to these forms of African 'socialism'. Based on
feelings which derived from their own experience and guided by men like
Sembène Ousmane and Oumarou Ganda, former Marseille and Abidjan
dockworkers, theirs remained a pragmatic approach.

THE MIRROR-SPACE

In order to decolonize the screen, the African audience had to be offered
a new vision of its own space. André Gardies has shown to what extent the
early film cultures of Black Africa attempted to recast the African space in
the image of the new sovereignties.[10] Colonialism had been a dispossession
of space, a deprivation of identity. The aim was to reclaim the territory so
that the audience could identify with it. By showing them images of home,
the cinema helped them to recover their cultural identity. When, in *Fad'jal*
(Senegal, 1979), Safi Faye shows long panning shots of the African bush, the
camera comes to rest, in the end, on human labour. Africa is now no longer
a backdrop, but the site of human activity. At a break in the harvest, the
children run off to their grandfather:

'Grandfather, tell us our history now.'
    'You're right. You ought to know it.'

In the prelude to the film, an inset quotation from Amadou Hampâté Bâ
sets the tone: 'In Africa an old man dying is like a library burning down.'
The story begins to the accompaniment of women dancing. Fad'jal is the
founder of the village, but it also means work: 'He who works will be happy.
He who does not work will be mocked.' *Fad'jal*, the day-by-day account of
a Serer village, does not so much tell a story as present a way of life. 'Unlike
Western cinema, which shows in order to tell, it seems to me that African

cinema tells in order to show', writes André Gardies.[11] The storyline is merely a pretext for the image to function as a mirror, disclosing a space and a behaviour which are presumed to be familiar and are to be reclaimed. To film Africa is to endow it with coherence for oneself and for one's fellow citizens. The space is the main character in the film. It has an almost fleshly existence on the screen, and gives coherence to the whole. For the African spectator, the accumulation of themes, which to us may seem bewildering, generates no confusion. The films are dense, but not confused. A man or woman recognizes him- or herself in them: the space is inhabited; people work there, relate to one another. The image is not a backdrop, but an art of living.

This is an ideological move. The desire to film African realities does not make cinema a pure reflection of reality: a certain image of the world is built up on the screen, and from this a political project emerges, pointing towards new imaginative possibilities. In *Un taxi pour Aouzou* (Issa Serge Coelo, Chad, 1994), Ali the taxi-driver plies the streets of N'djamena, picking up a whole gallery of characters on the way. There is the woman who is smuggling because her husband has no job, the glue-sniffer, the 'moaner' going on about greedy taxi-drivers, a woman with a fish which stinks the cab out... 'The taxi is democracy', says Ali. 'Anybody can get in, even if they stink!' When Ali learns that his wife has given birth, an amusing parade of taxis gathers around him, his colleagues expressing their solidarity, revealing the cement which holds their society together. The taxi provides a privileged vantage point for 'observing political realities, social distress, love – subjects which have their place in the cinema', comments the director.[12] The reality of life in Chad, which is so remote from us (though so present on the world's television screens in recent years) is conveyed with finesse and sensitivity. When, at the end of this 23-minute film, the camera pulls back to show the whole of N'djamena, the city already seems familiar. We have shared its turbulence, its tensions, its humour and the violence of a war which is still present, the everyday emotions of the place.

THE PRIMACY OF THE COLLECTIVE

Ali is merely the vehicle of a reality. At the beginning of the film he introduces himself:

> My name is Ali Mahamat Nour. They call me 'Arbatchar' after the torture I suffered during the war. I shall soon be a father. Here, if you're circumcised you become a man. And once your beard starts to grow, you get married and have children. And then, *inch'Allah*, you take a second wife. My idea is that if I've got a

son to carry on my name, two or three children are enough, because we haven't enough money to look after them properly.'

Even when Ali learns later of the birth of his child, the director focuses not so much on the psychology of his hero as on what his reaction says about the milieu in which he lives:

'Ali!'

'Taha, what are you doing here? You should be at school.'

'Uncle sent me. He's seen your mother-in-law with Achta at the hospital. Achta's had the baby!'

'Is it a boy?'

'No, it's a girl.'

'Is it really a girl? You're kidding!'

'I wouldn't dare.'

The film deals not so much with the man, then, as with the experiences and mentality of his milieu, with the group, the community. As Tahar Cheriaa stresses, the group represents the 'central character in African films. Indeed, I would say that the predominance of the group asserts itself very possibly without the director knowing it.'[13] It is as an effect of their cultural origins, then, that filmmakers stand out currently against a treatment of modernity that is confined to the individual – a tendency which is very strikingly marked, for example, among the younger French directors.

It is not that African cultures deprive individuals of their self-awareness. The question today is not one of an opposition between the individual and the group, but of a predominance of the one over the other. This does not prevent a certain individualization, since the inhabitant of a crisis-ridden Africa cannot, as in immediate postcolonial days, exist without representing his territory and the community to which he belongs. Weakened by the slave trade, racked with neurosis by colonial humiliation and alienated by the difficulty of living in today's Africa, the individual seeks a personal freedom to which he finds it difficult, none the less, to attribute a positive value, 'since it entails both resembling the colonialist and betraying the community.'[14]

Kini and Adams (Idrissa Ouedraogo, 1997), shot in Zimbabwe with South African actors, is thus typical of the current treatment of individuals in African cinema. Kini and Adams are two peasants trying to survive, who spend all their time dreaming of pastures new – in the city. They sink their time and their paltry resources into repairing an old banger which will be able to take them, and will enable them to earn money when they get there. Between the two men, however, jealousy, ambition and rivalry erect a wall which their friendship is unable to surmount. It is this wall which interests Idrissa Ouedraogo: the wall which goes up within each individual in a society torn between what it once was and what it is becoming. It is this cry from the heart (his previous film was called *Le Cri du coeur*) which is no longer an opposition between tradition and modernity, but the emergence of a new individual who feels dramatically both the fascination which Western technological success (and the corresponding consumer comfort) exerts on him and the vacuity and abnormality of the values implied by this model which is entirely subject to the logics of power, profit and the exclusion of the weakest. It is this split the film addresses – this dualization of society, this rent within every individual which will lead to the end of a friendship and a tragic dénouement for a man who cannot accept the impoverishment foisted upon him. We are far from the cowboy hero who is free to act as he chooses, unburdened by custom and free of state controls, a hero who can assume a destiny which it is within his power, if he so wishes, to define and magnify. The cinema has given Africans their fill of that type of hero, who is both fascinating and troubling, who clashes directly with their traditional ethical and aesthetic conventions. If Kini and Adams, with their social ambitions, are trying, each in his own way, to assert themselves individually, in the end they express their quest for individuality in a rejection of individualism. This is what interests me in African films today: the way they hesitantly and painfully weave this fabric of the 'revolt of the self' (as spoken of by such Arab critics as Khémais Khayati[15]) in a manner which is quite different from the Western model.

THE FREEDOM TO SAY NO

The quest for identity and the exploration of this contradictory personal development involve a confrontation with the elders which signifies neither passive acceptance nor rejection.

> 'The world is changing, young people exist.'
> 'The young want to run everything. The old aren't dead yet.'
> 'It isn't a rivalry between the old and the young. It's the times we are living in. I want to be village headman.'

This dialogue between the young and the old, brought together in *Fad'jal*, reminds us of the cultural freedom of the younger generation to reject the elders' management of affairs when they find it deficient. Indeed, had not the grandfather in the film already told the children that 'when the heir manages the property badly, it is taken away from him and given to the next in line'? The point here, then, is to show up the social order which emerged out of Independence, and to assert the freedom to say no: 'Our cinema must choose its path between immediate profitability, which condemns it to participate in the organized grinding-down of the continent, and contributing, at the risk of making itself unpopular, to the necessary thinking on freedom', writes Cameroonian director Jean-Marie Teno.[16]

Bad housing, urban chaos, unemployment and the vicious circle of poverty and resignation – this is the catalogue of horrors of neo-colonial modernity identified, in his view, with the filth and detritus piled in the streets of Yaoundé. Whose fault is this? That of the elites, of the governing politicians and their civil servants. The only possible answer is to regain a little freedom: to develop the informal sector, 'ducking and diving'; to start out from things as they are, but to have one's 'head in the clouds', to find a space of freedom. *La Tête dans les nuages* (1994) depicts an artist who finds components among this accumulation of detritus from which to fashion sculptures/totems of great plastic beauty – a recycling which symbolizes a possible African renaissance. The struggle for independence, which will enable everyone to exercise their initiative and creativity, is merely beginning: 'Freedom', continues Teno,

> means taking one's time; it means choosing to stand back from things, not moving, or moving only at one's own speed. Freedom means making documentaries or documents on video, especially when everyone thinks that is 'low status'; it also means refusing to enter that competitive whirl which prevents us from taking a view that extends beyond our very next film.

THE DUTY TO SHOW?

But how can you feel free when you know how much it costs to make a film today? What commercial legitimacy can there be for a cinema which, given low ticket prices, cannot be financed from its own audiences? What social legitimacy can there be for a fiction cinema which costs 800 million FCFA per full-length film?[17] Idrissa Ouedraogo stresses the enormous size of the sum: 'That's wells, schools, dispensaries!'[18] What cultural legitimacy can there be for a Western technology dominated by American industry? And what political legitimacy can there be for a cinema which has often had to take account of pressures from the authorities to remain in existence?

In these circumstances, legitimacy can only be ideological. It is 'night school', as Ousmane Sembène memorably put it, or – to quote Oumarou Ganda – it is 'a book which is, *par excellence*, read by everyone.'[19] A good film will be a useful film, but does a useful film necessarily make a good film? A good film will be descriptive of a new social order, so that an audience may bring that order about. But does the recognition of African reality

Poster for
La Noire de.../*Black Girl* (Sembène Ousmane, Senegal, 1966).

automatically imply knowledge of that reality? Filmic codes bring to the screen the image the director has of reality rather than reality itself![20] The time and space of cinema are closer to dreams and the imagination; they are closer to the author's personal representation than to reality. Any film conveys not *the meaning of reality*, but *its own meaning*.[21]

Young filmmakers are aware of this, and no longer seek legitimacy in too narrow an ideological justification. The Mauritanian director Abderrahmane Sissako sums up the situation: 'I don't have a duty to show!'[22] As thinking both on cinema and on the state of African societies progresses, there is a clear trend today: the aim is not so much to hold a mirror up to one's place in order to enable one's people to recover their identity but, rather, to offer a perception of the existing order in all areas of life and, as a consequence, to show a desire for a future order. The legitimacy of cinematic creation thus resides to a greater extent in the assertion of the role of culture in development.

Even when a film claims ideological legitimacy, however, its vision remains a profoundly ethical one, condemning evil, pursuing good. The cinema cultures of Black Africa, reflecting the social order which developed out of the colonial and immediate post-Independence periods, have been cultures of protest. In *Black Girl* (1966), for example, Sembène Ousmane denounces independence as a heavy, lifeless monument, on which Diouana and her boyfriend dance around insolently, answering only the promptings of their love. In this same vein, African filmmakers have passed a moral judgement on the present order and, in the mirror they offer up to contemporary African societies, set out a new ethics for political action and for life, a utopia for a world yet to be built.

NOTES

1. Jadot Sezirahiga, 'Entretien avec Sarah Maldoror', *Écrans d'Afrique* 12, 1995, p. 8.
2. Nwachukwu Frank Ukadike, *Black African Cinema*, University of California Press, Berkeley/Los Angeles/London, 1994, p. 5.
3. Fabien Eboussi-Boulaga, *La Crise du Muntu*, Présence Africaine, Paris, 1977, p. 143.
4. Jacques Chevrier, 'Sembène Ousmane, écrivain', *Cinémaction* 34 ('Sembène Ousmane'), 1985, p. 15.
5. Interview with Sembène Ousmane, *Africa International* 311, February 1998.
6. Melchior Mbonimpa, *Idéologies de l'indépendance africaine*, L'Harmattan, Paris, 1987, p. 48.
7. Amilcar Cabral, *Unity and Struggle*, Heinemann, London, 1980, p. 123.
8. Mbonimpa, *Idéologies de l'indépendance africaine*, p. 186.
9. Catherine Coquery-Vidrovitch, *Afrique noire, permanences et ruptures*, L'Harmattan, Paris, 1992.
10. André Gardies, *Cinéma d'Afrique noire francophone, l'espace miroir*, L'Harmattan, Paris, 1989, p. 8.
11. André Gardies and Pierre Haffner, *Regards sur le cinéma négro-africain*, OCIC, Brussels, 1987, p. 27.
12. *Écrans d'Afrique* 11, 1995, p. 17.
13. Tahar Cheriaa, 'Le Groupe et le héros', in Centre d'Études sur la Communication en Afrique, *Camera nigra, le discours du film africain*, OCIC-L'Harmattan, Paris, undated, pp. 109–10.
14. Mahmoud Hussein, *Versant Sud de la liberté, essai sur l'émergence de l'individu dans le Tiers monde*, La Découverte, Paris, 1989, p. 65.
15. Khémais Khayati, 'La liberté de l'individu dans les cinémas arabes', in *Cinémas arabes: topographie d'une image éclatée*, L'Harmattan, Paris, 1996, pp. 201–7.
16. Jean-Marie Teno, 'Liberté, le pouvoir de dire non', in *Cinéma et libertés*, Présence Africaine, Paris, 1993, p. 15.
17. There are 100 FCA francs to the French franc [*Trans.*].

18. Interview with Idrissa Ouedraogo, Paris/Ouagadougou, 1995.
19. Harouna Niandou, Interview with Ganda, *Nigerama* 3, 1975, p. 22; quoted by Maïzima Issa, *Un regard du dedans: Oumarou Ganda, cinéaste nigérien*, Editions Enda, Dakar, 1991, p. 51.
20. Gardies, *Cinéma d'Afrique noire francophone, l'espace miroir*, p. 176.
21. Christian Zimmer, *Cinéma et politique*, Seghers, Paris, 1974, p. 19.
22. Interview with Abderrahmane Sissako, Paris, 1995.

THREE

'PROVERBS WERE FLESH AND BLOOD': THE REFERENCE TO THE PAST[1]

> In what nostalgia
> Am I to recover my childhood
> Or against what cheek?
> Who, harming my sleep,
> Sang of monsters?
> I, my arm outstretched to the sea,
> What madness!
>> Tchicaya U Tam'si ('Marines')

There is a great ambiguity running through contemporary African history: the quest for authentically African values grounds a vision of an angelic, precolonial golden age which colonialism is supposed to have wiped out. In their concern to recover memory, some films have fallen prey to such a vision. A modern response to this is emerging, in the form of a fiction which explores the rationale for action and is not content with mere condemnation.

NECESSARY MEMORY

From the mid-1970s onwards, an increasing number of films have delved into the past to investigate Africa's deepest memory. Filmmakers are no longer content just to show the appearance of things in Africa today. It is no longer enough simply to condemn injustices. Confronted with the confusion of the current period, they are attempting to recover the deep values of Africa, the essential laws which govern relations between people, yesterday's values which can fuel progress tomorrow

notes the Tunisian Ferid Boughedir in his film *Caméra d'Afrique* (1983). 'But what if it were merely a myth?' he goes on. 'Can the soul of a continent be captured in images?'

On the Ghanaian coast, *Sankofa* is the drummer who summons up spirits. In the Akan language, *sankofa* also means 'to return to the past in order to go forward' – that is to say, to 'go back over one's past in order to wrest it from oblivion and thence to turn towards the future'. The film of the same name, made in 1993 by Haïle Gerima, an Ethiopian exiled in Washington, was a big hit in the USA, where it became a cult film for the black community. With the music of the *sankofa* beating in her ears, Mona, an African-American model, becomes possessed while visiting the Cape Coast castle in Ghana, from which thousands of slaves were shipped to the Americas. The spirits of her ancestors send her into the past where she becomes Shola, a maid on a sugar plantation, repeatedly beaten and raped by her master. She is in love with Shango, a rebellious West Indian slave, who urges her on to revolt. But Shola refuses to fight violence with violence. Nunu, an older slave, implores her to take flight. When the master discovers the plot, he punishes Shola and sends her to work in the fields. She then decides to struggle for freedom with Shango.

Mona, who originally sees herself simply as an American, irrespective of her blackness, will be able to construct her identity only after she has mentally inhabited the body and soul of her slave ancestor, and experienced her struggle. The past feeds into the present in a continuous spiral – *sankofa* – and clarifies the bonds uniting Africa and the black diaspora. Non-linear narration, stories within the story, repetition, different levels of music and voices and the use of mythic elements (such as a buzzard to mark transitions) all reinforce a different reading of History: whereas Hollywood-style presentation highlights the bodily and spiritual alienation of slaves, making them passive witnesses to an inhuman system, this film shows them as contradictory and dynamic actors in a liberation struggle. Re-establishing their African origin, it makes History a reference point for identity.[2]

Taking on historical subjects in the cinema thus makes it possible to restore a personal view of one's history and culture. Correcting the myths trafficked by Western images can help to change the view Westerners have of the continent and of black culture – and also the views of Africans themselves. In a period when humanitarian intervention (the only Northern presence in the South that can be admitted to) is being glorified, a film like *Le Grand Blanc de Lambaréné* (Bassek Ba Kobhio, Cameroon, 1994) is a useful corrective. The film, which covers the last thirty years of Albert Schweitzer's life, hovers between two opposing stances. Although initially conceived as a denunciation of colonial paternalism, in the end it presents a figure who cannot easily be shown as merely worthy of condemnation. It shows him by turns generous and racist, efficient and a megalomaniac, humble and egoistic.

When an admiring child says he wants to be a doctor, too, Schweitzer laughs in his face, telling him that a black boy isn't capable of that! The child will, nevertheless, go to Europe to study medicine, and return as a Member of Parliament at Independence. 'Schweitzer typifies Africa's humanitarian dependence', says Bassek Ba Kobhio. 'He chose to be the doctor of Lambarene, not to train Africans. He was clearly opposed to independence. He spoke many languages, but never studied the local language. He was a musician, but never showed any interest in African music.'[3] As a precursor of many Westerners' commitment in terms of humanitarian action, he exclaims in the film: 'I came to save the black man!' But he doesn't believe in anaesthetics, thinking that a black body reacts differently from a white one! Although he tends to the people's medical needs, his mind is on his surroundings: he writes books on African wildlife, and turns the dispensary into a Noah's Ark of different animals.

He will, however, choose to be buried at Lambarene. 'I'm from the forest of Cameroon myself', says the director. 'If someone tells me he wants to be buried in my homeland, I feel touched. I can't deny that.' There is fascination here, then, with the man in the bow tie, who put it on only for the photographers. And there is an honesty in this black-and-white vision which breaks with the Manichaean oppositions one finds only too frequently in a cinema with didactic intent.

The aim here is not, of course, to deny colonial alienation. 'If I made a film on Schweitzer, it's because his arguments are coming back into fashion!' says Bassek Ba Kobhio. A documentary like *Les Derniers colons* (Thierry Michel, Belgium, 1944) shows starkly how former colonialists who stayed in Zaire even after the rioting of 1991 and 1993 – and some Blacks also – remain nostalgic for a time when order and efficiency (of exploitation) reigned. The call for a modern recolonization of an Africa presumed incapable of managing its own affairs is, in a manner reminiscent of Holocaust-denial literature, a cancer on an ever-increasing body of writings. Hence the denunciation of colonialism remains on the agenda, as it is, for example, in *Camp de Thiaroye* (Sembène Ousmane and Thierno Faty Sow, Senegal, 1988), a film made without the support of French backers. The film was exemplary as a successful co-production between a number of African countries (Algeria, Tunisia, Senegal), and it was rewarded for its technical quality with the Special Jury Prize at the Venice Mostra. In that film, we see the so-called *tirailleurs sénégalais* (they were in fact drawn from various African countries) in their camp at Thiaroye near Dakar, demanding the same treatment and wages as European soldiers. The meeting between an African and an African-American sergeant (the latter evoking the black diaspora) reinforces the

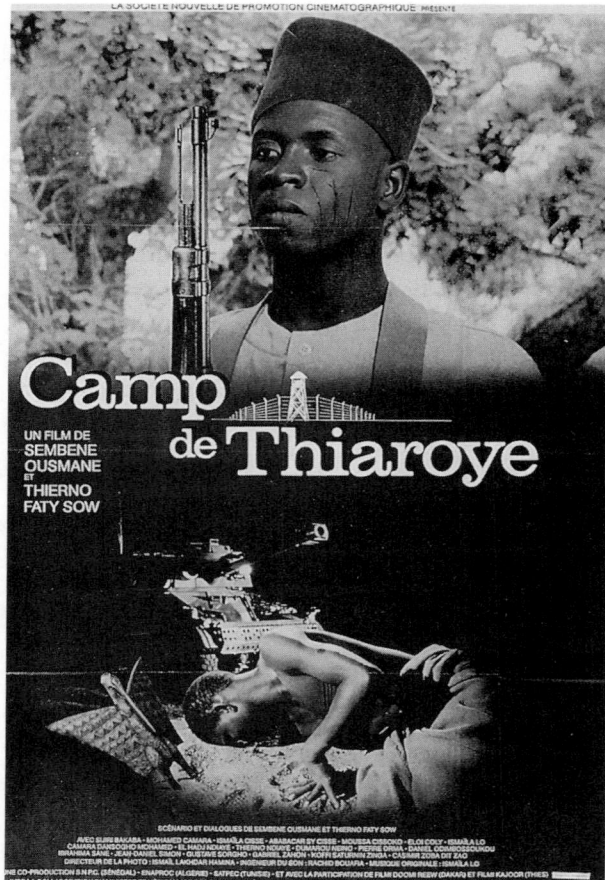

Poster for
Camp de Thiaroye
(Sembène Ousmane
and Thierno Faty
Sow, Senegal,
1988).

men's determination to reject this discrimination against them. After suffering the successive indignities reserved for 'colonial troops' – and, despite their engagement in the European war, they are still regarded as such – they mutiny. Their revolt is bloodily suppressed, and they are wiped out.

BLACK PHARAOHS

In the face of Western distortions, Africa has to restore an African vision of its history. As a Peul proverb has it: 'The child without memory will never shit hard.'[4] In order one day to be able to take a serene view of its identity, Africa needs a historical memory today, given all the troubles it faces. The impact of the work of Cheikh Anta Diop provides a good illustration of this need for history.[5] Diop has shown the importance of the Nubian, Black African, background in the development of Ancient Egypt, which, after its annexation by the Hellenic world and conquest by the Romans, was one of the seminal cultures of the West. In the view of the Mauritanian Med Hondo, Cheikh Anta Diop has 'scientifically re-established the historical continuity of Black African civilizations since the age of the pharaohs. His objective was not to find an alibi for our present tribulations but to restore the dignity of his own people.'[6] It is this continuity which is addressed in Hondo's film *Sarraounia* (Grand Prize, Fespaco 1987), adapted from the novel of the same name by Abdoulaye Mamani of Niger: the dynamism of African culture before and during colonization, the pivotal role played by women and the need for revolt against oppression. When Queen Sarraounia asserted the importance of resistance and autonomy, African audiences in Ouagadougou and Dakar did not miss the point, and applauded loudly. This queen of the Aznas of Niger, an initiate into the traditional secrets of her people, victorious in her campaign against the French colonial forces and loyal to her friends, is the perfect archetype of independence. She attempts to protect her kingdom both from colonial invasion and from Muslim conquest. At the end of the film she is immortalized by the griot: she has taught the African people to accept death before dishonour, and to see the struggle through to total liberation.

But good intentions are not enough. The ambiguity of historical films is that they run the danger of fostering myths. Many a revolution rooted in the idea of freedom has ended in terror. Many a liberation struggle has led to totalitarianism. Merely to call for liberation is not enough: one also has to specify what liberty is meant, and what it entails if dreams and myths are to be transformed into problems that require creative solutions. It is when memory of the past does not lead to a nostalgia for origins that it contributes to developing a critical stance.

It is the virtue of Cheikh Oumar Sissoko's film *Guimba, the Tyrant* (Mali, Grand Prize, Fespaco 1995) that it scathingly mobilizes the human and cultural diversity of Africa against the narrow political and sexual tyranny of a clan. The result is an acerbic critique of political power. The sandy, ochre tones of the walls of Djenné, jewel of medieval Sudan, where Black Africa meets Arabia, set off the dazzling colours of the traditional clothing, while the women from various African backgrounds express themselves in their own languages. This reference to a diverse, plural Africa highlights the madness of the tyrant's confiscation of power, and points forward to the current absence of political resolve to bring about genuine change. The setting of the film is not Mali but the ancient Mandé Empire, not the frontiers imposed by the colonial rulers but a supranational entity corresponding to a culture. This city of the Sahel, Sitakili, is ruled by Guimba Dunbuya and his dwarfish son Janguiné. From birth, Kani Coulibaly has been betrothed to Janguiné. To mark this bond, a rope was attached to the infant's left wrist. When she grows into a beautiful girl, Kani is greatly coveted, but no suitor dares declare himself in the climate of terror Guimba has created. During a courtesy visit to Kani, the dwarf Janguiné falls in love with Meya, mother of his fiancée. Meya's legitimate husband, Mambi, refuses to divorce her and, to satisfy his son's whim, Guimba has Mambi thrown out of the city. He takes refuge in a village of hunters, from which the revolt against the tyrant will be staged.

Thinking through the problem of freedom requires some introspection. A loss of identity on the part of the black colonial elites in part explains the current ambiguities of the neo-colonial period. In *Love Brewed in the African Pot* (Ghana, 1980), Kwaw Ansah had criticized his country's elite for rejecting their origins. In *Heritage... Africa* (Grand Prize, Fespaco 1989), he analyses how a civil servant in the colonial administration, Kwesi Atta Bosomefi – who, in imitation of his colonial masters, has turned himself into Quincy Arthur Bosomfield – is obliged to reject his culture as he takes on British ways. When his mother, whom he is ashamed to present to his friends, passes on to him the casket containing the spirit of his lineage, he hurriedly gives it away to the colonial governor. His mother, who eventually learns of this, appeals to ancient ancestral forces:

> You have wounded my soul.
> You have broken it.
> You have broken the bond with your ancestors.
> What has become of what you learned at school?
> Even your twin sister would have understood such a simple message!
> You will never be free if you do not recover the family casket.
> The ancestors will never leave you in peace!

In betraying his mother, he has betrayed 'Mother Africa'. His is a treason against the Africa of tradition as much as against the Africa of nations – the fatherland – which still remains to be built.[7] Could colonial recognition replace the love and protection he will have lost? A sense of all this will dawn on him after a series of humiliating confrontations with his mother, his wife and an imprisoned freedom fighter – all victims of the system he has contributed to constructing – and the experience of a terrifying dream. These events help him to see the need to seek out his heritage.

The countries which have undergone long struggles for their independence continue to celebrate the heroes of the liberation struggle to preserve

Poster for *Heritage Africa* (Kwaw Ansah, Ghana, 1989).

national unity. This might be said to be the objective of *Flame* (Ingrid Sinclair, Zimbabwe, 1996), the first film made about the Chimurenga which, after eight years of civil strife, brought down the Rhodesian apartheid regime. Two adolescent girls join the guerrilla forces in Mozambique. Life in the camps is hard, and the situation for women is far from enviable, but the two women each choose a *nom de guerre* – 'Flame' and 'Liberty' – and take their places in the common struggle. However, they continue to grow apart in the manner of their self-assertion: while Liberty pursues her desire to better herself socially through education, Flame passes through bouts of fighting and love affairs before finally returning after independence to her condition as a peasant and an alienated woman. At this point, she leaves her husband and goes back to the city to join up with Liberty again. The liberation struggle is seen here as a metaphor for women's struggle for independence. This was not to everyone's liking, and filming was interrupted at one stage by a debate on the historical veracity of the film, for though it is very accurate on the circumstances of the war, it also shows the achievement of equality between the sexes in the fighting forces. The problem was not so much that the film gave a mythic account of the liberation struggle but that it carried an unwelcome message for the times.

THE STRUGGLE WITH ONESELF

It is now that the generation of the children of Independence is making its voice heard, calling for Africans to take responsibility for themselves:

> Making a film about my father gave me a chance to ask how responsible we are for what is happening in Africa today. Westerners created this situation and the African countries have subsequently tried to take the easy way out... I live in a black *and* white world, in terms of both skin colour and morality. I can't say where good or evil lies: evil is mainly within us, as is good. It is a constant struggle with oneself,

says David Achkar of his film *Allah Tantou* (1990).[8] His father, Marof Achkar, was Guinea's ambassador to the UN. Recalled by the Guinean government in 1968, ostensibly to be given a new post, he was arrested as he stepped off the plane and imprisoned in the notorious Boiro camp. He did not get out alive. Switching between scenes of his father being interrogated in his cell, extracts from super-8 films made by his family, photographed letters ('writing to survive'), scenes of humiliation in prison and, at the end, the silent parade of the victims of the Sékou Touré regime, David Achkar explores the jigsaw of his memory: 'I didn't know my father much: only through what I've been told and what he wrote to us from prison.' The commentary blends the introspective 'I' with the son's 'you' before a final indictment of the regime couched in conventional political language.

Introspection is necessary if Africa is going to be able to define a future for itself. 'Africa must seek a certain Redemption', says Achkar.

> It must face up to its own evil. My film goes down well in the USA with young students who want to relocate their black identity in its overall context and not just as part of a dream of Africa with chocolate-box, Camara Laye-style images – pictures of a lost Africa you want to recover.

This is reminiscent of the criticism Mongo Beti made of Camara Laye's writings *(The Dark Child*[9]*)*, accusing him of pandering to colonial expectations of the good Negro intellectual.

AFRICAN RECALCITRANCE

This cliché of a hedonistic Africa dominates the blockbusters set in colonial Africa, such as *Out of Africa* (Sydney Pollack, 1985), as though the African imaginary were reduced to a mere desire for physical pleasure. In fact, this merely represents an 'exotic' Western vision of the continent. Such hedonism is described as 'an imported value' by Célestin Monga from Cameroon, as is that old stereotyped colonial image of African 'sexual permissiveness' which has become a dependable tourist standby.[10]

African cinema responds to the exotic gaze by affirming a dignity, an autonomy and a freedom. But, as Célestin Monga goes on to say, that freedom cannot be lived merely as a dream. It is the affirmation that in Africa

> man refuses to be the mere instrument of reason. The African, clothed in his spirituality, blessed with a practical, inventive vitality, tends to slip out from under that divine reason which people have been trying to impose on him for four centuries, and which feels in his daily life like a straitjacket. He restores contradiction to its proper place, which is an essential precondition for achieving the inner freedom that can alone make it possible to conceive other freedoms, to survive the everyday acts of cruelty, the totalitarianisms of political life, the fundamentalist manias of a traditional culture ill-adapted to the age, as well as the tyranny of an obsolete family yoke.

Many films assert the primacy of 'human happiness over repressive traditional practices',[11] but two masterpieces stand out. *Djeli* (Fadika Kramo-Lanciné, Ivory Coast, Grand Prize, Fespaco 1981) sets the love between two students, Fanta and Karamoko, against the tradition which prevents a son of a griot from marrying a Mandingo noblewoman, a conflict which inspires Karamoko to observe: 'We're talking feelings and they're talking marriage.' The conflict will be resolved only at the eleventh hour, when Fanta attempts suicide. In *Muna moto* [The Other's Child] (Jean-Pierre Dikongué Pipa, Cameroon, Grand Prize, Fespaco 1976), a love match between Ngando and Ndomé is prevented by dowry traditions. Ngando, an orphan, cannot pay: 'A woman is an ear of corn you can't bite into unless you have teeth!' Ndomé even goes so far as to lose her virginity to force the fiancé of her choice on her family – a fiancé who will give her a child. Ngando rebels: 'My uncle is stupid, Ndomé's parents are stupid and the stupidest ones are those who invented the dowry custom, not to mention the people who accept it! I'm stupid myself for not being able to change it!'

He kidnaps the child and is arrested, sentenced and imprisoned. African vitality, then, is a product not of hedonism but of an indiscipline, a recalcitrance[12] which can be seen in very many films, a vitality which Eric Fottorino, Christophe Guillemin and Erik Orsenna captured well in their book *Besoin d'Afrique*. They quote the Congolese writer Tchicaya U Tam'si, whom Sony Labou Tansi called 'the father of our dream', saying: 'Laughter is the only uniform I never wore in tatters at orgies.'[13]

HISTORY AS NOSTALGIA

That same Tchicaya U Tam'si had a character in one of his novels say that colonization was 'the first great African revolution'.[14] Leaving aside the element of provocation here, let us none the less attend to the question this raises. If Africa wishes to be aware, in building its future, of the forces which have shaped it, the upheavals brought to African societies by colonization and neo-colonialism cannot be conceived simply in terms of an antagonism with the West, with an outside entity. This is what the Senegalese writer Kä Mana asserts in his remarkable book *L'Afrique va-t-elle mourir?*:

> A neo-colonial subject, who sees colonialism as the beginning of a revolution he must himself deepen, has already sloughed off the lethal mentality which neo-colonial patterns of thought impose on him. He is no longer within a logic of structural antagonisms and violence. He is in a new logic, the logic of the creativity his new sense of being brings him for the transformation of his own destiny.[15]

It is not, then, the exactitude of the reproduction of historical facts and circumstances which gives a film veracity. This is, rather, to be sought in a thinking on History which cannot content itself with an alleged 'historical virginity' of the continent. The quest for essential values for the present cannot express itself in the idealization of historical characters who have successfully defended a supposed harmony by opposing external aggression. What is the point of mythifying the past – and reinforcing the myth of an angelic precolonial Africa for which the audience could only be nostalgic? What is the point, for example, of keeping silent about the slavery which existed before the arrival of Arabic and European slave-traders?[16] The dramatic stumblings of European history show how the mystification of the past leads to dead ends. Did not Goethe say in *Faust* that a people which does not reflect on its history is condemned to relive it? Black African cinema has not as yet made much of an effort to demystify precolonial Africa, whereas in the literary field such efforts go back to the 1960s and Yambo Ouologuem's iconoclastic novel *Bound to Violence*.[17]

Africa and the West share the same non-representation of slavery and the slave trade in the cinema. Films which deal with this subject are extremely rare. *Slaves* (Herbert J. Biberman, United States, 1969), *Aubes noires* (R. Lyod and D. Kraft, UK, 1978), *Your Children Come Back to You* (Alile Sharon Larkin, UK, 1975), *Tamango* (John Berry, with Dorothy Dandridge, from the novella by Mérimée, France, 1958) and *Solomon Northrup's Odyssey* (Gordon Parks, United States, 1980) remain isolated examples. As for Bernard Girardeau's *Les Caprices d'un fleuve* (France 1996), that is a film which falls into both cliché and the picturesque.

The showing of French director Christian Richard's *Gandaogo/Le Courage des autres* (Burkina Faso, 1987, with Sotigui Kouyaté) as the opening film at the eighth Fespaco sparked off a lively controversy. When black people showed Blacks being enslaved by Blacks, did that not justify the slave trade?[18] At the time, Richard was teaching at Inafec, the now-defunct Ouagadougou film school, and the film was produced by the likewise defunct Cinafric. It was an interesting film, practically without dialogue, showing the revolt of a column of slaves against their African masters. We find the same kind of memory-work in *La Côte des esclaves* (1994), in which Elio Suhamy sought out the social traces of the slave trade in Benin with the descendants of those who played an active role in it. But how is one to show that trade? It is with this question of the image that Cameroonian director François Woukoache's very fine film *Asientos* (1995) begins. On a shakily skewed television set, Western photographers are seen rattling out shots of the genocidal horror in Rwanda. History is stammering: 'It's beginning again.' The filmmaker surfs to find the right image, to avoid the pitfall of preoccupation with wretchedness, the sempiternal vision of enslavement and passivity. 'Why does the sea not throw back these corpses?' There is nothing to be seen of the slave trade. The camera fixes on the bare walls of Gorée. Only the plaintive cries of the sea can evoke those of the chained slaves. A child runs around to some lines from Aimé Césaire: 'In my memory there are gaps. My memory has its girdle of corpses...' 'It is a film about memory', says the director,

> a reaction to what is happening today. Africans seem neither to be masters of their destiny nor to be able to react to what is happening to them and redefine what they are. The slave trade is a trauma which has made Africa what it has become and will continue to define Africa in the third millennium if Africans do not take a good look at their history.[19]

The verdict is severe: 'The wave of filmmakers in the 1980s tried to change the image of Africa without investigating the moment when the image they rejected had emerged. This is the moment of the slave trade, when the black man was defined as an object by the Other.' And a voice-off concludes: 'Be quiet, he says, listen to the silence, relearn to look in order to see the unnameable.' The priority, then, will be to restore history. Since nobody does, let's talk about it! The Mauritanian Med Hondo replays the history of the West Indian slave trade in *West Indies: Les Nègres marrons de la liberté* (1979), daring to produce 'a musical tragicomedy' with the scenic unity of a ship as its backdrop – an interesting but filmically disconcerting option. The film is a theatrical dance-piece in the form of a radical chronicle, based on

a play by the playwright Daniel Boukman from Martinique: its aim is to re-
establish the truth of economic interest, to catalogue the abominations
committed, to confound the myths.

The Senegalese director Sembène Ousmane does not hesitate to show
slaves in the African society of his ode to resistance, the magnificent *Ceddo*
(1977), and he even has them branded with hot irons, as an indelible fleshly
mark of their condition. And, as we have seen, the Ethiopian Haïlé Gerima
calls up the spirits of the past in *Sankofa* (1993) to overturn the Hollywood
presentation of history. And it is no small undertaking to do so. When the
West Indian Guy Deslauriers (who had already dealt with this theme in
L'Exil du roi Behanzin, 1996) was preparing to film his docu-drama *Le Passage
du milieu*, it was the point of view of the hold, not of above decks, that he
took to describe the crossing of a slave ship, with its share of epidemics,
deaths, storms and becalmings which led the captain to sacrifice the weakest
slaves when he saw water and rations running low. And this point of view
is also that of the revolt of the slaves against the murder being perpetrated
on them. For this is the nub where memory is concerned: it was through
resistance that the slaves survived; it was through their uprisings that they
finally won abolition.

In their concern to contribute to the assertion of a positive self-image, it
has been the filmmakers of the black diaspora rather than those of Africa
who have made an ever-increasing number of historical films on escapes by
runaway slaves. The concern here is to reconstitute a dismembered past and
to reappropriate cultural codes. This is precisely the aim of the Brazilian
Carlos Diegues's trilogy, in documenting Afro-Brazilian resistance. *Ganga
Zumba* (1963) centres on a runaway slave discovering that he is the grandson
of the king of Palmares, the autarkic slave republic which was able to hold
out for a century (1595–1695) against the repeated onslaughts of the Dutch
and the Portuguese and which had, at its high point, 20,000 members on a
territory one-third the size of Portugal; *Xica da Silva* (1976) and *Quilombo*
(1984), also about Palmares, are conceived as *samba enredos* (plots constructed
like a 'samba school' with singing, dancing, costumes and words forming a
coherent folk narrative[20]), which in fact leaves them verging on a decorative
exoticism. This is also the case with Walter Lima Jr's *Chico Rei* (1982), a
Germano-Brazilian co-production about an enslaved African king buying
back his freedom. After successfully working a mine called Encardideira, he
becomes king of his region once again, while maintaining his non-violent
African methods. The black Cuban director Sergio Giral has also made a
trilogy, in which he attempts to restore an internal reading of slavery in
Cuba. The films concerned are *El Otro Francisco* (1975), *El Rancheador* (1976)

and *Maluala* (1979). Giral reverses the perspective adopted in the novel from which the first of these is taken:

> In camera terms, Suàrez y Romero, a descendant of a family of plantation owners, oriented the camera from his own angle, that of the slave-owner – focusing on the protagonists of his story and forgetting the other slaves on the plantation. My film turns the camera on these people, to see the same story through the eyes of those who apparently have no identity, but whose story this really is.

In the West Indies, Christian Lara – using as his source a study carried out by his grandfather, the son of a slave freed in 1848 – made the first West Indian historical epic, *Vivre libre ou mourir* (1980). In that film he squeezes the history of Guadeloupe into a courtroom where French colonialism is put on trial, and the heroes of Guadaloupe's struggle for independence defended. In *Sucre amer* (1997), he returns with a fictional work on the theme of revolt. This is still topical, for, as the Ivorian Diabi Lanciné asserts in *L'Africaine d'Amérique* (1991), 'the circumstances which also made you a hunted prey are no different.' This film, a didactic meditation on the recourse to African roots, puts the accent on the painful historic fissure in Black American history: 'All peoples despise us for our slave past.' This says it all. The memory has to be exorcized.

When, in *Les anneaux de la mémoire* (1994), the Ivorian director Kitia Touré questions a woman whose forebears were slavers sailing out of the French port of Nantes, he is shocked to find 'neither remorse nor compassion'. This film, which provides an edifying catalogue of the instruments of the slave trade, inquires into the impressive occultation of memory in this slaving port. For when all is said and done, its subject is not the slave trade, but memory, and dealing with memory means reopening questions of the present: Colbert's *Code Noir* (decreed by Louis XIV in 1685 and recast in 1724) continues its ravages, claims the Guadaloupean director Tony Coco-Viloin in *Le Cri des Neg marron* (1993), an impressionistic nightmare of a man of the black diaspora. 'The "*Neg marron*" is still running here':[21] so long as he is afraid of his history, so long has he has not exorcized it – which will be possible only when it is told from the inside and not from the outside. There is a contradiction in this: 'The paradox', says Coco-Viloin, 'is that when you're inside the yoke, you don't know the egg.' The thing then is to accept introspection, while preserving the question of origins – in short, to go 'back to the future', as in the Afro-American Julie Dash's admirable *Daughters of the Dust* (1991).

Breaking radically with the Hollywood aesthetic (of the *Amistad* variety – Steven Spielberg, 1997), which bolsters its faith in the continuity of progress with a linear temporal structure, this film translates into screen terms an oral tradition based on a cyclical conception of time. The identity of the characters emerges out of the rhythm of the close-ups of faces, the wide shots of landscapes and of an image which systematically binds the community to its surrounding space: Gullah Islands off the coast of South Carolina, the hub of the slave trade. It is in this space that black women will articulate their relation to Africa, their survival and their way of life in the USA. Dramatic confrontations mark out the experiences tearing apart the black man in America, before he comes in the end to settle on a multiple identity integrating the complexity of history. When the question 'Do you remember?' is put (in French) in the film, the answer comes back clearly: 'I express my memories in the language I learned here.' Here sharing and hybridization are ranged against a logic of authenticity, purity, confrontation and segregation. In linking a mojo and a Bible at the end of the film, however, Dash asserts that African culture can subvert the dominant culture, in an inverted syncretism. It is, then, an ethic of cultural resistance which the aesthetics of this crucial film presents – a film which, without ever showing slaves, defines the issues around slavery for the present age.

In his analysis of *Ceddo* (Sembène Ousmane, 1977), Serge Daney has shown how the element of inventing stories gives value to the living word as a collective statement which stands out against the myths of the Islamic colonialist.[22] *Ceddo*, which is set in the seventeenth or eighteenth century, depicts an African community confronted with two culturally alien forces competing for power: Islam (the imam) and Europe (the slave-trader and the priest). For Sembène, the ceddos are in fact resistance fighters [*des hommes du refus*]. They opposed Islamic penetration so that they did not lose their cultural identity. It is this force of protest which interests him, in keeping with the political message which runs through his work as a whole – the message of self-reliance:

> I wanted it to be above all a thought-provoking film, so that we Africans could have the courage to try to reflect on our own history and the elements which have come to us from outside, and I wanted us to stop making self-pitying films about our wretchedness or films to elicit other people's condescension.[23]

Yet it is when that reflection involves the presentation of the precolonial era as a golden age to be regained that what Marcien Towa from Cameroon terms 'the dictatorship of the past' appears: a tradition which is supposed to be reproduced as such, as though it were a question of restoring independence rather than establishing it, and a conception of the current situation which attributes it solely to external forces, as though it were decreed by the workings of fate. The subject of the most clear-sighted films is not, then, the past itself, but the contradictions of the past; it is not tradition itself, but the contradictory relationship with tradition. There is no golden age to go back to or step into: as the title of Ayi Kwei Armah's famous novel eloquently puts it: *The Beautyful Ones Are Not Yet Born.*[24]

LEGEND, A FALSE TRAIL?

The return to 'village films' (often dismissed as 'calabash cinema') is criticized both by the advocates of social analysis and by those who merely see such films as a way of responding commercially to the exotic expectations of Western audiences on the grounds that they develop a humanist, but ahistorical, ideology. The latter fear that the seductive effect of anthropology and folklore on foreign audiences may exert 'a magnetic influence' on a cinema which is financed in the main by the rich North, and that this will drive out all other approaches.[25]

But is this really a false trail? Should we deny the still essentially rural character of the countries of Black Africa? Three-quarters of their populations are still living in the countryside. When these country people leave the rural areas, they huddle together in enormous cities, but they do not deny their origins. Even if that huddling together constitutes one of the main social issues in present-day Africa, if not indeed its 'powder-keg', the rural origins of these city-dwellers remains crucial. Introspection cannot, therefore, be restricted solely to African cities. Are the Western critics who tend to accord greater importance to 'urban' films fully aware of this?

This criticism naturally arises out of a desire to see African cinema take on the challenges which the continent urgently has to meet today. The argument is that attention should be given to a salutary investigation of the urban conflicts which are going to determine the future, and where a social explosion may be feared, rather than carrying on with an epic cinema which is seen as too far removed from contemporary problems and in danger of providing a decorative image of Africa.

Yaaba [Grandmother] (Idrissa Ouedraogo, Special Prize of the Fespaco Jury, 1989; International Critics' Prize, Cannes, the same year), which was a great international success, was very much criticized by certain Africans and by the black diaspora in the American universities. The plot involves two children, Bila and Nopoko, who defy the proprieties imposed by the adults by befriending an old woman who is an outcast from the village on suspicion of witchcraft. When Bila calls an adult a 'bitch', the old woman retorts: 'Do not judge; she has her reasons.' The Malian writer Manthia Diawara sees in this philosophy a 'bourgeois humanist conception of tolerance', even 'a sort of French liberalism'.[26] The director has answered him by saying that 'the subject of the film' is indeed 'that people can be changed if you listen to them, and also that you shouldn't make arbitrary judgements'.[27] As a journey of initiation for two children learning to overcome prejudice, *Yaaba* is calling for a new view of the world, free of ideological assumptions. When the Nigerian Nwachukwu Frank Ukadike denounces it as 'elitist' and 'individualistic', asking whether it has 'a clear vision of the African future' and if it 'truly illuminates societal conflicts',[28] he clearly has in mind the requirement that a film should present an ideological vision. Yet this fictional work also speaks of the dignity of Africa, as the Senegalese cineaste Djibril Diop Mambety stresses in the rare commentary he appends to his fine, personal images of the making of *Yaaba* in *Parlons Grand-mère* (1989): 'Whether or not we are talking about film, Grandmother will avenge the child who is brought to his knees!'

Idrissa Ouedraogo acknowledges that he has 'in no sense any pretensions to represent my people or African values. It's easy to become pretentious when you set yourself up as a teacher or instructor.... Sembène's "night school" isn't fictional cinema!' And he stresses:

> Filmmakers, who have a power to say something, feel they have an obligation to communicate a political message, whereas a filmmaker is simply someone who wants to exchange a vision with others. We should give up this initial approach of wanting to be the consciousness of our peoples and assert our cinema more as the expression of our own consciousness. Our audiences often know a great deal more than we do about the conditions for their survival![29]

Cinema thus provides an opportunity to delve into one's origins: 'Africa will not invent the themes. They already exist. They are part of human life. The love of two children for a grandmother is universal, but we won't all talk about it in the same way.'[30]

The cinema cultures of Black Africa have not gone in much for formal innovation: the emphasis is on the human dimension. 'I am in pursuit of man, my erstwhile brother', wrote Sony Labou Tansi.[31] Similarly, Med Hondo – speaking in 1997, the year of *Watani, un monde sans mal* – observed:

> My concern remains a concern with the human being, immigrant or otherwise. *Watani* draws a parellel between two lives: a white man who is an executive in a bank and an immigrant dustman. These are the two situations of a single society: the supposedly rich person and the proletarian. The latter ends up being deported and the other being manipulated by right-wing extremists.

Recalling in this formally fragmented, discursively disrupted film the humanity of his culture of origin, Med Hondo presents that humanity not as an

On the set of *Samba Traoré* (Idrissa Ouedraogo, Burkina Faso, 1992).
© Félix von Muralt/Lookat.

alternative, but as an enrichment for a French society which desperately refuses to accept the grafting on to it of a foreign element.

In *Tilaï*, which won the Fespaco Grand Prize in 1991, Idrissa Ouedraogo once again takes up the call for tolerance which was evident in *Yaaba*, adding to this an examination of the theme of tradition. In this later film, Saga returns to the village of his birth after an absence of two years. His fiancée Nogma has become his father's second wife. Saga and Nogma still love each other. They make love. For the village this is incest, and Saga must die. Kougri, Saga's brother, should kill him, but instead he makes him promise never to return. The day Saga learns that his mother is dying he decides, all the same, to return to the village. He blows into his horn three times, as tradition demands when one enters the village and comes under its rules. Taking him for a ghost, the villagers run away. The father chases Kougri off and, in frustration, shoots Saga dead.

'I hadn't realized it, but it's a Greek tragedy!' the director was to say later.[32] But in fact this matters very little, for, although the particular does indeed open out into the universal, it is African reality Idrissa Ouedraogo is investigating, not the universality we believe we detect in his work. The film is part of a new take on history, which includes an investigation of human beings and their relations with tradition. This is no longer a simple battle between good and evil. Things are by no means seen in black-and-white terms, and the old rules are criticized in the very name of the values which inform them. This is what gives the film the pathos of an existential cry, the cry of a creature in crisis.

In such a context, do legends stand opposed to history, the folktale to social and historical investigation? The critical success of such films as *The Piano* (Jane Campion, Australia, 1993) or *Le Grand Bleu* (Luc Besson, France, 1990) is no doubt attributable in part to their treating contemporary themes in a mythic style: the emancipation of a woman whose alienation has led her to take refuge in silence or the return of the *puer eternus*, the 'eternal adolescent', who, no longer able to find a place for himself in this world, runs off to join the dolphins. When it is the vehicle for a range of collective problems, the legendary epic can have a therapeutic value for a society which is calling itself into question. At a time when academic learning is beginning to take precedence over the griot's memory, legend comes back in by the cinematic door. To the film which can be only the personal vision of a director it brings the breadth of vision of a collective imaginary.

'SHELLING' HISTORY

Let us say, rather, that legend, like the griot, manipulates History. The legend of Sunjata emerged out of a context of war, and served to legitimate the power of a king. Its repetition has always provided a justification for the exercise of power.[33] Legends do not strive for historical exactitude: their aims are moral, aesthetic and ideological. It is not surprising, then, that a cinema which is one of moral judgement, albeit still delivered at times in the guise of ideology, should draw on this cultural source material.

That material will, however, be used to meet current concerns. In *Keïta, l'héritage du griot* (Burkina Faso, 1995), which draws on the legend of Sunjata Keïta, Dani Kouyaté confronts the modern school system with the loss of Mandingo memory. But the film is not in any sense an epic, an African *Ben Hur*; the legend is told through the mind's eye of a child. To the despair of his mother and teacher, young Mabo Keïta gives up school to hear the griot Djeliba Kouyaté recount the origin of his name to him and, with it, the story of the foundation of the ancient Mandé Empire. He retells what he remembers to his friends, which allows the filmmaker to improvise playfully on eighteenth-century sets and costumes and not have to concern himself with historically accurate reconstruction of a kind liable to inflate the budget of this first feature film.

The status of griot is handed down from father to son. It is from his father, Sotigui Kouyaté, a famous actor and a member of Peter Brook's troupe, that Dani Kouyaté inherited the role of griot, and hence that of a repository of memory. To make History comprehensible, the griot introduces the dream element: 'Words are like groundnuts; you have to shell them!'[34] He plays with history, leaving the perspicacious to pick out the essentials. He is not against historical veracity, but calls for another conception of knowledge, as is stressed in the exchange between Djeliba and the schoolteacher when the latter comes to find him to suggest that he carry on the initiation during the school holidays:

> 'I was waiting for you. I know why you're here. You want to know why I'm keeping Mabo away from school.'
> 'No, old man, I know why. I just came to talk with you.'
> 'First tell me your name.'
> 'My name?'
> 'Yes.'
> 'Fofana… Drissa Fofana.'
> 'A fine name. Do you know its meaning?'
> 'No, I don't.'
> 'That's sad. You don't know! What can you teach children if you don't know your origins?… I shall hear what you have to say. But before I do, hear me out. There are 124,000 creatures between heaven and earth who breathe as you and I do. I know the origin of all those 124,000 creatures but two: the sheep and sorghum. Let us no longer tell Mabo, then, that he is descended from a gorilla! He is descended from a king, Maghan kon Fatta Konate, king of the Mandé Empire!'

The griot often introduces the plot of the film, and draws the moral from it. In *Keïta*, he addresses Mabo in grave tones: 'Remember always that the world is old and that the future comes out of the past!' If he does not appear, he can be replaced by a voice-off and a narrative structure which follows the pattern of the oral tradition, as in *Wend Kuuni* [The Gift of God] (Gaston Kaboré, Burkina Faso, 1982), a study in tolerance set in precolonial Africa which won the César award for best 'Francophone' film. A mute child is picked up by a traveller and adopted by a family who give him the name 'God's Gift'. The shock of seeing a hanged man causes him to recover speech, enabling both the adoptive family and the audience to understand his enigma. It emerges that after rejecting the custom which would have forced remarriage with an old man on her because her husband never returned from a hunting expedition, his mother was accused of witchcraft, and fled the village. She was a sick woman, and died of exhaustion as a result.

There is no desire to be didactic or demonstrative here, and there is no rigidity to the story, because a timeless Africa has been chosen as the setting. As described, the society is not static. In fact, the setting enables Gaston Kaboré to rehearse his theme in a period before the traumatic impact of colonization, and hence leaves him free to centre it on what the child's silence evokes: an inward reflection on behaviour and human relations issuing in a call for tolerance and social change. As we shall see, by drawing on the narrative mode of the griot, Kaboré develops a fiction which is not content merely to place action before an audience, but explores its whys and wherefores.

Buud Yam (Burkina Faso, 1997), which won Gaston Kaboré the Grand Prize at Fespaco, is shown clearly at the beginning as being set in the early nineteenth century in the loop of the Niger river. Its protagonists are the two children from *Wend Kuuni*, who have now grown up. The choice of a narrative structure not far removed from folktale represents not so much a pursuit of timelessness as a desire for universality. 'I love the folktale because its force lies in its apparent simplicity', declares Kaboré.[35] Simple here does not mean simplistic: 'It is from its stripped-down, stylized structure that the folktale draws its inner energy and dynamic.' A dynamic which reveals itself to be highly complex, so much is its perpetually renewed thinking enriched by syncretism. The different initiatory stages of *Buud Yam*, and also the telepathic symbiosis which Wend Kuuni maintains with his half-sister Pongneré (whose illness is merely the manifestation of Wend Kuuni's inner psychical disorder) or the conflict with his father, which he recasts, all pile up and become entangled, reaching a level of abstraction, a relativism and a detachment from reality which we, in our materialism, have great difficulty grasping. Yet the reference here is not to some ethereal, bloodless, ascetic or spiritualist form of culture. As Roland Louvel reminds us, it is no accident that, of all the movements of Western thought, Surrealism is the only one to have acknowledged any serious affinity with Africa.[36] The denunciation of mindless naivety, which one so often finds in Western criticism of African films, is thus amusing, given that – as Michel Leiris forcefully pointed out – African art is, paradoxically, one of the most intellectual forms there is.[37] The misunderstanding comes from the first contacts with Africa, when the West saw in the continent merely the physical weaknesses of a society that was economically unproductive by the standards of triumphant capitalism. In Adama Drabo's *Taafe Fanga* (Mali, 1997), the Dogon cosmogony, which is briefly traced out in the cave scene, casts light, despite its complexity, on the course of relations between men and women. The story itself is a secondary matter, so much does the myth immediately broaden out the subject. However, the laughter which shakes the cinema (both at Ouagadougou and Cannes) when the women's seizure of power reverses household roles indicates the topicality of – and need for – a film which has already left its mark in Africa: in Bamako, they speak of the 'Taafe Fanga effect', and this film, which advocates 'equality in difference', now serves as a reference point for marital conflict!

Adama Drabo could, of course, have got his message through by setting his narrative in a contemporary African city. That form of existential psychological probing would doubtless have been more in keeping with the conventions of French cinema. His decision to depict a myth no longer delights us in our quest for 'greater spirituality', a quest which once led untiringly to noble savages and timeless wisdom. The exoticizing idealization of Africa, which gained African films such success in the late 1980s, is no longer in vogue. Then they brought a serene freshness to a European cinema which was going nowhere, doubting its own future at a time when 'communications' was the watchword, and the audiovisual image was all-conquering. Since the early 1990s, however, the demand has been for social realism: the issues have all been clouded, and African films can no longer work their magic. We are in crisis; times are hard; racism is spreading, and violence and exclusion are becoming commonplace. European critics, looking for films which document their own crisis, no longer defend African films as being delightfully naive, but reject them for being negatively naive: outdated, academic, immature, consigned to a catch-all category of the 'bush film'.[38]

Yet fable is often the best means of delineating politics and current affairs. *La Genèse* [Genesis], directed by the Malian Cheikh Oumar Sissoko (1999), is an impressive lesson here. An African, who is in no sense a Christian, seizes on one of the founding texts of Western civilization because he finds in the fratricidal struggle between Jacob, the herdsman, and Hamor, the sedentary farmer, 'the human responsibilities which lead to ethnic conflicts'.[39] They will take counsel together beneath the *toguna*, the very first building the Dogon put up when they establish a village, and the place where they settle their disputes. 'Returning to the sources enables us to show that kinship does not prevent conflict', adds Sissoko, 'and never has done. *La Genèse*, like *Guimba*, shows the wealth of the cultural and human heritage on which Africa can draw to ensure civil peace and understanding between human beings.' The ancient text provides a path for conflict-resolution: 'a mysticism which man cannot master, but which he can use to make his happiness.'

THE AFRICAN CRY

The virulent criticisms which have been levelled against Idrissa Ouedraogo's cinematic development show just how strong the pressure can be. In *A Karim na Sala* [Karim and Sala, 1990], a film made for the French regional TV channel FR3 with Noufou Ouedraogo and Roukietou Barry, the two young actors from *Yaaba*, the exploration of the love between the two main characters goes far beyond the ritualization of feelings. The two are united by a great fluidity of interaction, a simplicity of attitude, a genuine warmth. Moreover, their evocation of complex family situations gives great depth to their relationship. The film takes us away from social documentary and into a serious consideration of human relationships. This is also the aim of Ouedraogo's short film on AIDS, *Afrique, mon Afrique* (1994), in which the pedagogic intent is directed more towards the fictional psychology of the characters than towards the physical solution (use a condom). The accent here is more on the 'African Cry'[40] – a terrible cry uttered in close-up by Naky Sy Savané, on whom the director calls to articulate his own suffering and revolt, to the accompaniment of a piercing score by Ismaël Lô:

> 'Africa, my Africa, is it you, this back bending and bowed beneath the weight of AIDS? No, no, pool of blood in your hands, pool of blood in your hearts. No!'[41]

Although it is built around a crime story (a man flees Ouagadougou after killing a garage owner in a hold-up, and goes to ground in his village with the loot), *Samba Traoré* (1992) does not so much guide spectators through a Hollywood-style plot as invite them, rather, to identify with the thief. 'In Burkina Faso, theft is a major transgression. Idrissa brings the viewer to understand why he stole. He breaks down the taboo of representation', observes Marie-Christine Peyrière.[42] Although the hero, Samba, is presented as a good-hearted crook, the film neither pardons his act nor spares him: he will have to atone for his theft. Here introspection bears on the conscience of a man divided against himself. The setting is not an ideal Africa. Even if the action does take place among traditional village huts, this is a very real place:

> Samba Traoré's native village cannot be exotic because it appears not within an opposition between the rich countries and the Third World, but as an element in a tension between town and country which carries the existence of the characters and the very life of the film.[43]

Samba is also a man riven by conflict: an individual in a spin, an individual with an African cry inside him. He is a loser, a 'rebel' in the James Dean mould, furiously searching for inner peace, but with no time to find it, who is overtaken by the extent of his own malaise and then, finally, by the police.

Fictional work explores the dizzying whirl of modern life. It was not in any sense surprising that Idrissa Ouedraogo's next film was called *Le Cri du coeur* (1994)! Moctar, a young African immigrant to France, is obsessed by a hyena which he thinks he sees roving around the streets of Lyon. His parents become worried and take him to a psychologist, afraid that he will bring them trouble. His meeting with a drifter – played by Richard Bohringer – opens up another way of understanding his condition, not as some personal defect but as his unconscious cutting in: 'There are millions of people who believe in the Virgin Mary; there are even some who've seen her! You just see hyenas!' In the end he, too, sees the hyena when Moctar opens the circle of fire in which he has captured it. Before it disappears, the hyena, which symbolizes the child's contradictory relationship with Africa, takes on the features of his grandfather.

Idrissa Ouedraogo, bitterly criticized first for indulging in folklore and, subsequently, for trying to make European cinema, concludes: 'I've come to the end of a line of argument. Perhaps we should now go back to our ancestors, back to a sort of historical epic, with far-seeing heroes.'[44] Idrissa is doubtless referring to the same 'seeing' as Moctar speaks of when he tries to explain the nature of Africa to his cousin, a seeing which could sum up the approach of African cinema: 'When you look, you see further.'

NOTES

1. Proverb quoted in the documentary *Le Roi, la vache et le bananier* (1994), made by Ngangura Mweze from Zaïre.
2. Mbye Cham, 'Le passé, le présent et l'avenir', *Écrans d'Afrique* 4, 1993, p. 21.
3. Bassek Ba Kobhio, Press Conference, Fespaco 1995, Ouagadougou.
4. Quoted by the Guinean writer Tierno Monenembo in Nancy Huston and Leïla Sebbar, *Une Enfance d'ailleurs, 17 écrivains racontent*, Belfond, Paris, 1993, p. 225.
5. See Cheikh Anta Diop, *The African Origin of Civilization*, Lawrence Hill, New York, 1991; *Civilization or Barbarism: An Authentic Anthropology*, Lawrence Hill, New York, 1991.
6. Ibrahima Signaté, *Med Hondo, un cinéaste rebelle*, Présence Africaine, Paris, 1994, p. 53.
7. Françoise Kaboré, 'Heritage Africa: rupture avec la patrie', *Sidwaya* 1223, Ouagadougou, 1 March 1989. Cited by Manthia Diawara, *African Cinema: Politics and Culture*, Indiana University Press, Bloomington, 1992, p. 159.
8. Interview with David Achkar, Paris, 1995. Achkar died at Conakry in 1998 at the age of thirty-eight while preparing to make his first feature film, *Un Fleuve comme fracture*, about a young man of mixed race, going in search of his roots in Africa.
9. Camara Laye, *The Dark Child*, Hill & Wang, New York, 1994.

10. Célestin Monga, *Anthropologie de la colère: société civile et démocratie en Afrique noire*, L'Harmattan, Paris, 1994, p. 64.
11. Ferid Boughedir, *Le Cinéma africain de A à Z*, OCIC, Brussels, 1987, p. 96.
12. The French term here is 'indocilité', as employed by Achille Mbembe in *Afriques indociles: Christianisme, pouvoir et Etat en société postcoloniale*, Karthala, Paris, 1987.
13. Fayard, Paris, 1992, p. 128.
14. Tchicaya U Tam'si, *Ces Fruits si doux de l'arbre à pain*, Seghers, Paris, 1988.
15. Kä Mana, *L'Afrique va-t-elle mourir? Essai d'éthique politique*, Le Cerf, Paris, 1991; reprinted Karthala, Paris, 1993, p. 114.
16. Claude Meillassoux, *L'Esclavage en Afrique précoloniale*, Maspéro, Paris, 1960, p. 15.
17. Yambo Ouologuem, *Bound to Violence*, trans. R. Manheim, Heinemann, London, 1971.
18. Patrick G. Ilboudo, *Le Fespaco 1969–1989: Les cinéastes africains et leurs oeuvres*, Editions La Mante, Burkina Faso, 1989, p. 113.
19. Interview with François Woukoache, *Africultures* 6 'L'esclavage aboli?', L'Harmattan, Paris, 1998; and on www.africultures.com.
20. Despite their name, the *escolas de samba* are not in any sense schools but, rather, the institutions which mount the lavish parade presentations at Rio de Janeiro's annual carnival. These presentations involve music, dance and outlandish costumes [*Trans.*].
21. The *Nègre marron*, the runaway slave, gives his name to the 'Neg marron' figure, who, with his (comically?) exaggerated Negroid characteristics, runs around the crowd at the Cayenne Carnival, threatening to hug frightened onlookers [*Trans.*].
22. Serge Daney, *La Rampe*, Cahiers du Cinéma, Gallimard, Paris, 1985, pp. 118–23.
23. Guy Hennebelle, 'Sembène parle de ses films', *Cinémaction* 34 ('Sembène Ousmane'), 1985, p. 29.
24. Ayi Kwei Armah, *The Beautyful Ones Are Not Yet Born*, Heinemann, London, 1992.
25. Rod Stoneman, 'Axe Sud-Sud… pour un cinéma fait par, avec et pour les Africains', *Écrans d'Afrique* 5–6, 1993, p. 21.
26. Diawara, *African Cinema*, pp. 162, 164.
27. 'Pourquoi juge-t-on les gens? Entretien avec Idrissa Ouedraogo', *Cahiers du Cinéma* 423, September 1989, p. 8.
28. Nwachukwu Frank Ukadike, *Black African Cinema*, University of California Press, Berkeley/Los Angeles/London, 1994, pp. 279, 282.
29. Interview with Idrissa Ouedraogo, *Africultures* 2, L'Harmattan, Paris, 1997.
30. Interview with Idrissa Ouedraogo, Paris, 1995.
31. Sony Labou Tansi, *Les Sept solitudes de Lorsa Lopes*, Le Seuil, Paris, 1985, p. 11.
32. Interview with Idrissa Ouedraogo, Paris, 1995.
33. See Tamsir Niane, *Soundjata ou l'épopée mandingue*, Présence Africaine, Paris, 1966.
34. Interview with Dani Kouyaté, Paris, 1995.
35. Interview with Gaston Kaboré, Cannes, 1997, published in *Africultures* 1, L'Harmattan, Paris, October 1997; and on www.africultures.com.
36. Roland Louvel, *L'Afrique noire et la différence culturelle*, L'Harmattan, Paris, 1996, p. 187.
37. 'Au-delà d'un regard: entretien de Paul Lebeer avec Michel Leiris', in *La Bibliothèque des arts*, Lausanne, 1994, p. 75.
38. Olivier Barlet, 'Cinémas d'Afrique noire: le nouveau malentendu', *Cinémathèque* 14, Autumn 1998, Cinémathèque française, Paris, pp. 107–16.
39. Interview with Cheikh Oumar Sissoko on the set of *La Genèse*, Hombori (Mali), 1997.

40. To quote the title of the famous book by the Cameroonian writer Jean-Marc Ela, *The African Cry*, trans. Robert R. Barr, Orbis, London, 1986.

41. This might be seen as a modern version of David Diop's lines from 'Africa':

> Africa my Africa, ...
> ... your blood flows in my veins
> Your beautiful black blood that irrigates the fields.

Gerald Moore and Ulli Beier (eds), *Modern Poetry from Africa*, Penguin, Harmondsworth, 1963, p. 58.

42. Interview with Marie-Christine Peyrière, Ouagadougou, 1995.

43. Laurence Giavarini, 'Éloge du proche', *Cahiers du Cinéma* 465, March 1993.

44. Interviews with Idrissa Ouedraogo, Ouagadougou and Paris, 1995. In 1999, Ouedraogo was to make an epic with 1,500 extras: 'It is a film about colonial penetration into Burkina, in order to set up the mechanisms of colonization, but also the contradictory ambitions of the Mossi chief, Boukary' (Interview with Idrissa Ouedraogo, Brussels 1997, published in *Africultures* 2, L'Harmattan, Paris, 1997 and on www.africultures.com).

FOUR

CLOSING YOUR EYES

I insult you, Occident,
But it's always mildly
I insult you –
For between you and me,
There's blood sloshing around together...
Sony Labou Tansi[1]

The contradictory relationship with the West, a relationship experienced both as dream and as nightmare, haunts African screenplays. It resolves itself today in an opening-up to splintered modern realities, to inwardness.

THE REFUSAL TO MIMIC THE WEST

Introspection entails a questioning of the relationship with the previous generation. Ousmane Sembène, who chaired the selection panel of Fespaco 1995, is regarded as the father of Black African cinema; his determination is seen as examplary, his commitment as imposing a duty upon his successors. In taking a new angle on the psychological damage done to their contemporaries, the generations of filmmakers who did not go through the head-on clash with colonialism have followed a different political and cinematic course from their oldest member. Yet they admire his films, respect his approach and acknowledge his importance. At Fespaco 1995, Dani Kouyaté, aged thirty-four, stressed the symbolic significance of receiving his prize from the hands of the 72-year-old Sembène, 'the forerunner of us all'. Even Idrissa Ouedraogo admits that 'when you see *Borom Sarret*, you have the impression you haven't progressed any further than that!'[2]

Borom Sarret, made in 1962, was a manifesto for Black African film, a beacon. 'Lucien Patry had invited me to take part in the Dinard Festival viewings. I saw *Borom Sarret* and I remember crying', confides editor Andrée

Davanture. 'It was a kind of cinema I found overwhelming, a cinema that went to the heart of things.'[3] Sembène's short is a film bubbling over with human life. Describing a day in the life of a *bonhomme charette*, a Dakar cartman, it lays down the thematic concerns for the films of the next two decades: the clash between old and new, between Africa and the West. As André Gardies has shown, it is a film structured around forms of separation and quest.[4] It follows out the stages of a journey fraught with one ordeal after another, a journey of initiation, a quest for the appropriation of space, and for identity. It is a quest which will end in failure for, upon finally reaching the part of the city which is forbidden to him ('le Plateau'), the cartman has the tool of his trade confiscated. The film lays down a programme for the cinema: to set out to conquer African space in the face of a modernity which is presented as a Western intrusion into the land of Africa.

Even in his last film, *Guelwaar* (1991) – a 'film of sober reflection for coming generations, which aims to demystify what is known as humanitarian aid'[5] – Sembène continues to preach disconnection from the West. The film depicts the narrow-mindedness of African Christians and Muslims on the occasion of the burial of a critical, idealistic campaigner against an Africa corrupted and enslaved by foreign gifts. At the end, the sacks of food aid are torn open and trodden underfoot. However, the idea that one should rely solely on one's own devices if one is to acquire dignity is one few African countries have made the basis of their policies. Attempts to do so have led historically to authoritarianism and violence. For example, as long ago as 1974, the difficulty of achieving self-sufficiency in foodstuffs in a traditional context plunged Nyerere's Tanzanian experiment into a violent voluntarism, with the army orchestrating the forced settlement of peasants on as yet uncleared lands.[6]

In the field of cinema, it has been the constant theme of a number of filmmakers, including Cheikh Oumar Sissoko from Mali, that dependence on the West should be reduced by pooling technicians and equipment from all the countries in a particular subregion, and mobilizing those resources jointly.[7] He pointed out recently:

> things are moving on. For example, Pierre Yameogo has produced films drawing on the technical resources in Burkina, Mali and the Ivory Coast. I'm convinced that Cinafric[8] can be started up again on a sound basis. A feasibility study has already been carried out in India for relaunching it with the aid of the state of Burkina Faso. Burkina is not far away: technicians could assist with the editing and mixing.... This would also make better training possible.[9]

This is, however, a demand to which others do not necessarily subscribe. They see it as part of the normal business of world cinema that they should work with European technicians, just as 'world music' does, to ensure production values are achieved which can enable them to reach the international market.

The rejection of dependence is part of a tradition of anti-colonial struggle glorified by films like the stunning *Mortu Nega* [Death Denied] (Flora Gomes, Guinea-Bissau, 1988). 'We are the generation of pain', says the central female character, whom the film follows in her determined efforts to support her freedom-fighter husband and in her passage through a country at war as it transforms itself into one that is learning independence. Her arrival at her husband's camp coincides with the announcement of the murder of Amilcar Cabral. They will have only a few moments to speak, for the struggle remains paramount.

History, for Cabral, is first and foremost a struggle which creates the unity of the world: it will lead to 'friendship, equality and peaceful co-operation between all peoples'.[10] If Flora Gomes still refers to Cabral today, it is more a question of 'putting his faith in the positive aspects of African society.'[11] In his next film, an urban comedy set in Bissau, *Udju azul di Yonta* [Yonta's Blue Eyes] (1992), the lovers have time to speak, but have difficulty meeting. A very beautiful girl is in love with a sad man who does not notice her, while a shy young boy dreams of her without daring to declare his love. He writes her love poems copied from a book, poems extolling her blue eyes, even though her eyes are not blue! Yonta will never have blue eyes: Africa is too absorbed in exotic dreams. 'You have to take advantage of the good things humanity can give us, but you have to know good from bad!'[12]

This is a delicate exercise: in *Sarzan* (1963) the Senegalese director Momar Thiam took a sardonic look at the difficulties of a sergeant of the 'colonial forces' returning to his village:

'The major asks you to combine the good things you saw in Europe with what's good in your village.'
'It sounds like you want to graft two mango trees!'
'That's it precisely, my friend!'

Knowing good from bad: rejecting the reductionist West, the West of the will to power, of materialism and profit, to take only the humanistically inclined West! In this vision, the West is no longer monolithic but contradictory, and it too is in search of a balance between power and wisdom, knowledge and meaning, rationality and depth.

As early as 1966, in *Le Retour d'un aventurier*, Mustapha Alassane of Niger played ironically on the fascination the West exerts on the African imagination. Returning from a trip to the USA, a boy gives cowboy outfits to his friends in his native village. Very soon the little gang has turned the village into a Wild West town! Making wonderful use of the African backdrop to create Western images, Alassane demonstrated the extent to which it is by parodying imported values that the young develop new forms of marginality. He was to take up this theme again in *F.V.V.A.* (1972; the initials stand for '*Femme, Villa, Voiture, Argent*'), in which Wife, Villa, Car and Money symbolize social success. Ali, a modest civil servant who falls victim to this mirage, ends up stealing to meet his financial needs, and going to prison.

The question of mimicking the West runs through the cinema cultures of Black Africa, much as it exercised Africa's social elites at Independence. The West exerts a fascination through its control of technology, its rational organization, its scientific and philosophical rigour, which gives humanity power over reality. But, as Aimé Césaire showed, it also represents contempt for human beings, dishonesty, and the betrayal of its own principles of humanism and freedom.[13] The modern form of the rejection of that model – resistance to the Westernization of the world – will be the assertion of a separate identity, a development caricatured in the rise of fundamentalisms.

OPTING FOR OPENNESS

The African, split between two cultures, is reluctant to wear both bubu and necktie, as does the African diplomat mocked by Daniel Kamwa in *Boubou cravate* (Cameroon, 1972). But this reluctance, this hesitancy, unnerves him. The uncertainties treated here as a comic theme can, in other cases, lead to neurosis. When the diplomat tries to throw off the shackles of tradition, he runs up against the perversities of the modern world. This is even truer for women when they attempt to escape patriarchal authority: like Étée in Jean-Pierre Dikongué Pipa's *Le Prix de la liberté* (Cameroon, 1978), they find themselves up against the 'black sharks' as the madman who wanders the streets of the town in that film calls them. The answer is clear: as Désiré Ecaré's *Visages de femmes* (Ivory Coast, 1984) also suggests, learning karate will enable a female friend to teach the rapist a lesson.

The struggle is an unequal one: Étée will slide into madness. In order to bring her back into the circle of the community, an exorcism is carried out. A chicken is killed over her head, and the blood runs down on to her face. Several years before this, the treatment of deviance was the theme of Ababacar Samb Makharam's magnificent *Kodou* (Senegal, 1971): having been rejected by the village for being unable to bear the pain of the tattooing of her lips in an initiation ceremony, a girl called Kodou goes mad. She flies into a violent rage and is, as a result, bound day and night. In the end her family take her to a psychiatric hospital managed by a European doctor. That approach proves unsuccessful, however, and her parents put her through a session of traditional exorcism.

André Gardies has shown how, beneath an apparent neutrality, the director uses the treatment of space to show his preference for the latter solution.[14] The full, balanced form of the circle provides a counterpoint to the angularity of the hospital. After breaking the circle of the community at her tattooing, Kodou comes back into it by joining the circle of the dance. Treatment by the group, the existence of divinities, healers and therapeutic objects and practices form the basis of an individual's cultural affiliation; they are a basis for their identity, and hence their mental equilibrium. Attempting to cure madness by treating the patient as a universal human being, not as someone from a particular culture, leads to denying them and, hence, to denying oneself. As Tobie Nathan writes,

> To refuse to think oneself in one's cultural specificity leads, by an inexorable logic, to destroying the humanity in the other person and, in the end, to destroying one's own humanity. The deepest difference between a Mandingo healer and a white psychoanalyst is that the healer will treat any patient 'in the Mandingo style', including a white Westerner, while the psychoanalyst will treat every patient 'with a universal approach', including a Casamance Mandingo, who is a village chief, but temporarily from necessity a maintenance worker in a Parisian administrative block – which produces catastrophes over several generations.[15]

'He who spits in the air must expect to get his saliva back on the end of his nose!'[16] In losing this awareness of belonging to a community and in denying it to the Other, whom it seeks to assimilate, the West is both weakening itself (the breakdown of law and order on the 'sink' housing estates is a sign of this) and endangering other cultures. 'It is not doubt that is at the origin of madness, but certainty', said Nietzsche. By claiming the specificity of an origin, while exploring its contradictions, African cinema cultures aid Westerners as much as Africans in their quest for identity. It is by being deliberately open about the tragedy of the African, about the dislocation of a being who is not 'wretched' but in crisis, both fascinated by and filled with hatred for his former conqueror and master, that the new African cinema plays a therapeutic role and promotes creativity.

TORN ASUNDER BY MODERNITY

'J'écris... je crie.'
Sony Labou Tansi[17]

The filmmaker who also has to cater for a Western audience, since distribution conditions prevent him from really reaching an African one, is on the horns of a dilemma: how is he to address two audiences with such differing perceptions? There is a danger that he will not reach either! Misunderstandings are inevitable. Are these necessarily an obstacle if the Western viewer accepts them as an expanding of his horizons? If you offer hospitality, then you should put yourself out for your guest...

But this demarcation line, to which we shall have occasion to return, does not simply run between North and South. Bouna Medoune Seye, who was born in Dakar and grew up in Marseille, is excited by things urban, which is where his roots lie: 'I'm better at defending myself against a lorry than against a snake! The village isn't my world, I don't understand it at all!'[18] This set designer, painter and photographer, who has sought to promote a serious African photography, wants to use cinema to capture not just the social divisions within the city, but also its tempo. In *Bandit cinéma* (1994), Laye, a young worker, has lost control of the prostitutes who are supposed to pay him a cut. In an effort to restore his fortunes, he sets up a new scam – buying up cinema tickets and selling them off at a higher price to an audience who will do anything to get into an American B movie! '*Bandit cinéma* offers an image of the city, and perhaps another image of African cinema, by stepping outside the village and the agrarian context to melt into the contemporary reality of a metropolis where the extreme is the rule.'[19]

Seye's short on AIDS, *Saï Saï by – dans les tapats de Dakar* (1995), uses a light, hand-held camera to follow the lonely life of a man who goes from door to door by night in search of drugs – an attempt to give the social outcast a human face:

'I love the night, with just the white of the moon and the light of men to light my desires and guide my steps.
  'I love the night with its snippets of muffled voices, always in the distance, with its doors closed by day which open across from me.
  'I love the night, which endlessly receives me, with its mysteries and my dreams.
  'The day should be the night.
  'Why these eyes full of pity and morality?
  'That's sod all to do with me! Get out of my head!
  'I won't go to die in the hospital. I shan't go again, ever!'

Saï saï by ('that little guttersnipe') is the Wolof name by which AIDS is euphemistically known in the '*tapats*' – areas built of corrugated iron and scrap metal on the outskirts of Dakar. It first oppresses you as a nightmare going round and round in your head before it reaches your body.

Temedy (Gahité Fofana, Guinea, 1996), another film in the series 'Black Artists and AIDS' initiated by the *Revue noire*, has no dialogue at all. Mouna, a twenty-year-old woman living in Conakry, 'or perhaps in another city', is

On the set of *Temedy* (Gahité Fofana, Guinea 1996).

left to speak with her face, gestures and attitudes. 'AIDS is in her. She knows it. With tomorrow so far away.' She too lives by night, in the scrubland and in the streets, then 'takes refuge in sleep because she is beginning to be afraid'. The camera, spontaneous and mobile, melts into the night of the street and its people and comes to rest, in the end, on Mouna in her bed, her only place of solitude. As the modern form of that inescapable fate of colonial conquest and locusts, tyrants and famines by which Africa has been beset, AIDS invites another kind of writing, a cinema of torn, fractured realities for split characters, a cinema reminiscent of the work of the Senegalese filmmaker Djibril Diop Mambety.

Amet Diallo was one of that same family of directors. Diallo, a 'free spirit who did just as he pleased, without asking anyone's permission',[20] died before his time from an asthma attack in a Dakar street. His astonishing *Boxulmaleen!!* (1991), produced with children from a shanty town [*l'an fer city*], drew on symbolism to orchestrate another descent into hell [*l'enfer*] – that of daily life. The institutions in which life is confined are caricatured here one by one in a surreally metaphorical saga.

Poster for
Touki-Bouki
(Djibril Diop
Mambety,
Senegal, 1973).

Djibril Diop Mambety had himself evoked social marginality in a very personal way as early as 1973 in the famous *Touki-Bouki*, which filmmakers often cite as a major influence on their own work, according it prophetic status both for its form and for its content.[21] Admittedly, the classic opposition between tradition and modernity runs through this 'hyena's journey' (the meaning of 'Touki-Bouki'), since the two young people – Anta and Mory, both attracted by life in the West ('Paris, Paris that little corner of Paradise', as Josephine Baker's song, a leitmotiv in the film, has it) – will come to different decisions in the end: the one taking the boat for France, the other returning to his roots. But the hyena, a rejected animal, is a symbol of marginality. Not that the film wishes to present the dilemma of leaving or not leaving as a marginal issue: it shows, rather, in a welter of surrealistic images, that nonconformism raises the question of origins for everyone, that it is a necessary passage and practice for thinking one's relationship to tradition. There isn't a good choice and a bad one, there is the inner dynamics of a tension. The director does not explore the difference, or even the clash between tradition and modernity, but the space which separates and connects the two, the riven nature of a society, all of whose members are split between their roots and a fascination for elsewhere. Although the film focuses on a particular social space, it does so through a journey of initiation, a quest, not by fixing its gaze on a referential tradition. The montage of *Touki-Bouki* is like a spiral located within the great circle of origins, which is symbolized from the beginning by long-horned zebus, linking the cosmos to the land of the ancestors. They are ridden by a shepherd boy representing the young Mory, who will later attach one of these horns as a trophy to the handlebars of his motorcycle.

By playing on ambivalence, by drawing deep on the imaginative resources of his cultural reality and employing parodic and ruptural techniques, Mambety reconstructs a battered psyche. He dispels the odour of an obsessive, stifling West to risk what the Zaïrian critic Vumbi Yoka Mudumbe calls 'the madness of Tiresias': the power to produce a different discourse outside the customary certainties, away from the normal run of things.[22] This is indeed an introspective gaze, an inward gaze. Speaking to a little girl in *Y'a pas de problème!* (Laurence Gavron, France, 1995), Djibril Diop Mambety says quite simply: 'I'll explain how you make a film: you close your eyes, you close them very, very tight...'

NOTES

1. Sony Labou Tansi, *La Vie privée de Satan*, cited in Jean-Michel Devésa, *Sony Labou Tansi, écrivain de la honte et des rives magiques du Kongo*, L'Harmattan, Paris, 1996, p. 146.
2. Interview with Idrissa Ouedraogo, Paris, 1995.
3. Interview with Andrée Davanture, Paris, 1995.
4. André Gardies, *Cinéma d'Afrique noire francophone, l'espace miroir*, L'Harmattan, Paris, 1989, pp. 17 ff.
5. Interview with Sembène Ousmane, Paris 1998, published in *Africa international* 311, February 1998.
6. *Une Afrique socialiste, la Tanzanie*, Éditions Ouvrières, Paris, 1976, p. 75.
7. To support an approach of this kind, *Elicia*, a database on cinema in Africa in the form of directories for each country, has been set up by the Médiathèque des Trois Mondes at 63 bis, rue du Cardinal Lemoine, 75005 Paris. We should also mention the pan-African directory published each year in Zimbabwe: *Africa Film and TV*, P.O. Box 6109, Harare, Zimbabwe.
8. Ouagadougou-based production and post-production unit which was forced to close down.

9. Interview with Cheikh Oumar Sissoko, Hombori (Mali), 1997.
10. Amilcar Cabral, *Unity and Struggle*, Heinemann, London, 1980, p. 162.
11. Interview with Flora Gomes, Paris, 1995.
12. 'Entretien avec Flora Gomes', *Écrans d'Afrique* 1, May 1992, p. 77.
13. Aimé Césaire, *Discourse on Colonialism*, Monthly Review Press, New York, 1972.
14. André Gardies, 'Le Discours de l'Espace', in André Gardies and Pierre Haffner (eds), *Regards sur le cinéma négro-africain*, OCIC, Paris, 1987, pp. 72 ff.
15. Tobie Nathan, *L'Influence qui guérit*, Éditions Odile Jacob, Paris, 1994, p. 219.
16. Proverb cited in *Djeli* (Fadika Kramo-Lanciné, Ivory Coast, 1981).
17. Sony Labou Tansi, *L'État honteux*, Le Seuil, Paris, 1981. The 'shameful state' is the 'ensavagement of the human, the incapacity to remain alive', Tansi declared to Guy Daninos (*L'Afrique littéraire* 57). Against this he ranged writing as a source of life: 'I write to be alive, to stay alive.'
18. Bouna Medoune Sèye in Laurence Gavron's film *Y'a pas de problème!*, France, 1995.
19. 'Entretien avec Bouna Medoune Sèye', *Le Film Africain* 16, May 1994, p. 9.
20. 'A propos du "documentaire-hommage"', *Regarde Amet* (Laurence Attali, France, 1995)', *Le Film Africain* 22, November 1995, p. 7.
21. For a brilliant analysis of *Touki-Bouki*, see 'Le montage comme fondement de la cohérence textuelle', in Gardies and Haffner, *Regards sur le cinéma négro-africain*, pp. 157 ff.
22. Vumbi Yoka Mudimbe, *L'Odeur du Père: Essai sur les limites de la science et de la vie en Afrique noire*, Présence Africaine, Paris, 1982.

FIVE

OPENING UP THE
CRACKS IN IDENTITY

I gave my heart to the party
And yet, if the party is grey
That's not my doing.
Where am I going to play this bugle
Which sticks to my throat?
　　　Tchicaya U Tam'si, *Le Suicide manqué*

The assertion of African cultural values can provide the basis of an identity. It is a question of getting back to what one knows as primary. But also of not becoming locked into that knowledge, so that one is not ensnared in the toils of identity. It is possible, by doubting one's origins, and possibly being unfaithful to them – as many women in the film scenarios are – to escape fixation on those origins (though this does not mean denying them), and hence move towards social change.

A UNIFIED WORLD

Rabi, a young boy in Burkina Faso, lives in a village with his father, a blacksmith, and his mother, a potter. One day, his father stumbles over a huge tortoise, which he gives to Rabi. The animal becomes the centre of his life – so much so that he loses interest in everything else. His exasperated father takes it back into the bush. In desperation, Rabi turns to old Pusga, his initiator and friend, who stares constantly at the hill in the distance where Rabi will in the end release the tortoise back into the wild. The hill 'is also the inner man, capable of looking up and down; it is the wisdom which enables us to discern what is good and what is bad.'[1] *Pusga* is the Mooré word for tamarind, a tree whose fruits and leaves are traditional foodstuffs. Old Pusga explains to Rabi that the savannahs of the Sahel were once covered with forest, where lions and hyenas roamed. In arguing against the destruction of the environment and the desertification of the Mossi Plateau, Gaston Kaboré is not content simply to show the systematic clearance of the area around the village by the timber trade. He contrasts the apparently static life of the village, where time is marked by the bellows of the blacksmith (a caste symbolic of union), with those imperceptible little shifts which splinter the community little by little. 'What I discovered in the rural world', he observes, 'is that it still accords great importance to meaning. Appearances are very much secondary to being. This has imprinted itself very deeply on my style of filming.'[2] To convey that difference not as a fixed certainty (the superiority of tradition over modernity), but as a dynamic space, Gaston Kaboré has recourse to myth, the tortoise emerging in the end as the voice of nature:

'Have you travelled a lot?' asks Rabi.
  'Not really, but my eyes have seen many things', replies the tortoise.
  'I want my eyes to take in the whole universe', retorts Rabi.
  'Do not limit your knowledge to the visible; be attentive to the pulsings of nature. They will teach you. Never forget that!'

Here there is neither nostalgia for a sacralized nature, nor simply a call for a more scientific management of ecosystems – these being the two ambivalent strands of the Western mythological visions of ecology, in which futurism and worship of the past are entangled.[3] The emphasis is on the invisible, on being, on a conception of the world in which man can draw from his relationship with nature an understanding of life and a mode of conduct. 'In Africa, the relation to the universe is very harmonious and spiritual, whereas the ecological approach in Europe is more secular', notes Joseph Gaye Ramaka from Senegal.

That spirituality confers on me a certain serenity in my positioning in the world. I don't need to know if it is scientifically possible to cause thunder by making a sound, but I find it splendid that the sound is sometimes answered with thunder. The approach to life this produces is extraordinary.[4]

It is this kind of understanding that is being referred to by Kaboré, who returns to the sources of his culture: 'In *Rabi* [1992], I make a sally into my subconscious, and delve into the foundations of my cultural heritage and upbringing.'[5]

In African symbolic thought, man is a product of a universe in which all is energy and everything is interconnected, born out of a 'primal force' which has spread a little of itself into all it has generated. As such, he is an element of the universe, and hence a force deployed in space and time.

On the set of *Rabi* (Gaston Kaboré, Burkina Faso, 1992). © Marc Salomon.

Consequently he must act in tune with other forces superior or inferior to his own, in order to gain their positive effects for himself.[6] Thus, respect for nature in all its dimensions is not a mere moral value, nor even a prerequisite for survival; it is a 'natural' consequence of man's positioning in the world, and a precondition if he is to thrive. It is this active sense of their place and role in the universe that Gaston Kaboré offers to those who know how to listen to stories about tortoises...

SYMBOLS IN MOTION

The Madagascan filmmaker Raymond Rajaonarivelo similarly expresses this symbolism of life opening up to a new way of behaving at the end of *Tabataba* (1987), when he places on the screen the following statement: 'You had to listen to the leaf, the waterfall. Like the wealth of men, felled trees are not all the same size.' You had to grasp better what makes up the movement of life to establish a new world after Independence. This was a way of telling the spectator who was still gripped by the force of this story of death: 'Watch out, you have to live differently now!' But the story was also one of resurrection, for Solo, the young boy, is at the end developing a general understanding of life. Set in 1947, the film recounts the uprising among the inhabitants of the village of Tanala on the east coast of Madagascar and the suppression of that uprising, which was part of the great revolt against French colonial power. Evil is afoot, and brings in its train hunger, pain, destruction and death. Yet the film has genuine metaphysical, poetic qualities: the young boy's initiatory quest takes place amid the beauty of the woods which surround the village, and on the hills all around, where mists hang as they do in Chinese prints, and beside the quiet river along which the whole of life flows. The forces of evil in question are not merely those which sparked the 1947 insurrection, but those still at work in the world and in Africa today. The answer lies in the leaf and the waterfall, which evoke trees and moving water, age-old symbols of African culture which recur repeatedly in the film.

> Malagasy is an allegorical language and its phrases are often translations of images. That is why there isn't a lot of talking in *Tabataba*: understanding comes in silence. Emotion is evoked by the presence of a tree, by the movement in the tree and the slight wind which causes it, striking fear. Only images can do this.[7]

'The tree speaks through the wind' says the proverb: take your learning from what you can know, while playing your part in the cycle of nature.[8] Trees – the home of spirits, the place for talk and rest, the link between the living

Poster for
Tabataba
(Raymond
Rajaonarivelo,
Madagascar, 1987).

upon the surface of the earth and the world of the ancestors – situate
human beings in time and space:

> 'Grandfather, how old are you?'
>> 'I don't know my age. I was born on a rainy day, a day of wind and lightning.'
>> 'In the rainy season, then!'[9]
>> 'And that day they planted that tree over there. Compare my tree with yours
>> and you will know my age.'

This exchange from *Fad'jal* (Safi Faye, Senegal, 1979), which begins with
a panning shot along the branch of the great tree, shows how much Africans
traditionally resort to symbolism to show their rootedness, their psychological, physical, spiritual and social union with that 'primal force', that
'primordial matrix' they define as the origin of the universe and of their own
existence. The reading of the films cannot, then, underestimate the importance of such simple, obvious elements as trees, water, earth, air and fire, in

so far as these are symbolic of an understanding of the world, and confer a deep meaning on the narrative.

All is force and all is interconnected, and time marks out cycles in a concentric universe: from one film to another a circle is traced out: a perfect *kara* circle appearing on the screen at the beginning of *Waati* (Souleymane Cissé, Mali, 1995); circles of madness and community in *Kodou* (Ababacar Samb Makharam, Senegal, 1971); a circle of origin in *A Lucy* (Maki J. Algen, Mauritius, 1995), a short in which Masai warriors go to Paris in search of the remains of Lucy, born in Africa three million years ago, in order to take her back to her native land. Thanks to the signs and symbols they find on their way and in the streets of Paris, they will follow her trail as far as the Musée de l'Homme!

In many films, dance (together with the organization of space and the camera movements) gives concrete form to the circles which, according to Alphonse Tierou, symbolize the three stages of spiritual development: a wide circle – of the village, the crowd and the body – marks out the domain of physical nature and the nature of the senses; a second, smaller, circle represents the intermediaries, the field of critical spirit and beliefs, the site of spiritual research; and a third circle near the centre symbolizes the spiritual world of the initiated, of masks, freedom and unity.[10] It is the function of the ceremony of the dead – a ceremony which brings the whole village together in dances of this type in a magical scene involving 3,000 extras at the end of *Mortu Nega* (Flora Gomes, Guinea-Bissau, 1988) – to question *Djon Gago*, the god of life and death, about what the future will hold in the period of newly won independence for those whom death has not claimed (the 'Mortu Nega'). Each woman in turn calls on him to give her a better life, offering up the lives sacrificed in the freedom struggle. Through the circles of the dance, the protagonists are able to experience and manifest their psychical equilibrium within the newly recovered social body which had been torn apart in the war.

READING WITH THE HEART

It is the desire to reclaim the postcolonial social space which underlies the recurrent opposition in Black African film between cultural tradition and an imported modernity. But contemporary African liberation thinking, which variously advocated the revolt of the vanquished against the victor, of the slaves against the master, the sons against the father, also informs that opposition. This dualism is often expressed in the films by a series of divisions: between town and village, Europe and Africa, present and past, money and barter, knowledge and ignorance, individualism and solidarity, debauchery and morality, speed and slowness, noise and quiet, fraud and honesty, and so on.[11] Today filmmakers are attempting to escape this dualism, which locks them into a conception which the Cameroonian writer Axelle Kabou regards as fallacious: 'It postulates the progress of mentalities towards an openness which is all the less probable when the demonization of the values of modernity has left African sensibilities frozen and inward-looking.'[12] Their concern is to resolve the tradition/modernity opposition in a relation of complementarity, a synergy. That opposition can be transcended not by systematically disconnecting from modernity, but by affirming one's cultural roots in one's manner of apprehending it: 'I am not speaking of modernity in the sense understood by the African person in the street, for whom having a car or a nice suit is modern', says Jean-Marie Teno from Cameroon. 'Modernity is always associated with the Western system; never is it seen as a form of progress that might not necessarily involve a mimicking of the West.'[13] Rather than fighting against the fascination with the West, the approach of African filmmakers today is to be open about contemporary fault-lines and fractures, and to advocate a new approach, anchored in culture, clear-headed about action, and in solidarity with all those throughout the world who are struggling for greater spirituality, drawing from the pursuit of essential values the hope for a different order, both in their own countries and between peoples.

For example, in *Ta Dona* [Fire!] (Adama Drabo, Mali, 1990) two complementary plots are developed. Sidy, a young Forestry Commission agronomist, is fighting the advance of desertification related to bush fires, and he sets out in search of a mysterious plant with curative properties. Standing out against a corrupt administration, he attempts to mobilize the local farmers. He is transferred to the remoter regions of the Sahel, where he is eventually vouchsafed the secret of the 'seventh canari'. This medicinal plant cures everyone, white or black. As with the number 7, which represents the conjunction of 4 (woman) and 3 (man), it contains a universal truth. By joining together, the two give life: the seventh canari is the medicine which brings society back to life. 'The preceding generation was happy to criticize; we want to move things forward!'[14] The reference to cultural foundations underlies a new vision of liberation: rather than seeing oneself as being in a struggle against the West, one is promoting freedom by co-operation between peoples and civilizations.

Deforestation is not presented here in catastrophic terms: the director does not use that emotional sensationalism, against a background of scientific demonstration, which is frequently misused in Western ecological discourse.[15]

Poster for *Ta Dona*
(Adama Drabo, Mali,
1990).

It is not a question of frightening people into acting but, rather, of changing the mental framework, as though it were a matter of learning to read – but reading something one already knew *by heart*! In this way, film can teach us how to see what is already in the collective memory: the values transmitted most often by the oral tradition of folktale. It opens up a perception reinforced by submerged intuitions which, with the aid of the emotion stirred up by the images, return to the surface to confront reality.

PASSING ON KNOWLEDGE

In Mali, as anywhere else, people no longer know who they are. What culture should they choose? What is really their own? What certainly isn't theirs? For this reason I chose to set my story ten centuries ago so that young people can recover a profound sense of their culture.[16]

Poster for *Yeelen*
(Souleymane Cissé,
Mali, 1987).

Cissé did not make *Yeelen* (Mali; Jury Prize, Cannes Film Festival, 1987) as a timeless film in order to summon up immutable values from the precolonial past. The film is, rather, strikingly contemporary in its concerns:

> It is a film in search of man's mysterious side. It evokes a number of African themes which may be universal. The lethal clash between a father and his son, this desire to kill.… Why reach the point of wanting to kill one's own flesh and blood? … Africa has a wealth of knowledge which can help humanity to advance.[17]

Yeelen enacts a process of initiation. The young Nianankoro (Issiaka Kane) will receive the knowledge which is intended to ensure that he masters the forces around him, that knowledge which the Bambara hand down from generation to generation. The father finds it hard to stomach the idea of his son becoming his equal. In order to escape the father's murderous madness, the mother sends Nianankoro away. In the course of his journey, the boy

gradually acquires the elements of ultimate knowledge, and of his new powers, which he will inevitably have to pit against his father's.[18]

To protect Nianankoro from his father's jealousy, his mother gives him
a fetish to take to his uncle, at the other end of the country, to enjoin the
uncle to calm the father's anger: this is the Koré Wing, the symbol of a
Bambara initiation society. Nianankoro has 500 miles to travel, and faces
various trials and riddles. When he is captured by the Fulani, he uses his
magic powers. The Fulani king is impressed, and gives one of his wives to
Nianankoro so that he may cure her of sterility. However, she becomes
Nianankoro's companion. When he returns to confront his father, who is
himself armed with the magic pylon used for punishing criminals, the two
merge into a blazing light. Father and son are mere instruments: Nianankoro's
child discovers two ostrich eggs in the desert sands and takes one to his
mother, who exchanges it for the Koré Wing reinforced with the power of
the pylon. He then returns, dressed in his father's clothing, to carry the
symbol of knowledge to the land of men. Through light, the world can be
reborn.

The film does not foreground magic, in which Cissé does not believe, but
stresses, rather, the power of knowledge understood as mastery of the universe. The hero is not merely a psychological entity: he symbolizes a people
in search of identity, a disorientated Africa in search of its origins. For the
Bambara, *Komo* is the incarnation of divine knowledge:

> It is based on the identification and knowledge of signs which have time and
> space as their reference markers. With the coming of the monotheistic religions,
> Africa sent its own theory of knowledge underground.... Our identity and our
> true independence cannot exist without a deep, clear, historical conception of our
> own culture. The response cannot come from an ethnology practised in the main
> by foreigners, but from the creative contribution of African artists.[19]

Light will come from confrontation, from violence, which is present throughout the film. Knowledge is held by a privileged caste from which it will have
to be wrested: to address African culture is to engage in political activity.
Without the correct transmission of knowledge, there is no identity.

BLOCKED TRANSMISSION

The political class has failed in this transmission of knowledge which would
lay the ground for African unity. There is nothing of the picture postcard
about the aesthetic beauty of *Yeelen*. Its function is to lend depth to a recurrent theme in Cissé's work: the stigmatization of a political class which was

prepared to do anything to defend its interests, and had no hesitation in sacrificing its own children. In *Baara* [Work] (Fespaco Grand Prize, 1979), a young engineer who attempts to improve the operation of a factory where he works is eventually butchered. In *Finye* [The Wind] (Fespaco Grand Prize, 1983), the students who refuse to renounce their ideas are savagely repressed. By denouncing the way the slightest aspiration towards democracy is brutally crushed, Cissé lines up, alongside many other filmmakers, in the battle for democratization, for a living space, a space of freedom where freedom would not simply mean, as Roland Barthes put it, 'evading the clutches of power, but also, and above all, having the strength to avoid subjecting others to its clutches'.[20]

In Cissé's latest film, *Waati* [Time] (1995), the disappointment at democracy's unkept promises parallels the bitter disillusionment already being felt on the African continent, where the various 'National Conferences' have often merely engendered a further dose of disenchantment.[21] It is his intuitive belief that if democracy is not to remain an abstract dream, the continent has to be unified, bringing together those forces which are moving down the democratic path. In the prologue, the grandmother tells the family gathered around the hearth how God created the world. How was he going to populate it? He questioned his counsellors, who asked for time to think over the question. During this time he created one animal species, then another, then a whole host of species. This diversity could not but be a source of conflict. The lion seized power, and that was soon contested...

The foundations of unity are thus to be sought in culture, history and the millennia of hybridization Africa has known. So it is on an initiatory quest for knowledge that Nandi, the heroine of *Waati*, sets out. Armed with her experience of humiliation while still a child in South Africa, she will study African civilizations to attempt to grasp the memory of the continent. 'Hang on to human values, to skills and knowledge', advises an inner voice, that of her grandmother. In an interlude in which the narrative breaks off – a sequence involving a dance arrangement by Were Were Liking – the matter of African masks is raised. These are to be regarded not as the expression of primitive thought, but as an eternal representation of humanity and its knowledge, as evidence of an age-old, but still living, culture, capable of expressing basic issues. Through these masks, Nandi learns to transcend her individuality, in order to broaden her struggle to include the other African peoples: she will go to help the dispossessed Tuaregs in the sands of the Sahara before returning to South Africa to take on her destined role, symbolically closing the circle of life and knowledge.

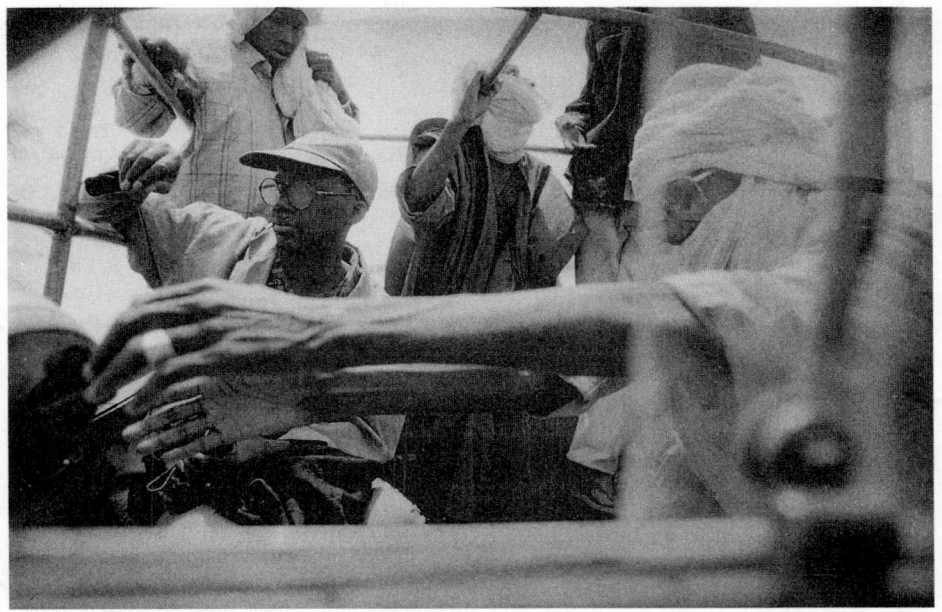

Souleymane Cissé near Timbuktu on the set of *Waati* (1995). © Françoise Huguier.

DRAWING STRENGTH FROM THE SOURCE

The grandmother tells her family – which is united, but poverty-stricken and desperate – the legend of the origin of the world. It is in this origin that Africans will find the strength to react to their problems. Democratization, even in a liberated South Africa, does not settle everything: problems remain, and have to be solved.

The solution is to be found in union, in the solidarity of a continent of multiple cultures. Reunification will come about on the basis of active cultures, not countries. In a sequence of great beauty, shot with a hand-held camera, Nandi is seen as a child at her school desk, learning to draw the world: she discovers that she is an actor in it, capable of conceiving and fashioning the world. Later in the film a television set will show the opposite image the Western media present of Africa: the misery of a crying child, abandoned to its hunger.

Nandi's gaze is serene but active. She can even channel her vital forces into action on her surroundings through the power of thought: she can stop a dog which is trying to attack her, disable the horse of the policeman who is going to kill her, or the airport guards who take her child away. Her 'supernatural' power comes from her inner strength, her harmony, her serenity. 'Nothing positive can come of violence, which represents a regression for us', says Cissé.[22] Political determination must not lead to adopting the enemy's violent tactics. The culture of respect for oneself and for the Other reveals a secret order of things, the relation to the universe or, 'to put it another way, what those who always want to simplify things call God. But we know very well that things are more complex…'[23] History fits into the circle of Bambara cosmogony: the hope for change remains, despite the pain and the ordeals.

AN ALTERNATIVE DEVELOPMENT

In Antoine de Baeque's view, 'as a filmmaker, Cissé has seen the trap the world is in danger of falling into: that of overexposure.' The light which invades the screen of *Yeelen* is a sign of the 'insatiable accumulation which ends up destroying the simplicity of the world in a grandiose confrontation between two opposing ambitions'. Excess, accumulation and growth are dead-ends: the universalization of the 'American way of life' is impossible, because the wealth of the North is based in part on the inequality and exploitation of the South. Moreover, ecological balances would not withstand such a process. As for the child in *Yeelen*, he reminds us of the wise old African dictum: 'We do not inherit the earth from our parents, we borrow it from our children.'

Foregrounding the knowledge of their cultural roots can enable Africans – and, hence, everyone else – to unpack the ideological aspects of the notion of progress, rethink the technological rat race and change the mental framework which sees the North imprisoned in the dogma of growth and the South in what Axelle Kabou calls 'Fridayism', a notion built on 'a mythical, anti-materialistic African, who is unaffected by money and lives on social warmth alone'.[24] A salutary echo of this position is sometimes found in the West. One thinks, for example, of the critique of anti-human development which politically committed European filmmakers like Marie-Claude Deffarge and Gordian Troeller expounded in the twenty films in their series *Au nom du progrès*, which developed the insights of François Partant's condemnation of the ideology of progress and his analysis of the economic crisis as the end of development.[25]

The Western conception of development, which African elites have taken over, remains based on the application of the model of industrial growth to

Poster for
Sango Malo
(Bassek Ba Kobhio,
Cameroon, 1991).

peasant societies in crisis. These societies are conceived merely as cases for the application of a universal model founded upon the three pillars of industrialization, modernity (urban, technical and scientific) and statization.[26] In the conviction that another type of development is possible based on a different conception, such as the autocentric development advocated by Samir Amin,[27] African filmmakers often use clashes between elites who are either corrupt or Westernized and individuals bent on innovation to convey the didactic burden of their films. In *Sango Malo* (Bassek Ba Kobhio, Cameroon, 1991), a young schoolteacher clashes with his headmaster because he bases his teaching on the practical acquisition of the local peasant culture (horticulture, animal husbandry, knowledge of nature, and a 'make-do-and-mend' approach):

> 'We're trying something new. We advocate an education adapted to local realities.'
> 'You talk like Sekou Touré in 1958!'

'What we need for our development are trained masses, thinking masses, not unwilling to use their hands.'
'It's scientists, doctors and engineers we're short of!'
'No, we need a people which knows how to use its hands!'

But how is one to sell autocentric development to young people who are in thrall to the consumer society? Young people today are not easily convinced. 'They have recognized our failure', says the Guinea-Bissau filmmaker Flora Gomes, 'and they no longer subscribe to our dream. In their eyes, only those who really act are credible, like Vicente in *Les Yeux bleus de Yonta*, who has shifted the struggle on to the economic terrain.'[28] Schooling, then, will be the best tool of emancipation, as we can see in this exchange from *Laada* (Drissa Touré, Burkina Faso, 1991):

'School does nothing for you.'
'The thing is to know how to write.'
'That'll make you a white...'
'It'll enable you to clarify what you know.'

There has been little advance, however, when it comes to registering the failings of the education system – a matter to which filmmakers are constantly drawn back, because the impasses of identity are linked to the impasses of transmission. In 1979, at the beginning of the film *Fad'jal*, Safi Faye criticized the place accorded to Louis XIV in the school curriculum, contrasting the teachings of the child's grandfather with such colonial irrelevancies. In 1994, the school in *Symbole*, a short by the Senegalese Ahmadou Diallo, was still not allowing pupils to use their vernacular language at all, permitting only French to be spoken, in the same way as only a few decades ago, in the French school system, a sign prominently displayed in the classroom used to inform Breton or Occitan children that 'they must not spit on the floor or speak patois'.[29]

THE ORIGIN IN DOUBT

The child in *Symbole* is doubly in a quandary. His mother interprets his French as an insult; the schoolteacher will not allow him to use his mother's language at all. His attitude to tradition, represented by a herdsman leading his animals between two baobab trees, is one of questioning. Which of the two cultures is he to choose? Let us hear Axelle Kabou once again: 'The young Africans of today lack one unquestionable certainty – the certainty that they can raise themselves up into a world power solely on the basis of their traditional values.' It is, as Cissé said, only through knowledge that the

Sembène Ousmane at the 1985 Fespaco. As is shown in the documentary *Burkina Cinéma* by Joseph Akouissone from the Central African Republic, many filmmakers took part symbolically in laying track on a railway which was being built at the time of this ninth Fespaco. © Françoise Huguier.

young could think of changing Africa and taking a role in the world. But it is not enough simply to draw on memory and knowledge, or to revive ancestral values, for there nationalist fundamentalism raises its head. 'History', Kabou goes on, 'particularly the history of precolonial Africa, offers no example of a society building up its power on the basis of its intrinsic genius.'[30] To remain stuck in one's origins is conservative: you have to know how to leave your origin behind and find something elsewhere which will enrich it, question it. As Daniel Sibony writes: 'It is the contamination, the adulteration, of the origin which rescues it from mindlessness.'[31]

This requires courage. It was dangerous enough to denounce the failings of development and the corruption of Africa's elites. After showing *Ta Dona*, a film which denounced the corruption of the authorities, at the Fespaco festival, and flying back to Mali, Adama Drabo was taken directly to see the dictator Moussa Traoré, and escaped serious difficulties only because the regime collapsed very soon afterwards.[32]

Nor has it always been particularly comfortable to stand out against the aims laid down for cinema by the intelligentsia, as Kitia Touré from the Ivory Coast discovered. 'At Sankara's first Fespaco, in 1985', he remembers,

> I had the temerity to say on the radio that African filmmakers are fighting the wrong battle when they make films. I said they saw themselves as guiding the people when in reality we are creators of dreams, sellers of dreams. The programme was stopped, and in the evening I had to go into hiding, as there were young revolutionaries after me.[33]

Today, however, it is introspective criticism which can expose the filmmaker to the keenest attacks; for, as the Senegalese Moussa Sene Absa says, 'The sense of rupture, of questioning, of subversion, is always regarded as a curse.'[34] Few people really risk this, and they are very soon accused of lacking authenticity when they do.

Pierre Yameogo from Burkina Faso defines that authenticity as 'dealing with individual social realities to achieve some progress'.[35] In *Laafi* (1991), a brilliant high-school graduate clashes with the bureaucratic machine in his efforts to pursue the medical studies which would enable him to serve his country. The brain drain is also a conduit for corruption. *Wendemi* (1993) denounces leniency towards prostitution, recounting the story of a young man in search of his identity, who does not know his father's name. But the debate on authenticity (moving social reality forward rather than responding to the Western demand for decorative images) ultimately conceals the question of what African cinema is. Does it mean films *on* Africa or films *from* Africa[36] – that is to say, films in which the director's imagination, in his confrontation with his origins, thwarts or fails to thwart the aesthetic and cultural expectations of an external audience? Filmmakers who state that they do not want to be confined to the 'ghetto of African cinema' in fact reject that ideological 'line' which insists on showing a social reality in order to contribute to modifying it. By seeking to distance themselves from the ghetto, they develop an inwardness which merely sends them back to the very cultural origin from which they sought to differentiate themselves. Otherwise, they are led to deny their origins in order to adapt to a commercial expectation, whether it be an appetite for exoticism or for a disembodied 'art for art's sake'. Thus authenticity is not a matter of belonging to a 'ghetto' or not, but, as in any true cultural creation, of opening up the cinematic field to the questioning of its own origin.

Nor is it a question of whether one resides in Africa or not. 'It is not living in the country which makes what you do authentic!' says Idrissa Ouedraogo.[37] Moreover, filmmakers confirm that it is very difficult not to spend a lot of time in Europe to gather the necessary production monies

Poster for *Laafi*
(Pierre Yameogo,
Burkina Faso, 1991).

and subsequently to follow up on the post-production. Authenticity has more to do with the approach to introspection: whether one is merely playing to the gallery or putting oneself on the line. Their situation as 'cultural half-castes' (the phrase is Congolese director David Pierre Fila's)[38] leaves directors astride two cultures. Already split between two languages, they *find themselves* between two places, well situated to developing new ways of questioning their origins. It is from this halfway house that they have to make their choices from the wealth of possibilities. 'Your dwelling has two hundred entrances', says the proverb. It is up to you to choose your path.

INFIDELITIES

One is struck immediately by a paradox: this cinema which is made, in the main, by men often uses women to question the virility of society. 'Nanyuma, we give birth to the world, and it does violence to us; our only course is patience and resignation', says a woman in *Finzan* (Cheikh Oumar Sissoko, Mali, 1989). The intention here goes beyond a mere dramatic logic concerned to include opposites. While modernity weakens patriarchy, women represent the perpetuation of that emulation which is the strength of the traditional village. The films willingly pay homage to them, showing them to be tough and hardworking. And they often take on a documentary dimension, lingering over the actions which make up the women's daily labours. In the port of N'gor near Dakar, the women shown in *N'gor, l'esprit des lieux* (Samba Félix Ndiaye, Senegal, 1995) hang the fish, soak it, salt it and dry it:

> Let me explain the situation to you: this work enables us to pay our way. We don't owe anyone anything. We'll do it as long as we have the strength. This work protects us, preserves us. It's a guarantee of independence for us and our families. It will go on as long as we live.

But women are, above all, those who rebel, who reject an established order which does them down. In *Finzan*, Nanyuma does not hesitate to flee from the circle of the community on several occasions to escape forced marriage, as do other women in *Le Wazzou polygame* (Oumarou Ganda, Niger, Fespaco Grand Prize, 1972); *Wend Kuuni* (Gaston Kaboré, Burkina Faso, 1982); *Histoire d'Orokia* (Jacob Sou and Jacques Oppenheim, Burkina Faso/France, 1987); or *Baoré* (Maurice Kaboré, Burkina Faso, 1992). An alternative course of action is to refuse to allow the marriage to be consummated, as in *Maral Tanié* [The Second Wife] (Mahamat Saleh Haroun, Chad, 1994), in which the seventeen-year-old Halimé tells herself: 'I'll make his life hell until he repudiates me. Then I'll be free!'

In so doing, the woman betrays her origin: she steps outside the circle of traditional rules. 'To be successful, you have to know how to betray', says Soma (Niamanto Sanogo) in *Yeelen* (Souleymane Cissé, 1987)! For this infidelity is a source of life: what is she being faithful to when she is unfaithful, if not to her very origins? Is not her betrayal of an identity frozen in conservative rules by which women are exploited a fidelity to her own identity – that of a living woman, capable of loving and giving life? Her example is, consequently, valid for the whole of society.

In rebelling against their condition, women break down the social consensus which determines that condition. Their infidelity makes such a breach in the play of established interests that the group unites to suppress their vital energy and bring them to heel. The village is then confronted with the drama created by the woman's obstinacy: it is in flight or death that women must find refuge. Mossane, the eponymous hero of Safi Faye's film (Senegal, 1996), is so beautiful that even the children are overcome by her looks, and abandon their football game ('As soon as they see her, those two, they set off in pursuit, and that's an end to the match!'). The classic plot of forced marriage for purposes of obtaining the dowry soon makes its appearance when her mother notices that she has a soft spot for Fara, a penniless student: 'When the earth produces nothing, that's an end to morality.' Only the grandmother is clear-sighted: 'Mossane isn't happy. You don't burn a tree which bears fruit!' But she is not heeded: the marriage is consummated, in spite of Mossane's rebellion. The only course open to her is flight, but she has to cross Mamangueth, that dangerous inlet which, if it could speak, really would have a story to tell...

The latest film by the Malian director Adama Drabo, *Taafe Fanga*, goes back to a Dogon legend which recounts the arrival on earth of the mask. A woman grabs it, the men are afraid, and oppressed womankind take advantage of the situation to seize back power: 'In our societies, when the mask appears, the women have to hide, and yet it is by their actions that we have masks today!'[39] By using a legend to argue for the recognition of women's role in African societies, and for greater sexual equality, the filmmaker draws the source of a certain modernity from his culture of origin. Does not equality mean education, autonomy, individualization, and therefore a challenge to the collective control of the community and the patriarchy?

To handle such a delicate subject, Adama Drabo chose humour, as many of the films made in Ivory Coast so successfully do. 'The African laughs at most things. Europeans take this for naivety, whereas I consider it a great philosophy!', says Henri Duparc.[40] In relating, in *Bal Poussière* (1988), how Demi-dieu [Demigod], a rich villager, takes a sixth wife but finds himself thereby confronted with a sassy, modern girl, Duparc is confronting the polygamy issue head-on. Whereas for men, having just a single wife is often regarded with contempt – like having only one eye or one shirt – monogamy is sometimes rejected by village women as synonymous with excessive chores and suffering for them: they have to do all the housework and the work in the fields on their own, and if illness comes they are left to face it alone. There is a danger, too, that repudiation will strip them of all their possessions, which revert to the husband.[41] *Bal Poussière* uses laughter to reveal the perverse features of polygamy, and to show that it is by no means a better solution. To avoid jealousies and rivalries between the wives such as characterize polygamous situations, where aggression cannot be directed against the husband, Demi-dieu carefully sets up a rota system, reducing the wives to the status of mere bodies to be exploited.[42] His wives have access neither to public life nor to knowledge and power, and so the hierarchy between the sexes is respected. If a woman attempts to resist, she can do so only by

Poster for
Bal Poussière
(Henri Duparc,
Ivory Coast, 1988).

refusing her body to her husband, thus reducing herself to the role of sex object. And since this also presupposes that she is to be chosen, and therefore attractive, the wife is hoist with her own petard: in fighting against an order of things, the women simultaneously reproduce its ideological framework.[43]

THE MARABOUTS' PROJECTIVE MECHANISM

Faced with their husband's infidelity, with illness or with phenomena beyond their comprehension, the women in a great many films run off to the marabout. When filmmakers have sought to criticize the shortcomings of traditional ways, the marabout has often been presented as a charlatan, ready to engage in any intrigue to obtain money: the marabout in *Saïtane* (acted and directed by Oumarou Ganda, Niger, 1972) manipulates superstition and people's credulity to such a degree that when he is found out, he kills himself.

Today, in our more introspective age, it is, rather, the projective mechanism used by the marabout which is at issue. The individual himself is rarely responsible for his affliction: the often impalpable evil comes from elsewhere. The marabouts have to name and identify this evil, and they have to find its place in the symbolic register of the community.[44] On the death of Assouan, the father of *Bouka* (Gnoan Roger M'Bala, Ivory Coast, 1988), a fetisher, pouring a little spirit on to the earth, announces: 'Assouan, come and drink. You died cutting down a tree. That death was not natural. It had a cause. Find the culprit. Strike him. Show the strength of your soul!' Those in attendance look each other up and down, afraid, before hurling themselves in relief on the most convenient victim, Kadjo, the dead man's brother!

In *Le Cercle des pouvoirs* (1996), the Cameroonians Daniel Kamwa and Jules Takam depict two types of marabout:

> There are two magic circles in the film: the evil witchdoctor who makes all who will listen to him believe he can help them to get wealth and power, in exchange for what are at first imprecise sacrifices, but which turn out to involve sacrificing a close relative to get out of the arrangement, and the healer Atchori, who represents the positive side of magic, who tries to help people in tricky situations, in which their lives are in danger.[45]

The hero, an upright journalist played by Kamwa himself, consults Atchori regularly, and gets genuine support from him for his campaign to denounce political and commercial sleaze.

Clearly, polygamy offers an ideal terrain for the marabout: who in that arrangement does not have a co-wife who wants to prevent him from having children? Every affliction has an external cause – often a spell cast by another jealous, malevolent family member. Thwarting it is simply a matter of identifying the perpetrator.

To question the projection used by the marabout is to privilege interiority and self-consciousness in women – and throughout society. In allowing women to express their lack of satisfaction, in valorizing monogamy or the intellectual work of some women, the filmmakers are challenging certain foundations of society. Here the individual escapes the influence of the group to determine his or her own life. She or he sets emancipated ways against the group's stereotyped, conservative behaviour.

The deceived wife in *Pouc Niini* (Fanta Regina Nacro, Burkina Faso, 1995) at first reacts angrily to her husband's infidelity: she consults a marabout and has her rival beaten. But once her sense of revolt has passed, she tries to understand why her husband prefers a courtesan, and, in an extremely unusual episode, visits her to discuss the matter calmly. In Mooré, *Pouc Niini* means 'open your eyes': here Fanta Nacro appeals to women to develop a new style of social behaviour in which the affirmation of one's own desire for life replaces a self-defeating rivalry.

FROM NUDITY TO MODESTY

In order to make its point the more forcefully and challenge current conventions, this short film presents some intimate scenes of a kind one seldom sees in a culture where any absence of modesty creates an immediate shock effect: 'African culture', notes Anne-Laure Folly from Togo, 'is more secretive, less externalized, more modest and restrained. Any unveiling is a violation. In this sense, cinema is transgression.'[46] Baring oneself, revealing what is hidden: the filmmaker will be tempted to show that which is not shown (or, as in the novel, to say what is not said). She or he transgresses the rules of the community. Now, when all is said and done, in Africa deviance suggests madness. The Senegalese villager refers to the village madman, who is often the mediator or possessor of a transcendental message, as 'the man who runs off naked into the bush.'[47]

Showing the unshowable might be said, then, to be the province of the mad, and this is what underlies a kind of taboo on nudity. Hence, in African film, what nudity unveils is generally kept secret; clothing protects the social cohesion of each human being. The filmmaker transgresses the taboo only for heightened meaning. It is undoubtedly, in part, to stress the importance of knowing one's origins that Souleymane Cissé presents the dancers of *Waati* naked, but the primary reason is to emphasize the courage required for such self-knowledge. Similarly, in *Finye*, filming the nudity of Bah and Batrou in close-up when the two young lovers, contrary to tradition, wash together, Cissé is attempting to remove the ambiguities between men and women: 'A society with a vocation to modernize must have no sexual boundary.'[48]

Claude Lévi-Strauss observed that 'people who live in a state of complete nudity are not unaware of what we call modesty: they define it differently.'[49] Modesty is correlative with respect for the individual's integrity within the group. It is not so much the naked body which is taboo as sexual relations in the naked state: in films and stories, sex is named, but not described.[50] To describe it is to invite incomprehension and scandal. *Visages de femmes* (Désiré Ecaré, Ivory Coast, 1984) was banned for a year in its country of origin for

Poster for *Finye*
(Souleymane Cissé,
Mali, 1982).

obscenity and gross indecency because it included a ten-minute scene depicting the adulterous copulation in a river between Kouassi and Affoue –
a ban which earned the film enormous publicity. Would we be right to
suspect here a sacrificing of authenticity for commercial ends, as Nigerian
writer Nwachukwu Frank Ukadike does,[51] or should we see merely a desire
to share the joy of transgression, the simplicity of a desire which, though
forbidden by the rules, seems quite natural, given the violence and self-
satisfaction of the husband? Not the eye of a voyeur – a stance the filmmaker
explicitly denies – but a 'contemplative gaze', conveying emotion and
fantasy.[52]

Respect for communal rules, asserted as ancestral and hence divine in
nature, may constitute an affirmation of self, in so far as one uses it to apply
a knowledge, and adopt an approach to the meaning of existence and an

On the set of *Touki-Bouki*. From left to right: Georges Bracher, Djibril Diop Mambety, Magaye Niang and Ousseynou Diop, Dakar, 1972. © Maya Bracher.

understanding of one's place in the world. It is not, however, something which can merely be taken for granted, as though it were biologically entrenched in a changeless, manipulative conservatism. As Jung said, 'He who does not question his belief falls victim to it.' It is by opening up the cracks in their identity, the fissures they sense within it, the contradictions between the essential values of their origins and the possible perversions of those values which tradition forces upon them, that women themselves advance, and also bring about social progress. African filmmakers' concern with this exemplary affirmation of the desire of woman – unfaithful as she is to cultural norms (without, for all that, rejecting them), but faithful, in her refusal of immobility, to her original life force – may, through the self-examinations it provokes, create fertile ground for social change. And is it not, indeed, a Dogon cross Anta grips in her hand as she copulates with Mory, her moans clothing the violence of their thrashing bodies, in the magnificent *Touki-Bouki* (Djibril Diop Mambety, Senegal, 1973)?

NOTES

1. Jean-Claude Biny Traoré, *Cinéma et histoire*, mimeo, Direction de l'enseignement secondaire des Hauts-Bassins, Bobo-Dioulasso, Burkina Faso, 1995.

2. Remark by Gaston Kaboré in Laurence Gavron's film *Y'a pas de problème!* (France, 1995).

3. Pierre Alphandéry, Pierre Bitoun and Yves Dupont, *L'équivoque écologique*, La Découverte, Paris, 1991, p. 266.

4. Interview with Joseph Gaye Ramaka, Paris, 1996.

5. Thérèse-Marie Desfontaines, 'Interview with Gaston Kaboré' in the booklet which accompanied the release of the film *Rabi*, Association française des cinémas d'art et d'essai, Paris, 1993.

6. Clémentine Madiya Faïk-Nzuji, *Symboles graphiques en Afrique noire*, Karthala, Paris, 1992, p. 32.

7. Interview with Raymond Rajaonarivelo, Paris, 1995.

8. Birgit Akesson, *Le Masque des eaux vives: danses et chorégraphies traditionnelles de l'Afrique noire*, L'Harmattan/Unesco, Paris, 1994, p. 5.

9. The period from June to September which, in the tropics, brings cooler weather and violent storms.

10. Alphonse Tierou, 'Danses d'Afrique', *Revue noire* 14, September 1994, p. 3.

11. André Gardies, *Cinéma d'Afrique noire francophone, l'espace miroir*, L'Harmattan, Paris, 1989, p. 31.

12. Axelle Kabou, *Et si l'Afrique refusait le développement?*, L'Harmattan, Paris, 1991, p. 96.

13. Interview with Jean-Marie Teno, Manosque, 1995.

14. Interview with Adama Drabo, Ouagadougou, 1995.

15. Hervé Kempf, *La Baleine qui cache la forêt, enquêtes sur les pièges de l'écologie*, La Découverte, Paris, 1994, p. 6.

16. Interview with Souleymane Cissé, press pack for *Yeelen*, 1987.

17. Ibid.

18. This is taken from Souleymane Cissé's synopsis of the film in Michel Boujut, 'Sous le soleil de Cissé', *L'Évènement du Jeudi*, 3 December 1987.

19. Souleymane Cissé, quoted by Ignacio Ramonet, 'Yeelen ou la magie des contes', *Le Monde diplomatique*, December 1987.

20. Roland Barthes, quoted by Kä Mana, *L'Afrique va-t-elle mourir? Essai d'éthique politique*, Karthala, Paris, 1993, p. 155.

21. The National Conferences were long debating sessions involving the various sociopolitical currents in those countries which launched the era of 'democratic openings' and African transitions after 1990 (Benin, Congo, Zaïre, Mali, Chad, etc.).

22. Jean-Marc Lalanne and Frédéric Strauss, interview with Souleymane Cissé, *Cahiers du Cinéma* 492, June 1995, p. 58.

23. Ibid.

24. Kabou, *Et si l'Afrique refusait le développement?*, p. 154. The term 'Fridayism' [*vendredisme*] is a reference to Defoe's Robinson Crusoe, and symbolizes both the 'noble savage' and the dependency complex of the primitive on the white man.

25. François Partant, *La Ligne d'horizon: essai sur l'après-développement*, La Découverte, Paris, 1988.

26. Catherine Coquery-Vidrovitch, Daniel Hémery and Jean Piel, *Pour une histoire du*

développement: États, sociétés, développement, L'Harmattan, Paris, 1988, p. 13.

27. Acting so that external relations serve the accumulation of the internal wealth of the country. Samir Amin, *Maldevelopment: Anatomy of a Global Failure*, Zed Books, London, 1990, pp. 157–8.

28. Thérèse-Marie Desfontaines, interview with Flora Gomes, *Écrans d'Afrique* 1, May 1992, p. 78.

29. The Occitan singer Marti tells of such a sign in the autobiographical story *Ome d'Oc*, Stock, Paris, 1977.

30. Kabou, *Et si l'Afrique refusait le développement?*, p. 178.

31. Daniel Sibony, *Entre-deux, l'origine en partage*, Le Seuil, Paris, 1991, p. 47.

32. Lucien Patry, Interview with Adama Drabo, *Films et documents* 378 ('Perspectives et réalités du cinéma africain'), December 1991, p. 18.

33. Interview with Kitia Touré, Abidjan, 1995.

34. Interview with Moussa Sene Absa, *Le Film Africain* 18/19, February 1995.

35. Interview with Pierre Yameogo, Paris, 1995.

36. Stéphane Balandrin, 'Les Cinémas africains en résistance', *Cahiers du Cinéma* 492, June 1995, p. 63.

37. Interview with Idrissa Ouedraogo, Paris, 1995.

38. In *Cinés d'Afrique*, a documentary by G. Debroise, S. Interlegator, O. Lichen (France) and Samba Félix Ndiaye (Senegal), 1993.

39. Interview with Adama Drabo, Ouagadougou, 1995.

40. Interview with Henri Duparc, Ouagadougou, 1995.

41. Marie-Denise Riss, *Femmes africaines en milieu rural*, L'Harmattan, Paris, 1989, p. 46.

42. The Senegalese director Moussa Sene Absa well illustrates in *Tableau Ferraille* (1997) the opposition between a first wife 'with Coca-Cola bottle curves', beautiful and pure, but sterile, and a second wife who is fertile, but does not hesitate to betray her husband. Between these two women, '*C'est la langue et les dents*' – a delicate choice between proxy motherhood and a polygamy which is anything but rosy.

43. Sylvie Fainzang and Odile Journet, *La femme de mon mari: anthropologie du mariage polygamique en Afrique et en France*, L'Harmattan, Paris, 1988, p. 162.

44. Dominique Lutz-Fuchs, *Psychothérapies de femmes africaines*, L'Harmattan, Paris, 1994, p. 231.

45. Interview with Daniel Kamwa, Paris, 1998, published in *Africultures* 7, L'Harmattan, Paris, 1998.

46. Interview with Anne-Laure Folly, Paris, 1995.

47. Interview with Zirignon Grobli, a psychoanalyst from the Ivory Coast, Abidjan, 1995.

48. Jacques Binet and Kitia Touré, interview with Souleymane Cissé, *Positif*, December 1987, p. 10.

49. Claude Lévi-Strauss, *Tristes tropiques*, trans. John and Doreen Weightman, Penguin, Harmondsworth,1976, p. 374.

50. Suzanne Lallemand, *L'Apprentissage de la sexualité dans les contes d'Afrique de l'Ouest*, L'Harmattan, Paris, 1985, p. 17.

51. Nwachukwu Frank Ukadike, *Black African Cinema*, University of California Press, Berkeley/Los Angeles/London, 1994, p. 222.

52. Désiré Ecaré, 'Quelques réflexions sur cinéma et liberté à propos de "Visages de femmes"', in *Cinémas et libertés*, Présence Africaine, Paris, 1993, p. 22.

SIX

AN OPENNESS OF APPROACH

Have I no other purpose on earth, then, but to avenge the Negro of the seventeenth century? ... There is no Negro mission. There is no white burden.[1]

**A detour through the English-speaking black diaspora enables us to grasp
the forward-looking character of hybridization. By denying its plurality,
French society refuses to integrate the Other present within it, and this
leads the society itself into a crisis of identity. In bidding farewell to
'negritude', the films of Black Africa help us to recognize the divided
nature of our origins.**

SOUTH AFRICAN INTROSPECTION

Who is more qualified to gauge the extent of the identity crisis of an oppressed people than the Blacks of South Africa, who have lived through
apartheid? It is symptomatic that the films made today by black South
Africans take that inner tragedy as their subject, and do so with a great
concern for openness. There are, however, still very few black filmmakers in
that country. Under apartheid, cinema was practically nonexistent for Blacks.[2]
The three million inhabitants of Soweto had only two cinemas to go to![3]
When films were made for the black population, the aim was to encourage
tribalism and primitivism in keeping with the ideology of apartheid. The
imitations of Hollywood films (hence the nickname *holyveldo*) which were to
follow in no way changed the sense of deprivation of their own images felt
by the black community penned into the 'townships'. When the Whites
showed black people in their films, they unashamedly reproduced the dominant discourse against all intercultural contamination – even when the intention seemed purely comic, as with Jamie Uys's highly successful *The Gods
Must Be Crazy* (1980). Under apartheid, only two feature films were made by

black directors. In 1975, Simon Sabela made *U-Deliwe* in Zulu. This was the story of a young orphan girl who became a model before returning in the end to her home. Despite its accurate depiction of the world of the black suburbs, the film's theme chimed with apartheid and, for that reason, received government subsidies. By contrast, Gibson Kente financed *How Long?* (1976) himself, but the film was banned and Kente was arrested.[4] For all the tribulations of distance and isolation it entails, exile has proved to be the only solution. Having taken refuge, like so many other directors, actors and technicians, in London, Lionel N'Gakane made *Vukani Awake* (1962), a documentary on the living conditions of South African Blacks; then a biography of Nelson Mandela; and, finally, a film on racism in Britain, *Jemina and Johnny*.[5]

Some managed to get around the censors' vigilance. One such was the American Lionel Ragosin, who, in 1959, clandestinely shot the classic *Come Back Africa*, a film which could not be shown openly in South Africa until 1988. This fictional work about a migrant worker and his wife skilfully blends in documentary footage of the city and the mines, and enables one to feel the warmth and atmosphere of the multiracial district of Sophiatown in the suburbs of Johannesburg (the area was razed to the ground in the 1960s and its inhabitants moved to Soweto, a considerable distance from the city). Similarly, *Mapantsula* (1988) was made discreetly by a white man, Oliver Schmitz, in collaboration with a Black, Thomas Mogatlane, the film's co-writer and principal actor. As is indicated by the nickname of the character Johnny – 'Panic' – the film described the fear rife among both Blacks and Whites in South African society, doing so under cover of a detective story – a factor which enabled it to slip past the censor. This *mapantsula* (a young tearaway from Soweto), though he is cynical and asocial, becomes a hero in spite of himself, refusing, at some risk to his life, to recognize neighbours on video footage shot by the police at a demonstration. More recently, *Wheels and Deals* (Mike Hammon, 1990), a film shot in Soweto using a fast, hand-held camera, tells the story of a trade unionist who is forced to resort to crime to survive.

It is these kinds of themes which are being developed by the small number of black South African filmmakers who are able to be active today. Rather than meeting the expectations of right-thinking Western opinion, which would prefer to see unspeakable Whites ranged against an idealized black community, they are attempting to exorcize the scars left upon the consciousness of black people by their history. Following the path marked out by the writer Njabulo Ndebele, the cinema has taken an interest in 'ordinary people', in their integration of violence into a society of violence.

'We owe what we are to apartheid', said the poet Lesego Rampolokeng. Mickey Madoba Dube, exiled in the USA, took on the issue of Black-on-Black violence directly in *Imbazo, the Axe*, exploring the relationship between a son and his father, who, to survive, had been a member of the squads of hired killers paid by the regime to terrorize the black ghettos. In 1997, Zola Maseko made a short fiction film, *The Foreigner*, on xenophobia towards the new immigrants who had come in from other African countries after the transition to majority rule. In *Fools* (Ramadan Suleman, 1996) – as Njabulo Ndebele, the author of the novel on which the film is based, observed – 'the purity of the wishes Zamani feels for the children in his class is proportional to his inability to free himself from the corruption which characterizes his own life'. Zamani is a respected teacher in the township, even though he once raped one of his young charges, something to which the community closed its eyes. A long time ago, Zamani rebelled against apartheid, but that is ancient history now. When Zani, the brother of the girl who was raped, returns from Swaziland, where he has had the opportunity to study, he is firmly resolved to change everything. In the early morning, in the waiting room of Johannesburg station, he bumps into Zamani, returning from a night on the tiles. Together they will return to the harsh reality of the township. Under the gaze of the women, who have never lost their dignity, Zamani will recover a little pride and Zani will, inevitably, lose some…

The new conditions make it impossible to think in binary terms: it is a time for introspection. 'With *Fools*', says Ramadan Suleman, 'I was trying to say that we cannot just externalize this hatred and that it is by this inner work that we shall be able to restore tolerance.'[6] One must go beyond resentment and scour one's own imagination in one's need to reconstruct one's self-image. Thus, without sinking into total forgetfulness, South African creative artists do seem to be avoiding what the writer John M. Coetzee calls the 'metaphorization of suffering'. Koto Bolofo's documentary, *The Land is White, the Seed is Black* (1996), which relates the humiliations of a black family during the apartheid years, is concerned not so much to denounce evils as to draw on the humanity Blacks were able to show in the time of their repression, in order to recover that humanity today. South African film directors, concerned as they are to document their times, are also intent, however, on not falling into the trap of simple reportage: in *Johannesburg Stories* (1997), Oliver Schmitz (with Brian Tilley) attempts a halfway house between documentary and fiction to portray a city engaged in an agonizing and fascinating transformation in which the old white order no longer has a place…

AFRO-AMERICAN RITES OF PASSAGE

While South African filmmakers are attempting to exorcize the marks history has left on black consciousness, the films of the Afro-American diaspora also reveal the filmmakers' efforts to piece back together an identity which has become fragmented in a community where unemployment, despair and rejection lead to extreme violence. 'One out of every twenty-one Black American males will be murdered in their lifetime. Most will die at the hands of another Black male', warns John Singleton as a prelude to *Boyz 'N the Hood* (1991). The film, which tells the story of a young man in the black ghetto, shows how lucky a young American black man can count himself if he reaches adulthood, beset as he is by gangs, drugs, police and depression. Taking this example from among the many films which follow a linear narrative thread through urban violence, Manthia Diawara observes that they conform to the classic structure of folktale: a young person confronted with imminent danger must go to see a close friend or relative who will teach him how to overcome it; his success makes everyone stronger.[7] These films also depict rites of passage through which a community in crisis can achieve a safer future. In *Boyz 'N the Hood*, the mother, who is separated from the father, hands her son over to him for initiation: he will learn not to lose his self-respect, not to reject school and, in order to stay alive, not to be led, through misplaced loyalty, into the spiral of violence. John Singleton returns to this initiatory narrative schema in *Higher Learning* (1995), in which a black student confronted with skinhead racism comes through the ordeal of violence thanks to his teacher's determination.

This 'new realism' is in stark contrast to the 1970s, when Black American cinema dealt with racism and black exploitation in the USA in a rather static manner, using black-and-white to give a faithful depiction of the psychological conflict underlying interracial relations in America.[8] Here again, denunciation is giving way today to the search for solutions. The films are now tending to develop a specific vision of problems which may extend beyond the mere framework of the black community, and to do so in a context in which box-office success is not necessarily ruled out. By grossing 8.5 million dollars with *She's Gotta Have It* (1986), a film which cost only 175,000 dollars to make, Spike Lee has rid independent black cinema of its inferiority complex, sloughed off the 'ghetto cinema' label and taken it into the mainstream. He has shown, as the director Arthur Jafa says, that it is possible to be 'both radically black and successful'.[9] In the tradition of *Sweet Sweetback's Badass Song* (1971), a provocative, chaotic, lyrical work by Melvin van Peebles,[10] the Charlie Parker of Black American cinema, *She's Gotta Have It* tackles head-on the issue of sexuality, which had previously been a more or less taboo subject in this type of cinema. However, rather than produce 'resistance' cinema, as Van Peebles did, in the spirit of the Black Power movement of his times, Lee approaches his subject in universal terms: can a woman love more than one man at the same time? His skill lay in exploiting the theme to depict the life of New York's Blacks in eclectic and explosive vignettes, and in an improvisational style reminiscent of jazz.[11] He would later return to that style to describe the difficulty communities have coexisting in *Do the Right Thing* (1989).

Spike Lee's success is a constant thorn in the side of an establishment which is not greatly inclined to support black protest campaigns, especially when Lee produced a Hollywood-style Malcolm X biopic (*Malcolm X*, 1992). The American myth of the melting pot merely provides a fig leaf for the fear of contamination with which American society is obsessed. Lee did, however, pave the way for a new generation of Black American filmmakers conforming to a classic Hollywood aesthetic, who have built their success on the popularity of hip-hop and gangsta rap among American youth. This has often produced images of extraordinary violence, as in *Menace II Society* (Allen and Albert Hughes, 1993), which depicts the nihilistic itinerary of Ken, a young man whose desire for fast living will inevitably lead to his death. Ken's expressions of reluctance to become involved in the spiral of violence seldom amount to more than lip service.

In stark contrast to these populist successes, independent black cinema has further pursued the quest for Afro-American roots in best 'Roots Movement' tradition. *Harvest 3000* (1976) remains the most successful of the films of this type and is a beacon, a historic landmark, for the whole of Third World cinema. Haïlé Gerima, an Ethiopian exiled in the USA, returned to his native land to direct the film, which, mingling realist narrative and political parable, describes the life of Ethiopian peasants in the year 1974, and their oppression by their landlord. Their young son runs away and identifies with other oppressed people: his emerging awareness heralds a new dawn. The character Kerebe, the madman, represents memory, and is a symbol of faithfulness to African culture in so far as this involves rebelling against injustice. The memory of Gerima's father is superimposed on the argument in the form of a song he wrote which runs as a leitmotiv through the film:

> Our bride (Ethiopia), our new bride,
> Your dress three thousand years old,
> How could it not be torn?
> Our Lady, our mistress,
> Your dress three thousand years old,
> Why is it not yet changed?

The exploration of origins makes it possible to get beyond the simple slave's conception of an opposition between freedom and subjugation. In *Daughters of the Dust*, Julie Dash stresses the need to know oneself better so that one can move away from that starting point, to know one's roots so that one can free oneself from them. In the early part of this century a family goes to picnic at Ibo-Landing, an island used in the past as a landing point for slaves. In a circular montage mingling the characters' stories and their questions, various possible courses of action are debated: should they remain anchored in their family community, go north and involve themselves in the modern world, or return to the Africa of their origins? The lyricism of the images and the rising tension lend a tone of pathos to the film. Afro-American identity seems fragmented into many facets. Nana, the grandmother, stresses ancestral values as a source of cohesiveness, and her wisdom will be a great resource. The reference to origins makes it possible to reconstruct a consistent identity, provided that one accepts the complexity of that identity – provided, in other words, that one takes on board the multiplicity of experiences which, from slavery to incorporation in North American society, have continued to shape it.

Here again, openness presents new vistas. In *The Glass Shield* (1994), Charles Burnett handles the theme of racism without reducing it to a mere black-and-white question by describing the painful compromises which have to be made by a black policeman fresh out of school, and showing his developing awareness of his situation. Introspection, described as an initiatory rite of passage, makes it possible to free oneself from the fantasy of a solid identity based on the recapturing of an origin. In the quest for identity, identity matters less than the quest itself. The films of Charles Burnett (*Killer of Sheep*, 1977; *My Brother's Wedding*, 1983) home in powerfully on this experience of the black minority, making that director one of the main representatives of 'documentary realism'. For example, his major success, *To Sleep with Anger* (1989), shows uncompromisingly how Harry (Danny Glover), who is both angel and demon, can play skilfully on the tensions and contradictions within the family which takes him in, to manipulate and exploit it. The title comes from an old African proverb, 'Never sleep with anger.' Harry symbolizes, then, the challenge to that fixed sense of comfort which the Black American middle class is concerned to preserve at all costs.[12]

HYBRIDIZED IDENTITY

Today's independent African-American filmmakers, under pressure from a market which wants images of revolt and violence, are trying to get beyond these stereotypes to explore their identity and demonstrate their humanity.[13] In *Naked Acts* (1995), Bridgett M. Davis tells the story of a woman who is determined never to show her body, so as not to reproduce the 'blax-ploitation' her mother underwent in the 1970s as a star in erotic films. She will discover that, in order to be able to lay bare her artistic emotionality, she will have to gain awareness of – and develop – the expression of her body.

In *The Keeper* (1995), directed by the New York psychiatrist Joe Brewster, an innocent Haitian (Isaac de Bankolé) is thrown in prison for rape: his jailer (Giancarlo Esposito), who shares the same origins, helps him to get out, but his life is thrown into confusion by the sudden re-emergence of a culture he had rejected in order to 'integrate'. The film's great achievement is that it goes beyond stereotypes to depict black characters in all their complexity – characters in whom one can see oneself. The re-emergence of Haitian culture through the aptly named Jean-Baptiste has a salutary effect on the prison warder and his wife, but this is not without its burden of pain and worry.... While that strain of films which attempted to purge the black ghettos of drugs and violence has, in spite of initial large audiences, begun to run out of steam, there is a new perspective here.

The questing for identity which had characterized the independent pro-ductions of the 1980s, centred on the experience of a minority community trying to find its way, is now being complemented by a vein of self-examination and exploration of responsibilities. One very exciting film illustrates this well. Through a psychodrama organized by a woman teacher with some of her difficult pupils, Darryl Lemont Wharton's *Detention* (1997) examines the personal obstacles to – and issues raised by – having the community take on responsibility for themselves. The film, which came out of a playwriting workshop, strikes exactly the required tone, and the actors express genuine emotion, lending force to words of such sharpness that one would be happy to have them heard in every inner-city area in the world.

The black diaspora in Great Britain is also preoccupied with this kind of memory. John Akomfrah left his native Ghana at the age of five: 'I was an Uncle Tom trying to be English!'[14] His films, particularly *Handsworth Songs* (1986) and *Testament* (1988), reflect the culture shock experienced by Blacks, and the black experience in a white country. The Black Audio Film/Video Collective which he runs, a product of the black minority video workshops set up in London before Thatcherism put an end to the Greater London Council, seeks to produce an independent black cinema combining memory, ideas, politics, sexuality and autobiography, as can be seen in such films as *Seven Songs for Malcolm X* (1992). These somewhat 'difficult' films leave audiences a little bemused at times: 'People say they're intellectual films', says Akomfrah, 'but that intellectualism comes out of a desire to reflect on oneself.'[15]

Although the video workshops still exist, many of their founder members have left to do other things. 'Black Audio' now operates as a normal production house, and has to find its own funding – from television, for example. A new generation of filmmakers is emerging who have no connections with the workshops. Whereas in the 1980s, Channel 4 and the BBC mainly commissioned documentaries, the tendency today is towards fiction: 'This makes it possible to concern yourself with characters without considering the colour of their skin', observes the Jamaican Menelik Shabazz, 'and so you gain in intimacy and meaning.'[16] Shabazz is the director of *Burning an Illusion* (1981), a sensitive and stimulating boy-meets-girl story set in the London Afro-Caribbean community. *Playing Away* (Horace Ové, 1986) was significant for the way it posed the problem of the return to Jamaica through the description of a Brixton cricket team invited to play a friendly match in Suffolk as part of a 'Third World Week'. The lack of interest on the cinema industry's part is so great that feature films are rare. With *Baby Mother* (1999) Julian Henriques has attempted an 'Afro-British' musical in Harlesden, a reggae area in north-west London. Anita and her friends take great care over their appearance and wear the most extravagant clothes, making the film something of a fashion parade. But Anita, who dreams of becoming a singer, also has to look after her two children on her own. As for short films, the Zimbabwean Manu Kurewa brilliantly describes in *One Sunday Morning* (1996) how the refusal to extend a Nigerian immigrant's visa wrecks his relationship.

The same desire for introspection which we find in Akomfrah's work sees Isaac Julien explore the passionate friendship between two young black disc jockeys against a background of intrigue and murder in *Young Soul Rebels* (1991). Their pirate radio station, 'Soul Patrol', broadcasts 'funk' music in London in the summer of 1977, the year of the Queen's silver jubilee, hurling their existential, black rebellion in the face of an England mired in social conservatism. Julien pursues this same introspection in *Frantz Fanon, Black Skin, White Mask* (1996), a distantiated, Baroque work in which he deepens the analysis of racism made by the psychiatrist Fanon – that white mask on black skin, that denial of the desire the White feels for the Black.

Bitterness and nostalgia are also facets of a minority identity. *Home Away from Home* (1993), a sensitive short by Maureen Blackwood (who, with Isaac Julien, runs Sankofa, another London collective), speaks, almost without dialogue, of rootlessness. Miriam builds a circular hut in her garden, like the ones in the village from which her people come, where she can huddle up when she feels lonely and her relationship with her elder daughter, who was born in England, is getting her down. Her neighbours will not stand for this. In building her hut, Miriam is not returning to her origins but symbolizing them in a kind of nostalgic blank period, a necessary stage in integrating her new hybridized identity and hence in understanding the contradictions experienced by her daughter, who is also torn between two cultures.[17] It is to this belonging to the world that Maureen Blackwood appeals when she is asked to define her audience: 'If you're willing to set aside perceived notions of what it is to be black, and if you're alive and in the world, then you're my audience.'[18]

FRENCH ASSIMILATIONISM

The support of the British Film Institute (threatened with budget cuts, beginning with the closure of its African Department in September 1996) and Channel 4 television has given black British cinema a freedom to experiment which would be unthinkable in the USA. This has allowed 'Black British Film' to assert itself as a genre, despite some far from commercial formal experimentation. Such a phenomenon is unknown in France, despite the fact that many black filmmakers live there. The attempt at a comic description of the Parisian black world by Thomas Gillou and the Guinean director Cheik Doukouré (*Black micmac*, 1985) and the fascinating cross-cultural reflections of Claire Denis hardly make up the shortfall.[19] 'Parisian' African films have been less concerned with the existential problems of a minority and more with the tribulations of Blacks arriving from the former colonies. In a humorous vein, *Toubab bi* (Moussa Touré, Mali, 1992) describes culture shock through the eyes of an African arriving in France and confronted with those who live there and their various dealings. The subject is the African's view of Western society, as it is also in *Lettre à Makura – Les Derniers Bruxellois* (Ngangura Mweze, Zaïre, 1995). In that film a Zaïrian describes the manners and customs of the Europeans in a working-class district of Brussels for the people of his home village, in a manner reminiscent of Jean Rouch's *Petit à petit* (1968). This reverse ethnology continues to present an external view, fascinating for the details it highlights and the different perception of society it reveals, but bearing witness only partially to the experience of a black minority in the West.

The latest film by Cheik Doukouré (*Toubab or not toubab*) does, however, attempt to grasp how emigrants who, like him, have been in France for thirty years have developed and helped French society to evolve: 'Missing from African cinema', he says, 'is that dimension of adapting to another culture without giving up your own.'[20] But would that dimension be accepted?

'There is also missing from French society', he goes on, 'an acceptance of the Other as someone who can contribute something different.'

The reasons for the absence of 'black' films in France are to be sought, then, in the lack of public interest – and consequently producers' interest – in the black community as such. It could scarcely be otherwise in a France which is traditionally assimilationist both in its colonial history and in its immigration policy. Giving a minority community support to express itself means acknowledging its existence, and therefore its right to difference. That would mean accepting the possibility of a change in our own identity, its enrichment by the experience of the Other and the confrontation between cultures. This, in particular, is what black cinema offers: taking account not merely of what we and the foreigner have in common – the reassuring elements – but also of those things we cannot integrate, those cultural elements through which the Other preserves his difference and troubles our convictions.

If we are able to deny the Other, this is because we believe that he is – as Joseph Gaye Ramaka from Senegal remarks – 'in a transit zone, here for a certain time before returning to Africa'.[21] The French person is incapable of taking on board the many identities settled on his territory. Ramaka goes on:

> Whereas the British colonial system was based on separation, prefiguring what was later to become apartheid, the French system was assimilationist. In Anglo-Saxon countries that separation leads to treatment on a quota basis, whereas integrationism is supposed to be based on equality. The danger in the Anglo-Saxon system is the ghetto, but if you compare this with the current French situation, in which there is no recognition of specific identities, the outcome is perhaps better.... France is not prepared to accept the cultural diversity it already enjoys!

The Afro-European is thus an insufficiently expressed reality, practically absent from the media and hence nonexistent for society.

For their part, however, Africans, even though they have chosen to remain in France, also accept in their own mind that they are in a 'transit zone': 'The "Other" does not pay us any heed because he doesn't know we're here. But we ourselves don't know we're here', says Ramaka. The dialectic is well known – between master and slave, between colonialists and colonialized peoples, who can break with their condition only by going over to the colonialists. Inner-city riots attest to a refusal to be confined within this dialectic, but also to the impossibility of any development beyond it, for how can one conceive of integrating the person one excludes?

FAREWELL TO NEGRITUDE

This detour through the English-speaking black diaspora shows to what extent identity is a process. It is a transit through the origin, but also the progressive integration of the many confrontations with the Other, and with one's own experience. Identifying with one's origin gives impetus but cannot be definitive if one does not want, as Daniel Sibony writes, to fall into the illusion of 'a single form and a solid image, the fragility of which one none the less perceives – an exasperating fragility which one tries to bolster up rather than giving in to it.'[22] The issue, then, is no longer one of rejecting the Other within oneself but of accepting having passed through otherness to become what one is today.

Cultural hybridization and economic differences have created a gulf between Africans and Afro-Americans. It was the certain knowledge that they could learn from each other, however, which prompted the Pan-African Festival of Ouagadougou to give considerable space to the films of the diaspora. There has gradually been a certain transatlantic convergence which the African-American Larry Clark, director of the legendary *Passing Through* (1977), welcomes: 'We didn't know each other, but now we are talking and getting to know each other. In cinema, we should end up mounting projects together.'[23]

By foregrounding introspection, and teasing out the subversive impact the clash of cultures can represent for the West and for themselves, such films are mostly challenging the confinement of identity in a monolithic value system. The return to the Promised Land, the 'beloved land' of the ancestors, advocated by the Jamaican Marcus Garvey and the Rastafarians of the 1930s, is no longer on the agenda! The journey through origin serves now only to throw the present into relief.

By according prime importance to a return to the wellsprings, as the fantasy of an identity which may or may not ever have existed, the Negritude school bore within it an immense nostalgia for the lost paradise.[24] Frantz Fanon was well aware of the futility of this desire to re-create origins because it is so redolent of a wish to deny what one has experienced without first mastering that experience. Aimé Césaire made the same point:

> I systematically defend our old Negro civilizations…. So the real problem, you say, is to return to them. No, I repeat…. It is not a dead society that we want to revive…. It is a new society that we must create… rich with all the productive power of modern times, warm with all the fraternity of olden days.[25]

Forward-looking filmmakers, sometimes at great pain to themselves, unblock the vision: by challenging the conservatisms of tradition, from the dogmatism of prelates to politicians' monologues; by giving precedence to lived experience through the use of scenarios constructed like letters to a friend; by subjecting ideals to reality-testing to avoid fundamentalisms; by promoting self-criticism to fight the miseries of the present. By often taking the viewpoint of women, they recognize them as midwives of a new world, and show them to be so. Bidding, with René Depestre, 'hail and farewell to negritude',[26] they explore the imaginary register of identity in order to confront it with reality and contribute to the resolution of the problems of the present. They dare to assert before their people, as Cheikh Oumar Sissoko did on Malian television,[27] that culture is of primordial importance for development, showing by the incessant questioning of their own creations that preparing the future is not the same as copying one's origins but, rather, knowing those origins in order to be able to leave them. In so doing, they open our eyes to our own identity fixations.

THE ANXIETY OF INTEGRATION

The process continues in a kind of cycle: forging one's identity involves the ever-renewed integration of the Other. Those filmmakers who have often known exile, having come up against racism and rejection, know how difficult Western societies find it to integrate impulses from elsewhere. Admittedly, accepting changes to what one regards as the integrity of one's personality requires some courage, for this presupposes that one can surmount – to quote Daniel Sibony once again – 'the fear that the Other may take you back to your origins through the anxiety he has about his own'.[28] But the game is worth the candle, because it is by overcoming the fear of seeing how much our origin is divided and hybridized that we can take inspiration from it without becoming fixated. Old Kansié in *Finye* (Souleymane Cissé, 1982) certainly reminded his grandson Bâ of his origins: 'Your father would not have acted that way.' But when he goes to the sacred wood to call on the aid and protection of the ancestors to get Bâ out of prison, the old man finds that he has to act alone. It is only then that he will burn his traditional dress and join the student demonstrations.

The most immediate impression among Westerners who go to Africa to widen their experience of life is the openness to others of those who receive them there. As the Mauritanian Abderrahmane Sissako says, 'We are more universal than the Europeans: the Other is less different for the African than the African is for the Others!'[29] Why should this be? Perhaps because, as Anne-Laure Folly from Togo observes, 'It is when you have found your master that you wonder who he is and what he's thinking. The Indians booted the British out of their country, and so interest was generated in their thought. The same has not been true of Africa.'[30] Only when the public has really discovered the wealth of African culture and thought, no doubt, and only when it has stopped looking at the continent in economic terms, will it really become interested in its films. And it is to such a discovery that African cinema invites us. 'When you begin to ask questions about points which you don't understand', says Flora Gomes from Guinea, 'that means you are interested in a difference: at that stage you have already understood something!'[31] Once one is stimulated by curiosity, one's way of looking changes. 'I found African cinema so different', remembers editor Andrée Davanture. 'I said to myself, "What is it talking about? What am I going to learn from it? What does it mean?"'[32] Without this openness and this readiness to look, our societies will remain walled up in their own concerns. Asked about his life in France, the Malagasay director Raymond Rajaonarivelo replied: 'It's very hard. There is so much incomprehension. People are so focused on themselves, so individualistic; they don't look at others. When you get to be a bit like them, suddenly you don't feel so good!'[33]

A CINEMA OF REVELATION

'With *Octobre*', explains Abderrahmane Sissako, 'I wanted to make a film about a mixed-race couple in Russia – a society which, without necessarily being racist, does not easily accept the Other. This conflict reaches a point of no return, and it is this moment I show.'[34] *Octobre*, an atmospheric hour-long feature, shot in black and white and bearing the stamp of the Moscow School where Sissako trained as a filmmaker, focuses on this breaking point when Irina, who is pregnant with Idrissa's child, is wavering over whether to keep the child, given the potential transience of the father. The dialogue becomes thinner and thinner, because everything has already been said: the confusion and pain of our divided origins are expressed with the full force of sound and image. The film's *originality* lies, without doubt, in the fact that it opens up our imaginations to this inner world, this silence, in which the conscious images of the limits of a society collide with that other division of our wholeness which Freud revealed to us: the existence of an unconscious.

It is, however, the recognition of a divided origin uniting human beings which those filmmakers concerned with hybridization disclose to us. They outline potential collective identities on a continental or planetary scale, opening up universal visions. Cissé roves through Africa from South to North in *Waati*, while Sissako travels North–South in *Rostov–Luanda*, a journey into the interior of the continent and into his own interior, to meet up again with Baribanga – a friend he met in Russia – in that man's native Angola, a country scarred by thirty-four years of warfare. Despite the cultural differences between a Mauritanian born in a country which has not known wars of liberation and an Angolan from a resistance background, *Rostov–Luanda* attempts to let a sense of a common destiny show through. The form is an open one, the approach being resistant to any sense of immobilism: this provides a wonderful opportunity for meetings which tend to show once again that it is simple people who say the truest things. Anne-Laure Folly from Togo also went to Angola to make *Les Oubliées* [*The Forgotten Women*] (1997), which focuses on the victims of a country at war. In one of his poems, Brecht asked: 'Who built the Great Wall of China?', immediately giving the ironic answer: 'The Emperor of China, of course!' It is the essential inversion implied in this which Anne-Laure Folly achieves: in talking about history and politics, she listens to the people, not to the leaders – the people, and particularly the women, whom she shoots in close-up to read in their faces the marks of thirty years of war. And when these women hold out their children to demonstrate the need for aid, the commentary becomes bitter: 'They used the lens the way I use it myself. The only difference is that they believe their suffering can still move people and change the course of their destiny.' The emotion stays with us: one does not forget *Les Oubliées*.

'I knew nothing of Angola', admits the director honestly at the beginning of the film. 'I say this so as not to deceive anyone or make any spurious claims. I think most audiovisual works take a more or less external approach. The important thing is to know who is looking at what. The fact of being a black woman doesn't give me the culture of a black woman in general, once I'm outside the little area of my particular upbringing. Contrary to the staggeringly immodest assertions one sometimes hears, being African doesn't mean being culturally aware of the whole of Africa, but simply that one has a culture which comes from Africa! Being a Zulu does not give you the keys to Yoruba culture! I am simply the product of my own culture and I don't claim anything else!'[35]

Who can say precisely where the boundary between documentary and fiction lies? 'I can't manage to draw a clear boundary between fiction and documentary', says the Senegalese director Safi Faye.

Fiction is acted, but it comes as much from everyday life as documentary does. You set things up artificially to respect the conventions of cinema time. For example, in Mossane, the wedding scene lasts eight minutes! When I film sequence shots in a documentary, I shoot them so as to tell a story, so that there's a beginning and an end.[36]

Even the journey into the reality of the Iranian earthquake in Abbas Kiorastami's *And Life Goes On* (Iran, 1990) was a reconstruction. Let us simply note in conclusion the acceptance of fragility, the openness to self-doubt, the rejection of a fixed identity in Abderrahmane Sissako's approach. This comes from an inner vision, as Drissa Touré from Burkina Faso puts it so simply: 'For me, the ideal is to make the films I feel, those which come from inside. If I can succeed in doing this, I shall encounter the human element. This is important. At that point you attain to universality. Human beings are the same everywhere: the same feelings, the same drives.'[37] This is the very opposite of navel-gazing: a gaze which is directed towards, but not confined to, oneself.

In the style of Roberto Rossellini – thanks to whom, as Jean Douchet reminds us, 'cinema returned to its initial function, that of looking: forcing us to see or to await revelation'[38] – the cinema cultures of Black Africa, when they achieve this inner migration, propose an innovative, ethical, utopian gaze, opening out to a universal vision in which everyone's problem is my problem: 'I feel as much concerned in the problems of Liberia as in those of the former Yugoslavia', says the Senegalese Joseph Gaye Ramaka. 'Wherever there is suffering, I feel close to that pain.'

What, then, is the memory of a people in crisis? 'Dignity feeds on memory, and vice versa', adds Ramaka. The question of memory is not resolved by reawakening memories. Where is a collective memory to be found in a state of oppression, or an individual memory in an identity crisis? The history of oppressed peoples and minorities gains in depth what it loses in events. It comes down to a quest for, and an affirmation of, human dignity which connects with that of all excluded people. Drawing on the origins, but perpetually developing, it is at the source of creativity. It merges with the memory of the world: 'Memory is not a question of the past; it is living and active; you carry it with you on a daily basis', concludes Ramaka. 'It is a part of our essence.'

Djibril Diop Mambety's father, a famous imam, tells how, for a time, his young son could not sleep:

> He wrote all night and tore it all up the next day. He gave up school, going back occasionally for an odd day, and shut himself away again with his writing. I thought: 'Something strange is going on.' He wandered around the house aimlessly, staring off into space. Puzzed by all this, I asked him what was happening. He said, 'It's nothing, Father. I'm just trying to understand the world.'[39]

Djibril Diop Mambety and Mansour Diouf on the set of *Hyenas/Ramatou* (1992).
© Félix van Muralt/Lookat.

This understanding of the world makes independence an interdependence and liberation a co-operation between civilizations to create a new order of things. In that understanding, the origin is a transit opening up to hybridization, and identity is a never-ending process. These styles of filmmaking transform evocative myths into problems to be solved for a new Africa and a new world.

When, in *Hyenas/Ramatou* (1992), the circle of the inhabitants of his village closes in on Draman Drameh, singing laments because the Queen of Death, Lingeer Ramatou, has offered them 100 billion francs for his life, it is the greed of these human beings turned hyenas which shows through. We see a world in which people as different as Swiss playwright Friedrich Dürrenmatt, author of *The Visit*, and the Senegalese filmmaker Djibril Diop Mambety, who adapted it for the cinema in *Hyenas/Ramatou*, meet to assert a world culture respecting both individual and collective identities:

> I don't see any distance between Dürrenmatt and me; the only distance is age. We have something in common: it is disquiet or, rather, more than disquiet, derision. We even share something more than derision: a certainty that we shall not get out alive and that that is the way things are.[40]

NOTES

1. Frantz Fanon, *Black Skin, White Masks*, trans. Charles Lam Markmann, Paladin, London, 1970, pp. 162–3.
2. See Les Écrans de la liberté, *Afrique du Sud: Cinéma sous influence – cinéma de résistance*, La Cinémathèque française, 1990; Keyan Tomaselli, *The Cinema of Apartheid*, Routledge, London, 1989.
3. As Anne Khady Sé points out forcefully,

   > Following the 1994 elections, a new complex was built at Dobsonville, a sub-
   > urb on the outskirts of Soweto. However, the – white – developers had got
   > their market research wrong. 'These cinemas get audience figures of no more
   > than 6 per cent', explains Ramadan Suleman. 'It happens to be the case that
   > the young person in Soweto does not like the ghetto ideology. He prefers to
   > leave his suburb, take a taxi, and travel the 18 miles or so to the city centre to
   > see a film. For years he was forbidden to sit in town among the Whites.
   > Suddenly he's free. More people go to the city-centre cinemas now…'

   'Afrique du Sud: années zéro pour le cinéma noir', *Africultures* 14 ('Produire en Afrique'), L'Harmattan, Paris, 1999.
4. Lionel N'Gakane, 'En attendant avril 1994', in *Le Cinéma et la vidéo en Afrique du Sud* (dossier d'Écrans d'Afrique 5–6), 1993, p. 112.
5. In 1997 Lionel N'Gakane announced: 'I came back to South Africa two and a half years ago. At first I tried to understand what was going on to see what role I could play. I've got two screenplays ready at the moment. I'd like to make two films, then retire.' (Interview with Lionel N'Gakane, Ouagadougou, 1997, pub-lished in *Africultures* 4, L'Harmattan, Paris, January 1998; and on www.africultures. com).
6. Interview with Ramadan Suleman, Paris 1997, published in *Africultures* 1 ('La Critique en question'), L'Harmattan, Paris, 1997.
7. Manthia Diawara, *Black American Cinema*, Routledge, New York and London, 1993, p. 20.
8. Clyde Taylor, 'Les Grands axes et les sources africaines du Nouveau Cinéma noir', *Cinémaction* 46, ('Le Cinéma noir américain'), 1988, p. 88.
9. 'Philosophy with cinematographer Arthur Jafa, edited by Kodwo Eshun', *Black Film Bulletin*, Autumn/Winter 1993/94, British Film Institute, London, p. 23.
10. 'I didn't do this as a black man', says Melvin van Peebles, but it just so happens that Melvin is black, and is also a bit of a joker. 'I just took over the worst nightmares of American whites! This is my suicidal streak! You can see in it whatever symbolism you like. Otherwise, in society, not much has changed! A few blacks have made some headway and there are some improvements at times, but when there's a step forward, there's often two steps back…' (Interview with Melvin van Peebles, Paris, 1998).
11. Imruh Bakari, 'Le Facteur X du nouveau cinéma afro-américain', *Écrans d'Afrique* 4, 1993, p. 51.
12. Stephan Hoffstadt, *Black Cinema: Afroamerikanische Filmemacher der Gegenwart*, Hitzeroth, Marburg, 1995, p. 174.
13. 'Showing who we are' was the leitmotiv of a round-table discussion chaired by Mbye Cham at the Milan Festival in March 1996. The participants were the writer Clyde Taylor, the director of the Los Angeles Festival Ayuko Babu, and the filmmakers Bridgett M. Davis, Linda Goode Bryant (*My Am*, 1995) and Joe

Brewster (*The Keeper*, 1995).

14. Interview with John Akomfrah, London, 1994.

15. June I. Givanni, 'Cinéma et libertés: divergence ou dichotomie, entretien avec John Akomfrah', *Écrans d'Afrique* 7, 1994, p. 13.

16. Interview with Menelik Shabazz, Paris, 1998.

17. This inevitably puts one in mind of the practice of the Senegalese N'Doep, which consists in naming the spirit causing the disorder one is experiencing (the spirit is supposed to be in love with the sick person), then erecting an altar to it in the yard where it is given meals and gifts. Unlike Western therapies, which set out to eliminate the disorder, this practice aims at managing it, controlling it, if not indeed valorizing it so as to be able to live with it. We find this same practice in various forms throughout the world in all possession rites of African origin (see *Africultures* 13 ('Africanité du Maghreb'), L'Harmattan, Paris, 1998; and on www.africultures.com).

18. 'Home from Home: Maureen Blackwood Resurfaces', *Black Film Bulletin*, Autumn–Winter 1993/94, p. 26.

19. *Chocolat* (1987), *Man no run* (1989), *S'en fout la mort* (1990), *J'ai pas sommeil* (1993).

20. Interview with Cheik Doukouré, Paris, 1996.

21. Interview with Joseph Gaye Ramaka, Paris, 1996.

22. Daniel Sibony, *Entre-deux, l'origine en partage*, Le Seuil, Paris, 1991, p. 341.

23. Interview with Larry Clark, Paris, 1998.

24. Melchior Mbonimpa, *Idéologies de l'indépendance africaine*, L'Harmattan, Paris, 1989, p. 93.

25. Aimé Césaire, *Discourse on Colonialism*, Monthly Review Press, New York, 1972, p. 31.

26. René Depestre, *Bonjour et adieu à la négritude*, Seghers, Paris, 1989.

27. On the Malian television programme 'Ciné-Tribune', Fifi Bala Kouyaté, Falaba Issa Traoré, Souleymane Cissé, Cheikh Oumar Sissoko, Tahar Cheriaa and Med Hondo took part in a round-table discussion on African cinema on the occasion of Fespaco 1991.

28. Sibony, *Entre-deux, l'origine en partage*, p. 73.

29. Sissako makes this comment in Laurence Gavron's film *Y'a pas de problème!* (France, 1995).

30. Interview with Anne-Laure Folly, Paris, 1995.

31. Interview with Flora Gomes, Paris, 1995.

32. Interview with Andrée Davanture, Paris, 1995.

33. Interview with Raymond Rajaonarivelo, Paris, 1995.

34. Interview with Abderrahmane Sissako, Paris, 1995.

35. Interview with Anne-Laure Folly, Paris, 1997, published in *Africultures* 2 ('Les Africaines'), L'Harmattan, Paris, 1997.

36. Interview with Safi Faye, Cannes, 1997, published in ibid.

37. Françoise Balogun, *Cinéma et libertés*, Présence Africaine, Paris, 1993, p. 105.

38. Jean Douchet, 'Rossellini ou l'évidence', *Cahiers du Cinéma* 427, January 1990, p. 49.

39. From Laurence Gavron's film *Nikinanka, le Prince de Colobane* (1991).

40. Lucien Patry, interview with Djibril Diop Mambety, *Films et Documents* 378 ('Perspectives et réalités du cinéma africain'), December 1991, p. 24.

PART II

AT THE WELLSPRINGS OF NARRATION

SEVEN

BLACK HUMOURS

Humour preserves. It calms you down. Humour is our weapon, the weapon of the weak. The weak laugh at themselves to unsettle their opponents. Humour is a weapon.

Tchicaya U Tam'si[1]

African humour is at the opposite pole to Western humour. Rather than developing cynicism and projection, it is a tragicomic self-derisiveness which restores emotion, and hence has therapeutic value.

A POLITICALLY COMMITTED PASTICHE

Gnamien Ato, sometime swineherd and animal castrator, and welder in his spare moments, is his village's jack-of-all-trades. He is also the butt of its humour. One night, when he has drunk more than he should have, his pals throw him in the water. When he comes out, he goes into 'hypnotic convulsions'. He sees visions of a white monkey and a red tortoise, accompanied by a 'heavenly' voice. This leads him to regard himself as a 'liberator' marked out by God, and he wins the confidence of the people through a number of miracles to which he alone has the key. He is given the name Magloire the First, and claims to be the son of Christ. Visitors come from all over the country, seeking advancement on the political ladder, improved business turnover or cures for sterility and paralysis. Magloire the First takes advantage of the situation to demand half of the harvests or to exercise a *droit de seigneur*. In the end, however, he is hoist with his own petard, insisting on being ceremonially shot at in order to prove that he has eternal life…

Although *Au nom du Christ*, a parody of that tribe of false prophets who have invaded Africa, won the Fespaco Grand Prize in 1993 and did well in that continent, it flopped in France. Was this, as its Ivorian director Gnoan

Roger M'Bala observes, because it raised the question of sects at too early a stage for the West, whereas African culture, by contrast, is deeply imbued with fetishism? Or was it because images imprinted deep in their consciousness prevented a Western audience from laughing at a black man on a cross?[2] For what is black remains negative, as language reveals, whether it be in black markets or black moods, black magic or the black economy, black days or black humour. Since André Breton produced his 'Anthology of Black Humour', even the humour of black people has become black![3] It is omnipresent in Black African film, doubtless because, as Amadou Hampâté Bâ once put it, 'Always being overserious isn't a very serious way of going on.'[4]

There is a need to entertain an audience which is excessively pressured by everyday concerns, but for these committed filmmakers, laughter and forgetting are not synonymous. The entertainment, as Pierre Yameogo from Burkina Faso says, conceals the message: 'You have to know how to slip in the information, find the right mix, because it isn't always very palatable. Entertainment doesn't necessarily prevent you from confronting real issues!'[5] In his film *Wendemi/The Gift of God* (1993), when young Wendemi meets a friend from his village, 'Berger [Shepherd]', now called 'Fils de l'homme [Son of Man]', he finds that he has become a pimp procuring young girls for rich clients. However, the character played by Abdoulaye Komboudri, an actor adored by Burkina Faso audiences, brings gales of laughter from an audience which is there to have fun.

Admittedly, laughter is culture-specific. 'Things which make an African laugh don't necessarily amuse a European or a Chinese', says Pierre Yameogo. 'When a film shows a well-off family grown fat from eating well, Africans laugh, whereas Westerners tend to be more saddened than anything!' Ahmadou Diallo, the director of *Symbole* (1994), was shocked to see his film raising laughs in Senegal: 'I thought I'd made a serious film! I was afraid I'd got things badly wrong!' This was surely not the case, since this short feature belongs essentially to that vein of tragedy which elicits laughter from a concerned audience. Its originality lies in its making us wince at reality; it is a heart-rending eye-opener which 'produces an urge to laugh', as Tchicaya U Tam'si put it in *Les Méduses*, 'in order to conceal the urge to cry. To cry with rage and contempt! To calm your nerves, to ease your fretting and fuming.'[6]

When Henri Duparc from the Ivory Coast made a comic film about AIDS, he began by making a thorough study of the subject. The product of that research, *Rue Princesse* (1994), is much more effective among predominantly illiterate populations than the giant billboards one sees in the

Poster for
Rue Princesse
(Henri Duparc,
Ivory Coast, 1994).

African cities and countryside proclaiming 'AIDS = fidelity or condom'. In that film, a musician from a good family prefers a pretty prostitute to the classy but 'tarty' girlfriends who are forced upon him. Their thwarted loves, which contributed to normalizing the use of condoms, were a great popular success: 'I start out from the idea that a sense of humour always overcomes intolerance.'[7] In an area where laughter is more effective than speeches, word of mouth will do the rest.

There is no ribaldry in all this: the humour draws on a tradition of subtle, decorous suggestion which, while not avoiding subjects, evokes their ambience poetically. When Fara, returning to his village because the university is on strike, meets Mossane, only a few words are spoken, but everyone there understands how deeply they are in love (*Mossane*, Safi Faye, Senegal, 1996). Only a single phrase is heard, prompting audible laughter: 'Close your eyes, it's night-time!'

'Why should we just be intellectual when Louis de Funès gets laughs in African cinemas?' asks Ivorian Fadika Kramo-Lanciné.[8] Ali, the hero of *Wariko/The Jackpot* (1993), wins the big prize in the national lottery with a ticket his wife had to buy to get some change at the market. Unfortunately, after the result is announced, the winning ticket cannot be found. With family members beating a path to his door to claim their part of the windfall, Ali turns the house upside down in his desperate search for the ticket. This is a typically Ivorian skit on the hopes of thousands that they can improve their social condition. There is exaggeration for parodic effect: Ali is a comical police officer who stops the *paca*, the cheap little Abidjan municipal buses, to extract a bribe from the drivers. But, beneath the pastiche, the message is clear. After calculating what he will have to give his family if he manages to find the ticket again, he tells his wife that it isn't the jackpot that will solve their problems. She asks him what would, and he whispers a reply unheard by the audience.

LAUGHING AT ONESELF

The atmosphere in African cinemas is unforgettable, so fond are African audiences of a good belly laugh. When the hero of *Gito l'ingrat* (Léonce Ngabo, Burundi, 1992) has to escape dressed as a woman because his two mistresses – one black, the other white – have got together to steal his clothes, there are gales of laughter, and members of the audience jump to their feet, shouting, to exult in this scene, unimaginable in an African context. Gito is the butt of everyone's jokes, but his humiliation has its effect, since being caught out like this brings home to him the macho nature of his behaviour. All the male spectators appreciate that it could happen to them, and the message gets through.

African traditions of hospitality require that a stranger arriving at a mealtime is invited to share his host's food. *Dunia* (Pierre Yameogo, 1987) begins with just such an occurrence, but the family is forewarned of the Fulani's arrival. They quickly hide the meal they were about to eat. The clever Fulani returns a little while later when the food has been brought out again. The situation is one everyone recognizes. They are not laughing at others here, but at themselves and their own culture. It is a form of self-ridicule reminiscent of the humour of modernity defined by Baudelaire: 'the ability to step outside oneself rapidly and look on at the phenomena of one's ego as if one were a disinterested spectator'.[9]

This emperor without clothes whom the black humorist shows on the screen is none other than himself. We are a long way from the contemptuously ironic references to showbiz personalities that are the stock in trade of the television comedian. It is, in fact, with a pastiche of a television interview that Gnoan Roger M'Bala's *Amanié* (1972) begins. If this highly amusing portrait of an inveterate womanizer hits the mark, that is because it caricatures the wily macho which Westernization brings out in every man. Kwassikan, a peasant who has turned to labouring on the Abidjan docks, knows how to win the ladies, and is quick to slip on a tie and present himself as a 'junior official in the Ministry of State': 'To get the girls, you have to shoot them a line. You have to dress well and impress them!' The fish soon takes the bait. Nicole telephones her girlfriend: 'I've just found a real treasure, an absolute marvel! I'll introduce you. No one's going to take this one from me!' Her suitor cleverly uses his charm to relieve Nicole of considerable sums of money, though this does not prevent him pursuing other women without, however, satisfying all their requirements:

'Have you got a car?'
   'Yes, a Ford.'
'Have you got a villa?'
   'In Cocody.'[10]
'Have you got a TV?'
   'Yes, a Thomson.'
'You don't have any wives, do you?'
   'No, not even a girlfriend!'
'Are you on the telephone?'
   'No.'
'That's a pity!'

After being unmasked and going back to being a labourer, he tries a second time:

'I hardly know you, but I seem to have been in love with you for centuries!'
   'What's your name?'
'Cassius Clay.'

DERISION AS A STRATEGY

Getting laughs by exaggerating certain features amounts in the end to appealing to clichés, commonplaces and stereotypes, and exaggerating them to excess. In short, a particular reality is denounced by forcing the spectator to laugh at it. It is easy, in this approach, for politicians and the country's cosseted elite to be depicted as grotesque, as is often the case in the African novel. And there are indeed some ferocious satires. In *Ablakon* (Gnoan Roger M'Bala, 1984), a well-to-do family's servant boys wear waistcoats bearing the words 'Dressing Boy', 'Polishing Boy', 'Cigarette-Lighter Boy',

Poster for *Ablakon* (Gnoan Roger M'Bala, Ivory Coast, 1984).

'Trainee Toilet Boy', and so on. And the film is equally scathing in its mockery of peasants and their ignorance of the modern world. The first part shows Charlemagne Ablakon's artful con-tricks; when he returns in the second part to his native village, the villagers are so impressed that he prepares to extract a large sum of money from them in exchange for the promise of a building plot. Apo, won over by his charm, decides to leave her fiancé, Yapi:

> 'Apo, what's wrong?'
>> 'Let me go!'
>> 'Are you mad at me?'
>> 'Do you want to know?'
>> 'Yes!'
>> 'You're not for me any more. I'm going out with civilized people. I've developed.'
> [She goes]
>> 'That's neo-colonialism!'

In a fit of pique, Yapi goes off to the city to swell the exodus from the countryside. However, aware of the pitfalls of this 'development' towards modernity, he returns to the village in time to denounce Ablakon's fraud.

In this way cinema tends to become theatrical, and – to use Mikhail Bakhtin's terms – 'dialogical' and 'carnivalesque'.[11] Cameroonian director Daniel Kamwa employs a torrent of dialogue in *Notre fille* (1980) to produce a successful comedy capable of 'telling truths and improving standards of behaviour'.[12] This film, based on Guillaume Oyono-Mbia's play *Notre fille ne se mariera pas*, veers wildly between farce and fable to describe a father's desperate efforts to make his daughter, the only one of his thirty children who has really succeeded in life, give up the marriage she has just announced in order to help her family. She herself feels a sense of indebtedness, because it was only thanks to African solidarity that she was able to complete her studies. Each of the characters is an outrageous stereotype in the purest traditions of that satirical comedy Ferdinand Oyono introduced into African literature in 1956 with *The Old Man and the Medal*.[13] Derision is a strategy here – a strategy of rebelliousness. In his suffering, the African has developed a great self-awareness from which he draws the disputatiousness, indiscipline and recalcitrance on which his capacity for resistance is based. Whereas imagining, for the Westerner, means first of all denying reality and detaching oneself from it, fleeing into unreality to escape the straitjacket of existence, Africa mocks that reality to appropriate it, subverts it so as to be better able to bear its burden.[14]

With *Une couleur café* (1997), the Ivorian director Henri Duparc ran up against the criticism that his satire was perhaps questionable. An immigrant worker in France, an orderly in a Paris hospital, married with no children, decides, when he is on holiday in Africa, to take a second wife. However, the French Embassy refuses to grant his new wife a visa, since polygamy is tolerated but not actually legal on French territory. The man falsifies the documents and Kada is changed, for official consumption, from a second wife into a daughter. When they get to France, even though she is still at school, she becomes pregnant. Who is the father? The law becomes involved, and the father/husband is accused of incest.... This is, in fact, a serious subject. Duparc has one of his characters ask: 'I wonder if there really is a place for immigrants in French society!', and the film ends with the wife being expelled from the country. 'I've lived from hand to mouth for so long that my hand's got stuck in my mouth', exclaims his hero, when bitterness finally pierces the comic veneer. The subject is so serious that the film was regarded with sufficient suspicion for the usual institutional funders of African cinema to get cold feet, despite the undeniable success of Duparc's previous films. In the end, he was able to make it only thanks to a South–South production deal and post-production in a Moroccan laboratory.

A strategy of derision is dismissive of any taboo. There is no question of censoring anything on the pretext of remaining serious: 'When there is tragedy', declares Duparc, 'I treat it with derision to give it the least possible importance. The only tragedy there can be on earth for an individual is death. Beyond that, the rest is merely a human comedy!' And it is this which triggers the laughter: the ridiculous contradictions which ensue from apprehending events on two levels. *Une couleur café* denounces the reality of immigration while exaggerating the clichés surrounding the image of the Black: it mingles reality and exaggeration, the tragic and the extravagant. By exaggerating to the point of caricature, it produces a counter-discourse, and denounces intolerance and stupidity. This is a dangerous exercise, because mockery can be misconstrued: more than one African felt directly offended when the hero enjoys the dog food which his wives serve up for him on one occasion ... and more than one European has felt embarrassed by the parodic display of clichés he would like to reject. But surely the humour is not questionable when the only danger is that of laughing at oneself. 'If I caricature', Duparc continues, 'this is to have the courage to look at us as we are, so that we can become better; otherwise, we are burying our heads in the sand!'[15]

A VITAL LAUGHTER

Beneath their mockery of traditional conservative ways, black styles of humour conceal a disenchanted vision of a bruised and battered society. Here, laughter and tears go well together. As Gérard Genette wrote, 'comedy is merely tragedy seen from behind'.[16] In *Haramuya* (Drissa Touré, Burkina Faso, 1995), the imam's sheep eat the 'grass' brought in by the beggar children of the Koran school, but this turns out in fact to be cannabis. 'Bandits' (to use the local term) dumped it on the children during a police raid. Like the dumbfounded imam, amused filmgoers watch as the sheep, drugged to the eyeballs, zig-zag around, butting each other. The cruelty of the Koranic school, which the director experienced in childhood, is evoked here with a sardonic humour which brings out its mindlessness.

The public takes the very heavy hint, as it does in *Obi* (Idrissa Ouedraogo, 1991), where, before poignantly recounting her fate as a woman driven from her home by her husband, with her four children in tow, and working in the Buda goldmines, the eponymous heroine stares directly at the audience and says: 'Are you still there? I'm warning you, the last thing I'm going to talk

about is my husband. If that's all right with you, we can start!' At the end
of her tragic story, Obi turns once again to the camera and snaps: 'Let me
get on with my work! *You* aren't going to put food on my plate!'

At the worst moments of tension, humour defuses the tone of pathos
which threatens to take over. After planning to destroy old Kansayé's house
and leave him destitute, Sangaré, the dreaded governor in Souleymane Cissé's
Finye (1982), remarks: 'Even the toothless will laugh at him!' With this, a
distance is re-established, and it helps to demystify the situation. After the
funeral of Nanyuma's husband in *Finzan* (Cheikh Oumar Sissoko, Mali, 1989),
a man remarks ironically: 'A gravedigger with a hard-on is thinking of the
widow!' Laughter dispels the sense of tragedy: the 'sorcerer' at a local festival
in *Macadam Tribu* (José Laplaine, Zaïre, 1996) asks a young woman in the
audience to put a condom on the erect penis of a traditional statue, bringing
laughter from an urban crowd who are well aware of the dangers of AIDS.
Even during an initiation, the message is accompanied by humour: 'The
termite will seize on the unfaithful man's penis', warns the old sage in *Laada*
(Drissa Touré, Burkina Faso, 1991).

Film gives one permission to laugh at what the collective consciousness
does not allow to be unveiled. Humour is immodest, and hence subversive.
In *Guimba* (Cheikh Oumar Sissoko, Mali, 1995), it even attacks a subject
cinema has generally been wary of addressing: precolonial Africa, which
Negritude had portrayed as an idyllic golden age and a key reference. *Guimba*,
a film about power, plays on the grotesque character of the tyrant, the
ludicrous nature of his sex-crazed dwarfish son and the comical aspect of
his obsequious griot, whose eloquence knows no bounds: 'Shit is not a
thorn, but he who steps in it hobbles along!'

Whereas realist discourse can grate, humour, when it is a laughing at
oneself – a self-mockery of that other which is actually just a part of oneself
– has therapeutic value. The women of the Gambian Kanyalang secret societies shown in *Die Macht des Lachens: Kanyalangfrauen in Gambia* (Ulla Fels,
Germany, 1994) engage in systematic mockery of themselves and of those
they regard as pretentious, whingeing or arrogant. They do whatever comes
into their heads without anyone really having any cause to feel offended by
them. Their laughter is contagious! They dress in bad taste for parties,
because they believe that if they make themselves ugly and are laughed at,
the spirits and death will not take them seriously, and will leave their children
alone. In this same way, using self-mockery and collective laughter, they help
previously sterile women to have children.

Similarly, the rites of the Lebou fishermen of Senegal described by Joseph
Gaye Ramaka in *Baw-Naan* (1984) and referred to in *Nitt... Ndoxx/The*

On the set of *Touki-Bouki* (Djibril Diop Mambety, Dakar, 1972). © Maya Bracher.

Rainmakers (1988) are intended to 'reduce God to tears of laughter' in order to bring rain. As Jean Rouch's commentary points out, it is said that he cannot in the end deny these little climatic favours to people who have such a hard time surviving on this earth...

A CATHARTIC PARODY

With less concern now for ideological legitimation than was evident in their early years, the film cultures of Black Africa are throwing off the seriousness of an obligatory realist veneer. In literature, from the late 1960s onwards, Yambo Ouologuem and Ahmadou Kourouma produced the first landmark works of a satirical tradition which paralleled the one already developed by such English-speaking writers as Amos Tutuola and consolidated in the recent work of Chinua Achebe.[17] In a similar vein, Sony Labou Tansi was to follow in the footsteps of Tchicaya U Tam'si in the Congo. In the cinema, it was undoubtedly Djibril Diop Mambety who led the way. Beginning with his *Contras'city* (1968; a wild romp through the streets of Dakar) and *Badou Boy* (1970; the 'adventures of a slightly amoral street urchin who resembles me a lot') and, above all, with his magnificent *Touki-Bouki* (1973), African cinema moved away from the simple representation of reality that had previously been the norm towards a highly paradoxical form of enunciation, edited in such a way that the argument is fragmented into cycles, underscoring a very free use of images that is not far removed from visual lyricism.

We find this unrestrained, sensitive and captivating filmic language once again in *Le Franc* (1995), which describes the tribulations of Marigo, a musician whose landlady has confiscated his instrument, a congoma, because he never pays his rent.[18] Marigo gets himself a lottery ticket and sticks it on his door so that no one will steal it from him, hiding it behind a poster of Yaadikooné Ndiaye, 'defender of children and the weak'. The ticket wins the jackpot and Marigo lifts the door on to his back to carry it to the lottery booth. This teeming of metaphorical images, with what appears on the screen eventually representing only Marigo's imagination, builds a vision whose intention is no less than to reinvent cinema: 'It's a choice to be made. You either have to be very popular and talk simply to people, or seek out and find an African language, excluding chatter and concerning oneself more with sound and image.'[19]

The basis of this radically new language is parody, an art of superimposition or counterpoint. *Le Franc* brings together a number of heterogeneous elements which are typical of the urban experience of the 'little man's' relationship to money: devaluation and the national lottery, piles of rubbish in the streets and the skyscrapers of the big banks. Putting the two together generates a sense of emptiness, which is offset by the close-up shots of the passengers' faces on the Dakar bus, and a disorder to which the sun's reflection on the waves restores harmony. A shot from the film can be taken as representative of its tenor: Marigo and a dwarf decide to put into practice the slogan 'The currency has been devalued: buy African!' by choosing to eat at a street-vendor's stand. The image at this point is skewed, and the diagonal line of the pavement evokes the precariousness of their situation – that precariousness which affects the whole of Africa. The return to equilibrium will not be achieved by the mere representation of reality. Against the power of money, the only recourse of the 'homme franc', the decent man, is mockery, reverie and serenity. Marigo's wanderings lead him down to the sea, that preternaturally flat line, that source of life and stirring of origins with which the poster of his childhood hero comes to mingle. But it is also a boundless ocean, a sign of death. The cycle of life is completed. The rhythm of a cyclical, repetitive montage, the comical nature of the character, wildly exaggerated images and a score which binds the images together all engender in the spectator a catharsis akin to that of the theatre

Poster for
Le Franc (Djibril
Diop Mambety,
Senegal, 1995).

of cruelty: treating madness with madness, in order to arrive at a purification of emotion. This will not destroy the madness of the world, but the crazed swirl of images, by acting on the viewers, will open their eyes and shake them out of their inertia.[20]

Because this cinema language is an artificial one and never an end in itself, because it draws its 'stories of ordinary folk' from the daily experience of 'decent people', this wrestling with the image is akin to a tragicomic self-mockery, the poetry of which touches the heart and quickens the pulse.

Styles of black humour reveal to us, then, how much our Western cynicism undergirds a laughter which, as the philosopher Henri Bergson put it, 'is incompatible with emotion'.[21] By contrast, in their capacity to laugh at states of regression and madness, at those states from another age which sometimes surface again so painfully in contemporary confrontations, these styles of humour restore the tension between present and past, between what is and what has been forgotten but remains possible, ready to resurface when crises lend it the opportunity; and show more than ever how therapeutic and salutary they are. Rather than promoting the projection of their own difficulties on to other peoples or social groups, black styles of humour guide human beings in unravelling the inextricably tangled threads of their destiny.

NOTES

1. Quoted by Nicolas Martin-Granel, *Rires noirs, anthologie romancée de l'humour et du grotesque dans le roman africain*, Sépia/Centre Culturel français de Libreville, 1991, p. 26 (this is an excellent work, and it has guided my thinking here on humour).
2. Interview with Gnoan Roger M'Bala, Abidjan, 1995. The scenario of the film was written with Akafourou Bertin and the 'Bossonist' Ivorian writer Jean-Michel Adiaffi, who, while remaining a monotheist, attempts a modernization of animist beliefs by arguing for the existence of spirits known as 'bossons.'
3. André Breton, *Anthologie de l'humour noir*, Livre de Poche/Biblio, Paris, 1986.
4. *Amadou Hampâté Bâ*, an interview filmed by Ange Casta and Enrico Fulchigioni (1969).
5. Interview with Pierre Yameogo, Paris, 1995.
6. Tchicaya U Tam'si, *Les Méduses ou les orties de mer*, Albin Michel, Paris, 1982.
7. Clément Tapsoba, 'Entretien avec Henri Duparc', *Écrans d'Afrique* 8, 1994, p. 16.
8. Interview with Fadika Kramo-Lanciné, Paris, 1995.
9. Charles Baudelaire, 'De l'essence du rire', *Oeuvres complètes*, vol. III, Éditions de la Pléiade, Paris.
10. The residential district of Abidjan.
11. Mikhail Bakhtin, *Rabelais and His World*, trans. Helene Iswolsky, MIT Press, Cambridge MA, 1968 (the carnivalesque); *Problems of Dostoevsky's Poetics,* trans. Caryl Emerson, University of Minnesota Press, Minneapolis, 1984 (the dialogical).
12. Daniel Kamwa, quoted by Pierre Haffner, 'L'Ésthétique des films', *Cinémaction* 26, 1981, p. 68.
13. Trans. John Reed, Heinemann, London, 1982.
14. Célestin Monga, *Anthropologie de la colère: société civile et démocratie en Afrique noire*, L'Harmattan, Paris, 1994, p. 72.
15. Interview with Henri Duparc, Montreal, 1998, published in *Africultures* 12 ('Rires d'Afrique'), L'Harmattan, Paris, 1998.
16. Gérard Genette, *Palimpsestes, la littérature au second degré*, Le Seuil, Paris, 1982,
17. Yambo Ouologuem, *Bound to Violence*, trans. R. Manheim, Heinemann, London 1971; Ahmadou Kourouma, *Les Soleils des indépendances*, Le Seuil, Paris, 1970; Amos Tutuola, *The Palm-Wine Drinkard*, Faber & Faber, London, 1952, and *My Life in the Bush of Ghosts*, Faber & Faber, London, 1964; Chinua Achebe, *Anthills of the Savannah*, Heinemann, London, 1988.
18. *Le Franc* was intended as the first part of a trilogy on 'ordinary people'; it was followed in 1998 by *La Petite vendeuse du soleil/The Little Girl who Sold the Sun*. A

third part, *L'Apprenti voleur,* was planned but never completed [*Trans.*].

19. 'Entretien de Catherine Ruelle avec Djibril Diop Mambety', *Cinémaction* 3 ('Cinéastes d'Afrique noire'), p. 43.

20. See Françoise Browne, 'Sony Labou Tansi: une écriture nostalgique d'unité', in Anny Winchank and Philippe-Joseph Salazar, *Afriques imaginaires, regards réciproques et discours littéraires, 17e-20e siècles,* L'Harmattan, Paris, 1995, p. 254.

21. Henri Bergson, *Laughter: An Essay on the Meaning of the Comic,* trans. Cloudesley Brereton and Fred Rothwell, Macmillan, London, 1911, p. 139.

EIGHT

'MEN DIE, BUT WORDS REMAIN': AT THE ORIGIN OF NARRATION, ORALITY[1]

> I,
> Appointed to cry out for all men,
> From a single mouth,
> In a single shout
>
> Sony Labou Tansi[2]

The reference to the oral tradition establishes the specificity of the films of Black Africa. In their concern for social development, filmmakers do, however, position themselves differently from the masters of the tradition. Their voices are superimposed on the spoken word in a paradoxical *écriture*. Whereas tradition is merely a series of successively incorporated modernities, myth remains foundational and therapeutic – fiercely topical.

FIRST, SILENCE

The strength of this cinematic language relates to its symbolism, which consists in a surrealism that is both mystical and metaphysical. The films of Black Africa deliberately mingle the esoteric and the sociological gazes. Symbols invade the images. These take the form of gestures, attitudes, rhythms, colours, sounds, local or Western objects, rituals, and so on, combining with the words – or even with proverbs. By an analogical process of reasoning, they invite the viewer to participate. Symbols do not merely represent, they suggest a meaning and ultimately create a unity, a participation in the play of vital forces which rule the world. Thus, for Souleymane Cissé, intuition is more important than the screenplay. The poetry comes from nature itself. 'I do not create', he says; 'I participate in something.'[3]

When, in *Stromboli* (Roberto Rossellini, Italy, 1950), the fishermen sail in singing on a calm sea, their nets filled with jumping, flapping tuna fish, we have within us a resonance of what the symbolism of a represented event can summon up: a sensitivity to the deep forces at play within human beings and the world. We find this same duality – both sociological and esoteric – in *Le Franc*, but, despite appearances, it produces not so much a dizzying whirl as a sense of unity. Marigo sings as he sets his door out to sea, and cries and laughs crazily, as though knocked senseless by the waves. With all his gangling body, he understands the forces under which he labours. The emotion the image produces is not sentimental but poetic. It is a participation, a communion, with the force which drives the universe. 'The vertical, Judaeo-Christian vision is the opposite of our horizontal, fusional vision of man as part of nature', points out Imunga Ivanga from Gabon. 'Human beings modify nature in order to exist, but not to destroy it or for their own pleasure. They do not exclude themselves from nature. This is a spiritual approach, but also a purely intellectual one; it is not a matter of living in the past.' The unity thus expressed does not emanate from the will to dominate nature, as seen in European cultures, nor from the effort to escape the world seen in some Asian ones. It is an alliance and a participation with the great natural forces. The lottery ticket seems in the end quite derisory when the ironic movement of the waters leaves it sticking to Marigo's forehead, for here we are no longer dealing with the dream of wealth it represented during the film, but with the symbolism of life and of the order of the world.

The filmmaker could have spelt out this truth more clearly, but 'to define a thing is to limit its possibilities', as one of the characters in Tchicaya U Tam'si's *Les Cancrelats* has it.[4] The openness sought here is the openness of paradox, but – unlike in the case of the Surrealists – these images, which may initially seem incomprehensible, are not the product of the free or arbitrary associations of automatic writing, but are drawn from the real world and the perceptions of 'little people'. Djibril Diop Mambety's symbolic universe has its coherence, reflecting his observation of the world and his conception of it. Underlying the ambivalence of the images is a profound wisdom, a wisdom which stands outside the system of rationality and has its source in the observation of natural and cosmic forces, a wisdom which requires symbol and paradox for its expression.

Freeze-frame: the human being returns to his solitude, distances himself from reality in order to see it anew. In *A Karim na Sala* (Idrissa Ouedraogo, 1990), Karim, working as a shoeshine boy, stops suddenly. The camera homes in on a close-up of his face, and the background loses definition. He looks at the streets of Bob-Dioulasso with a fresh eye: 'What a town! How sad the people look! And they don't even wear leather shoes...' (to be polished).

Making way for silence: *Wend Kuuni* has been struck dumb by a traumatic experience (Gaston Kaboré, Burkina Faso, 1982). His actions, his glances and, at the end, his recovered speech will be all the more significant for that. In the Sudanese cultural zone, words take on significance only when they are shrouded in shadow. Only when they are incomplete do they express themselves fully. Is this why the cinema of that region is so rich, in spite of the poverty of the states concerned? There is a comfortable fit between the place silence and reserve occupy in Mandingo thought and a filmic language to which the play of simplicity and complexity lends a certain grace: an image without overblown signs; a dialogue without verbiage; counterpoints sought in actions, movements and glances; a filmic texture playing, like language, on more than one level of understanding; fragmented scenarios and exploded editing structures. 'In spite of the enormous differences between the filmmakers', says Andrée Davanture, 'there is a basic culture which unites them: a way of constantly saying one thing and its opposite, or indeed three things at once. All Malian films have an exploded structure and hence are not linear.'[5] There is a subtle, tightly woven fabric of events, situations, interchanges and dialogues, lending the films a particular sharpness.

The Malian director Souleymane Cissé goes off into isolation in the bush for several weeks or months before starting a new project:

> If I go off into the bush to find the quiet I need for meditation and to organize my work, I do this so as the better to stand back from it, to achieve that necessary distance that enables me to see things more clearly. There are moments which require solitude. 'Alone with God', as the Bambara say. It's a way of freeing the spirit.[6]

Alone with God, for the preliminary to the film (which is itself a moment of speech) is a moment of silence, a moment of emotional inwardness. 'In an African culture, it is more important to experience something than to express it outside yourself', says director Anne-Laure Folly from Togo.[7] It is from just such a personal experiencing of her subject that her documentaries on African women draw their quality of attention and emotion. And the women successively filmed in *Saïtane* (Oumarou Ganda, Niger 1972) would not contradict her on this. They look on over their yard walls as Safi is beaten by her husband, and their silence tells us more than any – unthinkable – rebellion.

The ritualization of feelings, as in greetings, allows emotion to be expressed while retaining a sense of propriety. The apparently restrained character of African greetings cannot disguise the richness and intensity of relationships. How could we forget the silences of the Tuareg women in *Waati* (Souleymane Cissé, 1995) who, rather than offering endless advice, express their trust to Nandi in a few simple phrases studded with long silences? Their deep gaze stays with us long after the film has ended.

THE PATH OF SIMPLE SELF-EVIDENCE

As a prime site of symbolic analogy and rereading of reality, dreams cannot but be a source of inspiration. As Souleymane Cissé observes,

> In my deep, dream-filled sleep things appear to me, mingling and intermingling, like clouds which suddenly clear to let through a piercing light. Things then light up and take shape. Characters appear and a dialogue begins between us in my dream. After we have spoken I can at last write on a few blank sheets of paper. This is the beginning of the story, always inspired by life itself and by what is around me.[8]

As a result, the film will be the final expression of an inner questioning. 'There are shocking situations and I am deeply distressed by them', Cissé goes on. 'When these facts build up in my heart and my head, I am distraught. That's the moment when I have to write. That's how it all begins.'

The demand for good screenplays, which is so often said to be a necessary precondition for African cinema to make progress, does not automatically lead to the Americanization of screen writing. 'The only rule, if there has to be one, is to have a good story', says the director Imunga Ivanga from Gabon,

> because that is the root of the film. Afterwards, there are ten thousand ways of telling that story. There are some very fine films which aren't action films. You think you're going to be original, but what is originality? Is it what has never been done before? Digital technology enables us to create new effects on top of what are often sketchy story lines. This is not how I see humanity going forward![9]

When all is said and done, the *originality* of films from Africa is that they respect human beings and open up an understanding of their place in the universe. Souleymane Cissé manages this 'very well', as Serge Daney writes,

> not by aestheticizing the world, but by slotting bodies directly into their environment. To such an extent that the transition from the 'natural' to the 'supernatural' is effected without any great hullabaloo, a glance is enough to transfix a rival or possess a woman, and the beauty of the actors has the elegance of those things which are sufficient unto themselves.[10]

Neither the picturesque nor exoticism! Exoticism requires chocolate-box images: the kind of backdrops designed to serve our desires and our fantasies – fantasies of the barbarian, the savage, the primitive. By contrast, the simplicity and clarity of images, whose only purpose is to advance the theme

Fadika Kramo-Lanciné

Nar Sene and Moussa Sene Absa

Mohamed Camara

Samba Félix Ndiaye

Cheik Doukouré

Fanta Nacro

Dani Kouyaté

Jean-Marie Teno

Abderrahmane Sissako

Flora Gomes

Gnoan Roger M'Bala

Djingarey Maïga

Salif Traoré

Cheikh Oumar Sissoko

Adama Drabo

Anne-Laure Folly

Bassek Ba Kobhio

Drissa Touré

of the film, leave the characters endowed with the naturalness and grace of their presence in the world, as masters of the meaning of their acts and the rhythm of their being. In fact, Cissé addresses this question in an interview with Rithy Pahn:

> The positive impression you derive from seeing a person or a thing and which remains in your heart and mind for a long time is something the Bambara call *damu*. Perhaps it is what is known as grace. When you see a human being living, you observe all that he is, everything around him. When you can understand him, you must show him with *damu*.

No doubt it is this sensitivity to reality, this complicity with human beings, animals and things, which gives Cissé's films their powerfully convincing moral force.

It is difficult to imagine anything more static than a sculpture. None the less, the Madagascan filmmaker Raymond Rajaonarivelo sets his presentation of the works of the sculptor Ousmane Sow in time, structuring his documentary *Le Jardin des corps* (1994) between morning, noon and evening. Just as Chris Marker and Alain Resnais repositioned African statues in the context of their appropriation by the colonialists (*Les Statues meurent aussi*, 1955), thereby lending them a historical density which magnified their beauty, Rajaonarivelo does not separate the sculptures from the shadow that is the story of their memory. Life is breathed into the static work and aestheticism comes alive...

THE PRIMACY OF ORALITY

A young Guinean, born in France because his parents had to flee the Sekou Touré regime, is curious about the memories which remain from the adults' stories. He decides to go to Guinea to see his grandfather. The result, *Tanun* (1994), is a funny, lucid dialogue between yesterday's world and the camera examining it:

> 'You want to see me close up, but you won't see me! [He laughs] I frighten you. [Staring off into the distance] 'Comrade, God does as he pleases in this world!'

'My approach was to use cinema', says Gahité Fofana. 'Our collusion enabled him to understand what a film was. So he is, then, also an old man speaking about cinema in a village in Africa.'[11]

> 'If God gave me life until today, it's my duty to tell you all this so that you know it. So that you can express it in your turn, pass it on to your children.
> 'Our ancestors are happy with each other. They did not know they could take photos as you do. We do it now and when I'm dead and in the hereafter, if you want me to speak, I'll speak. God has shown you that trick!'

There is no use of the shock image here: 'It's a failing of my film that it asks a lot of the viewer. The Guinean audience understood it better. People here aren't in the habit of listening.' And *Tanun* does, in fact, allow time to pass slowly. It is an inner vision which does not deny its sources:

> I try to take my inspiration from the oral tradition: not to repeat, but to repeat all the same, to hover around things without passing judgement, and yet to assert truths all the same. A series of images surrounding the topic rather than the topic itself...

There are few filmmakers who do not refer to this orality lying at the wellsprings of their cinematic language. The Malian director Adama Drabo, for example, says: 'I was very struck in my childhood by the public story-telling sessions of the griots, who often stepped out of their tales to make connections with reality.'[12] Even when they grew up in an urban environment, they stress the oral nature of the culture that was around them: 'As children we spent hours telling each other the stories of films', says the Cameroonian director Jean-Marie Teno.[13] Like his audience, the African filmmaker has profoundly grasped the techniques of the oral tradition – and also the collective imaginary it implies. Visual markers (gesture, costume) or auditory signs (declamation, words, song, music) give rise to a particular kind of perception.[14]

Peoples with oral traditions are not retarded! The distinction to be made is not between oral and written language but, as Ferdinand de Saussure pointed out, between *langue* and *parole* – that is to say, between a system of signs, which is a logical and impersonal instrument, and the use each person makes of this to communicate with others. 'Language' is ageless, whereas 'speech' in the Saussurean sense is located in history. Cultural discrepancies do not mean that the 'primitive' has not, thanks to language, crossed the threshold between nature and culture, as the civilized person has done – the culture achieved is common to both, the culture of 'speech.' As Amadou Hampâté Bâ put it, 'a people without writing is not a people without culture.' Writing lives off language, but it is not another language. Oral communication passes on knowledge just as surely as writing does. Where necessary, the oral languages can be written to meet the demands of modernity. In *Finzan* (Cheikh Oumar Sissoko, Mali, 1989), the chief of the Bambara village counters the scorn of the new district officer with the question: 'Did you not know that our language could be written?'

The Westerner, whose forefathers deprived Africans of their speech, often regards African language as mere chatter, background noise, 'babble'. Yet if he were prepared to, the civilized man could see himself as fellow to the

On the set of *Wazzou polygame* (Oumarou Ganda, Niger, 1970).
Courtesy of Argos Films Production.

'primitive', since they share the same basic myths, and these myths are found
in the Africans' speech. The shared need to find reference points in the
current state of the world thus confers a highly modern status on orality
within the universal consciousness. The filmmakers' concern to revive
memory fits into this perspective: they stage speech in the field, often con-
spicuously, by framing the narrator in the centre of the image. This is done,
for example, with the king in *L'Exilé* (Oumarou Ganda, Niger, 1980), who
is placed on a stage and given time to speak, as though it would be sacrilege
to interrupt him. In so doing, they ritualize speech, confirming the sacred
status it already has in the social order. It is because it becomes spectacle
that it detaches itself from the merely verbal and confirms its noble rank as
knowledge, as the message of tradition for the present and the future.

Cinema is thus the prime means for magnifying speech, and it thereby
acquires new legitimacy, as a prime cultural vehicle perpetuating and mod-
ernizing African speech. In societies where writing generally made its appearance at a late stage, cinema assumes its full value. As André Gardies

points out, it gives 'the combined verbal element and image the force and power of speech'.[15] The filmmaker then becomes a cultural energizer, a griot of modern times.

This does not confine the filmmaker within tradition: the choice of the image is an opening-up to a new writing, a rewriting capable of integrating external elements, as Imunga Ivanga puts it, particularly 'those elements of Western culture which we carry with us from the cradle, while our culture of origin is very threatened and shaky'.[16] It is here that the discourse is new: through the cross-fertilization of cultures, the confrontation of ancestral speech with the realities of the modern world produces a new speech in which modern humanity, both African and non-African, can recognize itself.

When the images do not furnish the verbal element with the metaphors to raise them to the level of speech, however, the film sinks into explicative verbiage. If the cinematic writing does not incorporate cultural elements of *mise-en-scène* which give a metaphorical dimension to its themes, the demonstrations fall flat.

CONTRAPUNTAL SYMBOLS

It is not at all surprising, then, that African directors, in their concern to put their realist vision in the service of memory, are obsessed by symbols, and show great concern where these are perverted. As early as 1966, in *Black Girl*, Sembène Ousmane used the fate met by an African mask to signify the cruel nature of contempt. We first see the mask being made by Diouana's young brother. Then, after she has been taken on by a couple of VSO volunteers to look after their children, she gives it to the wife as a mark of the warm relationship between them. She in turn hangs it on the dining-room wall as decoration during their stay in France. Diouana, disgruntled at being treated as a mere maid, takes it back. But, crushed by loneliness and lack of understanding, she kills herself. The husband goes to take the mask back to her family. Diouana's brother dons it and follows his sister's former employer in an effort to drive him out of the area. The mask, having become the symbol of Diouana's Africanness, takes on 'a connotation of political protest and cultural resistance'.[17]

This puts one in mind of those Masai masks made in large numbers in Kenya for the tourists, even though the art of carving masks is not part of the Masai tradition.[18] The craftspeople are attempting to meet the Western expectation of an African art of 'mysterious masks' and woodcarving. If the tourists allow themselves to be 'had', they do so because they want to bring home as a souvenir an object which is regarded in the popular mind as a symbol of Africa, without knowing what constitutes its specificity: namely, the social and ritual motivations of a people which gave birth to it.

In *The Battle of the Sacred Tree* (1994), the Kenyan director Wanjiru Kinyanjui shows an association of Christian women bent upon cutting down an ancient tree which now represents for them only the superstitions of a bygone age. In this case, by contrast, it *is* the tree's cultural specificity which the Christians are attacking – the density of its history, the behaviour and motivations of the ancients, criticized for their obscurantism. It is not the tree as symbol they reject, but the meaning it has assumed for their group: 'Everyone is a little bit afraid of the tree, of touching it, of what it can signify', points out Wanjiru Kynianjui. 'No one is trying to defend the past as such', she continues. 'Everyone is, rather, attempting to preserve not the tree in itself, but a part of themselves. They laugh at the women, but they are afraid of touching the tree.'[19]

In addition to their universal signification, symbols thus possess a particular resonance which is typical of a cultural specificity that is sometimes tricky to decipher for a spectator alien to the culture. Clémentine Faïk-Nzuji Madiya cites the example of *Sarzan* (Momar Thiam, Senegal, 1963), in which a chicken is sacrificed in the rain to celebrate Sergeant N'Diaye's return to his village.[20] The understanding of this symbol requires a specific knowledge of the local culture. In the films that come out of Africa, there are many sacrifices which may offend the sensibilities of Western viewers but will be fully understood by African spectators. We cannot, however, assume that the meaning will be the same for all Africans. Africa is a pluralistic continent, and the diversity of cultures makes symbols which are too specific to an area or an ethnic group difficult of access – and, indeed, the same sacrifice may take on different meanings. The boundaries to interpretation may begin at the next village. But in fact they lie, no doubt, at some other point, for may not symbols be seen, in fact, as an invitation to another way of apprehending reality? They widen the horizon. They are like a rhetorical figure in a piece of writing, the metaphor of a vision, a cosmic pause for breath, the grain of subjectivity which enables fiction to achieve a universal dimension. A magical rite makes its point by the impression it produces; in no sense does it appeal to deductive argument.[21] 'You just have to accept symbols', says Flora Gomes, 'and every time you remember them, you set about trying to decipher them again.'[22]

In *Po di Sangui/Tree of Blood* (Guinea-Bissau, 1996), symbols open out the fiction from the outset: the village is fighting the flames and calls in the old witchdoctor Calacalado to help. Africa is burning because it cannot, as birds do, distinguish the living from the dead. Hamidou was born a twin. Tradition dictates that at every birth a tree is planted which accompanies the child throughout its life. When Dou returns to the village, his twin Hami has just died, but it is Dou's tree which has died, and this greatly perplexes him. He wavers over claiming his heritage, over taking on Hami's household, with his wife and daughter: Hami's shirt is too big for him. What did he die of? What scourge is afflicting the community? Why does Dou's mother not recognize him? Covered in clay and moving among sheets of fabric marked with red, the colour of power in the animist tradition, three women will carry the twin pitcher as a mark of reconciliation. The mother goes into a trance, crying and trembling. Before bringing forth the reconciliatory pitcher, she exclaims: 'The ancestors said one of you must die, but your father and the imam would not have it.' There is a reference here to African responsibility, which prevented sacrifice. It will take the initiatory rite of a collective exodus for the village to pick up again the red threads woven by the spider of life around the remains of the witchdoctor: the original word remains central, but a new reading is required....

The intense use of symbols does not, then, lead inevitably to opacity. It is, rather, the opposite which happens when the camera manages to grasp the complexity of the African gaze, that symbolism which both conceals meaning and reveals it, which suggests while occluding, which unveils while adding to the mystery. In *A Banna* [It's over] (Kalifa Dienta, Mali, 1980), for example, the cinematic language uses fire, a storm and raging waters to symbolize tension and confrontation, playing on the universal meaning of threat these represent and elevating them to their poetic dimension.[23] The accent placed on objects, gestures, looks or backdrops by the use of light, camera movements, acting or staging enables an image to tell a story or become charged with meaning. The Western spectator often finds it hard to get beyond the decorative view of what he will regard either as a beautiful image or as a relatively banal presentation of natural elements. Since he is unused to this symbolism, it is often hard for him to perceive the emotional force of elements as simple and immediate as trees, sky, water, fire or wind, and so on. It is, however, this subtle use of symbols which, when it is successful, endows the image of Black African films with a meaning that goes far beyond what they appear to state directly.

Gesture then takes precedence over the spoken word. The precision of the daily gestures involved in preparing a meal or working in the fields symbolizes the force of tradition. Consulting the gods in *Emitaï* (Sembène Ousmane, Senegal, 1971) or exorcizing madness in *Kodou* (Ababacar Samb Makharam, Senegal, 1971) belong to a traditional register of gesture in which the significance of words yields before the meaning of movement.

More than ever here, silence is golden. It begins to speak. In *Tabataba* (Raymond Rajaonarivelo, Madagascar, 1987), the arrival of the soldiers puts an end to all sound. The noises of the forest artificially give way to pure silence, disturbed only by the drumming of the soldiers' boots. The sound here counterpoints the image. The viewer is gripped by a complex emotion which forces him or her to think.

The symbolic counterpoint nudges the image towards its opposite: the obvious conclusion ('that's what he's getting at') resolves itself into something quite other, producing a questioning; the spectator is then open to another understanding, to another emotional response. Beneath the realist mask of denunciation, we can discern a moral vision of the world: the satire is suffused with affection; the sensuality becomes mystical; the local is elevated into the universal. The shots are steady here; there are few tracking or panning shots, but when they do occur they are slow, so that the image becomes charged with another natural force – the force of a deep, moving reality. The world appearing on the screen is revealed as the screen itself succeeds in being forgotten.

Within the framework of the documentary, the use of counterpoint makes a kind of didacticism possible. It gives precedence to thinking over behaviour and eschews demonstration. 'In my films', notes Jean-Marie Teno,

> the text isn't a commentary on the image. The images often tell a story, the story today's Africa puts before our eyes. Behind those images there is a context, with so many stories which aren't told and would be far too long to tell. My work at the level of the text enables me to situate things in their context, but at the same time it provides a distance, a space for reflection.[24]

Teno, having set out to film the informal sector of the economy, could find no way to place his camera so as not to have his view obstructed by the piles of rubbish which clutter the streets of Yaoundé. In this way, the rubbish forcibly asserted itself as the symbol of a particular reality, giving Teno's *La Tête dans les nuages* (1994) a demonstrative power a mere realist approach could not have achieved.

CULTURAL SPECIFICITIES OF THE IMAGE

Focusing primarily on human beings implies an overall vision of the individual caught up in his environment, whereas the Western approach tends to present only a selective vision, stressing the psychological dimension. Thus the close-up is used more to link two shots than to reinforce a dramatic situation. When they film conversations, African filmmakers prefer to use

Gaston Kaboré on the set of *Rabi* (Burkina Faso, 1992). © Marc Salomon.

long shots or mid-shots taking in elements of the backdrop rather than the traditional shot/reverse-shot approach. Two people will be filmed talking over a backyard wall in a static shot, without the camera having to change angle. The framework provided by the walls separating yards and alleyways often reinforces the director's sociological point by illustrating the compartmentalization imposed by traditional rules. As the Tunisian filmmaker Ferid Boughedir notes, this makes it possible to get to the heart of the question:

> Black African films have taught me to brush away things which are not needed in the cinema and to try to get down to a certain undemonstrative essentiality – not shooting someone going up and down stairs, going around them, cutting in on the person from the left, then from the right as Westerners like to do. When you keep a camera on the level, it's what's inside that fixed frame that counts: the movements, the space and the framing.[25]

However, such a framing of the actors produces something of a theatrical effect. This is sometimes taken to excess, as in *Notre fille* (Daniel Kamwa, Cameroon, 1980), which was indeed taken from a stage play, in which, in one long scene, four characters sit in a line talking, all facing the camera.

But how could shot/reverse-shot – the alternation between close-ups of each protagonist as they speak – be used when the very culture is opposed to it? 'In the Mossi region', as director Maurice Kaboré (Burkina Faso) points out, 'it is not proper for a woman to look a man in the eye. When a young couple converse, the woman will be attentive, but her head will be lowered.'[26] If such a scene is filmed in the shot/reverse-shot style, the woman will almost seem blind and the scene will assume another meaning. Kaboré mainly makes short fiction films which are educative in intent, designed to be shown in remote regions. In *Baoré* (1992), for example, the eponymous heroine runs away from her village in collusion with her lover, so that she does not to have to marry the man she has been promised to for many years. The latter follows her, and tries to bring her back, but is arrested by the police. In this context, the meaning of gesture assumes its full importance. 'You look each other in the eye only when there is conflict', adds Maurice Kaboré. 'No one would understand how two lovers could look each other in the eye: do they love each other, or are they at daggers drawn? The viewer would be disorientated!'

A film like *Totor* (Daniel Kamwa, Cameroon, 1994), the story of an orphan taken in by pygmies, has an impressive number of vertical tracking shots along trees to mark transitions between shots. Rather than using a 'dissolve', for example, the directors choose to raise their camera gradually to the top of the tree, the opening to the sky which connects us to the cosmos. Idrissa Ouedraogo takes up this old convention in *Le Cri du coeur* (1994), but gives it a quite special significance: Paulo (Richard Bohringer) buys a bunch of balloons in a park – not to give them to Moctar (Saïd Diarra), the black child he has befriended, but to release them to fly up into the sky. As the camera follows their flight, the thrust of the film becomes clearer.

GRIOTS OF A NEW KIND

In an oral culture, in which words fade quickly if they are not passed on, cinema can find a new legitimacy by perpetuating memory. Dani Kouyaté saw himself as the bearer of the stories handed down to him by his father and mother, who were both griots. But being a griot was now nothing more than a label for him, the traditional meaning of his name. In making *Keïta, The Heritage of the Griot* (1995), in which he ventured to adapt *Sunjata*, the most famous of the Mandingo legends, for the screen, he was attempting to get back to the oral tradition, for which 'the future comes out of the past.' When, at the end of the film, an enormous baobab tree has grown magically outside Mabo's house, the child tries to walk round it. We see then that we have each to seek out the end of the story of Sunjata Keïta for ourselves, since – as Amadou Hampâté Bâ put it – the knowledge is within us. There is an echo here of an Amerindian legend which Sotigui Kouyaté relates, in which at the beginning of life on earth, human beings so greatly abused the share of divinity granted to each living creature that God decided to hide it where it would be most difficult to find: inside ourselves![27]

At his press conference at Fespaco 1995, Dani Kouyaté specified the four types of knowledge:

> There is the person who knows and knows that he knows. He is a 'knower'.
> There is the person who knows, but doesn't know he knows. A sleeper.
> There is the person who doesn't know and knows that he doesn't know. A searcher.
> And there is the person who knows, but knows he doesn't know. A danger to all and sundry.

It is often through humour, then, that the griot, like a court jester, asserts himself as the one who knows and dares to say what everyone must know. By the force of his words, he defuses conflict and ensures social cohesion. In Burkina Faso, the *Zi* travel around Bobo country, 'assess the tensions' and, in collective sessions of declamatory art, explain the strength of the different clans and the hierarchy between them, praising heroes and calling for respect for the elders and for custom.[28] The wandering griot minstrel thus has the same function as the palaver: he reduces conflict by way of language. In spite of its codes (precedence granted to age, prohibition on interrupting) the palaver, which is often depicted in films as taking place in the shadow of a baobab tree, implies absolute frankness and the total freedom of the participants.

However, in *Finzan* (Cheikh Oumar Sissoko, Mali, 1989), when Nanyuma's father is furious with her for stubbornly refusing to marry her dead husband's brother, the palaver does not resolve the conflict. The tension is heightened all the more by the fact that this should, culturally, produce unanimity. The exchanges now come in the form of well-known sayings:

> 'Hey, you're going at breakneck speed!'
> 'That's because of Nanyuma! Children have no respect any more!'
> 'That's not it. But times have changed!'
> 'Is that a reason? She'll do as I've decided!'
> 'Why don't you want my Bengali?'
> 'Don't talk to me about him!'
> 'I'm going to talk about him. He's my son. You whipped him and I said nothing. I think you're up to something.'
> 'Calm down, N'Golo!'
> 'I will not! I don't like what you're implying. If he doesn't watch out, I'll put his lights out! The ram with his head down knows exactly where he's going!'
> 'N'Golo! What a thing to say!'

The filmmaker is no longer a griot releasing tension here, but he takes his inspiration from the way the griot uses audience participation to transform his story in accordance with his listeners and current events. 'This technique which enables the griot to exploit imaginative resources to the full by mingling reality and fiction is at the centre of my artistic thinking', observes Dani Kouyaté.[29] It is this type of griot – the involved storyteller – with whom filmmakers identify, often placing such figures at the beginning of their films. *Guimba, the Tyrant* (Cheikh Oumar Sissoko, Mali, 1995) begins and ends with a panning shot of a griot beside a river. In this case, he is the narrator who will be faded out as the film continues with his story. However, Sambou (Habib Dembele), the tyrant's griot, is merely a retailer of proverbs, whose main concern is to reinforce the power of his chief. He is just a caricature of the Senegalese *farba*, the Fulani *mabo* or the Malinke *djeli*, those master wordsmiths attached to the great families or the royal family, serving them as mouthpieces and hymning their past great deeds, while also acting as counsellors in present matters.[30]

Similarly, the news-bearing griots – often wandering guitarists like the Fulani *gawlo* or the Malinke *nyamakala* – who attempt, through humour, toadying or threats, to extort money from people, are often denounced both in the novel and in films. *Borom Sarret* (Sembène Ousmane, 1963) gives his paltry earnings to the griot who sings his praises out in the street, while his wife is waiting for him at home, penniless. The griot here is a living allegory of the perversion of the spoken word, an allegory of flatterers of all kinds, including the politicians who demagogically abused the values which inspired the Independence movements.

Doubtless the filmmaker recognizes himself in the old-time griots, who were feared for the virulence of their speech, unrestrained by responsibility. Traditionally, the griot is in a culturally exceptional position: he is not really a man, since he does not fight in war, and his lower-caste status prevents him and his family – as in *Djeli* (Fadika Kramo-Lanciné, Ivory Coast, 1981) – from coveting a woman of higher birth. And yet, as a cleansing force and humorist, he is at the heart of society. Aware that people find some truths hard to swallow, he takes the burden of them upon himself: 'He wears the shirt so well that it suits everyone!' says Moussa Sene Absa from Senegal.[31] His ambiguity makes him a mediator and an arbitrator, and this confers on him a certain spiritual position which is backed up by his songs and his words. He draws on initiatory traditions, in much the same way as the Malian Souleymane Cissé uses Malinke esoteric knowledge on the birth of light in *Yeelen* (1987).

Can we, perhaps, call the filmmaker the griot of modern times? Although he does take inspiration from the griot's technique, he does so with the opposite aim in view: his intention is not to enhance the group's cohesion, but to move it forward. 'What the griot does', says Senegalese filmmaker Djibril Diop Mambety, 'is what I do; it is the filmmaker's role in society. "Griot" is a Wolof word which means more than a mere storyteller. The griot is a messenger of his times, a visionary and the creator of the future.'[32] Whereas the traditional griot is committed to maintaining and legitimating existing sociopolitical structures – and is efficient at doing so – the filmmaker borrows his ethical mission of 'active wisdom' and turns it around into a weapon for reducing cultural alienation. In this respect, he is – like the griot of *Jom ou l'histoire d'un peuple* (Ababacar Samb Makharam, Senegal, 1981) – an agitator, a 'stirrer': not in the sense of delivering a revolutionary message, but in the sense of stirring up a pot of reality full of crisis and misery, so as to bring it to the boil. And he does so not so much by raising awareness as by affirming his vital impulses – sexuality, power, death and adoration. Thus he appropriates for himself the movement the spoken word generates:

'The griot', says actor Sotigui Kouyaté, 'is the inspiriting person, the one who drives people on, who motivates them. He is a stimulator.'[33]

But how is this to be transposed into cinema? 'I have to find a writing, a verbal expression which gets people talking, sets them thinking', says Sembène Ousmane.[34] 'I can't tell them what they have to see in it, but I offer a space for thinking. Even if people don't like the film, the important thing for me is to make them think. I'm looking not for emotional involvement, but for participation.'[35]

To this end, the griot proceeds with subtlety. He draws here on the oral tradition, which never defines the true and the false precisely, and appeals to the maturity of the spectator. 'In the oral tradition, you never know what is truth and what is a joke', says Sotigui Kouyaté's son Dani. 'You always have to decode it yourself.' In so doing, the griot himself willingly becomes a therapist of his society – not just to dispel depression, as in traditional socio-therapies (the Serer *Lup* or the Wolof *N'doep* described in the 1972 film of that name by Michel Meignant, and referred to by Samba Félix Ndiaye in *N'gor, esprit des lieux*, 1995), but also to cure society of its inhibitions and its perversions.

By translating the word into action, filmmakers avoid both fiction and ethnology. They swing between retailing impersonal myths (denounced as 'epic cinema') and personal fiction (rejected as 'Western psychological cinema') to anchor a local story in the history of their society, if not indeed the history of the world – to cross, as Gilles Deleuze put it, 'the boundary which would separate [their] private business from politics, and which *itself produces collective utterances*'.[36] In giving life to the word, they reject not only the domination of a fixed past but also the dictates of cultural neo-colonialism, to contribute to the invention of a future for the people to whom they feel committed. This means their own people, of course, those among whom they were brought up, but also – and above all – all those throughout the world who share their determination.

THE VOICE-OFF: THE CONSCIOUSNESS
OF THE FILMMAKER

The voice of the griot lends substance to the spoken word. The 'old man' (the African expression has no pejorative connotations) does so too. Both state moral principles. At the beginning of *Wariko/The Jackpot* (Fadika Kramo-Lanciné, 1993), the griot sings: 'Money is no good! Money has spoiled the world today!' Old Pusga will tell Rabi (*Rabi*, Gaston Kaboré, 1992): 'The tortoise was your father's. He could do as he liked with it.' To emphasize how much the griot and the 'old man' are one with the spoken word, they are filmed in the centre of the image, with a certain fixity. The absolute opposite to this might be found, perhaps, in the restless movement of the youths from the urban ghetto in Matthieu Kassovitz's *Hate* (France, 1995), who pour out their hatred in a flood of twisted words, a disembodied, dead-end language – an expression of the violence of their social exclusion. The African filmmaker is in search of a voice between these two opposite extremes. He or she is attentive to words, because they represent knowledge, but also to the outcasts, the women, the children who have no voice with which to confront the conservatism that freezes speech in disembodied principles. In *Njangaan* (Mahama Johnson Traoré, Senegal, 1975) a six-year-old child is condemned to silence, separated from his mother by the high-handed action of his father, who sends him to a Koranic school to become a *talibe*, a beggar-disciple: 'I'm not asking your opinion, I'm telling you. To go against my decision would be sacrilege.' The child will eventually die beneath the wheels of one of the town's cars. The dialogue becomes thinner, allowing the filmmaker to express himself through the metaphors of the image and, at times, in that 'voice-off' which is superimposed upon it. Far from being, as it usually is, a distancing technique, the voice-off here becomes a consciousness with which the spectator is invited to identify.

The voice-off of the cartman in *Borom Sarret* (Sembène Ousmane, 1963), a founding moment in African cinema, is a literary voice, the voice of the novel, the voice of a man who says 'I' in a world which says 'We'. It is an existential affirmation, the opening to a new imaginary dimension in which the 'ego' can emerge. The inner voice of Diouana, the maid in *Black Girl* (Sembène Ousmane, 1966), is a voice of desire, a doubting, fleshly voice. It is the voice of an individual refusing alienation even in death. By lending her voice to the part, the late Haitian actress Toto Bissainthe gave unexpected breadth to the performance of a non-professional.

THEATRE IS A MERE WAYSTATION

The voice-off is not, however, a counterpoint. From *F.V.V.A* (Mustapha Alassane, Niger, 1972) to *Muna Moto* (Jean-Pierre Dikongué Pipa, Cameroon, 1975), these personal voices merely reinterpret the action. Yet even when it is physically absent, a voice-off which is the consciousness of the filmmaker marks the filmic *écriture*, and it is there, rather, that we have to look for a counterpoint. It is to be found in the humorous and grotesque features which punctuate the narrative, the all-purpose proverbs (used for laughter, for argument, to defer or to conclude), the forced attitudes and eloquent gestures, the metaphors contained in the images and representations. It is to be found in the sidelong references to everyday reality in every narrative, references made in the style of the larger-than-life, satirical theatre of Africa, which, despite all these things, is sometimes extremely profound. It is a theatre – *Koteba* in Mali, *Yoruba* in Nigeria, *Makobe* in Zaïre – in which everyone sees their everyday problems depicted – adultery, patriarchy, family quarrels, power games, and so forth. Malian popular films, like the films of Falaba Issa Traoré,[37] are profoundly marked by this traditional theatre in which, on the village square in the evening, souls are bared against a familiar canvas, without any actual conclusion being necessary, as indicated in the Malinke term '*koteba*', which means 'unending story'. One also finds traces of such theatre in a film like *Guimba the Tyrant* (Cheikh Oumar Sissoko, 1995). In Nigeria, there is a whole industry distributing Yoruba theatre productions on video, and Ola Balogun drew on that style in *Ajani-Ogun* (1976) to ensure the success of his fable about power. 'Yoruba theatre has interesting techniques which can produce good results in the cinema', he explains. 'It uses folklore, draws on cultural resources and mythology, religious belief and magic; it mingles dance, song and bodily expression; it leaves room for improvisation and is a travelling theatre which goes out to meet its audience throughout the Yoruba area.'[38] It is a form of theatre, combining different genres ranging from drama to comedy, which has very deep roots in Ancient Africa, as Ola Balogun goes on to note: 'They don't just play out a magic scene without first having done real research among the witchdoctors to get the genuine wording of the incantations.'

So the filmmaker borrows the evocative power of the oral tradition. To avoid coming under suspicion of being a technique wholly associated with the colonialist West, cinema doubtless had to take that route and use the different traditions of popular theatre. But theatre could be only a waystation. It can still – as the Abidjan-based Cameroonian playwright Were Were Liking says – 'bring a quality of invention which transcends banal reality to a cinematic image that lacks imagination'.[39] The point is, of course, not to fall into that oft-denounced theatricalization of attitudes and gesture in which the dialogues feel artificial and calculated.[40] Today, African theatre is experimenting with a cinematic style in which, as in Were Were Liking's shows, verbal language represents merely one part of a total theatre of music and gesture. Similarly, it is when cinema is able to distance itself from verbal theatre that it ceases to be collective therapy, asserts its 'voice-off', and becomes a personal expression.

LETTING THEM TELL YOU STORIES

Although it sometimes goes so far as to reproduce the rite in which the spoken word is passed on, cinema always tends to develop a critical consciousness. It replaces the griot's epic by a clash of personal destinies, in the logic of tragedy, in which everyone says 'I' without any third party necessarily intervening to restore harmony. Even when the film is invaded by the verbal dimension, subordinating the significance of camera angles and length of shot, establishing the narrative through a series of juxtaposed playlets, personal affirmation comes in through the door of the narrative. Thus, in a film such as *Adja Tio* (Jean-Louis Koula, Ivory Coast, 1980), which is theatrical in the extreme, the intention is clear. The errors of tradition can be remedied first by the hospital, then by the law. While the fisherman, Mango, who is sick, is sent to a fetisher who only makes him worse, his daughter, who has settled in Abidjan, takes him to the hospital where he is cured. Urged on by Akreman, Mango's sister-in-law, the fetisher poisons Mango and his brother, who is his legal heir. Akreman's intention is to inherit all his goods, as custom dictates, but a trial will restore the rights of Adjoba, Mango's wife. There is heavy didacticism in this, but at least the filmmaker takes a clear stance in the topical debate between tradition and modernity. Strikingly, this way of opposing customary law and the law relating to the appropriation of goods and children by the dead man's family is taken up again in a very similar way in the more recent Zimbabwean film *Neria* (Godwin Mawuru, 1990). With all its didactic intent, considerable scope is also allowed here for dialogue and for the debates at the trial, though realist description here takes precedence over the exemplary nature of fable.

The revolt against the perversions of custom, found in both these films, sits easily with the affirmation of a specific ethic which many films will seek to support by reference to traditional stories and sayings. The folktale or proverb, which are positively *inlaid* into the narrative, pull together scattered elements, just as the griot does, and offer the possibility of a universal understanding. In *Samba Traoré* (Idrissa Ouedraogo, 1992), Samba tells little Ali the story of Moriba:

> 'Samba, tell me another story!'
> 'Another one? You're asking a bit much... All right then, but this will be the last.'
> 'All right.'
> 'We're going to talk about Moriba.'
> 'Who's Moriba?'
> 'Don't you know him? He's like you. Stubborn *and* stupid!'
> 'Don't call me names!'

Idrissa Ouedraogo on the set of *Samba Traoré* (Burkina Faso, 1992).

© Félix von Muralt/Lookat.

'I'm joking… You're brighter than Moriba.'

'Right, that's better.'

'Now, listen. One day, Moriba went off to market and bought himself a pair of trousers. The feast days were coming. When he got back home, he realized the trousers were big, very big, and too long for him. Moriba begged his father to shorten his trousers. But his father refused, and his mother too, and all his sisters, because Moriba was a stubborn boy. Late that night Moriba went to sleep, unhappy and bitter. Without telling anyone, his father decided to shorten the trousers. His mother did the same thing. And so did the sisters, again in complete secrecy. The next day, Moriba put on the trousers but they had become small, very small. Guess what comes next…'

'I know. On the feast day, Moriba had just a pair of underpants!'

With the story of Moriba's shortened trousers, Samba sums up the thrust of the film: his own difficulty in tailoring his existence to the right size, the problem of finding his place in the world.

Drawing on the oral tradition is not without its dangers with a Western audience which tends to see oral literature as 'folktale' and folktale as relating to childish imagery. Not having entirely thrown off colonial ideology (according to which – to take the 1932 Larousse dictionary entry for 'Negro' as a guide – the 'intellectual inferiority [of Negroes] means we have a duty to protect them'), the Westerner finds it hard to appreciate the complexity of oral references and their contemporary quality. He or she tends to see the folktale as a pleasant, innocuous anecdote, adding a little local colour to the narrative.

Yet, as director Fanta Nacro from Burkina Faso points out, 'the tale is not a gratuitous, unmotivated thing, because it takes its cue from daily experience'.[41] Her short *Un certain matin* (1993), a metaphorical piece on the reception of cinema, has the density of a folktale, and uses its narrative devices: repetition, symmetry, surprise, appeal to the imagination, the use of signs, objects and hence of space rather than dialogue. A peasant hears shouts, and sees a man chasing a woman. When the scene repeats itself, he intervenes and shoots at the man, who falls. We then hear the word 'Cut!', because this is a film being shot in a remote area. When he catches up again with his father, who has run away for fear of reprisals, the son asks him in the night: 'Daddy, what's cinema?' Through its cinematic transcription of the oral tradition, producing a contemporary folktale, the film provides its own answer. The folktale weaves its magic: the viewer enjoys it and comes back for more.

In *Clando* (Jean-Marie Teno, Cameroon, 1996), Chamba has been in Germany for ten years. When his father is at last able to speak to him on the telephone, he does not ask him to justify himself but to listen to a story – the story of a hunter who does not want to return to the village empty-handed. 'The hunter story doesn't exist', says Jean-Marie Teno, 'I invented it. It's a symbol of immigration. You go off thinking you're going to come back, but you don't feel you've made it, and that stops you going home.'[42] The story of the hunter, punctuating the narrative as it does like an advance in understanding, confers the force of moral self-evidence on it.

Two children go begging through a town. Ablaye is begging for his father; Madou for the imam of his Koranic school. Their wanderings bring them up against the indifference of the rich, the compromises and fears of adults. They also take them across a nuclear waste dump which has left the surrounding area devastated. To music by Wasis Diop and the voice of Youssou N'Dour, a folk ballad accompanies them:

> There was once a caiman and a bird whose mother had gone off to feed.
> The caiman said to him: Come down, I'm your mother's friend.
> But the bird replied:
> You are trying to trick me,
> Mother will not come.

Oh Mother, oh Mother!
Mother, come and get me!'

'*Picc Mi* [Senegal, 1992] is a product of experience', says its Senegalese director Mansour Sora Wade. 'The children in prison, the destruction of the environment, the misappropriation of food aid, the African heads of state behaving like beggars in North–South relations – these are things I want to talk about, but not violently.'[43] The folk ballad provides the occasion for an explicit warning: 'Modou, there are caimans everywhere. Don't drop your guard or they'll eat you!' Just as Haïlé Gerima invoked Ethiopia as a bride in *Harvest 3000* (1976), or as the writer Nuruddin Farah evokes woman, in the tradition of Somali poets, as a symbol of Somalia, the folktale in *Picc Mi* appeals allegorically to Mother Africa...

WHAT SLOWNESS?

The oral storytelling tradition imbues African films with a specificity which is easily missed when Western criteria are applied. If one is to respect the Other's culture, one requires a quality of attention which film editor Andrée Davanture obviously possesses: 'I understood right away that the priorities of the African filmmaker were not necessarily the same as mine. My initial reactions were French ones: a way of building up a story, an inclination to pull everything together...' When all is said and done, what is at stake is respect for the audience. 'You can be wrong sometimes, you can have the impression that what the director is trying to say could be said more simply. This is often a trap, because what seems easier to you may appear more abstract to an African audience.'[44]

Editors would often like to remedy what seems to them the lack of pace, the slowness of a film. 'A fast-moving film', says Davanture, 'imposes a way of looking on the viewers, a point of view, whereas a slow film allows them the freedom to see what they want to see, to involve themselves, to make discoveries. Their imaginations can get to work.' This was the path taken by the Senegalese director Ababacar Samb Makharam, who died in 1987:

> I'm going to try to domesticate the technology with the way of feeling of an African.... We should start out from our oral traditions, push slowness of pace to the point of exasperation, a slowness which comes from the very depths of our culture and which I don't intend to deny.[45]

For Idrissa Ouedraogo from Burkina Faso, it is the image which sets the pace of a film:

When they say Africa means sitting under the 'talking tree', and that takes a long time, I don't agree. If you have a one-minute crane-mounted tracking shot, you don't notice the minute passing! But when the camera is still for a minute, you accept it only if the actors are very good; if they aren't, you can't take it![46]

The Senegalese director Moussa Sene Absa similarly rejects 'semiological clichés' which could be said to confuse movement with speed: 'The public can be extremely annoying, but they aren't stupid. They want to find their own heartbeat in a film. There are two ways of knocking at a door: hard or softly. It isn't a question of slowness!'

The result is a certain grace, which Ferid Boughedir, the Tunisian director who is also a great connoisseur of Sub-Saharan film, explains as follows:

When Gaston Kaboré films *Wend Kuuni* and, by comparison with the classical rules of editing, holds the close-up of the boy longer than is usual, at that moment suddenly something magical occurs: it was a great lesson for me! He realized that you had to cut later, and those few seconds 'too long' generated an emotion I hadn't encountered elsewhere.[47]

For an audience weaned on American audiovisual products, which are invariably action-based – the more so as they must make sure their viewers don't switch channels during the commercial breaks – boredom is the major fear. It has even become the main criterion. Yet if a film bores me, it does so because it seems to be of no interest, to be banal or predictable. I consider myself above all that – more intelligent, superior... Or it may be that it is too complicated for me, or that it lacks action, which comes back to the formal question of a pace I regard as too slow. In all cases, as in a conversation, boredom is a way of not hearing what the film is telling me. Yet it so happens that films which are regarded as boring are not perceived in the same way some years later. It isn't the film which bores, but I who (actively) *feel* bored. I can, admittedly, be bored with a film which comes from my own cultural family, a film which produces a terrible impression of 'déjà vu'. But if watching a film from another culture meant not necessarily having to understand, but simply to open oneself up to something, the boredom one felt could change into uncertainty and meditativeness. Boredom might then, as Raoul Ruiz suggests, be the secret weapon of a different cinema...[48]

The question of time also brings us back to origins: 'When, in *Emitaï*, the people are under the tree, it is time passing, infinitely', says Sembène Ousmane. 'The story takes place over twenty-four hours, but it is the tree there which signifies this infinite time of dialogue.'[49] Traditionally, rites combat the deterioration which ensues from the passage of time. They restore primordial time, the time which enables us to deny death and overcome anxiety. The *longueurs* of the film can express the passage of time, its cyclical and repetitive logic, the presence of the past in the present event. The breaks in the filmic *écriture* of *Waati* (Souleymane Cissé, 1995) mark its different phases. Moving from a jumpy style of filming with a hand-held camera for the South African scenes to long tracking shots and contemplative sequences in the Sahara Desert, the film plays on time to the point where that is, in the end, its only subject. The defence of Nandi's university thesis is illustrated by a dance routine, choreographed by Were Were Liking, in which masks and a naked man and woman evoke the movement of origins and its significance for the present. This marks a pause in the narrative, a shift to a deeper level, accentuating the importance of the knowledge contained in ancient wisdom for the understanding of the contemporary world. Reality is fiercely interwoven with the movement of the universe, and that movement helps us in understanding it, in getting it into proportion, yet without denying it. In short, it serves to show it as part of a universal harmony. As a result, the anachronistic nature of the racist heresy – and, indeed, of all intolerance – is strikingly revealed.

SPACE–TIME

The camera embraces landscapes and bodies, setting them in both their geographical and political environments. The African space, which is often filmed in panoramic long shots, is indissociable from passing time. Thus still shots of landscapes, sunsets or people standing still have nothing static about them. They represent time – the time of the narrative or the time the narrative subtends, a vision of the world registered in movement. 'Time does not pass in the same way in the desert as it does in the forest', says Imunga Ivanga from Gabon.[50] Space is the measure of time, as in those movements from one hut to another, or from the village to the town, which would be left out in Western films. African cinema shows these in their full extent, for otherwise it would lose this fundamental sense of time, as Fatima Sanga, the grandmother in *Yaaba* (Idrissa Ouedraogo, Burkina Faso, 1989) felt she was doing when, reluctantly having to make car journeys for the making of that film, she was no longer able to see the landscape passing.

The image thus gives body to time, not only by the length of the shots but by its spatial economy: the place accorded, for example, to depth of field, which, as in painting, inscribes the subject in space, in the end making the latter the central subject of the film. When, in *Blanc d'Ébène* (Cheik Doukouré, Guinea, 1991), which is set in 1943, the villagers leave after a confrontation with the French adjutant Mariani, a long shot from above shows the adjutant alone in the foreground and, at the foot of a great baobab tree, the tightly knit group of villagers shuffling off. The village community thus transcends the simple cohesion acquired during the time of the film and, despite the display of its divergences, demonstrates the timeless nature of its solidarity. When, in *Dunia* (Pierre Yameogo, Burkina Faso, 1987), at the midday break in the fields, the men and the women eat in separate groups under the same tree, with the men in the foreground and the women in the background, this arrangement of the image has more than merely sociological objectives. The time of tradition appears on the screen with the weight and self-evidence of eternity. It is in this sense that African films are films *from* Africa – not because they are set in that continent, but because they form a part of it. Africa is no longer merely the Africa shown by the image, but also the Africa of memory, the Africa of a space–time in which the past lives in the present. Then, on occasion, we see slowness transmuted into grace: in the work of Cissé, for example – the grace of a naturalness of emotions, a profound fit between space and time.

A CYCLICAL COMPOSITION

A change is, however, making itself felt, and it is not one we can attribute solely to the pressure of American images or the increasing penetration of television. Young filmmakers today are attempting to break away from linear narrative and looking for a new pace to their films, a pace which is all their own. With the development of society playing its part – the unfulfilled hopes of the Independence years having given way to democratic questionings – the filmmaker's relationship with the viewers has become more subtle: it is no longer a question of taking them down a well-worn path, but of frustrating them, in order to take them to a different place – to an understanding which is not a product of didacticism, but more akin to a reflection on themselves, their experience, their society. With *Haramuya* (1995), Drissa Touré from Burkina Faso attempted a composition without plot or dénouement, centred on events in the lives of a group of people typical of the life of the capital city, Ouagadougou.

> I said to my editor, the Tunisian Kahina Attia, that I wanted a circular structure: make a circle, but make it join up, so that the audience isn't totally lost. She took a pen and a sheet of paper, drew the circle and said, 'This is what I suggest.' That's how we started.[51]

This whirl of intermingling episodes involving social outcasts, Libyan shopkeepers, a Koranic school and street children is imbued with a gentle humour and a seriousness of tone. Jean-Pierre Bekolo's *Quartier Mozart* (Cameroon, 1992) has a similarly exploded structure. This, too, is a contemporary chronicle of urban Africa, the story of a young girl magically transformed into a young man in a poorer area of an African city. She falls for the daughter of a polygamous police superintendent who rids himself brutally of his first wife, while an unknown man makes men's genitals disappear by shaking their hands!

These genuinely enigmatic films maintain the structure of the oral tale to some extent, but they do so not by the interweaving of subplots which is characteristic of so many African films and novels but, rather, by the effects of a repetitive, circular montage. They thus avoid that juxtaposition of scenes which sometimes gives the impression that the director is waiting for some-one to finish speaking or moving before changing the shot. The spiral montage confers a certain coherence on an otherwise apparently chaotic narrative.

Previous generations had prepared the ground. The documentaries of the Senegalese director Samba Félix Ndiaye are based on this spiral logic, as is his feature film *N'gor, l'esprit des lieux* (1994):

> I made up my mind that it wasn't necessary to show everything, that I could build up the film like a puzzle with mazes and little side alleys. If the viewer likes, I'll give him my hand and take him inside. When you climb mountains, you some-times ask yourself what you're doing there. And then you reach a peak and the thing opens up before you. You're filled with a sense of wonder.[52]

As early as 1973, Djibril Diop Mambety employed a cyclical compositional style in *Touki-Bouki* – something he further developed in *Le Franc* (1994). The effort required of the viewers to piece together the narrative makes identification less likely, but shifts them towards a new view of reality. The images induce a reality effect in much the same way as do the photographs included by André Breton in his work *Nadja*. The viewer will attempt to find a coherence among those images. The irony of the narrative then sharpens the critical faculties and one's reflection on one's own actions. The themes and the symbolism point the viewer towards an overall understanding. He is then summoned to situate himself in the world, within a general logic which the circular narrative structure imposes as a metaphysic: set against Time, a life is merely a transient episode, but one which inscribes itself in Time, through multiple rites of passage, as a permanently creative act.

RATHER THAN HEROES, THE ART OF THE PARADOX

What point could there be, then, in relying on suspense, as Hollywood cinema does? The problem is not to raise the tension in the audience by announcing in advance what the hero is to discover or what is going to

Abdoulaye Komboudri running on the set of *Samba Traoré* (Idrissa Ouedraogo, Burkina Faso, 1992). © Félix von Muralt/Lookat.

happen to him. Even with a plot based on detection, such as the one which underpins *Samba Traoré* (1992), Idrissa Ouedraogo prefers the surprise effect which grips the audience only during the action. If the few shots which show the policemen hunting for Samba clearly throw an air of menace over the calm of his newly rediscovered village life, this is more to emphasize the precariousness and ambiguity of the place he is seeking for himself than to stress the fear of hypothetical reprisals. The arrival of the policemen closes the film, but does not provide a conclusion to its basic argument. The intention is not to facilitate identification with the hero but to offer a moral reflection on the state of crisis and on human behaviour.

If, in *Ceddo* (1977), two 'heroes' might be identified – the people resisting collectively and the princess who, isolated far from the village, comes to an understanding of the course she must follow – Sembène Ousmane maintains the distance between these two kinds of narrative – between the description of resistance and the fiction of liberation, between the collective and the individual, between the people and its hero – right up to the final scene (when the princess returns, with tears in her eyes, to kill the imam). Thus, as Serge Daney observes, 'the princess is not Zorro'![53]

Distance from what might be perceived as a hero is also maintained in a film like *Niiwam* (Clarence Delgado, Senegal, 1992). Thierno sees his child die in hospital because he cannot afford the necessary medicines. He takes the bus to go and bury him at the cemetery and there, in turn, each of the passengers tells their story, presenting a sociological tableau in which linear argument gives way to a series of anecdotal narratives. The film, adapted from a short story of the same name by Sembène Ousmane, lingers over life in Thierno's village and the reasons for his son's death, whereas the book hardly mentions these things. In this way, the viewer can feel with Thierno the cruelty and individualism of urban life. He will identify with him not as a person, but for what he represents socially.

The 'road movie' is particularly well suited to this descriptive intent. The Ghanaian director King Ampaw used the device of a lorry crossing the country in his *Kukurantumi* (1983) and Moussa Sene Absa from Senegal once again adopted the idea of the interlaced narratives of bus passengers in his *Yalla Yaana* (1995). Each passenger has his character and his story. Those of *TGV* (Moussa Touré, Senegal, 1997) reflect the opposing forces within Africa today. 'TGV', which links Dakar to Conakry, is an express bus driven by Rambo. After an uprising among the Bassari at the Guinean frontier, only some ten passengers are left. They are soon joined by a sacked minister and his wife, then by white ethnologists. In the face of the danger, each asserts his or her personality, and relationships are formed. There is nothing here of the Hollywood logic in which a hero – often an avenging hero – confronts some kind of disruptive outsider. The actions of characters in African films have more to do with revealing something about their society. They leave their usual environment (hence the many journeys in films) to confront another place which poses a problem for them (the city, Europe, modernity, etc.), or their arrival disturbs the existing order (the village community, custom, tradition, etc.).

Thus the logic is more that of paradox than of a conflict, embodied in a hero, between two clearly defined terms. There is a considerable difference between these two things, for paradox offers an opening to something else. A society with a written culture develops the syllogism, a rigorous form of reasoning in which the conclusion is deduced directly from the premisses. In a society with an oral culture, truth has multiple dimensions which cannot be pinned down in closed rational systems. 'Words are often deader than dead unless they lie', wrote Sony Labou Tansi.[54] To solve the puzzle which faces them, characters in African films will often have to appeal to a wisdom based on the observation of natural and cosmic forces. They do, of course, go to see the marabout, who perhaps divines from cowrie shells or kola nuts a message which takes the story forward. But it is, first and foremost, from a natural reading of the world that they come to understand what is happening to them. The Dogon traditionally watched their children's play to know whether it was going to rain. The Fulani used the way the different coats of the oxen were distributed about the landscape to divine the future. Nature offers human beings an imaginary dimension from which they derive order, harmony and rhythm. Human beings integrate themselves into that dimension, playing to that rhythm. It is in this sense that Ababacar Samb Makharam could assert that Africans have their own rhythm for speaking, telling stories and behaving.[55] Symbols and paradoxes abound in these films to express the dynamic relation which exists between human beings and the world. They are aids to understanding the very complexity of existence.[56]

THE TOPICALITY OF MYTH

Although they base themselves on these cultural elements, however, African films are not about promoting inertia. In his analysis of *Wend Kuuni* (Gaston Kaboré, Burkina Faso, 1983), Manthia Diawara shows that the film borrows from the oral tradition (length of shot, voices-off, apparently linear narrative) to reinforce the verisimilitude of its argument. But Kaboré, by overturning the order of what the oral narration of his story would have been, also reverses its meaning. Centring his plot-line on a child who has been struck dumb, he stresses the child's acquisition of autonomy, which echoes that of his mother, who refuses a forced remarriage. Rather than appealing for custom to be respected, the film becomes a call for self-assertion. The boy recovers his voice when, in shock, the images of his mother's flight come back to him. His relationship with Pongneré, the daughter of the peasants who have taken him in, will mark a turning point in the narrative: she relates a dream to him in which he could speak, introducing a previously unknown subjectivity into the account. The camera moves in closer here, using wide-angle shots and shot/reverse-shot. Wend Kuuni no longer seems merely an orphan to us, but an autonomous individual. In this way, tradition is denounced when it is archaic and justifies the dictatorship of the community over the individual. In calling for a new social order, cinema asserts itself as a subversive art.

The child was given the name Wend Kuuni ('Gift of God') like all foundling children. In Africa, to choose a name is to force destiny. The griot-actor Sotigui Kouyaté explains that he called his film director son Dani because

Gaston Kaboré on the set of *Rabi* (Burkina Faso, 1992). © Marc Salomon.

the name means 'seed'.[57] The symbolism of names asserts itself by daily repetition. It places the individual in the group. It does not simply name, it explains. By the name of the child alone, *Wend Kuuni* opens on to a metaphysic of change. The film calls for a different social order, and hence a different political and economic order, but it is concerned to set that order within the general order of things. Starting out from myth – anchoring itself in the spoken word only to call for that word to be rewritten – it weaves a tale that prefigures the future, which is a way of reminding the viewer that modern consciousness has something to gain from listening to myth.

Whereas tradition can be seen as a series of modernities, accumulating to form a whole, with today's modernity becoming integrated into that whole to forge a new tradition (which in some ways casts a new light on the sempiternal opposition between these two terms), myth enunciates the values, valid for the whole of humanity, which arise from man's confrontation with nature and with himself. Tradition offers a reading of these which modernity revisits. By holding up a mirror to this rewriting, the films put reality to the test of a double analysis: confrontation with the founding myths and a modern critique of the tradition which came out of them.

Whereas the West claims to possess a universal truth without acknowledging that it simply forges its own truths, the cinema cultures of Black Africa continue in this way to affirm the topicality of the founding myths common to all humanity. Far from conserving them as inert memories, they revivify them, incorporate them into the social rhythm, connecting fragments of reality in an attempt to deliver a message which is valid for their community. They play out and clarify the paradox of a mystification which is indispensable because it is structural and a demystification which is equally indispensable if the myth is not to become fixed, preventing any social evolution. In the end, they assert that myth – with the essential values it affirms – remains valid, but that the form given to it must change! This requires both courage and determination. 'Who am I to have distorted the words of the ancestors?' asks old Calacalado in *Po di Sangui/Tree of Blood* (Flora Gomes, Guinea-Bissau, 1996) before sending his village out, in an initiatory exodus, to find a path to renewal.

When the Westerner realizes that African mythology echoes his own, revealing to him that even his own discourse, which has become scientific, contains archetypes common to the whole of humanity, he recovers his bearings and the energy to advance when he was beginning seriously to flounder. Myth is necessary: if you don't feel you can pull through, where are you to find the energy to do so? Without confining anyone to the past, myth restores a meaning where the shortcomings of modern development leave us reeling in mental chaos and existential anguish. Myth thus asserts its therapeutic force, as a light on the path of hope and life. It is, no doubt, towards this type of dynamic poetry that a child recovering speech is trying to point us.

NOTES

1. Proverb quoted in the Zaïrian Ngangura Mweze's documentary *Le Roi, la vache et le bananier* (1994).
2. Quoted by Jean-Michel Devésa, *Sony Labou Tansi, écrivain de la honte et des rives magiques du Kongo*, L'Harmattan, Paris, 1996, p. 164.
3. In Rithy Pahn's film *Cinéastes de notre temps: Souleymane Cissé* (1991).
4. Tchicaya U Tam'si, *Les Cancrelats*, Albin Michel, Paris, 1980.
5. Interview with Andrée Davanture, Paris, 1995.
6. In Pahn's film, *Cinéastes de notre temps: Souleymane Cissé*.
7. Interview with Anne-Laure Folly, Paris, 1995.
8. In Pahn's film, *Cinéastes de notre temps: Souleymane Cissé*.
9. Interview with Imunga Ivanga, Paris, 1995.
10. Serge Daney, 'Cissé très bien, qu'on se le dise', *Libération*, 9–10 May 1987.
11. Interview with Gahité Fofana, Paris, 1995.
12. Interview with Adama Drabo, Ouagadougou, 1995.
13. Interview with Jean-Marie Teno, Manosque, 1996.
14. Tshishi Bavuala Matanda, 'Discours filmique africain et communication traditionnelle', in Centre d'Étude sur la Communication en Afrique, *Camera nigra, le discours du film africain*, OCIC–L'Harmattan, Paris, undated, p. 169.
15. André Gardies, *Cinéma d'Afrique noire francophone, l'espace miroir*, L'Harmattan, Paris, 1989, p. 128.
16. Interview with Imunga Ivanga, Paris, 1995.
17. Quoted by René Prédal, 'La Noire de...: premier long métrage africain', *Cinémaction* 34 ('Sembène Ousmane'), 1985, p. 39.
18. Jutta Ströter-Bender, *L'Art contemporain dans les pays du 'Tiers Monde'*, trans. Olivier Barlet, L'Harmattan, Paris, 1995, p. 37.
19. Interview with Wanjiru Kinyanjui, New York, 1996.
20. Clémentine Faïk-Nzuji Madiya, 'Symbolisme et cinéma africain', in Centre d'Étude sur la communication en Afrique, *Camera nigra*, p. 220.
21. Yvette Biro, *Mythologie profane: cinéma et pensée sauvage*, L'Herminier, Paris, 1982, p. 27.
22. Press conference for the presentation of his film *Po di Sangui*, Cannes, 1996.
23. Clémentine Faïk-Nzuji Madiya, 'Symbolisme et cinéma africain', p. 221.
24. Interview with Jean-Marie Teno, Manosque, 1995.
25. Interview with Ferid Boughedir, Paris, 1998, *Africultures* 13 ('Africanité du Maghreb'), L'Harmattan, Paris, 1998.
26. Interview with Maurice Kaboré, Paris, 1995.
27. Sotigui Kouyaté interviewed by Jadot Sezirahiga, *Écrans d'Afrique* 13–14, 1995, p. 14.
28. Louis-Vincent Thomas and René Luneau, *La Terre africaine et ses religions*, second revised edition, L'Harmattan, Paris, 1995, pp. 56, 198 (first published 1975).

29. 'Rencontre avec Dani Kouyaté', *Le Film Africain* 18–19, February 1995, p. 11.
30. Amadou Koné, *Des textes oraux au roman moderne, étude sur les avatars de la tradition orale dans le roman ouest-africain*, Verlag für Interkulturelle Kommunikation, Frankfurt-am-Main, 1993, p. 48.
31. Interview with Moussa Sene Absa, Paris, 1995.
32. Djibril Diop Mambety interviewed by June Givanni, *African Conversations*, BFI/Screen Griots, 1995.
33. Sotigui Kouyaté, *Écrans d'Afrique*, 9–10, 1994, p. 22.
34. Interview with Sembène Ousmane, Paris 1998, published in *Africa International* 311, February 1998.
35. Ibid.
36. Gilles Deleuze, *Cinema 2: The Time Image*. trans. Hugh Tomlinson and Robert Galeta, The Athlone Press, London, 1989, p. 222.
37. *Premières lueurs d'espoir* (1978); *An be no don* [We are all guilty] (1980); *Duel dans les falaises* (1985); *Le Pagne sacré* (1990).
38. Interview with Ola Balogun, Paris, 1996.
39. Interview with Were Were Liking, Ki Yi village, Abidjan, 1995. In *Were Were Liking*, Issiaka Konaté from Burkina Faso sketches a portrait of Ki Yi village, which is home, in the centre of Abidjan, to some hundred people, participating in the same economy through various activities ranging from craftwork to the clothing business. The theatre company bears the name Ki Yi M'Bock, which means 'ultimate knowledge of the universe': here knowledge of self contributes to developing a sense of responsibility which goes beyond differences to produce harmony.
40. Matanda, 'Discours filmique africain et communication traditionnelle', p. 172.
41. Fanta Nacro interviewed by Françoise Balogun in *Cinéma et libertés*, Présence Africaine, Paris, 1993, p. 98.
42. Interview with Jean-Marie Teno, Manosque, 1996.
43. Interview with Mansour Sora Wade, Ouagadougou, 1995.
44. Andrée Davanture interviewed by Françoise Balogun in *Cinéma et libertés*, pp. 118, 120.
45. Quoted by Matanda, 'Discours filmique africain et communication traditionnelle', p. 166.
46. Interview with Idrissa Ouedraogo, Paris and Ouagadougou 1995.
47. Interview with Ferid Boughedir, Paris, 1998, *Africultures* 13.
48. Raoul Ruiz, *Poétique du Cinéma*, Éditions Dis Voir, Paris, 1995.
49. Quoted by Antoine Kakou, 'Les gris-gris d'un conteur', *Cinémaction* 34 ('Sembène Ousmane'), 1985, p. 64.
50. Interview with Imunga Ivanga, Paris, 1995.
51. Interview with Drissa Touré, Ouagadougou, 1995.
52. Interview with Samba Félix Ndiaye, Paris, 1996.
53. Serge Daney, 'Qu'est-ce qu'elles se disaient?', in *La Rampe*, Cahiers du Cinéma/Gallimard, Paris, 1983, p. 121.
54. Sony Labou Tansi, *La Vie et demie*, Le Seuil, Paris, 1979, p. 124.
55. Ababacar Samb Makharam, interviewed by Pierre Haffner in Pierre Haffner, *Kino in Schwarzafrika*, Institut Français de Munich, Munich, 1989.
56. Betty O'Grady, 'Le parler–écrit: L'exemple de Tchicaya U'Tamsi', in Anny Wynchank and Philippe-Joseph Salazar (eds), *Afriques imaginaires: regards réciproques et discours littéraires, 17ème–20ème siècles*, L'Harmattan, Paris, 1995, p. 262.
57. Interview with Sotigui Kouyaté, Paris, 1998.

NINE

'IF YOUR SONG IS NO IMPROVEMENT
ON SILENCE, KEEP QUIET!'[1]

> Lumumba
> Like rumba, conga!
> Lumumba
> Like rumba, Congo!
> Tchicaya U Tam'si[2]

**In music, dance, sound and song Africa expresses its difference. But do
we know how to listen?**

DANCES OF RESISTANCE

When the footballer Roger Milla danced a few *makossa* steps after scoring a
World Cup goal for Cameroon, and when Nelson Mandela began to dance
as the election results which made him the first black President of South
Africa came through, was this simply because they have 'natural rhythm' or
were they, as Célestin Monga suggests, asserting a claim to dignity?[3] Dance,
like laughter, is here the assertion of a resistance, of a difference, a rejection
of discipline. The visceral, fleshly aspect of African music today is in fact
based on a history of suffering and struggle: 'My dance and my laughter,
crazy dynamite, will explode like bombs in your faces', wrote Léopold Sédar
Senghor.[4]

How can we explain why the most famous Zaïrian musical double-act of
recent years has involved a fat man and a dwarf? In disturbing the supposed
norms of the social order, Pépé Kallé and Emoro express a rediscovered
freedom and originality in both their music and their bodies. It was they –
together with Papa Wemba – who assured the success of the film *La Vie est
belle* (Ngangura Mweze and Benoît Lamy, Zaïre/Belgium, 1985). In that film
a young singer and musician mingles humour, charm and resourcefulness to
make it big in Kinshasa. Another comedy – the first Zimbabwean full-length

feature film, *Jit* (1990), directed by Michael Raeburn, a Rhodesian who went into exile in opposition to the Ian Smith regime, and returned at Independence – describes, to the *jit-jive* rhythm of Oliver Mtukudzi, one of the country's most famous musicians, the farcical efforts of the young UK to amass the dowry for a pretty girl against the wishes of an ancestral spirit. The film was a great hit in Zimbabwe.

Are we to see these two musical comedies' relaxed attitude and unconcern for realism as indicating a purely commercial intent? Combining humour, rhythm, music and satire, they certainly have all the ingredients for real popular success. But, as Ngangura Mweze points out,

> Popular films aren't necessarily commercial films. They work to set formulas, using sex and violence, etcetera! I think it's possible to make films about things everyone enjoys in everyday life. The messages can come later from those who analyse the films![5]

The idea for *La Vie est belle*, he says,

> came to me when I was waiting for a bus one day and a young man at the bus stop was telling a really crazy story about a servant who'd borrowed his employer's suit to impress a woman he was chasing. Everyone laughed as they heard the story. A girl was listening and they went off together in the end, the young man having used the story to get off with her! I said to myself: why should I just stick to traditional plot-lines?

TALKING DRUMS

Léopold Sédar Senghor gave indications as to which instruments were to 'accompany' his poems, hence defining the atmosphere he wanted to be created. If Idrissa Ouedraogo turned to the Cameroonian composer Francis Bebey to write the music for *Le Choix/Yam Daabo* (1986) and *Yaaba* (1989), he did so to contribute to the emotional dimension of those narratives.[6] On the other hand, for *Tilaï* (1990) he turned to the South African Abdullah Ibrahim (Dollar Brand) to achieve a jazz ambience, opening the film out to a wider world.[7] However, straitened finances often prevent real attention being given to music, and the danger then is that it will appear to have been simply tacked on to the film. 'You mustn't fall into the trap of using the music you enjoy listening to', says the Mauritanian director Abderrahmane Sissako. 'Then the music forms a kind of screen in front of the image. It prevents you from seeing, and is no longer an element of the drama.'[8]

When the music is right for the visual content, there is a sense of formal collusion. In a scene from *Hyenas/Ramatou* (1992), Djibril Diop Mambety uses music and choreography from a Senegalese rite of exorcism in which

Musician Wasis Diop and stylist Oumou Sy on the set of *Hyenas/Ramatou* (Djibril Diop Mambety, Senegal, 1993). © Félix von Muralt/Lookat.

the person is soaked in the blood of a sacrificed animal and washed, using steeped roots, beside a river as the drums send him into a trance.[9] Might the viewer unfamiliar with this reference merely read this as pleasant music? Certainly not. Just as they will be sensitive, in their own way, to the symbolism of the shot which shows a woman in a red pagne dancing opposite a bull which is going to be put to death, they cannot but appreciate the fit between the original function of the music and the expression sought in the film.

Hence music is never gratuitous. When it comes from a traditional source, it contributes to the film's aim of perpetuating memory. When the film describes a painful reality, the music plays its part in conjuring away the anxiety and the difficulties. Supporting the director's intentions, it even turns out at times to be truly subversive, as in the case of reggae, which expresses the need of oppressed peoples for freedom. It then becomes 'a weapon' in the service of change. As the title of one of the most famous albums by Nigerian musician Fela Ransome Kuti has it, 'Music is a Weapon.'

Music *speaks*, like those talking drums which send coded messages from old, forgotten languages.[10] Fadika Kramo-Lanciné reminds us of this in the opening shots of *Wariko/The Jackpot* (Ivory Coast, 1993) when he opens his film with subtitled drumming:

> The talking drum welcomes you:
> Anouka! Good evening!
> Moh klona! Thank you!
> Mougnan gnoan moutié.
> Come and hear the message.
> Moutié, moutié, moutié.
> Listen, listen, listen.

The use of an instrument may go far beyond mere accompaniment. The Dyula drum we hear in *Keïta, l'héritage du griot* (Dani Kouyaté, Burkina Faso, 1995) illustrates the legend of Sunjata, and signifies: 'So long as one is alive, one must go on fighting.' Similarly, André Gardies cites the example of the molo which is heard at the end of *L'Exilé* (Oumarou Ganda, Niger, 1980) when Sadou sacrifices himself: 'Culturally, this tune is played in honour of the death of chiefs. But this sequence also marks the end of the film. The molo provides a lament here to a threefold disappearance: the disappearance of the chiefs, of the film and of authentic speech.'[11]

THE SONG OF THE PEOPLE

Music adds an independent connotation to the spoken language of the film, doubtless complementing it in African films more actively than it does in Western cinema where, as sound mixer Dominique Hennequin remarks, 'spoken language conveys 98 per cent of the information'.[12] And for purposes of greater 'legibility', songs are often foregrounded. Far from being there merely to add exotic colour, they make a collective statement on behalf of the people which thus becomes a key character in the film, situating the anecdote from the outset as part of the collective experience. When, in *Visages de femmes* (Désiré Ecaré, Ivory Coast, 1984), we are following the commonplace story of a husband jealous of the romance between his wife N'Guessan and his brother Kouassi, the song of the dancing, laughing women elevates the argument joyously into one of women's liberation. These women's song accompanies the story, explaining to the viewer what he can otherwise only surmise from the unspoken dimension of the images:

> They left,
> Kouassi to go to his village,
> N'Guessan to her mother's,

> But the villages were very close together,
> Less than a kilometre, they say.
> So she spent most of her time
> In Kouassi's arms.
> And her husband came to hear of all this.

The women strike their hands on the ground in rhythm with their song, alternating the palms and the backs of the hands, as though telling a child a story. After N'Guessan is more and more roundly accused by her husband in the following shots, they stand up to clap their hands in a circle, with each woman in turn dancing in the centre:

> Men never have faith in us.
> Yet there are so many trustworthy women.
> Yes, so many trustworthy women.
> Men don't know how to appreciate that.
> They see wrong everywhere.
> Especially where there is none.
> What does a man who has no faith in you deserve?
> He deserves only one thing.
> What's that?
> To be cheated.
> Yes, to be cheated!'

One woman stays in the middle of the circle and dances, joyfully singing:

> I'm going to tell you what I do to mine,
> That husband who's always spying on me, suspecting me,
> Follow me and you'll see life.

There then begins that long and much-criticized love scene in which N'Guessan and Kouassi are filmed in a river, showing an abandon which echoes the women's song. Although the husband later sets a trap for his wife by dressing like Kouassi to catch them at their usual trysting place, the women have earlier come to an opposite conclusion:

> Do you think the husband will suspect anything?
> He'll swallow everything you tell him.
> Everything. All you tell him.

The women are not greatly troubled that they get this wrong, for their songs traditionally represent a chance for them to let their hair down and tell of their daily suffering. They are not consciously imagining another life. By coolly depicting adultery and, later on, economic success and the use of karate for self-defence, the film is clearly calling on the women to react against the abuse they are subjected to.

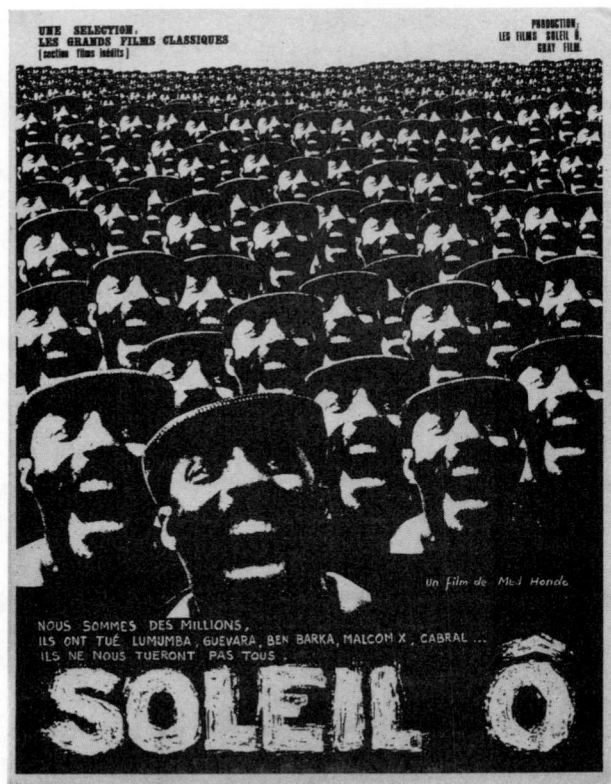

Poster for *Soleil ô*
(Med Hondo, 1969).

By removing the need for heavy, didactic statements in films of this kind, song, which is originally a product of the popular 'voice', provides a new outlet for that voice. These sung pauses in the story, these rhythmic halts in which the story is reflected on once more, sit easily with the form of film narration. Here cinema makes it possible to achieve something which is difficult in literature, where any message stated as clearly as this assumes a ponderous, overdirect quality. It is no doubt this limitation on the novel which is responsible for the desire the Kenyan writer Ngugi Wa Thiongo has repeatedly expressed in articles to follow in the footsteps of Sembène Ousmane and take up cinema in order to put the people on stage.

In *Soleil ô* (Med Hondo, 1969), a song is heard over shots of a café pinball table:

Some men have flown away, Apollo,
To the moon in search of summer days, Apollo,
Going where others have feared to go, Apollo,
But their song has had no echo, Apollo,
Leaving the Earth and its misery.

I don't know why, Apollo,
They went flying so high, Apollo,
Did they want to acquire, Apollo,
A diamond or a sapphire, Apollo?
Leaving the Earth and its misery.

Without passports, they left home, Apollo,
Heading for the great unknown, Apollo,
Couldn't stay under orders, Apollo,
Within our narrow borders, Apollo
Leaving the Earth and its misery.

But the fighting is still rife, Apollo,
On the Earth between the tribes, Apollo,
And there's hunger coming now, Apollo,
In the cities all around, Apollo,
On this Earth with its misery.

Love is there, with outstretched arms,
Why leave when we cannot heal?
The immensity which dazzles with its might,
Day and night.

A Gambian kora player, Foday Musa Suso, also wrote a song at about this same time in which the word 'Apollo' recurred as a leitmotiv at the end of each line:[13]

Ah, *dindin ka nyin*, Apollo,
Ah, the young woman [lit. 'child'] is beautiful, Apollo,

Dindin kunsinyi ka nyin, Apollo,
The woman has beautiful hair, Apollo,

Dindin kan fala ka jan, Apollo.
She has a beautiful long neck, Apollo

Dindin nyin kese ka ge, Apollo.
She has lovely white teeth, Apollo.

In both cases, whether mentioned in relation to immigration or to love, the fascination exerted by the moon landing of the Apollo spacecraft in 1968 makes it possible to raise the tone to an almost cosmic level. Immigration was, incidentally, presented earlier in the film using a 'voiceover': 'Sweet France, I am whitened by your culture, but I remain thoroughly black, as at the beginning. I send you greetings from Africa.'

Song thus attains to a symbolic dimension, opening up to an emotionality which is further reinforced by the music. As is stressed in the prologue to *Xew xew/La Fête commence* (Cheikh Ngaido Ba, Senegal, 1982), music in Africa is always 'a unifying force'. In that film, music, in the form of the group Xalam, enables parents to bridge the generation gap dividing them from their daughter. Similarly, at the end of *More Time* (Isaac Meli Mabhiwka, Zimbabwe, 1992), in which an adolescent girl discovers that love may, in this age of AIDS, mean gambling with her life, a rap song picks up the moral of the film: that you should give yourself more time for your love-making. The message is encapsulated in rap rhythms so that it no longer seems like the old refrain of yesterday's generation.

AFRICAN SOUND

An ochre-hued desert extends across the full width of the screen. The camera moves towards it gently, enabling us to pick out the cracks where the earth has been eroded, the geological strata, the valleys. The sounds become clearer, too. At first we hear only running water, then a diffuse drumming; but the sounds grow louder, with animal cries and human voices. A *komo* text is displayed on the screen (*komo* is the Bambara secret society): 'The world is a mystery, an incomprehensible mystery. Life is a mystery, an unfathomable mystery.' Between image and sound, the world is there, with all that it contains: men and animals, trees and stones. And, the better to locate his narrative in time – 'the convulsive present of Africa, its past of misery and magic, its inevitably better future'[14] – Souleymane Cissé has the grandmother in *Waati* [Time] (1995) relate a causal account of the origins of the world. Here, once again, the sound illustrates the fragmentation effected by time, but also possible reunification. The film locates apartheid within the wider split in the universe and seeks – through a woman, Nandi – the reconciliation of those who ought never to have separated: human beings and the creatures of nature.

The music and the soundtrack find a rhythm which corresponds to the perfect *kara* circle drawn on the screen at the opening of the film. Similarly, in the films of Djibril Diop Mambety, music binds the shots together into a vital cycle. In *Le Franc* (1994), a jazz saxophone accompanies 'the dream of an Africa great and free' of the hero of the poster that is pinned to the winning lottery ticket, and competes with the muezzin's call to prayer; an *a cappella* voice mingles with the wind and the buffaloes to illustrate the garbage of all kinds; and the shots are linked into a kind of Baroque symphony by the sound of the congoma, the voice of a troubled, pathetic inner loneliness.

Two film-music sleeves: *Aiye* (Ola Balogun, Nigeria, 1980, based on the famous Yoruba theatre play by Hubert Ogunde, who also wrote the music) and *Ceddo* (Sembène Ousmane, Senegal, 1977, with music by Manu Dibango).

Djibril Diop Mambety acquired this extreme sensitivity to sound in his childhood:

> I grew up in an area called Colobane, where there was an open-air cinema called the ABC. We were very young, eight years old, and not allowed out at night because the area was dangerous. But in spite of this we escaped and went to the cinema. We had no money to buy a ticket, so we listened to the films from outside. They were mainly Westerns and Hindu films.... Maybe that is why I attach a lot of importance to sound in my films, as I heard films for a number of years before I saw them.[15]

To indicate fear and stifling oppression, filmmakers are quick to return to that primal rhythm, the beating of the heart. Senegalese cineaste Clarence Delgado uses this device twice in *Niiwam* (1992): first when Thierno and his wife enter the morgue to recover their son's body, and later when a bus passes a hearse coming out of a mosque. Sembène Ousmane had pointed the way in the text on which the film is based: 'Fear enveloped him, he was suffocating. He felt he shared this suffocating feeling with Niiwam. His heart beat louder and louder.' In *Tumult* (1996), the Ethiopian director Yemané Démissié uses the impossible escape of a revolutionary after a failed *coup d'état* to illustrate the harsh history of his country. As the vice tightens around the hunted man, the beatings of his heart accompany, at some length, his last stirrings of life.

'A baobab will never be a cherry tree. You can't have a European vision of time, light and sound in Africa', says Sarah Maldoror. 'I'm very sensitive to African sound, which you don't find anywhere else. Let's respect African sound!'[16] One good way to do this is to leave the image entirely to that sound, for the seriousness of the gaze often imposes silence. How can we forget the hands of the women in Flora M'Bugu Schelling's *These Hands* (Tanzania, 1992), breaking rocks all day long on the edge of quarries where enormous machines do the same work? The commentary is sparse, and at times nonexistent, fading out to leave only the women's singing.

African cinema tells us, then, that we can gain not only from looking at Africa, but also from listening to it. For, as Jacques Attali reminds us, a society speaks more through its noises and music than it does through its statistics.[17] When the images speak for themselves, what is the point of overlaying them with commentary? That commentary happily gives way to street sounds in Idrissa Ouedraogo's *Ouagadougou, Ouaga, deux roues* (1984), a ballet of images on the two-wheeled traffic of Burkina Faso's capital. This is a wordless documentary, as are those celebrations of traditional handicrafts *Les Ecuelles* (1983) and *Issa le tisserand* (1984):[18]

These were impressions, shots, images driven by an idea, because at the time I was wanting to make film which was socioeducative in character, targeted at an audience that was 90 per cent illiterate. That meant a style of cinema in which the image was preponderant, which could be easily understood by an audience speaking forty-two different languages.[19]

Easily? Does not Ouedraogo's work already prefigure the current pursuit of a documentary form in which the absence of commentary compels viewers to make their own effort of interpretation? Being required to read an image without the intermediary of words discourages viewers from having their eyes glued too tightly to reality, and encourages them to respect a distance which forces them to think. We are a long way here from militant documentary and *le cinéma direct*.

When, thanks to this silence, the sounds of life become music once again – when, in *Les Malles* (1989) by Senegalese director Samba Félix Ndiaye (a documentary in his gripping *Trésors des poubelles* [Treasures of the dustbins]) series, the hammering of metal drums lends a rhythm to the film in the manner of the African 'talking drum' – an obvious but moving fact emerges: above and beyond the extraordinary African skill which is able to transform tar barrels into painted trunks decorated in sparkling colours, what is asserted here is a different temporality of objects. In that world, and in contrast to our consumer society, another logic applies, a dance between one function and another, which is reminiscent of that waltz of objects the Georgian director Otar Ioseliani treated fugally in *Favourites of the Moon* (1984).

Whereas, in Western cinema, the image too often forgets the sound – '*écoutons-voir ce cinéma qu'on n'entend pas!*'[20] – in African cinema it has some happy surprises in store for us: a joyous irony, as in the use of the piece of classical music which gets stuck in the opening sequences of *Contras'city* (Djibril Diop Mambety, 1968) against images of buildings of the colonial period; a hybridized counterpoint when Bouna Medoune Seye records the sounds of the Paris metro to illustrate scenes shot in the Senegalese capital for *Rouge-feu*; a healthy derision when the voice of Josephine Baker repeats in an endless loop the illusion of a fascination with the West – 'Paris, Paris, this little corner of Paradise' – in Mambety's *Touki-Bouki* (1974).

For the meanings of things and situations can appear only when they are linked to the harmony of their sound envelopes. In a screenplay which is still in search of a producer, *Le Train bleu* by the Senegalese director Joseph Gaye Ramaka, the locomotive of the train in question is made up of women, the drumming of percussion instruments and the hissing of tenor and alto voices. These are all so many elements which will give flesh to the train, for in an African culture, Ramaka points out, 'flesh and music intermingle, whereas in the Judaeo-Christian religious sphere the praise of God had to be extracted from the sinful body; therefore, the music had to be cut away from its fleshly envelope.'[21] It then becomes a question of transcribing in the film how sound, the body and movement are structured in the head. 'Making cinema', Ramaka goes on, 'means going out to meet my mental structure.'

NOTES

1. Quoted by Adama Drame and Arlette Senn-Borloz, *Jeliya: être griot et musicien aujourd'hui*, Paris, L'Harmattan, 1992, p. 342.
2. Tchicaya U Tam'si, *Le Ventre*, Présence Africaine, Paris, 1978, p. 143.
3. Célestin Monga, *Anthropologie de la colère: société civile et démocratie en Afrique noire*, L'Harmattan, Paris, 1995.
4. Léopold Sédar Senghor, *Oeuvre poétique*, Le Seuil, Paris, 1990, p. 224.
5. Interview with Ngangura Mweze, Cannes, 1996.
6. The famous writer, poet and composer/performer Francis Bebey made a brilliant foray into cinema in 1974 with *Sonate en bien majeur*, the moral trials and tribulations of an immigrant in Paris.
7. Jacques Samé, 'Entretien avec Idrissa Ouedraogo', *Le Film Africain* 22, November 1995, p. 8.
8. Matthieu Krim and Jean-Pierre-Garcia, 'Rencontre avec Abderrahmane Sissako', *Le Film Africain* 22, November 1995, p. 8.
9. Interview with Jean-Servais Bakyono, Abidjan, 1995.
10. For a transcription of the language of drums, see Birgit Akesson, *Le Masque des eaux vives: danses et chorégraphies traditionnelles d'Afrique noire*, L'Harmattan/UNESCO, Paris, 1994, pp. 169 ff.
11. André Gardies, *Cinéma d'Afrique noire francophone, l'espace miroir*, L'Harmattan, Paris, 1989, p. 157.
12. 'Entretien avec Dominique Hennequin', *Cahiers du Cinéma*, special number 'Musiques au cinéma', 1995, p. 80.
13. See Wolfgang Bender, *Sweet Mother: Modern African Music*, trans. Wolfgang Freis, University of Chicago Press, Chicago and London, 1991, p. 20.
14. From the text of a press release on *Waati*.
15. June Givanni, interview with Djibril Diop Mambety, in *African Conversations*, British Film Institute/Screen Griots, London, 1995.
16. Interview with Sarah Maldoror, Paris, 1996.
17. Jacques Attali, *Noise: The Political Economy of Music*, University of Minnesota Press, Minneapolis, 1985.
18. These films are already on the way to being fictionalized documentaries. It was at the point when he realized that cinema, given its current resources, would never reach rural populations that Idrissa Ouedraogo turned to purely fictional filmmaking.
19. 'Interview with Idrissa Ouedraogo, *Cahiers du Cinéma* 423, September 1989, p. 8.
20. Noel Akchoté, 'Écoutons-voir ce cinéma qu'on n'entend pas', *Cahiers du Cinéma*, special issue 'Musiques au cinéma', 1995, p. 100.
21. Interview with Joseph Gaye Ramaka, Paris, 1996.

TEN

SPEAKING YOUR OWN LANGUAGE

> he ka bo ni bue
> ni tala banda
> ni tala londe
> na ku makanga
> ni dingi dingi
>
> Maxime N'Debeka[1]

A major contradiction: Africa has many languages, but Africans do not read subtitles. Which language do you choose to reach a particular audience? And what if the most important thing were emotion and respect for plurality?

THE EXPRESSION OF LIVED EXPERIENCE

In *Aube noire* (Djingarey Maïga, Niger, 1983), Omar comes back to Niger to work, accompanied by his new wife Jeannette from Togo. She can communicate only in French, and translation is required for some members of the family. Incomprehension and religious differences make the integration of this 'unsuitable' woman impossible. In Black Africa, language and religion are factors of extreme diversity, whereas in the north of the continent they are pillars of unity: 'North African cinema has a considerable advantage over the cinema of Sub-Saharan Africa', notes Idrissa Ouedraogo, 'the unity of language.'[2]

Whereas classical Arabic is so imprinted by the Koran that it is the language of God, and does not afford the possibility of intimate incursions into the fantasies of human beings, the French which African writers discovered at school displays – in novels, for example – a form of first-person singularity. If Arab-speaking writers choose to use French, they do so because it allows them to use 'I', which is so out of place in a divine

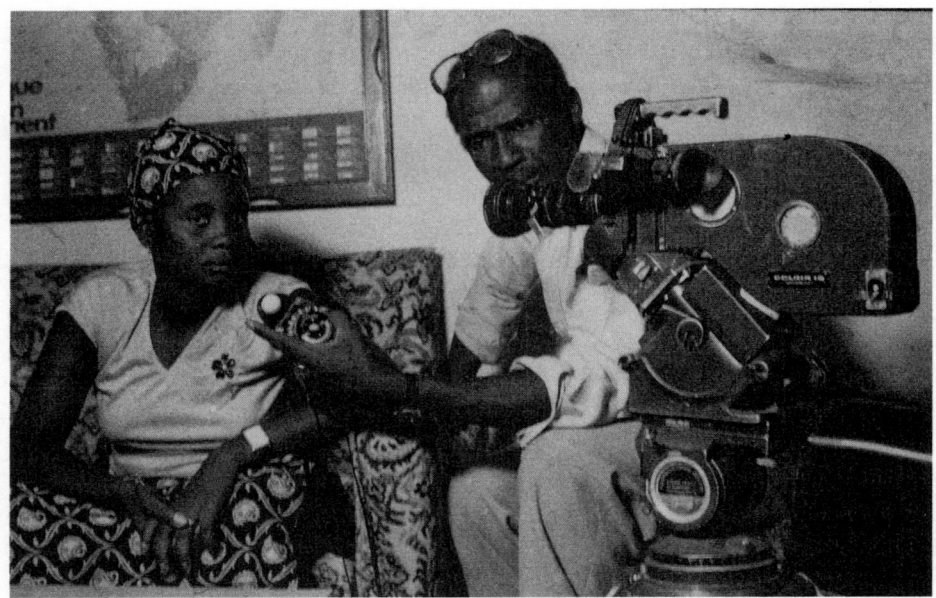

Kadidia Babi and Djingarey Maïga on the set of *Aube noire* (Niger, 1983).

language. There is no great wrench involved in leaving their mother tongue behind and slipping into a language which allows them to express desire, doubt and the flesh, and hence to exist as individuals.[3] For a writer or filmmaker from Black Africa, the division is more often seen in terms of historical and social experience: Amadou Hampâté Bâ wrote his autobiography in French to express a vision of the world characterized by colonial experience, but he retained the use of Fula to transcribe texts from the oral tradition. Similarly, in a play like Wole Soyinka's *Death and the King's Horseman*, 'each world', as Alain Ricard notes, 'speaks its own language, but the stereotyped language of the colonial administrator's humanitarian goodwill stands opposed to the dense and subtle language of the horseman and his griot, expressing the central values of a culture of solidarity and sacrifice which administrative philanthropism cannot grasp'.[4] Thus, in this play the British speak English, the soldiers pidgin; while the villagers, the horseman and the griot speak an artificial language reproducing Yoruba linguistic diversity, from the poetry of the griot to the popular, satirical language of the marketplace.

As a result of subtitling, cinema is free of the linguistic artifice required by theatre. Each person speaks his or her own language, and this has a realistic ring to it. The problem is that whereas subtitles are no discouragement at all in the art cinemas of Europe, the African audience does not read them. 'I am a doctor of letters and of cinema, but I don't like subtitles because I can't read and watch the film at the same time!' says Ivorian Kitia Touré.[5] 'We are told', he goes on, 'that making a film in French means alienating African culture to the French language. Bullshit!' The Ivorian urban public is more used to French as an everyday language than many other countries, but what Kitia Touré is rejecting here is an argument about being in thrall to the colonial tongue. He is not out to deny the past, but one has to realize that one is the product of one's history. When Congolese writer Sony Labou Tansi was asked if French was a foreign language in Africa, he threw back the question, asking if Coca-Cola, Toyota or the wearing of khaki were foreign to Africa? 'The fact that we have been colonized – and that includes being colonized in our language – is part of our history', says the Nigerian Funmi Osoba. 'English is the language I speak best. It's better to film in the language I'm most at home in!'[6]

A REVISITED FRENCH

After all, French and English are no one's property. They belong to all who use them. You can't make an omelette without breaking words… Following the pragmatic guidelines laid down by Léopold Sédar Senghor, Maxime N'Debeka and Sony Labou Tansi laid claim to French as the language of their poetry, not hesitating to manipulate it as they saw fit ('writing distract-edly').[7] Med Hondo asserts a similar claim: 'It has become my language and my tool. I sweated blood to acquire it, and no one's going to take it away from me. It wasn't a gift, it was an achievement.'[8] The important question is what you do with the language. 'Even though I am a user of French', he goes on, 'I don't feel any calling to become an activist for the French language.'

The inhabitants of Africa's cities did not wait for artists to show them the way before taking over the language of their former masters. The ritualization of speech takes on a new form here, with symbolic references shifting towards cultural stereotypes and individual fantasies that combine caricature and mythic images. The urban French of Cameroon used in *Quartier Mozart* (Jean-Pierre Bekolo, 1992) is a good example of this. The writer David Lehn has drawn up a list of some of the expressions used, and condensed them into a highly personal lexicon:

Bordelle (s.f.): woman of little virtue, or even less.

Caroline (of Monaco) or *Lady* (Diana): commonplace reference to be thrown into a conversation as and when necessary. Can be used for any purpose.

Chose: (1) *Faire la chose*: no need to draw you a picture. (2) *Je m'en vais coucher pour moi ma chose tranquille*: I'm just off to bed.

C'est un dix heures dix: his feet turn outwards like the hands on a watch showing ten past ten.

Est-ce que nous sommes des drapeaux?: are we salsify, dustbins, rags, burst tyres, for you to go by without paying us any attention and without coming to say hello, you rude thing?

Grand frère: (1) Todger of the real man, the man with real balls. (2) Policeman's gun, whether the officer in question has balls or not.

Gérer: to conduct a romantic affair with a woman to its most complete physical fulfilment.

Gombo: a scheme, a good plan or undertaking with low costs and big dividends. And that's really all you need to know about it, my darling.

Chaud gars: he has the hots for women. He's very resourceful and always primed for action.

Mesure préservative: latex device, currently the height of fashion.

Un garçon est mort le jour où il est né: he's a man, and a man has no reason to fear death (he's already passed that way; he has nothing more to fear).

Mettre du sable dans le riz de quelqu'un: to disturb or annoy someone, spoil his plans.

Mettre de l'huile jusqu'à faire le sous-marin: to drown food in oil, glug-glug, till, hey, it's completely disappeared!

Où est la télévision qui est souvent là: African litotes for 'always'.[9]

Jean-Pierre Bekolo worked long and hard on these expressions for his film, in order to exclude anything which might be seen as 'pidgin', as incorrect turns of phrase, though they are, of course, merely produced by spontaneous translation into French from African languages.[10] In its day, Amos Tutuola's acrobatic syntax gave rise to a real debate on the quality of his prose before the Nigerian author was recognized as a talent to rank alongside such writers as Joyce. The strength of his work lay, in fact, in his adapting English to Yoruba syntax and constructions. The value of a film like Henri Duparc's *Bal Poussière* (Ivory Coast, 1988), filmed mainly in French, also lies, as Jean-Pierre Garcia writes, in 'the inventiveness and originality of its reworking of the French language'.[11] There is a great deal of punning in the film, much of it harbouring meanings which go far beyond words. Beneath a caustic humour, we can see a sharp analysis of social relations:

'Chilli pepper, what an aroma! It must be as powerful as our friend Demi-dieu. I can't sleep at night for thinking of the old rogue with his six wives!'

'You know, that's all about food. In the citrus fruits, there's vitamin C. Have you heard of vitamin C? In meat, it's vitamin M and peppers have vitamin P. When you eat sugar you get vitamin S. S for strength. So you see, these European languages aren't stupid. And Demi-dieu's nobody's fool! Do you know why he's always eating bananas? That's vitamin B! That's for bonking!'

This hinterland of language is no doubt more marked in Africa, where apparently simple statements often require several levels of interpretation. This means that we have to go beyond a mere word-based aesthetic and be attentive to the African context if we are to escape oversimplified notions of purely ludic wordplay. When, in 1995, an Abidjan taxi-driver greeted the tip I gave him as 'a contribution to overseas aid', his humour evoked the harshness of the devaluation of the local currency, the CFA franc.

FAILING TO REACH YOUR AUDIENCE?

The use of French seemed natural to the first Francophone filmmakers. Whereas the Belgian and British colonialists had accepted African languages in their primary schools, the French had chosen their language as sole vehicle of education, strictly excluding African languages. In this they were merely reproducing what they did at home, where the French tongue had an official existence, but Breton and Basque did not. It was when he showed his first films to village audiences that Sembène Ousmane became aware of the language problem:

> My attitude then was that there was nothing wrong with imposing the French language on the films, because the French language was a fact of life. But on the other hand, the peasants were quick to point out to me that I was the one who was alienated, because they would have preferred the film in their own language, without the French.[12]

Choosing French or English, a move which is often justified by the concern to use a lingua franca to break out of the narrow linguistic boundaries of most African languages, can mean that you don't reach your audience. 'To reach a broad African audience', says Senegalese director Ahmadou Diallo, 'I have to film in French, but it's a double-edged sword: in Senegal people won't go!'[13] In similar vein, Françoise Balogun notes that whereas Nigerian films in English have difficulty pulling in an audience, films in Yoruba enjoy considerable success.[14] Does this mean that if a filmmaker wants to reach an African public he has to work in its language? Although the Nigerian market is big enough for films in vernacular languages to be profitable, this is the exception in Africa, where a single national territory often covers several major language areas. As Justin K. Kakambega, chief executive of Sonacib (Société nationale d'exploitation et de distribution cinématographiques du Burkina Faso), points out: 'As the Mossi (who speak Mooré) often have some grasp of Dyula, a film in Dyula will be easier to market than a film in Mooré, which can be shown only on the Mossi plateau.'[15] This does not mean that no subtitled African films perform well outside their own language areas, but such successes are often linked to the fame of the director or the popularity of the subject.

PRIORITY TO THE EMOTIONS

Is it not preferable, then, to accept the existing linguistic pluralism, and for everyone to stay in the language closest to them? In *Waati* (1995), the actors speak in their mother tongues. The film moves from southern to West Africa and the languages spoken include Zulu, Sotho, English, Afrikaans, French, Bambara and Tamashek. 'I've always been concerned in my films', says Souleymane Cissé, 'to respect the languages in which people express themselves. It's my intention to allow people to convey their emotions naturally. This is what gives a film its power.'[16] With the actors speaking the language of their own culture, the fit between word and action guarantees lively dialogue, natural attitudes and truth of emotion.

Whereas it might seem natural to film in French in an Ivorian urban context, for example, to many other filmmakers this would seem anachronistic. 'I can't film in French', says Raymond Rajaonarivelo from Madagascar. 'It isn't my culture. France isn't where I spent my childhood, it isn't where I felt the wind on my feet or in my hair. It isn't where I saw the landscape.'[17] Both for actors and for the director, language is a factor of authenticity. Once again we are invited to 'listen to' the image: 'There is something strange, something magical, about editing a film when you don't understand the language it's in', says editor Andrée Davanture. 'You pay attention to lots of signs; you aren't taken in by a direct understanding of the text. You're forced to look!'[18]

When language is used in an authentic way, it reveals the social hierarchy, real or mystified. *An be no don* (Falaba Issa Traoré, Mali, 1980) is a film shot almost entirely in Bambara, but the trial of Aminata takes place in French, a language she does not understand. In African films, characters often have to ask civil servants who address them in French to speak in their own language. In *Finzan/A Dance for the Hero* (Cheikh Oumar Sissoko, Mali, 1989), for example, the village headman asks the new district commissioner to speak to the village in Bambara. In *Xala* (Sembène Ousmane, 1974), El Hadji, with the weight of his patriarchal authority behind him, argues with his daughter in French, while she replies in Wolof. However, when, at the end, he wants to give the members of the Chamber of Commerce a piece of his mind, he asks to be allowed to address the meeting in Wolof. In reply, he is told that the only language of business is French, and he is called 'racist, sectarian and reactionary'. As the chairman adds, 'Even insults will be made in the purest French-speaking tradition.'

OPENING UP TO MULTICULTURALISM

Beneath the choice of language lies the question of communication. 'The man in a hurry bites his own tongue', says old Inazel in *Le Médecin de Gafiré* (Mustapha Diop, Niger 1983). In that film the new doctor, Karounga (Merlin N'Diagne), who believed only in white medicine, becomes the disciple of the healer Ouba (Sidiki Bakaba). But what language is he to use to pass on his knowledge? 'When will they stop believing in a single truth, a single cosmos? How can I speak to them?' Whereas the conflict between Karounga and Ouba might be a mere clash between tradition and modernity, the film develops a different theme by way of a parallel story which brings together the village sage and his adopted son in a field with a large shea tree towering over it:

'Is this the day, old Inazel?'
  'This is the day, Gaoussou.'
  'At last I'm going to know my father.'
  'This is your father's field. This shea tree is your father.'
  'What?'
  'Yes, he sees you, he hears you.'
  'I don't understand.'
  'Don't try to understand. Accept that truth for what it is! When your father died, we buried him here. We planted seeds in his belly. Only those who have done more good than evil in their lives can be born again like your father. I'll leave you, Gaoussou. Speak to your father. He will reply. Perhaps you will not understand him. Be patient. It takes time to understand the language of the dead.'

Karounga learns patience in order to understand the language of the dead – of his ancestors – not in order to move from one type of knowledge to another, but in order to cross-fertilize his culture. Drawing a higher strength from this self-enrichment, he defeats the poison Ouba has made him take. The village headman can cry out at the end: 'Now the disciple has outstripped the master.' In this way the value of intercultural hybridization in solving the problems of modern times is demonstrated. Many contemporary African artists have called for the development of this kind of synergy. One such is Wole Soyinka, the Nigerian Nobel Prize laureate: 'In Africa we are inheritors of several languages, and I think we should celebrate in our work this two- or threefold heritage.'[19]

IS DUBBING THE ANSWER?

If the costs were not so high, the dubbing of films into the main African languages (Hausa, Fula, Dyula, Swahili, Lingala and Arabic) would greatly facilitate their distribution.[20] As for dubbing into French, aid monies are available from the 'Agence de la Francophonie' (former ACCT),[21] but these have not been much used: whatever the language chosen, the distribution of African films ought to be done on a regional or subregional scale, but this is not yet the case. Television channels sometimes dub their films. This should, however, be done by African actors. Then we would not have actors with Parisian accents appearing on African television screens, as happened with Idrissa Ouedraogo's *Yaaba* (1989)!

This raises once again the eternal question of respecting the Other's culture. When it was presented in Africa, *Le Ballon d'or* (Cheik Doukouré, Guinea, 1993) astonished the audience. Although it was filmed mostly in French – a necessary lingua franca for a film which began in the north of the country in the Malinké region, and moved round eventually to Conakry – the producers demanded that the African voices be dubbed on the grounds that the African accent was incomprehensible. 'The work was altered beyond recognition!' exclaimed the director.

> This is part of the difficulty of opening up to Africans who are supposed to have been educated in French culture. When Japanese people speak, they are allowed to do so in their own language because we are not on conquered territory there. The African is a noble savage; he is underdeveloped, and so, therefore, is his cinema![22]

SAVE THE ACTOR!

The small quantity of films produced in Africa means that there are few roles for African actors. In Europe, they are confined to playing the 'Black'. 'The West uses us more for our colour than for our talent', observes Cameroonian actor Gérard Essomba.[23] Confined to stereotyped roles which conform to European imaginings, they play supporting or minor characters: the actress Darling Legitimus from Martinique, who created the first black actors' company in Paris in 1933, had to wait until the age of seventy-six to be given a leading role, the part in *Rue Cases-nègres* (Euzhan Palcy, 1983) for which she won 'Best Actress' at the Venice Film Festival. Black actors run up against the persistence of colonial conceptions. 'European theatre directors can't seem to understand that there are black women who speak with a French accent', says Cameroonian actress Félicité Wouassi, 'just as in the

On the set of *Hyenas/Ramatou* (1992). © Félix van Muralt/Lookat.

USA there are little black boys who speak American!'[24] Incredibly, Alex Descas was criticized for not being a black man in *Le Cri du coeur* (1994). 'The distributors and exhibitors tell me he doesn't have the basic attitudes of an immigrant, and that it won't be acceptable!' rages Idrissa Ouedraogo.[25]

Given the shortage of roles in both theatre and cinema, actors often make the move to the other side of the camera, while continuing to work as actors when they can. The Ivorians Sidiki Bakaba and Mory Traoré, the Guineans Cheik Doukouré and Mohamed Camara, and Umban Ukset from Guinea-Bissau are all in this position. Strong links with the theatre still exist. Many directors began their careers on the stage, including the Ivorians Timité Bassori, Désiré Ecaré and Henri Duparc, the Mauritanian Med Hondo, the Senegalese Djibril Diop Mambety and Moussa Sene Absa, the Cameroonian Daniel Kamwa, Philippe Maury from Gabon and Dani Kouyaté from Burkina Faso. Actors are still being pushed towards directing by the shortage of roles. 'I set up a little production company to be able to work on projects which interested me and which I wasn't necessarily being offered by directors', says Ivorian actress Brigitte Hanny Tchelley.[26]

African actors often criticize directors for upstaging them – a point which the Senegalese director Moussa Sene Absa concedes: 'African directors have crushed their actors – undermining them, preventing them from becoming stars by speaking on their behalf. The Fespaco [Ouagadougou Festival] programme doesn't even list actors' names! African cinema gobbles up actors!'[27] Admittedly, actors are rarely given prominence in the promotion of a film: no 'star system' operates in the search for an audience – except in Nigeria, where the success of some films is based on the fame of the stars of Yoruba theatre (Françoise Balogun managed to ensure the success of *Ajani-Ogun* by drawing on Duro Ladipo's company of actors).

The films are not written for actors, and filmmakers, wary of overtheatrical poses or rigid acting styles, often prefer to use non-professionals. 'In the beginning', confides Souleymane Cissé,

> I wanted to give the major roles to actors from Malian amateur theatre. I soon found we didn't have the same conception of acting, that their acting did not suit my films. Since that first experience I looked to the interior of Mali for people who don't know anything about cinema, who have never acted. Spontaneous people, with no narcissism, who meet my needs.[28]

Djibril Diop Mambety filled the leading roles for *Hyenas/Ramatou* (1992) with people from the bars of the port of Dakar, including Aminasa Diakhaté, who was impressive as the old lady, Lingeer Ramatou. 'When Djibril introduced me to the woman who was going to be the great princess', says his

Abdoulaye Komboudri

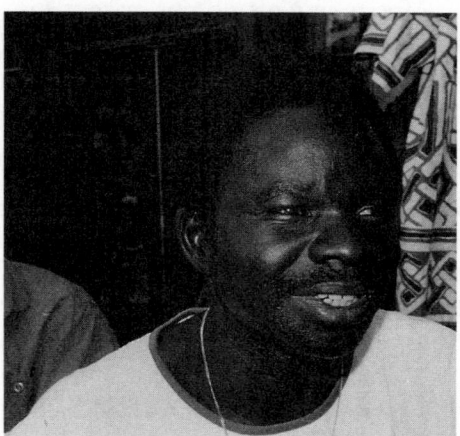

Habib Dembele

Naky Sy Savané

brother Wasis Diop, 'he just said, "Tell her the plot as though it was a folktale".'[29] The leading actress in this adaptation of a play by Friedrich Dürrenmatt could not even read.

However, as Idrissa Ouedraogo says, 'they are people who give of themselves to us spontaneously, who can at times and in some cases bring off something remarkable, but you have to admit they are not actors'.[30] As a result, filmmakers have to be highly skilled at directing actors, since physical resemblance to a character is no substitute for acting experience. 'The central character in *Rue Princesse* was played by a non-professional', says Henri Duparc. 'We rehearsed until things were ready. Then I did two takes per shot – no more.'[31] It is absolutely not a question here of imitating European acting. 'We speak with more life', says the Ivorian actress Naky Sy Savané. 'In European cinema, the actors often seem to us to act like robots!'[32]

African customs do not make it easy to establish a 'star system': it is regarded as impolite to approach people and it is difficult, as a result, to advertise one's talents as an actor. African actors do not have agents like their European counterparts. They complain of being badly paid, and indeed a legendary actress like Zalika Souley from Niger has never been paid more than 500,000 francs CFA for a role![33] 'One cannot make a living from art in Africa: we know the films are made on small budgets and we accept low wages', says the actor Abdoulaye Komboudri, from Burkina Faso, with regret. 'But our strength', he continues, 'is the general warmth. I am loved. I get help when I'm in trouble. There are difficulties, but on the set we're one big happy family. On the ground, it's still Africa!'

'The star system and media coverage are our aim! The public has to come to see the actors they like. It's the image of the actor we should sell', exclaims Burkinabè actress Georgette Paré, who, since 1997, has been running 'Casting Sud', an association in Abidjan which produces promotional directories of actors for each of the countries of the region.[34] It is understandable that African actors should dream of the kind of star system which exists in the West, or in India or Egypt, even though the number of beneficiaries of such systems is small. A real 'star system' would require a cinema industry and enough films to enable the actor's image to become fixed in the public mind. It would also need magazines to maintain the myth on- and off-screen. But what is the nature of this fascination? Is it the myth of the star that African actors are interested in, or the desire to be able to do their jobs as actors in better conditions? Do African actresses dream of being those 'syncretic personalities' described by Edgar Morin, in which you can't distinguish between 'the real person, ... the person fabricated by the dream factories and the person invented by the spectator?'[35] Do we find in Black African cinema those ruthless women who seem to be driven by some inner compulsion, those extraordinary destinies in which revolt against the taboos of morality and the established order produce a tragic loneliness? As we have seen, directors with a tendency to foreground social reality are after a different order of myth, though this does not preclude actors and actresses from being appreciated by their public today.

The relationship with the actor is of another order here, as is clearly seen by those who have not let success go to their head. 'Human beings are like the five separate and different fingers on a hand', says Naky Sy Savané. 'You are always in the middle. You aren't before or after the others. Fame passes. You have to keep your feet on the ground!'[36] The actors draw this attitude from their roots: 'Before acting in a film', says the Benino–Ivorian actor Isaac de Bankolé, 'I need to recharge my batteries, to go back to my family, to the working-class district where I lived, to meet up again with the people I love and who I can chat with about anything and everything. This gives me renewed confidence to face new challenges.'[37]

The warmth of the public can become a problem, because in some cases identification with the characters lasts after the film has ended! Ivorian director Kitia Touré tells how, after the actor Bamba Bakaré had played a character who was HIV-positive, some former acquaintances had shunned him.[38] Playing a prostitute in the early years of her career had given Naky Sy Savané similar problems.[39] In *Denko* (Mohamed Camara, Guinea, Short Feature Prize, Fespaco 1993), a woman makes love to her blind son to restore his sight. The woman who agreed to the incest in the film did not want it to be shown in her native region.

It can even be dangerous to be an actor on a film set! Sidiki 'Sijiri' Bakaba from Ivory Coast tells how, during the making of his feature film *Les Guérisseurs* (1988), in which he was himself playing a drunkard, some of the extras started chasing off this dangerous madman who was disgracing them on the set...[40] And in a scene in which Joseph Kumbela, the star of *Gito l'ingrat* (Léonce Ngabo, Burundi, 1992), ran off into a market, the people there took him for a real thief and raced after him. The actor had to be rescued![41]

NOTES

1. Maxime N'Debeka, *La Danse de N'Kumba ensorcelée*, Publisud, Paris, 1988, p. 7. The author gives no translation of his Bantu language in this book: he simply allows the words to speak for themselves by their rhythm and phonic qualities. This simplicity and clarity of the sign are at the opposite pole from what we call exotic. No exoticism is to be got from signs which operate only through the

imaginary. To be able to develop the alien – whether creature or thing – as the backdrop to our desires, fantasies, utopias or dystopias, we need the *image* of the savage, the barbarian and the primitive, the impression of the jungle and a 'dark continent' or a sandy beach studded with palm trees and bamboo huts. (Hans-Jürgen Heinrichs, '*Sprich deine eigene Sprache, Afrika!': von der Négritude zur Afrikanischen Literatur der Gegenwart*, Dietrich Reimer Verlag, Berlin, 1992, p. 33.)

2. 'Rencontre avec Idrissa Ouedraogo', *Le Film Africain* 9, p. 4.
3. See Mohamed Kacimi El Harani, 'Langue de Dieu et langue du Je', *Fractures*, 1994.
4. Alain Ricard, *Littératures d'Afrique noire, des langues aux livres*, Karthala–CNRS, Paris, 1995, p. 210.
5. Interview with Kitia Touré, Abidjan, 1995.
6. Intreview with Funmi Osoba, London, 1994.
7. Sony Labou Tansi, 'Foreword', *La Vie et demie*, Le Seuil, Paris, 1979, p. 9.
8. Ibrahima Signaté, *Med Hondo, un cinéaste rebelle*, Présence Africaine, Paris, 1994, p. 82.
9. David Lehn. This text was communicated to the author by Jean-Pierre Bekolo.
10. Interview with Jean-Pierre Bekolo, Paris, 1995.
11. Jean-Pierre Garcia, *Le Film Africain* 14, p. 19.
12. Sembène Ousmane, interview with Kwate Nee Owo, quoted by Lizbeth Malkmus and Roy Armes, *Arab and African Film Making*, Zed Books, London, 1991, p. 171.
13. Interview with Ahmadou Diallo, Paris, 1995.
14. Françoise Balogun, *Le Cinéma au Nigeria*, OCIC–L'Harmattan, Paris, 1984, p. 46.
15. Interview with Justin K. Kagambega, Ouagadougou, 1995.
16. 'Entretien de Clément Tapsoba avec Souleymane Cissé', *Écrans d'Afrique* 7, 1994, p. 10.
17. Interview with Raymond Rajaonarivelo, Paris, 1995.
18. 'Entretien de Françoise Balogun avec Andrée Davanture', in *Cinéma et libertés*, Présence Africaine, Paris, 1993, p. 120.
19. Interview with A.R. Abeokuta, quoted by Ricard, *Littératures d'Afrique noire, des langues aux livres*, p. 176.
20. I am drawing here on an idea dear to Cheikh Anta Diop, who saw these as possible linguae francae of a future federal Africa.
21. Agence de Coopération culturelle et technique, an international body for the promotion of the French language overseas. Interview with Robert Lombaerts, Paris, 1995.
22. Interview with Cheik Doukouré, Paris, 1996.
23. 'Entretien de Clément Tapsoba avec Gérard Essomba', *Écrans d'Afrique* 13–14, 1995, p. 18.
24. Alessandra Speciale, 'La triple galère des femmes africaines actrices', *Écrans d'Afrique* 7, 1994, p. 27.
25. Interview with Idrissa Ouedraogo, Ougadougou, 1995.
26. 'Entretien de Lamine Saad et Mathieu Krim avec Brigitte Hanny Tchelley', *Le Film Africain* 21, August 1995, p. 17.
27. Interview with Moussa Sene Absa, Paris 1995.
28. From Rithy Pahn's film *Cinéastes de notre temps: Souleymane Cissé*, 1991.
29. 'Entretien de Lucien Patry avec Djibril et Wasis Diop', *Films et documents* 378 ('Perspectives et réalités du cinéma africain'), December 1991–January 1992, p. 25.
30. Interview with Idrissa Ouedraogo, Paris, 1995.

31. Interview with Henri Duparc, Ouagadougou, 1995.

32. Naky Sy Savané, press conference, Fespaco, Ouagadougou, 1995.

33. Ali N'Keury N'daw, 'Zalika, star des films nigériens', *Écrans d'Afrique* 5–6, 1993, p. 31. 500,000 FCFA = approximately £500.

34. Interview with Georgette Paré, Namur 1998, published in *Africultures* 12, L'Harmattan, Paris, 1998.

35. Edgar Morin, *The Stars*, John Calder, London, 1960, p. 105.

36. Naky Sy Savané, press conference, Fespaco, Ouagadougou, 1995.

37. 'Entretien de Clément Tapsoba avec Isaac de Bankolé', *Écrans d'Afrique* 13–14, 1995, p. 24.

38. 'Entretien de Françoise Balogun avec Kitia Touré', in *Cinéma et libertés*, Présence Africaine, Paris, 1993, p. 83.

39. Speciale, 'La triple galère des femmes africaines actrices', p. 29.

40. Sijiri Bakaba, 'Devant, derrière le caméra', in Fédération Panafricaine des Cinéastes (FEPACI), *L'Afrique et le centenaire du cinéma*, Présence Africaine, Paris, 1995, p. 354.

41. Léonce Ngabo tells this story in *Cinés d'Afrique*, a documentary directed by G. Debroise, S. Interlegator, O. Lichen and Samba Félix Ndiaye.

ELEVEN

TOWARDS A CRITICISM
BASED ON THE NEED TO EXIST

I've never read what's been written about *Hyenas*. I'll do it when my head is clear. Let me relate an anecdote. It's the story of a man sentenced to death. Just before the blade of the guillotine falls, a telegram arrives. He says, 'Put it in the basket, I'll read it when my head is clear.'

Djibril Diop Mambety

Western criticism is prey to every conceivable prejudice. The state of African cinema means that we ought to look to subjectivity to identify a film's need to exist, quite apart from the comparison with our own cinema.

THE WESTERN DIKTAT

When Hollywood took over the colonial stereotypes of Africa, they went into the making of some forty Tarzan films over a seventy-year period. Today, Hollywood is more likely to offer liberation films in which Blacks are upstaged by white liberals. *Cry Freedom* (Richard Attenborough, 1987), for example, shifts the focus from black leader Steve Biko to a white journalist, Donald Woods, wrestling with his conscience. Françoise Pfaff has shown how such a strategy is directed at achieving commercial success, but is not a demystification of African realities.[1] If Western cinema is not grappling with that particular agenda, the cinema cultures of Black Africa certainly are attending to it, but they lack an audience.

Even what are generally regarded as the most thoughtful newspapers sometimes publish some amazing value judgements on African film. Abderrahmane Sissako was angered when *Libération* discussed his film *Octobre* (1992) in terms of its director's 'charm'.[2] And in the *Cahiers du Cinéma*, Charles Tesson, writing about *Yeelen,* summed up 'what gives African cinema its charm and irreducible otherness: it is a cinema of origins, naive and primitive'.[3] This is almost beyond belief. 'Authenticity', 'ingenuousness', 'natural-ness', 'naivety' – the clichés rain down from sloppy journalists in a hurry, who can't be bothered to take more trouble over their writing.

The reception in France of *Le Cri du coeur* (1994) by the Burkinabè direc-tor Idrissa Ouedraogo was highly revealing in this context. Ouedraogo, a filmmaker with a fine reputation for the quality of his 'African tales' (*Yaaba, Tilaï, Samba Traoré*), ventured to Lyon to film the relationship between an immigrant child (Saïd Diarra) and a hard-bitten drifter (Richard Bohringer), who none the less opens up to him. The director has acknowledged that his film may have certain faults – it 'may perhaps be too demonstrative'[4] – but he is saddened that it has been judged against his earlier work. The critics were disappointed by a camera 'which did not manage to recover its African grace',[5] and advised him to 'have a serious rethink and take up again a path he has made his own'.[6] This African ought to make 'African films', and not 'leave the landscapes and villages of his homeland', since he so 'enchant[ed] us in his previous films'.[7] The film, which was released in only two Parisian cinemas, had total audience figures of just 1,180 in its first week.

Do French directors get told to make 'French' films? 'People say our cinema doesn't develop because we're always doing the same thing', says the Guinean Mohamed Camara, 'but when I do something different they tell me it's not African enough!'[8] The relationship to artistic creation in the countries of the South is still terribly marked by a neo-colonialist attitude in which artists are required to show 'authenticity'. This attitude takes the form of a stunning ignorance of the existence of contemporary art in those countries, and the rejection of any autonomous expression which does not correspond to Western 'exotic' expectations. A painter like the Indonesian Dede Eri Supria depicts scenes of life and survival in Djakarta with great verve. Despite his crucial influence in his own country, and the success he enjoys there, Western art lovers criticize his 'Westernized' style, which they see as being too close to American pop art.[9] An Indonesian should produce Eastern art…

When you seek to confine the Other to his or her difference, there is nothing special to say about him or her which can be coherent. It is in order to sidestep this demand for cultural difference, which slips surreptitiously into film criticism, that young directors living in Europe reject the term 'African filmmaker' with such vigour. 'I thought I was becoming a filmmaker', said the Guinean David Achkar, who died in 1998,

> and the colour of my skin made me an African filmmaker from the very outset.…
> So a particular kind of criticism keeps me in a particular sort of academicism, a style, a tone, a way of filming. I would advise the critics concerned to go back to

the cinema and see that Sembène has never made a village film.... We are up against a great deal of ignorance. Which critics go to the Fespaco?[10]

TOWARDS A SUBJECTIVE CRITICISM

On the other hand, when an African ventures to evoke magic as the cultural expression of an ancient knowledge which is able to cast light upon the present – a magic in which he himself declares that he does not believe[11] – Western critics see this as a 'majestic mystery, inducing contemplation'.[12] Souleymane Cissé rails against this perception of *Yeelen* (1987): 'It is a profoundly political work in which you have to get beyond the surface of the image.'[13] *Yeelen*, the first African film to receive the Jury's Special Prize at the Cannes Film Festival (1987), has at times been regarded as inaccessible and at others praised to the skies as a masterpiece of African cinema. None of this has led, however, to a real understanding of the film: 'Everyone told me "It's very fine", and that was the end of it because no one had understood.'[14] The critics, fascinated by the film's symbolic power, mostly liked it, as did the general public, though it remained difficult of access. It would have been logical and positive for them to have attempted to understand it. However, as Nixon K. Kariithi shows in his critique of the errors committed by Western critics in their attempts to explain the film, it was not so much the – ultimately understandable – lack of knowledge of African traditions that was the problem as the incapacity to read a foreign film without applying their own interpretative grids.[15]

It is the very process of criticism that is at issue here: it is tempting to apply an analytical method to a film rather than to give free rein to one's subjectivity by asserting a personal opinion which translates the emotion one felt when viewing it. Sheila Petty observes that if you apply a feminist or psychoanalytic grid to reading *Hyenas/Ramatou* (Djibril Diop Mambety, 1992), you find you are confronted with problems of interpretation which can hide the real meaning of the film.[16] Only personal subjectivity can attempt to perceive the deep cause of the film, its real 'need to exist', not its objective genesis. Filmmakers draw that 'need to exist' from their culture, experience and deep knowledge of their own situation. This is where the emotional power of a work and its topicality meet. Critics must allow space for improvisation!

Here again, however, the road to hell is paved with good intentions. A widely shared tendency is to apply a universal reading, to the detriment of the culture one is trying to explain. 'At what point does the universality of a theme reveal itself to be the product of a cultural misunderstanding?' asks

Stéphane Malandrin.[17] In 1992, Mohamed Camara made *Denko*, his first short. In order to break the curse on him, a mother sleeps with her blind son in order to restore his sight. Camara was praised for his astute reversal of Sophocles' *Oedipus Rex*. 'It begins as a dialogue of the deaf', says Malandrin. 'The listener takes over the speaker's words to hear what he already knows. The person telling the story in a sense loses paternity of the images he invents, because the person hearing asserts that he already knows them.' It is this misunderstanding which makes it impossible to grasp the spirit of a work, to take what the filmmaker attempted to put into it, not what you think you recognize in it. It would be better to allow oneself willingly to lose one's bearings, to let oneself be carried along by emotion, to replace a deductive approach by an intuitive perception of the film, and let oneself learn what the Other is teaching that is new. Respect for a different cinema requires this detour if we are to avoid liking it for what it is not – and if we are not to prevent it from existing as what it is.

THE DEAD WEIGHT OF CRITICISM

The realist option adopted by African cinema is said to have taken it down a road which is often denounced as monolithic, excluding ambivalence and representation through an appeal to stereotypes. Michel Serceau asserted only recently that as a result of African cinema's rejection of modernity, genres and the *cinéma du réel*, the African spectator was dispossessed of the specificity of his own gaze: 'he is called upon to do nothing less than espouse the filmmaker's view'.[18] Basing his argument on what he regards that cinema as *not* being, on what it 'refuses' to import from the West, Serceau deduces that African film lacks its own system of representation. By freeing itself from the narrative modes imported from the West, however, Black African cinema cultures could, according to André Gardies, open up to 'an imaginary anchored in African cultural reality'.[19] Is this not precisely what they are doing? Taking on the contemporary history of the continent, they are questioning at every step a relationship to self which combines disorientation and an appetite for life, and a relationship with the West experienced both as dream and as nightmare. The result is a fragmented pursuit of self-knowledge and self-assertion opening out to a cross-fertilization within Africa and, subsequently, with the rest of the world.

Delicately balancing an African audience force-fed on television films and B-movies with a Western 'art cinema' audience which is itself ambiguous, but wants ambivalence in its films, African filmmakers are moving beyond didacticism in the documentary sphere to develop a certain inwardness; in fiction, they are achieving forms of play on identification which open up a new system of representation. It is tempting for academics and Western critics to lay down a set path for this development, a path read off quite sincerely from their own way of conceiving cinema, which is, in many cases, characterized by the elaboration of allegedly universal systems. We must hope that these cinemas will be able to develop a modernity based on what they are and not on what others would like them to be. For this to happen, some genuinely African theoretical reflection on cinema is needed. The secretary general of FEPACI, Gaston Kaboré, calls for precisely such thinking:

> We tend no longer to decode ideas, but just to repeat them, as though they were part of us. Africa is either oversimplified or made so complex that it amounts to the same thing! If we are not to remain tied to simplistic equations, anthropologists, sociologists and academic intellectuals will have to write about cinema in order to nourish it! Unfortunately, most of the existing books were written by Western critics who are not unaffected by their own social history.[20]

Let us not forget that, on the pretext of imposing correct French, a particular kind of literary criticism and certain publishing houses have – as the Zaïrian Pius Ngandu-Nkashama points out – forced African authors into self-censorship 'on the fallaciou pretext of correcting grammar, thus forcing us to shift what might be considered the "fundamental truth of the text" into another register'.[21] This is to regard 'Africanisms' as a misuse of language! Anything that did not fit into the 'correct' style of writing taught in the schoolroom was rejected as misuse, error, mixing of registers, interferences, and so on.

This 'critical dead weight', which is still so present in Western periodicals, has a directly political effect. Anything that does not conform to Western narrative norms is regarded as incorrect. Any deviation is an error. 'African directors as a whole have great difficulty in constructing their narratives properly', wrote Daniel Serceau in 1985. 'The sense of concision and ellipsis, the question of repetition, the arrangement of dramatic effects are so many elements making up the cinematic narrative which they have not really mastered.'[22] Although things have moved on today, this permanent comparison with the Western norm is still widespread in the approach to the whole of African creative art. While that art is often regarded as superfluous – though critics rarely dare to put it in such terms – there is praise for the Africans' efforts to 'catch up'. What is the point of throwing off paternalistic condescension if comparison with the West is not discarded too? 'Rule number one', wrote Éric Libiot, 'is not to talk about African cinema as "minor and imperfect, but so nice". Rule number two: don't hesitate to

shout out loud and clear that some African films are worthless.'[23] I can feel
that a film is worthless if it seems artificial or gratuitous. If, on the other
hand, its sincerity has not achieved the standards in vogue in my kind of
cinema, is that a reason to deny the need for the film? 'Perhaps we are not
yet free enough in our heads', writes editor Andrée Davanture, 'to spot in
the stumbling progress of these difficult beginnings the aspirations to a real
freedom.'[24]

AFRICAN CRITICISM

In 1979, the pioneer of African film criticism, Paulin Soumanou Vieyra,
wrote of *Baks* (Momar Thiam, Senegal, 1974):

> The film was ill-conceived and poorly prepared. The filmmaker's aim was to
> denounce the damage done by *yamba* (cannabis). And yet the audience found itself
> confronted with a glorification of the drop-outs who smoke that drug with such
> sensual delight that they make you want to try it![25]

Stressing the contradiction between a realist approach and educative intent,
Vieyra here conforms to the moral norm. Could he have done otherwise,
had he so wished? He himself emphasizes the impossibility of 'expressing
political opinions contrary to the doctrine of a regime: they would not get
past the censor'.[26] African criticism will thus acquire a real freedom of
opinion only with the emergence of a non-state press linked to the democratic openings of recent years.

African criticism finds it very unfortunate today that it can intervene only
after opinions about films have already been forged in the West. Where the
films of Black Africa are concerned, it criticizes Western critics for not
differentiating between the origins of films, when African cultures and
experiences are many and varied. There is broad agreement within African
criticism that value judgements and peremptory affirmations from the West
are to be rejected in respect of a culture African critics can claim to know
better and interpret more accurately. Taking a position as a necessary intermediary between the film directors and their audience, those critics generally
stress the primacy of the African audience and attempt to contribute to
training that audience to decipher images. They are, however, aware that
written criticism does not make much of an impact in Africa, whereas 'word
of mouth' is effective, being responsible – according to a survey commissioned by Sonacib (Société nationale de distribution cinématographique) in
Burkina Faso – for the choices made by 47 per cent of those questioned.[27]
African critics, concerned that African cinema should make a breakthrough

with the African public, are often wary of films which give pre-eminence to formal innovation which the cinema-going public will not understand; though on the other hand they do not tend to denigrate them. Convinced that Africans can only transpose into images an African culture and reality which are their own, the critics are quick to attribute the deviations they perceive – avant-gardism or exoticism – to a desire to please Western audiences or the concern to meet the expectations of financial backers.

'An African fiction cinema', says the critic Clément Tapsoba from Burkina Faso,

> has to be based on cultural and social realities. If the film talks about the audience, the audience will embrace it. That audience is subject to many influences, but it remains attached to its values. They love to talk about the social situation, and are amazed if a European who has come to Ouagadougou for Fespaco knows nothing of the country's political situation after spending a week there![28]

The perception of the cinema-going public is crucial: 'People feel drawn in by a linear or logical structure and find it hard to grasp non-classical structures.' The Ivorian critic Jean Servais Bakyono, in contrast, is sensitive to the disruptive tendencies in film écriture, but remains open to all discourses: 'In my criticisms, I borrow a little from everywhere. The fact that I've been a literary critic helps me to reread films. Music, too, is a help, as is the tradition of folktale and initiation.'[29] In his analysis of Les Guérisseurs, for example (Sidiki Bakaba, 1988), he brings out the five musical themes in the film (sung by Sori Kandia Kouyaté, Salif Keita, Nayanka Bell and Alpha Blondy) and relates them to the five main characters, thus reinforcing the ideas which underlie the narrative.[30] In Bakyono's view, a press article must not discourage the public from going to see a film, but may urge them to go and see it right away! It attempts to answer the questions the public is asking itself by analysing the filmmaker's aesthetic: 'In Africa, film criticism is not received in the same way as in Europe, where they put a mark against it and say "Not that one!" We'll often encourage people to go and see films, but the good films are seldom shown here!'

African criticism is, admittedly, extremely diverse, but it often presents the public as a supreme judge that is to be trained in the reception of images. It does not confine itself, however, to the transmission of a *knowledge*. It is rare for articles to be purely descriptive of a film, subjecting it to scholarly analysis. They are often accounts of emotional responses. There is a personal involvement, appealing to a perception beyond any spirit of system. If a critical distance is still maintained, it is on the level of an individual retranscribing his or her own perceptions, an individual whose opinion, because it is personal, may have exemplary status. This open attitude implies a favourable predisposition towards film, for the cinema cultures of Black Africa are still finding their way. The critic aims to participate in this experimental dynamic, both in extolling the filmmaker's approach to the spectators and as a mouthpiece for the public and its views.

It is in this context that the debate on the avant-garde comes down to a debate on the film's need to exist. African critics, who have been of one mind in praising works which are as innovative as those of the Senegalese director Djibril Diop Mambety, make a distinction between formal experimentation done for its own sake – a kind of narcissistic 'art for art' which they reject in Western cinema as being merely an aesthetic of the beautiful – and a true avant-garde of creation, in which formal disruption is able to express content – an approach whose *originality* lies in a questioning of origins without artificiality or gratuitousness. 'What does avant-garde mean?' asks Djibril Diop Mambety. 'It could indicate that man who, even before dawn, gets up to meet the sun while others continue to slumber. That is to say, he who is not satisfied and who is still searching; it is a perpetual search, a thirst impossible to quench.'[31]

NOTES

1. Françoise Pfaff, 'Hollywood's die-hard jungle melodramas', in Fédération Panafricaine des Cinéastes (FEPACI), *L'Afrique et le centenaire du cinéma*, Présence Africaine, Paris, 1995, pp. 194–9.
2. Michel Amarger, 'Les cinéastes africains et la presse se mettent à table', *Écrans d'Afrique* 12, 1995, p. 39.
3. Charles Tesson, 'Genèse', *Cahiers du Cinéma* 397, June 1987.
4. 'Entretien de Carlos Pardo avec Idrissa Ouedraogo', *Libération*, 8–9 April 1995, p. 35.
5. Olivier de Bruyn, 'Hyène de vie', in *Les Inrockuptibles* 4, 5–11 April 1995.
6. P.M., *Le Monde*, 6 April 1995.
7. C. Helffer, *Le Monde de l'Éducation*, May 1995.
8. Mohamed Camara, press conference, Fespaco, Ouagadougou, 1995.
9. Jutta Ströter-Bender, *L'Art contemporain dans les pays du 'Tiers monde'*, trans. Olivier Barlet, L'Harmattan, Paris, 1995, p. 176.
10. Interview with David Achkar, Paris 1997, published in *Africultures* 5 ('Jeunes créateurs africains'), L'Harmattan, Paris, 1998.
11. Souleymane Cissé, quoted in Ignacio Ramonet, 'Yeelen ou la magie des contes', *Le Monde diplomatique*, December 1987.
12. Bernard Genin, 'Le Voyage du fils', *Télérama* no. 1977, 2 December 1987, p. 31.
13. From an interview with Souleymane Cissé by Philippe Elhem and Claude Waldmann, *Cinergie* 1987.
14. 'Entretien de Marc Lalanne et Frédéric Strauss avec Souleymane Cissé', *Cahiers du Cinéma* 492, June 1995, p. 5.

15. Nixon K. Kariithi, 'Misreading Culture and Tradition: Western Critical Appreciation of African Films', in FEPACI, *L'Afrique et le centenaire du cinéma*, pp. 166–87.

16. Sheila Petty, 'Whose nation is it anyhow? The Politics of Reading African Cinema in the West', in ibid., pp. 188–93.

17. Stéphane Malandrin, 'Les cinémas africains en résistance', *Cahiers du Cinéma* 492, June 1995, p. 61.

18. Michel Serceau, 'Le cinéma d'Afrique noire francophone face au modèle occidental: la rançon du refus', in Nwachukwu Frank Ukadike (ed.), *Iris, revue franco-américaine de théorie de l'image et du son* 18 ('New Discourses of African Cinema'), Spring 1995.

19. André Gardies, *Cinéma d'Afrique noire francophone. L'Espace miroir*, L'Harmattan, Paris, 1989, p. 174.

20. Interview with Gaston Kaboré, Ouagadougou, 1995.

21. Pius Ngandu-Nkashama, *Écriture et discours littéraires. Études sur le roman africain*, L'Harmattan, Paris, 1989, p. 272.

22. Daniel Serceau, 'Emitaï: L'échec d'une transposition dramatique', *Cinémaction* 34 ('Sembène Ousmane'), 1985, p. 43.

23. Eric Libiot, writing in *Première* on the release of *Hyenas/Ramatou* (Djibril Diop Mambety, 1992), a film he welcomed with great emotion: 'Rule number three: don't hesitate to shout out loud and clear that *Hyenas* is a gem.'

24. Andrée Davanture, 'Une indépendance nécessaire', in FEPACI, *L'Afrique et le centenaire du cinéma*, p. 391.

25. Paulin Soumanou Vieyra, 'La critique, la critique africaine et la critique de la critique', in *Réflexions d'un cinéaste africain*, OCIC, Paris, 1990, p. 173.

26. Ibid., p. 171.

27. Clément Tapsoba, 'De l'orientation de la critique du cinéma africain', in FEPACI, *L'Afrique et le centenaire du cinéma*, pp. 157–63.

28. Interview with Clément Tapsoba, Milan, 1996. Tapsoba is editor of the journal *Écrans d'Afrique*, and secretary-general of the Burkina Faso Cinema Critics' Association.

29. Interview with Jean-Servais Bakyono, Abidjan, 1995. Writing as Francis Bagnon, he regularly publishes criticism in the Abidjan daily *Le Jour*.

30. Jean-Servais Bakyono, 'L'Afrique des sages', *ID* 911, 24 July 1988, Abidjan, Ivory Coast.

31. June Givanni, Interview with Djibril Diop Mambety, in *African Conversations*, British Film Institute/Screen Griots, London, 1995, p. 31.

PART III

BLACK PROSPECTS?

PART III

TWELVE

'HE WHO WANTS HONEY HAS THE COURAGE TO CONFRONT THE BEES': THE DIFFICULTY OF MAKING FILMS[1]

We have to fight the death of life, because it is more odious than the death of individuals.

Sony Labou Tansi[2]

Making films in Africa is a gamble, yet it is one that people take! The director turns into a one-man band, and low budgets and the unforeseen problems of production also have their effects. Inevitably, this produces fantasies of autonomy.

THE TRIALS AND TRIBULATIONS OF FILMING

Whereas the other arts become an industry only after the point of creation, film, like television, has the ambiguous privilege of being so from the outset.[3] The cinema cultures of Black Africa do not, in the main, have the good fortune as yet to have a genuine cinema industry in their own country.[4] Is this wholly unfortunate? For a filmmaker to make a film is a tremendous ordeal, but the films that are made often gain a density that is the product of sheer necessity. The danger, on the other hand, is that a single film is overloaded in its content as a result of the director's poor prospects of making another. An account of the hurdles to be got over in making a film would merit a book in itself.

There are many filmmakers who can make films only as a second-string activity, or must have a second job in order to make a living. The Mauritanian Med Hondo earns his living by dubbing the black voices in American films. The Ivorian Fadika Kramo-Lanciné publishes catalogues and advertising brochures, and Drissa Touré from Burkina Faso works as a packer to pay his rent. The aim of each is to survive so that they can continue to write and film. Many African directors are producers, editors, properties men, trainers,

Near Timbuktu, on the set of *Waati* (Souleymane Cissé, Mali, 1995).
© Françoise Huguier.

and so on, or make videos and films on commission. *Soleil ô* (1969) was made at weekends, using reels of film bought by Med Hondo out of his wages as the filming went along. Djingarey Maïga from Niger cannot film outside Niamey for lack of resources. All the transporting of actors and equipment is done in his car. 'I'm an average worker living in a poor area of Niamey', he says. 'Every morning I see what's going on. That's what I want to put on film.'[5] His latest film, *Miroir noir*, finished in 1995, was filmed in 1985:

> I had wanted to stress the themes of democracy and polygamy, but scenes filmed ten years ago had lost some of their currency. I had to cut them at the editing stage. When I'd submitted the screenplay, the Niger Ministry of Culture had promised me financial assistance. It never arrived and I had to wait...

It took Malian director Souleymane Cissé four years to make *Yeelen* (1987) and seven years to finish *Waati* (1995). Five weeks after shooting had begun on *Yeelen* in November 1984, it was interrupted by terrible sandstorms. These were so prolonged that the crew had to break up. Two months later, just as they were able to begin again, the main actor, Ismaïla Sarr, died of a heart attack. Then, to cap it all, the film stock which Fuji had given them turned out to be out of date, and they had to start all over again. Shooting began again in November 1985. Six weeks later, the French cinematographer got a whitlow which became infected, and he had to be flown back to Paris as an emergency.

The realities of Africa have to be taken into account at every stage. In *Waati*, when the fleeing Nandi is discovered on the river by the South African police, everyone has to dive into the water to escape. Cissé tells the story of how his assistant came to find him: 'Souleymane, there's a problem. The actors can't swim!' As for Lineo Tsolo, the non-professional actress who played Nandi, she refused to crawl along the ground: '"You crawl to get away from the police, to avoid them seeing you, to dodge the bullets!" "No, I won't." The argument went on like this, but she didn't give in. It was, as they say, only a film. But for her it meant humiliation. In real life she would rather be shot than crawl on the ground!'[6]

The practical problems of filming in Africa are unimaginable for Europeans. Actors aren't on the telephone. How do you get in touch with a PO Box in an emergency? And when custom demands that they should be present at a wedding, should you let them go? African cars are 'tired'; the power goes down when there are storms or surges of current blow the lights; generators are unreliable or inordinately expensive; transport is chaotic and exhausting; there are constant breakdowns in all things mechanical; the light is infernal; the technical resources are inadequate; the political and customs authorities are irksome; and illness is never very far away... But a solution can always be found!

Ivorian director Jean-Marie Koula tells how, when he was assistant direc- tor on *Djeli* (Fadika Kramo-Lanciné, 1981) and they were filming in the north of the country, the camera operator wanted beer even though alcohol was not allowed. The conflict became embittered and in the end he went back to Abidjan, taking with him the camera, which belonged to the tele- vision station and which he had charge of. They had to go and find him there.[7]

As the films are often made with mixed crews, the presence of European technicians can pose specific problems. Not the least of these is adjustment to the climate. But the effects of collaboration are generally rewarding for all concerned, as it means pooling experience, teaching each other new skills, and discovering Africa. The opposite, however, can also be the case. 'After *Muna moto*', says the editor Andrée Davanture,

> we wanted to give Jean-Pierre Dikongué Pipa the resources he needed, so we managed to get three French technicians for the crew of *Prix de la liberté* [1978]. I recommended a cinematographer who had a great sense of light and who had

A Cinafric lorry (Ouagadougou African Cinema Company) on the set of *Samba Traoré* (Idrissa Ouedraogo, Burkina Faso, 1992). © Félix von Muralt/Lookat.

worked all over the world. There were weaknesses in Dikongué Pipa's screenplay, but you felt that these could be sorted out. However, the team of French technicians were unbearable. They were narrow-minded, sectarian and stupid, and they approached things with the attitudes they might have had if they had been working at Gaumont. They were unable to understand the difference in the situation, and criticized everything that wasn't done their way. The director had the ground completely cut from under his feet. The cinematographer didn't even want to view the rushes! At that point I questioned everything I was doing, and I almost chucked it in. I'd been extremely naive. The cinematographer was totally unwilling to take on board the difference in the situation, on both artistic and economic levels, and his remarks were incredibly aggressive. When Dikongué Pipa came to edit his film, he wasn't the same man he had been with *Muna moto*. I understood the hurt he felt. I felt horrendously guilty, and the editing was a terribly painful process.[8]

The low level of budgets involved very often forces directors to operate in 'one-man band' fashion. *Cendres et soleil* (Canada, 1994), Stéphane Drollet's film about the Malian director Falaba Issa Traoré, shows how he produces, directs, edits and distributes his films himself. The titles of Djingarey Maïga's films (Niger) are simple because he does everything: screenplay, image, direction, editing. 'What I would like would be to have a producer so I could concentrate on directing', says Drissa Touré from Burkina Faso. 'You're always trying to do two things at once. It's exhausting.' For Kitia Touré from the Ivory Coast, however, that concentration of tasks has some beneficial aspects: 'You need two hands so that the one can wash the other!'[9] Yet there are limits to what can humanly be done: 'I'm going to make a fifth film, then I'm stopping', says Djingarey Maïga. 'Making films in Africa is suicide!'[10]

THE DREAM OF FINANCIAL AUTONOMY

Cinafric, which was set up as a private undertaking in Ouagadougou, was, in the words of Malian director Cheikh Oumar Sissoko, 'a jewel'. It had a projection room, a dubbing studio, editing suites, costumes, make-up provision, a large studio, filming equipment and custom-built vehicles. The post-production on Sissoko's film *Finzan* (1989) was done entirely in 'Ouaga'. However, Cinafric, which was underused and unable to get distribution for the films it made, went to the wall. As director of the National Centre for Cinematic Production in Mali, Sissoko dreams of a technically independent Africa which would be able to control its own costs. To that end, he has called for an inventory of the technical and human resources available in all the filmmaking countries: 'How many cameras, lights and camera dollies are locked away in National Cinema Centres, in TV stations, and used only for small productions or left to rot?'[11]

Whereas the services of European film laboratories represent almost a third of the cost of African films today, Cinafric could, if it were refloated, carry out the post-production and dubbing for West African films, with the laboratories in Harare, Tunis, Rabat and Algiers covering the other countries of Africa. If the political situation opened up the frontiers, the laboratory at Jos in Nigeria could also be brought into the equation, since that was where Brendan Shelen's film *Kulba na Barna* was processed. In the meantime, West Africans look longingly towards southern Africa, where, for example, *Flame* (Ingrid Sinclair, Zimbabwe, 1996) was processed by the Central Film Laboratories in Harare and completed in South Africa, at Johannesburg. Two centres for film copying and subtitling are also projected for southern Africa, with the support of an Italian charitable foundation.[12] Given the lack of a sufficient level of film production, such structures can be financed only on a regional, if not indeed continental, scale.

The Burkina Faso example is something to marvel at. DIPROCI (Direction de la production cinématographique) is financed by a 10 per cent levy on ticket sales, centralized ticketing having existed there since nationalization in 1972. The equipment DIPROCI has been able to acquire by this means is used in almost all the films made in the subregion.[13] Cheikh Oumar Sissoko also drew on DIPROCI technicians to make a first cut of *Guimba* (1995), before completing the post-production in Paris. The policy in Burkina Faso shows that state taxation of tickets can provide cinema with the necessary foundations for its development. It was the great demand of the filmmakers who met at Niamey in 1982 that this example be followed in other countries, but this has not so far happened to any great extent.

Filmmakers dream of technical autonomy so that they do not have to pay high prices for post-production in Western countries, and can therefore establish their independence. Many consider this an indispensable precondition, the first step in creating a cinema industry, the foundations of which have not yet been laid. There is no lack of arguments for entirely African crews, for South–South co-productions, for regional or continental structures which would make films easier to make and promote independence. What could be more legitimate than to call for the means to work in the right conditions? In this context, however, other filmmakers have to justify their decision to choose technicians for their quality, not for the colour of their skin, otherwise they are suspected of betraying an African solidarity with surreptitiously tyrannical overtones. The ambiguity between national and international, authentic and multicultural, integrity of identity and hybridization re-emerges here, in a little world in which the reality of funding and the filmmakers' personalities impose a vast array of different individual solutions.

THE TRIALS AND TRIBULATIONS OF FUNDING

The more difficult the conditions, the harder it is to predict the costs of a film. Unexpected problems tend to mount up, non-professional actors take longer than would normally be the case; there are insufficient resources for time to be managed efficiently. In some cases, filming is interrupted because the initial budget has been spent and the director has to go running around to find additional funds. Souleymane Cissé is a specialist in such filmmaking marathons. After a package of 13 million francs had been put together from the French culture and co-operation ministries, from la Sept-Cinéma and from Canal Plus, the filming of *Waati* had to be interrupted before he was able to film among the Tuaregs. The producer, Daniel Toscan du Plantier, threw in the towel at this stage:

You have to understand, Cissé is sometimes difficult to follow. One morning, I get a phone call from Abidjan: 'Daniel, could you send me a lion, please?' I'm flabbergasted. 'Aren't there any lions in Africa, then?' He says there aren't. At least, no trained ones. So the lion you see in the film, visibly discomfited by the heat – a lion which terrorized the Ivorian extras – was imported at enormous expense from Marne-la-Vallée.[14]

Support from the European Union made further funds available, but after two months' filming the coffers were empty again. The cast and crew were broken up, and Cissé spent nine months finding the necessary additional finance. Claude Berri, already involved as distributor, viewed the rushes and got more involved. It was finally possible to film the last shots, using an aircraft with its doors taken off; these are the images with which the film opens: the Namibian desert, the dawning of the world...

African filmmakers need unflinching strength and determination to see their projects through. To make *Sarraounia* (1987), Med Hondo had made a 50–50 co-production agreement with Niger state television. A month before filming was due to begin, Niger reneged on the agreement without explanation. All the barrister Jacques Vergès was able to obtain was an acknowledgement of Niger's responsibility in halting the production. Hondo suffered such strain that he had a minor heart attack; he also lost 75 million FCFA. Thanks to the support of Thomas Sankara, who had just come to power, the state of Burkina Faso came in with financial aid for the project and allowed Med Hondo to film on its territory. The film was made. While provision was made in the distribution contract for the film to be shown in fourteen cinemas, *Sarraounia* was shown in only five. The receipts were inadequate, and Hondo had to wind up his company. 'Since then I've set up another company, and life goes on!' he says.[15]

Yet, compared with Western productions, Black African films are made on extremely low budgets. Whereas the average budget of a French film in 1995 was 28 million francs (18 million in 1991), and Jean-Paul Rappenau's blockbuster *Le Hussard sur le toit* cost a record 176 million to make, the budget for *Wariko* (Fadika Kramo-Lanciné, Ivory Coast, 1993) was 3.5 million French francs. For *Guimba* (Cheikh Oumar Sissoko, Mali, 1995) it was 4 million; for *Rue Princesse* (Henri Duparc, Ivory Coast, 1994) 6.5 million. '*Yaaba* cost 6 million, *Tilaï* 5 million and *Le Cri du coeur* 13 million because it had Richard Bohringer in it, and the hyena had to be trained', says Idrissa Ouedraogo.

Going beyond this requires enormous energy... I don't have any illusions about that. If I make a 15-million-franc film with 8 or 9 million, I won't make a good film. A stick of wood can stay in the water for twenty years, but it won't become a caiman! You can make films with a message which are not pretentious either in form or in content. On *Le Choix* we worked with all our hearts: 800,000 francs, a single car ... and no nights![16]

Many a filmmaker has got into debt in an effort to finish a film. The hazards of distribution and general wariness on the part of television stations prevent them from covering their costs. Time passes, and the search for funding replaces cinematic work. The Senegalese director Ababacar Samb Makharam, who died in 1987, took four years to pay back the debts he ran up while making *Et la neige n'était plus* (1965). It took him two more years to get the necessary finance together to make the magnificent *Kodou* (1971). And after *Jom* (1981), he was saddled with a debt of 50 million francs. 'I prefer an average film which covers its costs to a masterpiece for which I have to carry the debt for the rest of my life', he confided bitterly to Pierre Haffner, though he immediately added that money played no part in the form of his films, and he did not 'prostitute' himself.[17] In contributing to setting up FEPACI (la Fédération panafricaine des cinéastes), Samb had vigorously defended a committed cinema – committed not to negritude or authenticity, but to being faithful to one's own subjectivity. He was, however, aware of the danger of merely addressing a minority audience.[18]

Low budgets are not without their effects on the images produced. In making *Tumult* (1996), the Ethiopian Yemané Démissié had to borrow, film, stop for lack of money, then start again. In such circumstances, the actors may no longer be available: 'The sequence in which Yoseph helps the van driver who is going to give him a lift to pick up his fallen load was shot from a distance simply because I couldn't get the actors back together again!'[19] The decision to film in close-up, which characterizes the rest of the film, corresponded in part to a desire to produce a sense of claustrophobia – Yoseph being, after the failed coup d'état, a 'dead man' condemned to wander. But it was also an economic necessity: 'I had to get close to my actors and the action because I couldn't have a backdrop which didn't correspond to the story – most of the film having been shot in Los Angeles!'

Yet young filmmakers manage to come to terms with the low level of their budgets, accepting them as the 'New Wave' directors did. David Achkar summed up their position:

> We share common views on cinema with a group of young directors: films which may possibly be difficult, made in difficult production conditions! Our concerns are the same in the sense that it's the film which is important, not the person making it. The aim is to say what you can as best you can with the budget you have, in the knowledge that our financial circumstances are very difficult! This has created a particular tone: use of 'voice-off', lots of ellipses as in Jean-Pierre Bekolo's films, mixing documentary and fiction, as Jean-Marie Teno does, as well as mixing

past and present, and at times a non-linear composition which plays around with time. And all this in a desire to get beyond the tradition/modernity debate and probe the contemporary problems of our society (water, ecology, violence, sexuality, etcetera.).[20]

THE TRIALS AND TRIBULATIONS OF PRODUCTION

'Every time a producer has dealings with an African, there are problems of cultural difference!' says Idrissa Ouedraogo.[21] African filmmakers have responded to this situation recently by developing solidarity between like-minded individuals. For example, Idrissa Ouedraogo produced *Guimba* (Cheikh Oumar Sissoko, Mali) and Pierre Yameogo produced *Keïta, l'héritage du griot* (Dani Kouyaté, Burkina Faso). It must be said that some had already had their fingers burnt with unfortunate experiences in which certain producers turned out to be charlatans. After spending nine years looking for funding for his new film *Wariko* (1994) – in spite of the fact that his *Djeli* (1980) had been a critical success – Fadika Kramo-Lanciné at last became confident that his film would be made when the French Co-operation Ministry granted him a subsidy of 700,000 French francs. The Swiss DDA followed this up with 120,000 francs. To manage this Swiss funding, the cineaste signed a contract in the Ivory Coast with a French producer, the World Film Company, which took the money and then shortly afterwards declared itself bankrupt – only to re-emerge later as Atlantis Films. Additional assistance of 300,000 francs from the French Agence de la Francophonie (the erstwhile ACCT) and 150,000 francs from the Ivory Coast FIAC (Fonds d'Intervention pour l'action culturelle) enabled the film to be made after all.[22] Gnoan Roger M'Bala had a similarly unfortunate experience, as the producer brought in to manage funds from a number of French government ministries ran off with the money. It took an eighteen-month trial to reacquire the rights which made possible a last-minute rescue of the rushes of *Au nom du Christ*, as the colour was beginning to deteriorate.[23] For Senegalese director Safi Faye, it took a six-year court case against her producer to get *Mossane* (1996) released:

> The French associate producer I had taken on had, without my knowledge, appropriated all the rights income from the film and all the funding I had found. The finance from Switzerland and Italy disappeared and was never seen again. For six years, I had to battle on alone while awaiting the outcome of the legal proceedings. My film was shot entirely in 1990. Mossane was fourteen at the time. How would things stand if sequences were missing now, with Mossane twenty-one? I would like to forget those six years. *Mossane* is finished, and I'm happy I managed to make it. I like the film a lot.[24]

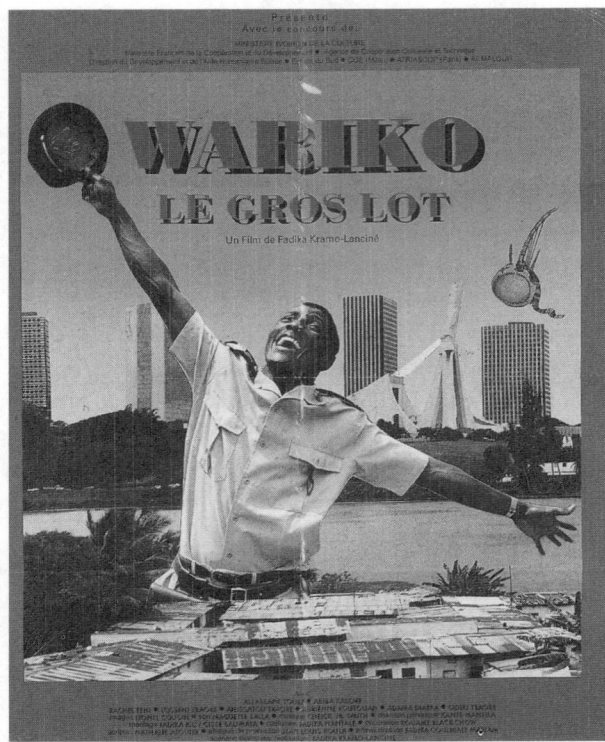

Poster for *Wariko/
The Jackpot* (Fadika
Kramo-Lanciné,
Ivory Coast, 1993).

Because they are in a minority, African production companies have the impression that they are producing for others: the takings do not go to them. 'We didn't even own the copy of *Yonta's Blue Eyes*!' (Flora Gomes, 1992) points out Maria-Cecilia Fonseca of the Arcoiris Co-operative in Guinea-Bissau.[25] There is no comparison between the life of an African producer and that of her Western colleagues! 'I have an office, a table and a telephone', she says. 'To send a fax, you either have to pay or use the French cultural centre. It's the same for photocopying – endlessly going backwards and forwards...'

With no real market, the African producer is – in the words of Ahmed Attia, a Tunisian producer campaigning for the existence of an African cinematography – like a 'trapeze artist without a safety net'.

NOTES

1. Wolof proverb.
2. Sony Labou Tansi, *La Vie et demie*, Seuil, Paris, 1979, p. 152.
3. Christian Metz, *The Imaginary Signifier: Psychoanalysis and the Cinema,* Indiana University Press, Bloomington, 1982, p. 75.
4. The presence of a film industry does not solve the cinema crisis. In *Le Cinéma, entre l'art et l'argent* (L'Harmattan, Paris, 1989), Pierre-Jean Benghozi shows how the endless trade-off between aesthetic concerns and economic constraints at all stages of production means that cinema cannot but be in crisis and perpetual turmoil.
5. Interview with Djingarey Maïga, Ouagadougou, 1995.
6. Olivier Margot, 'A Pietermaritzburg, l'actrice de *Waati* n'a pas voulu ramper', *L'Équipe*, 7 June 1995.
7. Interview with Jean-Marie Koula, Abidjan, 1995.
8. Interview with Andrée Davanture, Paris, 1995.
9. Kitia Touré, 'Les structures des films', *Cinémaction* 26 ('Cinémas d'Afrique noire'), undated, p. 80.
10. Interview with Djingarey Maïga, Ouagadougou, 1995.
11. Cheikh Oumar Sissoko, interviewed by Clément Tapsoba, *Écrans d'Afrique* 9–10, 1994, p. 13.
12. *Zoom – Zeitschrift für Film*, Zurich, November 1993, p. 23.
13. Interview with Justin K. Kagambega, acting chief administrator of Sonacib, Ouagadougou, 1995.
14. Daniel Toscan du Plantier, quoted by Danièle Heymann, 'Souleymane Cissé, l'Africain pluriel', *Le Monde*, 8 June 1995, p. 12.
15. Ibrahima Signaté, *Med Hondo, un cinéaste rebelle*, Présence Africaine, Paris, 1994, p. 47.
16. Interview with Idrissa Ouedraogo, Paris, 1995.
17. Pierre Haffner, 'Kino in Schwarzafrika', *Revue du CICIM*, 27–28 Institut français de Munich, 1989, p. 133.
18. Ibid., pp. 122, 126.
19. Interview with Yemané Démissié, Milan, 1996.
20. Interview with David Achkar, Paris, 1997, published in *Africultures* 5 ('Jeunes créateurs africains'), L'Harmattan, Paris, 1998.
21. Interview with Idrissa Ouedraogo, Ouagadougou, 1995.
22. Interview with Fadika Kramo-Lanciné, Paris, 1995.
23. Gnoan Roger M'Bala interviewed by Lamine Saad and Jean-Pierre Garcia, *Le Film africain* 17, October 1994, p. 14.
24. Interview with Safi Faye, Cannes, 1997, published in *Africultures* 2 ('Les Africaines'), L'Harmattan, Paris, 1998.
25. Interview with Maria-Cecilia Fonseca, Paris, 1995.

THIRTEEN

THE AFRICAN AUDIENCE IS
ANYTHING BUT HOMOGENEOUS

I have thrilled to all of Africa
and taken root
in this salt of rocky memory
Since the childhood of the Omo,
Since Karnak

Théophile Obenga[1]

African film and its audience have difficulty coming together: the conditions for this to happen do not exist. The meeting is possible, but myths are difficult to dispel.

THE AGONIES OF DISTRIBUTION

Since films made by African filmmakers remain largely unseen on the screens of that continent, filmmaking in Africa is still a paradoxical activity! When countries were gaining their independence, in the 1960s, film distribution everywhere, in the best colonial tradition, was in the hands of foreign companies, but subsequently not all parts of Africa were to share the same fate. Whereas a fiction cinema appeared and developed in Francophone Africa, the English- and Portuguese-speaking countries continued for the most part with the policy of didactic documentary set in place by the colonial regimes. Even today, distribution in those countries is in the hands of foreign – American or Lebanese – companies, or of multinationals based in South Africa, so that the rare filmmakers who do exist have to be their own distributors. In French-speaking Africa, on the other hand, the history of distribution shows up the expectations filmmakers have had of their states, and the contradictions and disillusionment which have ensued.[2]

In 1960, the market of the fourteen countries of French West and

Equatorial Africa was divided between two companies: COMACICO (la Compagnie marocaine du cinéma commercial) had 85 cinemas; SECMA (la Société d'exploitation cinématographique africaine) had 65; these cinemas were supplied by two companies based in Monaco, in order to avoid the French tax system. These companies, with a monopoly of distribution and exhibition, repatriated 40–50 per cent of their turnover to Monaco. In order to reclaim these profits, the African states had to nationalize the importation and distribution of films. The filmmakers who formed FEPACI (Fédération panafricaine des cinéastes) called on the government for protectionist measures. Some countries – Algeria, Burkina Faso, Mali, Senegal, Benin, Tanzania, Madagascar, Congo, Somalia and Sudan – nationalized their cinemas and gradually, through the 1970s, brought film importation and distribution under the control of national companies. The foreign companies responded by boycotting those countries. After five years, the all-powerful Motion Pictures Export Association of America (MPEAA) negotiated a choice of films and screenings for its local production with Algeria. Upper Volta (now Burkina Faso), after seeking in vain for other sources of supply, had in the end to give in to a deal with COMACICO and SECMA for the exclusive programming of its cinemas.

Senegal, however, managed to force the two companies to pay back half of their takings. The tide was apparently turning for the foreign companies, which now modified their strategies. Under pressure from the French government, which feared that the nationalization of distribution might lead to anti-French attitudes, COMACICO and SECMA sold up at the end of 1972 to the UGC (Union générale cinématographique), which immediately offered the nationalized companies partnership in the newly created SOPACIA (Société de participation cinématographique africaine). Thus, in 1974, Senegal, the driving force of African cinema, created SIDEC (la Société de distribution et d'exploitation cinématographique), the ownership of which was split 80:20 between the state of Senegal and SOPACIA. However, UGC, with its 20 per cent, continued to dominate distribution in Senegal. Its network of 110 cinemas and 130 private clients assured it of 75 per cent of the Francophone African market, the rest being shared between other distributors, with AFRAM Inc., an American company, having the lion's share of 22 per cent. How could Senegal make a profit from purchasing films to show in the country, when such giants as these obtained them at wholesale prices? SIDEC was merely a semblance of Senegalese sovereignty, and SOPACIA continued to control the market in best neo-colonial fashion. SOPACIA, which now derived its main profits from importing and distributing films, became the UAC (Union africaine du cinéma). It sold off its cinemas to African private individuals, but continued to import films, which it bought cheaply and exploited for enormous profit on African soil.

The filmmakers continued to press for increased control of the cinema industry, and in 1979 this led the states of OCAM (Organisation commune africaine et malgache) to create the CIDC (Consortium interafricain de distribution cinématographique), based at Ouagadougou. The idea was to establish a kind of 'common market' of distribution between fourteen countries, with CIDC acting as a purchasing co-operative which could insert African films into its packages. The profits from the CIDC were also to be reinvested in production through an inter-African film production consortium: Ciprofilms.

At first all seemed to be going well for the decolonization of African screens, as UGC ceded its cinemas and its film list back to CIDC in 1980, while it continued to play a part in the purchasing office set up in Paris. However, as its director, Inoussa Ousseini from Niger, was to say, 'Hell isn't other people, it's ourselves!'[3] Cinema proprietors preferred the sure-fire success of spaghetti Westerns, Indian melodramas and karate films to the African films in the packages delivered by the CIDC. Nor were the national distribution companies which came out of the wave of nationalization exempt from commercial aims, often putting the profit associated with foreign films before the promotion of African film, which they regarded as a 'cultural' product. The member states of CIDC did not plough back into cinematic activity the – at times exorbitant – taxes which they levied on distribution. Many did not pay their subscription to CIDC, to the point where the latter could not pay back its debt to UGC. A legal and political imbroglio preventing the Africanization of the Parisian office, and revealing dissent between the different states, and various acts of embezzlement, finally sounded the death knell for CIDC in 1984. The suppliers of American films have since had no trouble occupying the market which its demise opened up. This they have done through a Swiss company, Socofilm, which was sold in 1989 to the CFAA (Compagnie franco-africaine de l'audiovisuel) – a holding company formed by banks such as Crédit Lyonnais and Banque Populaire. If French interests have now been protected, this has been with a complete disregard for the films of Black Africa.

In the heyday of the CIDC, however, African films had some out-and-out successes: *Finye/The Wind* (Souleymane Cissé, Mali, 1982) and *Djeli* (Fadika Kramo-Lanciné, Ivory Coast, 1981) achieved record receipts in their own countries and were also commercially successful elsewhere. The prospect of sustained distribution momentarily made production easier. Today it is difficult to obtain copies of films except directly from the filmmakers. The creation of common distribution markets, bringing together a sufficient number of cinemas in which African films could be given preferential treatment, remains, then, an important goal today. All concerned have called for new, regional, less centralized CIDCs. But if a federal structure is to be preferred, in order to avoid some of the difficulties of centralized organization, which bodies are to form part of it? The national distribution companies of Mali, Benin, the Ivory Coast, Niger and Cameroon have ceased to exist. In southern Africa, the South African Lionel N'Gkane also advocates a new regional structure negotiating directly with overseas independent distributors and producers rather than being entirely beholden to South African distributors.[4] But no such structures are yet in place.

By demanding the nationalization of the sector, the FEPACI filmmakers had thrown themselves into the lion's mouth: nationalization brought excessive bureaucracy and, in many cases, a state control which prevented the making of films that upset the status quo, and at times led to the enforced production of propaganda films. Gathering at Niamey in 1982, the filmmakers called for their states to take control of distribution only. The absence of national legislation in fact left the CFAA in control of a market organized into sectors: the French company, for example, supplied some fifty films a month to the 'centre sector' for a monthly fee of 7 million FCFA. These could be shown for around three weeks in each of the countries in the pool (Ivory Coast, Burkina Faso, Niger, Togo, Benin).

The Niamey manifesto sought to escape state control by calling on African states to support national production, but to allow private producers to choose the subjects of the films. The question of tax was central: the filmmakers wanted African cinema to be supported by tax breaks, and by redistributing the income from box-office taxes on distribution and exhibition to bodies responsible for supporting the rehabilitation of cinemas and production.

The example of Burkina Faso has been a beacon. African films have been exempted from taxation in that country, increasing incomes within the profession by 25 per cent. Conversely, the taxing of foreign films enables this poor state to have one of the most dynamic cinema industries on the continent. SONACIB (la Société nationale d'exploitation et de distribution cinématographique du Burkina Faso), formed as part of the nationalization measures of 1970, is supposed to pay 15 per cent of its box-office receipts into a fund for the promotion and extension of cinematic activity. That fund, which has been a real success, has played a part in the production of many films and has financed DIPROCI (la Direction de la production cinématographique), whose equipment is used in making almost all the films in the subregion. SONACIB's recent difficulties – in the last five years it has not been able to pay into the production fund – arise from a fall-off in audiences linked to the proliferation of clandestine video showings and to fraud-related losses where money was taken at the door but no ticket was issued, or tickets were taken back intact from inside the auditorium and resold at the box office. A study showed that the company was losing 25 per cent of its revenue in this way. Action by ticket inspectors operating on oath has increased the takings by 27 per cent since 1993![5]

Fraud in Africa runs at levels unimaginable to a Westerner used to a properly supervised national ticketing system. Distributors therefore tend to charge a flat-rate fee rather than accepting a percentage. Since the risks are not shared, who would still dare to put on a difficult film? To be sure that they will be paid their share of the takings, filmmakers have to accompany their films when they are shown. Jean-Louis Koula from the Ivory Coast tells of how he

> went to a Lebanese proprietor's cinema. It was full. There were even people in the aisles. The receipts were for 400 tickets. We went into the auditorium to count the spectators with a torch: there were a thousand! The manager told us the other people were relatives! Africans do have large families, but even so...[6]

In turning themselves into distributors, filmmakers are beset both by fraud and by censorship. Françoise Balogun tells how, in Nigeria,

> we tried to distribute Henri Duparc's *L'Herbe sauvage*. We bought the rights, but the censorship committee banned it. We tried again with Kwaw Ansah's *Love Brewed in the African Pot*. A press showing at the National Theatre assured us of a good reception, but we never got a certificate from the censor! Kwaw Ansah then took back his film and his rights, and had another go. In the end, it was passed and was a great success, but Kwaw Ansah left without making any money because he was defrauded out of box-office takings and the film was seized at the airport![7]

In this connection, the content of films is not a neutral factor. *Silmandé* (Pierre Yameogo, Burkina Faso, 1998) was released without any problems at Ouagadougou (where it had record audience figures for Burkina Faso), at Cotonou and at Dakar, but in Abidjan the Lebanese cinema-owners who own half the country's cinemas boycotted it, considering themselves slandered by certain scenes. However, the film, which denounces corruption on all sides, treats all communities alike. Indeed, it approaches each in its psychological complexity. The Lebanese are shown as bearing the marks of their history of exile and insertion into a foreign society. No one emerges as a 'fine, noble soul' from the very human clashes, and this is the value of this profoundly political film – political in the sense that, rather than criticizing from the sidelines, it takes us inside these conflicts.

As head of CIVCA (la Compagnie ivoirienne du cinéma et de l'audio-visuel), the fiery cineaste Kitia Touré wanted to establish a new policy in the Ivory Coast, based on the axiom which is the refrain of all African film-makers: financing cinema out of cinema takings! The aim was that out of the 10 per cent of tax (excluding VAT) on cinema tickets, 5 per cent should go to film production, 2 per cent to distribution, 2 per cent to exhibition and 1 per cent as royalties. Touré hoped in this way to do something about the dilapidated state of cinema buildings, and give a boost to new production. Unafraid to face up to the vested interests ranged against him, he set out to apply the strategy of the African house rat:

> He contrives to eat you in your sleep. When you wake up your toes are half-eaten. How does he do this? He begins by blowing on your toe to dull your sensitivity, then he begins nibbling. When you move, instead of scuttling off, which would wake you up, he stops and blows again and again. This is the strategy we must adopt! It's a long haul in which we have to combine courage and political will![8]

When I met him two years later, he had admitted defeat in the face of the interest groups which had opposed his policy. The ministerial hierarchy had not taken the idea on board, and it had been impossible to make any headway.

DILAPIDATED AUDITORIUMS

The numbers and condition of African cinema buildings are not improving. Ivory Coast, which could once boast some seventy-five cinemas, now has barely thirty in a fit state of operation. In Mali, Bamako had twenty or so cinemas. 'Today', says the Malian director Salif Traoré, 'they are in a dis-graceful state of dilapidation. A gentleman would be reluctant to sit down in one for fear of getting dirty or tearing his trousers!'[9] In Lagos, the capital of Nigeria, only the National Theatre and university cinemas are in an ac-ceptable condition. The foreign cultural centres are still almost the only places where you can see African films. Namibia has only seven cinemas. Guinea-Bissau has something like ten, all of which belong to sports clubs. N'Djamena, the capital of Chad, has three cinemas, two of which operate more or less decently, but, for want of a film supplier, they show videos. Soweto in South Africa emerged from the apartheid years with only two cinemas for its three million inhabitants.

The privatization of the cinemas in Senegal, Mali, Benin and Niger has not necessarily solved the problems. The chaotic state of affairs in Mali shows that the withdrawal of the state often amounts to a sell-off at knock-down prices and does not guarantee that the cinemas will be kept going. Filmmakers then have to act to protect independent cinemas and stop them becoming supermarkets.[10] In Senegal, five popular cinemas in Dakar were recently turned into shops or warehouses.

Apart from the rare cinemas which have been renovated and had air-conditioning installed, the auditoriums are usually in a run-down state. One could ignore the hardness of the seating if the projection conditions did not make viewing a film an epic, and often frustrating, adventure. The in-experience of some projectionists and the age of the equipment make for a great many breaks in projection, which are met with a hail of howls and whistles. The copies of the films are returned to the distributor in a dis-astrous state: marked, burned or torn. In the popular cinemas, the image is often too dark and the sound is either shrill or inaudible. In such conditions, how can film hope seriously to stem the rise of television and video?

THE VIDEO MONSTER

Whereas a cinema ticket costs between 150 and 1500 FCFA (1.5–15 French francs), depending on the particular cinema and the country, a video show-ing, organized privately in the living-room or back yard of a person with a video-recorder, costs the initiate only 50 or 100 francs.[11] Why go elsewhere? In Abidjan, a video can be rented for 1,000 FCFA, less than the price of a cinema ticket! In Nigeria, videos can be rented or bought almost anywhere on an entirely informal basis: a short by Ola Balogun made for Canal Plus shows that they can even be found in hairdressing salons!

It must be said that in Nigeria video has developed enormously, and has almost replaced independent cinema. More than 250 video features are made a year, but virtually no films. Since videos are cheap to make (between 100,000 and 150,000 naira, or 30,000–45,000 French francs), it is easy to make a return on stories on popular themes filmed in Yoruba, Igbo or Hausa, even though the hit-and-miss quality of this production makes it unexportable. The situation is the same in Ghana, where at least one video feature comes out every fortnight. Although the screenplays are adequate, the technique and direction are sometimes below par. The public does, however, like the simple dialogue, and enjoys seeing familiar places and stories.[12]

Pirate video-hire clubs flourish in African towns and cities, and there is no legal control on them whatsoever. Indeed, in some cases they compete with film distributors in importing top US action movies. For example, *Jurassic Park* (Steven Spielberg, USA, 1993) was widely viewed in Ivory Coast on video before it was released in the cinemas, where it reached only a third

Cover of a
Nigerian video
monthly (October
1994).

of its potential audience. Few countries effectively combat a piracy which
prevents any proper organization of film distribution. In Nigeria, however,
use of the Nigeria Copyright Council label and substantial policing have
restrained piracy appreciably.[13] In South Africa, the efforts of private
operators reduced piracy from 93 per cent in 1981 to 17 per cent in 1994.[14]
In a country where it is estimated that there are a million video-recorders,
the stakes were enormously high. The end of the apartheid regime has
enabled the Film Resource Unit to distribute films on video in the townships, with the best sales being recorded for *Ulibambe Lingashoni/Hold up the
Sun* (Laurence Dworkin, 1993), a series of five one-hour videos on the history
of the ANC. These are sold door-to-door and also directly to societies and
churches.

Frontage of the Les Studios cinema in Abidjan.

ACCOMPANYING ONE'S FILM

There are, however, highly motivated cinema managers who promote Black African films. Pascal Diekebre, programmer for the 'Les Studios' cinema in Abidjan, meets directors at Fespaco in Ouagadougou and invites them to bring along their leading actor, and come and present their films.[15] The press, summoned for the occasion, supports the film's release in the country. Les Studios can then programme the film in its provincial cinemas, and show it over a three-year period. 'My experience', observes Michel Janin, who has managed various cultural centres in Africa, 'is that when a filmmaker comes with his film he can fill a cinema for ten days twice daily with an audience of ordinary people'. In this way, African filmmakers spend their time following their films around, making sure they get an audience, rather than preparing their next film. But they do so with some success, thus apparently proving that Africans still want to see their films!

Salif Traoré from Mali – who was assistant to Souleymane Cissé for a long time, before becoming a director himself with the excellent consciousness-raising short *Siguida/The Environment* (1995) – took copies of Cissé's films and went to see the exhibitors one by one. In Togo, he prepared for the release of *Yeelen* in Lomé with advertisements in the newspapers, television interviews with Cissé, and even a town crier! 'Now I always employ a public crier who goes through the town from morning till night – and it works! And I send the poster out in advance so that people know beforehand that the film is coming.'[16]

The logic here is akin to that of the 'ciné-buses', which took cinema into the remotest areas. As cinemas were built and television spread, these buses gradually disappeared. They still exist, however, in those countries most deprived of cinematic structures and in the poorest countries, where they play an educational role. 'My aim was to make shorts which exposed a peasant audience to modernity and changes of behaviour', says Maurice Kaboré from Burkina Faso. 'I wanted them to stop following tradition blindly, but to retain those positive aspects which are the basis of their identity.'[17] When he went along on the ciné-bus which was presenting his film *Etre femme au Burkina*, he saw how lively and passionate were the debates to which it gave rise:

> When you arrive in a place, you play music and a loudspeaker announces the show will take place in the village square. Then you set up the equipment, show the film and discuss it. The show's free, being financed by the Ministry of Culture. It was the ciné-bus which exposed me to films and made me want to make them.

Today, such initiatives are made easier by the use of lighter video equipment: within the framework of the 'Southern Africa Communications for Development', programme, which has support from a Canadian organization called 'Vidéo Tiers-Monde', a free video film festival was able to tour Namibia, South Africa, Zimbabwe and Mozambique.[18]

Each filmmaker has their own way of getting their films distributed. Lucien Patry, who headed the technical unit at the French Ministry of Co-operation, tells how Djibril Diop Mambety asked him at Cannes to suggest a distributor for *Touki-Bouki* (1973):

> I told him I would think about it so as to find somebody really dependable. Next day I went to the Blue Bar in the Ancien Palais, where everybody from the festival foregathered. I saw a big sign: 'For *Touki-Bouki*, speak to the barman!' I went to find the barman and he confirmed that he'd been contacted by Djibril and had undertaken to note down all the contact addresses.... The press even published a photo of the sign![19]

A PLURALISTIC AUDIENCE

In *Laafi* (Pierre Yameogo, Burkina Faso, 1991), a secretary is replying on the telephone to suggestions from her boyfriend, who wants to take her to the cinema.

> 'I don't like the pictures. And it's an African film.'
> 'You don't see those every day, African films!'
> 'I only like Hindu films. They have dancing in them, and there are nice songs too. African films are rubbish. They're always going on about how bad things are. I don't like them!'

Yet films from Black Africa do find their audience. The films of the Ivorian director Henri Duparc are smash hits in French-speaking Africa. In Abidjan alone, 150,000 people saw *Abusuan* (1972) in just four months.[20] When *Rue Princesse* (1994) was shown in Ouagadougou, extra showings had to be arranged at midnight and 2 a.m.! Pascal Diekebre can remember people fighting to get into *Yeelen* (Souleymane Cissé, 1987) in Abidjan. Fifty thousand people saw the film in Bamako, where there had already been forty thousand to see *Finye* (1983)! Similarly, *Samba Traoré* (Idrissa Ouedraogo, 1992) was an enormous hit in the popular cinemas of Ivory Coast. Forty thousand people went to see Gnoan Roger M'Bala's *Au nom du Christ* (Fespaco Grand Prize, 1993) in that country: 'That will just make us enough to pay the actors and wipe off our debts, but it won't pay the total costs of the film. And yet that's the biggest audience you get for a successful film.'[21] Even if it is a success, a film cannot make money simply from the box-office receipts in its own country: whereas production costs are spiralling upwards, ticket prices remain very low. Access to other markets is needed, including other African countries, Western countries and television.

The African public does, none the less, like to see its films, though it prefers those from its own culture and in its own language. But we should not conclude that Africans rush to the cinema as soon as an African film appears. Like any other audience, they generally favour action and entertainment films over more thought-provoking productions. Whereas some countries practically never have access to Black African films, since no distributor offers them, the countries which do support them nevertheless take commercial demands into consideration. Whereas the Ouagadougou public rushes to see African films during the Fespaco competition, they tend to neglect them in the intervening period, preferring films intended solely as entertainment. Apart from internationally recognized films, which stir up the public's curiosity, only films which 'send up' modern life or national films made in the local lingua franca are outright successes. 'When directors make films like that', says Justin K. Kagambega, the manager of SONACIB, 'we're prepared to show them, but you can't take up an 8.30 showing with a film that brings in only twenty or thirty people!'

In a crisis situation for cinemas, how can one expect a manager to programme a difficult film during peak hours? It would take specific financial assistance to do so. A programme is currently being examined in those French ministries that support African cinema which would take the form of subsidies for pilot cinemas in exchange for concerted programming of Francophone and African films. Education in African cinema is certainly needed, and the vehicle through which this will be done is clearly television. To this end, the French Ministry of Co-operation is setting up an experiment in conjunction with Canal France International to show one recent African film a month, accompanied by analysis and debate. But it is no easy matter even to find twelve films per year. Once all the recent films have been shown, it will be necessary to go back in time to find others.[22]

Eyes are turning now towards South Africa, which represents a substantial potential market, but the audience there has been very much shaped by Hollywood. 'It's a question of education and promotion. One of the biggest distributors released Isaac Meli Mabhiwka's *More Time* [Zimbabwe, 1992], but it didn't do well', observes its producer, Ben Zulu. 'South Africans have TV stations with wall-to-wall American programmes. They know the actors and who's got the Oscars. African films are unknown. That's not something that can be changed overnight!'[23] These remarks are tempered by the comments of another Zimbabwean producer, Joel Phiri:

African films will take time to catch on. *Flame* came out in eight South African cinemas. It didn't take off right away, but it did better as time went on. It's a matter of time. You have to stick at it. The public isn't used to these images yet. SABC and M-Net are making a start by showing some French-speaking African films.[24]

Black African films – which are often guided by a desire to reflect critically on their society, and are thus akin to a non-commercial *auteur* cinema – have the same difficulties on the ground as 'art films' in the West. Only a few break through into the mainstream. If it wants to reach levels of profitability which can sustain it, this kind of cinema has to meet the quality standards of the international market. It will then have to take its chance as craft-based cinema, alongside all the other different forms, in the face of the Hollywood steamroller. On the other hand, filmmakers do know how to reach a sizeable local public with 'theme' films which are often quite humorous, simply because the audience recognize themselves in them. Such films are not, however, necessarily exportable beyond the African continent. To make a profit from such films in conditions where there aren't many cinemas, where the ones which do exist are badly run down, where ticket prices are cheap and box-office practices not consistently policed, means making films with a great economy of means. This raises once again the questions of technical autonomy for the countries of the South, which would enable them to bring their costs down, and a commitment on the part of African states.

African cinemas consume a great number of films. They often project different films at each showing, with five or six being shown in a day where the cinemas are not in the open air (there the usual number is three, beginning at around 6.30, when night falls). The programmes also change very rapidly. The rare African productions get lost in a tide of films which compete with them at the box office. A country like Burkina Faso, for example, needs more than seven hundred films per year, whereas only around fifty African feature films are available and only five to ten are made each year: 'The African films which have a certain audience appeal are bought by SONACIB', says its director, François Vokouma, 'but they are shown so often that people get sick of them.'[25] African film will continue for many years to represent only a small percentage of an already small domestic market. The question is not, then, whether Africans like their films or not: they go to see what they enjoy, whether it is African or not. They may or may not be hungry for their own images; any generalization is of the order of myth.

Since Black Africa has a pluralized cinema culture, and because African societies are divided into different social strata and vary from country to country, the African cinema-going audience, like that of any other continent, has no real unity. At best we can say which films have the greatest success. Generally the biggest hits are films that parody social roles and pastiche the deviant forms of behaviour which accompany the modernization of African society. This does not mean there is no audience for more experimental works, but distribution conditions have prevented an African 'art cinema' from appearing. There is still a consensus for regarding the African cinema-going public as homogeneous on the strength of its cultural roots: the African public is supposed to share an intrinsic knowledge of the sociocultural codes present in the films, which might be said to establish a kind of community of perception. The filmmaker's problem is then supposed to be one of going out to the audience, which has long meant reproducing an allegedly authentic (non-Western) angle on people and things. To carry on rehashing this myth of the unity of the African public today does not make the filmmaker's task any easier. Since this fictitious audience is supposed to be hungry both for profundity and for entertainment, directors would have to make films which challenged the social order, while at the same time being popular, so as not to be cut off from the masses. If they were also trying to keep a potential Western audience in mind, this would be a really interesting balancing act. The few 'serious' films which have made it into the mainstream serve only to perpetuate the myth.

Yet the deculturation of the inhabitants of African cities increases visibly each day. One can, admittedly, attempt to identify the features of a specific imagination – the African public not being either the Western or the Asian public – but it is none the less the case that that public is developing, and that imagination is becoming hybridized. It has gone, with the help of video recorders and satellite dishes, from kung fu and Westerns to American action films and television series. It calls now for greater pace and faster cutting. In its efforts to identify with the characters, it is less satisfied with pure action and is concerned to understand the process underlying it: it wants fiction now, not just crime or fighting.

In order to address an audience fed on a non-stop diet of heroes and American-style psychology – but also psychologically damaged by the crisis they have to cope with in their everyday lives – African filmmakers have to take a subtle approach, exploring the motivations for behaviour. In putting 'action' into their films, they have gone along with their audiences, the better to lead them down a different, more thought-provoking path. It is clear that such an approach can be attractive or disorientating depending on the particular film or audience. In order to create an ambivalent moral climate, for example, Mahamat Saleh Haroun adopts a Hitchcockian narrative logic in

Goï-Goï (Chad, 1995). A dwarf, who neglects his wife and goes drinking and playing cards, discovers that she is cheating on him. He is advised to put flour in her loincloth, and follow the trail. In this way, Goï-Goï catches his wife with her lover. She runs off, and he kills the lover. He is then himself killed by his wife's sister, with whom the wife had taken refuge. The sister is not the sort to have second thoughts: 'Cut him up and put him in the river! Like they do in the movies!' The suspense continues when the police become interested in the two women...

A SCHOOL OF LIFE

Popular cinemas (in which African film is a scarce commodity) are still genuine meeting places where the spectators restore that active participation which all African spectacle traditionally demands. They are places where the spectators assert their sociability and their membership of a clan. The person who does not participate is a dropout, a sad individual.[26] The programmes are split between action movies (second-rate Hollywood products are gradually winning out over karate or ninja films, detective movies and war epics), pornography and Hindu films. These last are watched in the main by women, who happily join in with the songs and sometimes bring their babies on their backs. They generally have happy endings and tell tales of family feuding, in which children avenge their dead parents, or love stories which turn out well once the cheating partner has been punished. The sumptuous costumes and beautiful sets, which are often temples or other sacred places, make these films fairy-tale celebrations of a hero's derring-do.

Those under eighteen years of age are theoretically banned from seeing pornographic films, but since the regulations are not enforced, people of all ages can get in. These films are watched in relative silence, whereas action films trigger off chain reactions in the cinema. In his study of cinemas in working-class districts of Abidjan, Yao Konan reports:

> fights between the hero and his adversary end in a total apotheosis, with the audience on their feet, clenched fists raised, shouting, whistling and applauding the hero as he finishes off his enemy. In such a situation, there are only pictures. Even the soundtrack is drowned out by the audience's shouts and the noise of the metal chairs.[27]

The atmosphere is generally relaxed. Some are bare-chested, others smoke or eat sandwiches, while the lolly-sellers clink their coins in the relative darkness to show where they are. At the ten o'clock showing, even the newspaper-sellers turn up to try and unload their last remaining copies. The

The Ciné-Palace open-air cinema at Ouahigouya (Burkina Faso). The posters advertise films entitled *L'Espionne qui venait du soleil levant, Le Dragon noir de Shaolin* and *Les Exécutrices.*

comments and conversations, chair noise, shouting and applause drown out the voices of the actors, which are difficult to hear in the first place because of the poor acoustics. When the film climaxes in a fight scene, the audience, after shouting and applauding the action, sometimes leave the cinema before the film is over. The film is 'read', then, by picking up on a combination of key images and snippets of dialogue.

For young people, who are the main audience in the popular cinemas, films provide a school of life: they don't go to hear what is said, but to see what goes on. Action cinema is a window on to the outside world, on to a West which fascinates them. And they go not so as to get to know it better, but in order to understand its 'weaponry' – namely, the 'weapons' which enable you to cope with a life in which 'ducking and diving' is the norm. These they will try out in the frequent brawls which occur as soon as they get out of the cinema. In their search for models, they often imitate the American heroes in dress and behaviour or in their intensive body-building.

In this way, they build a form of group behaviour out of their individual imaginary perception of the film.[28]

Is it the case, then, that youth violence has been imported by way of cinema into a society which respected the old adage 'If you don't want your father to be hit, you must not hit another's father'? Or should we not, rather, attribute this development to the uprootedness of urban life and the inactivity, despair and distress it has brought with it? Violence, which has a logical place in an art in which the dynamic of the narrative is most often based on confrontation, becomes morally contemptible – if not indeed dangerously contagious – when it is aestheticized.[29] It is precisely this aestheticization of violence (and sex) which is rejected by the immense majority of African filmmakers, who show it only when it is significant and serves the narrative.

NOTES

1. Théophile Obenga, *Stèles pour l'avenir*, Présence Africaine, Paris, 1978. Obenga, a disciple of Cheikh Anta Diop, sees the future of an Africa without frontiers as lying in a poetic melding of the land of the ancestors and the new culture.
2. The historical account which follows draws on Emmanuel Sama, 'Le Film africain étranger sur son propre territoire', *Écrans d'Afrique* 4, 1993, pp. 54–67; and Ferid Boughedir, *Le Cinéma africain de A à Z*, OCIC, Brussels, 1987, pp. 11–33.
3. In Ferid Boughedir's film *Caméra d'Afrique*, 1983.
4. Lionel N'Gakane, 'Developing Film Distribution and Exhibition in Region', in FEPACI, *L'Afrique et le centenaire du cinéma*, Présence Africaine, Paris, 1995, p. 294.
5. Interview with Justin K. Kagambega, acting manager of the board of SONACIB, Ouagadougou, March 1995. SONACIB owns a large proportion of the cinemas in Burkina Faso, but does not control the rare private cinemas such as the Neerwaya in Ouagadougou. A private cinema is not subject to the ticketing system which exists in all the SONACIB cinemas. It enters into monthly fixed-rate contracts, and a filmmaker is allowed to share his or her receipts directly with a private cinema. A national ticketing system is envisaged, but it is not yet operative. The contracts made between SONACIB and African filmmakers are based on a 50:50 share of receipts, which is a much better rate for filmmakers than in most other countries, where they often receive only 30 per cent. Many directors negotiate a contract with SONACIB during Fespaco and leave a copy of the film with them.

Since SONACIB had a monopoly on film imports, it did tend to give preference to its own cinemas. However, by splitting the management of distribution from that of exhibition, a fairer collaboration with the private cinemas has been restored. Since these cinemas could not previously get access to the profitable films, they had been unable to pay the fees due under the arrangement.

There are plans to privatize SONACIB, now that its profitability has been restored, but these plans have run up against the problem of its unsettled debts (one billion FCFA). It is anyone's guess whether a privatized SONACIB will continue with its policy of support for African cinema.

6. Interview with Jean-Louis Koula, Abidjan, 1995.
7. Interview with Françoise Balogun, Paris, 1995.
8. Interview with Kitia Touré, Abidjan, March 1995. Apart from introducting a generalized ticketing scheme, Touré's plan was for regulation of video-hire clubs, state loans for cinema managers with an obligation to renovate the cinemas, co-operation with France on exchanges and training, and partnership/twinning arrangements for cinemas.
9. Interview with Salif Traoré, Paris, 1995.
10. Bemba Kabiné Diabaté, 'Exploitation et distribution au Mali: le chaos originel', Écrans d'Afrique 4, 1993, pp. 72–6.
11. The devaluation of the CFA franc in 1994 radically changed the situation, doubling the costs of a cinema industry in which everything is made abroad. 'We don't understand the French language very well', remarks Kitia Touré ironically. 'We didn't understand that when you devalue by 50 per cent, prices increase by 100 per cent! Seat prices could not be increased when the monthly income of an Ivorian civil servant is 330,000 FCFA. The only solution was to reduce the tax burden' (interview with Kitia Touré, Abidjan, March 1995). Before devaluation, seat prices had not increased for ten years, even though the cost of films had been rising constantly.
12. Nii Laryea Korley, 'Le boom des vidéos', Écrans d'Afrique 7, 1994, p. 67.
13. 'Nigerian Video Market Booming', in Africa Film and TV 1994, Z Promotions, Harare, p. 45.
14. Richard T. Ismail, 'Les films africains en Afrique, une histoire d'ironies', Écrans d'Afrique 8, 1994, p. 70.
15. Interview with Pascal Diekebre, Les Studios cinema, Abidjan, 1995.
16. Interview with Salif Traoré, Paris, 1995.
17. Interview with Maurice Kaboré, Paris, 1995.
18. Pedro Pimienta, Mozambican producer, interviewed by Ines Anselmi in Zoom – Zeitschrift für Film, Zurich, November 1993, p. 23.
19. Interview with Lucien Patry, Paris, 1995.
20. Victor Bachy, Le Cinéma en Côte d'Ivoire, OCIC–L'Harmattan, Paris, 1983, p. 46.
21. Gnoan Roger M'Bala, interviewed by Lamine Saad and Jean-Pierre Garcia, Le Film Africain 17, October 1994, p. 14.
22. Interview with Frédéric Bontems, director of the Media Bureau in the French Ministère de la Coopération, Paris, February 1996.
23. Interview with Ben Zulu, Ouagadougou, 1995.
24. Interview with Joel Phiri, Brussels, 1997, published in Africultures 14 ('Produire en Afrique'), L'Harmattan, Paris, 1999.
25. Sama, 'Le Film africain étranger sur son propre territoire', p. 64.
26. Prosper Kompaoré, 'Le Spectateur africain et le spectacle cinématographique', Revue du VIIème Fespaco, pp. 17–19. This argument is quoted and further illustrated in M'Pungu Mulenda, 'Avec les Spectateurs du Niger', in CESCA, Camera nigra, le discours du film africain, OCIC–L'Harmattan, Paris, 1984, p. 150.
27. Yao Konan, 'Cinéma et marginalité sociale: l'exemple des quartiers populaires', DEA thesis, Institute of Ethno-sociology, Faculty of Letters, Arts and Human Sciences, Abidjan, 1990, p. 29.
28. Cinema has always triggered off fashions among the urban young. In Kinshasa a whole generation was influenced by Westerns. They were called 'the Bills'. They

could be recognized by their clothing and their language, 'hindubill' (*Cinémaction* 26, p. 149). Mulenda's 'Avec les Spectateurs du Niger' shows how the arrival of kung fu films launched the fashion for imitating Bruce Lee.

29. Serge Daney demonstrated this in a famous text which drew on Jacques Rivette's judgement of a tracking shot in *Kapo*, a film on the concentration camps made in 1960 by Gillo Pontecorvo. See Serge Daney, *Persévérance – entretien avec Serge Toubania*, POL, Paris, 1994, pp. 13–39. This piece was also published in *Trafic* (POL, Paris) 4, Autumn 1992.

FOURTEEN

A FICKLE AUDIENCE
IN THE NORTHERN HEMISPHERE

No one can lend you his heart.
Mozambican Proverb

The Western audience blows with the wind. It is all a question of the way of looking. As vital palliatives to the shortcomings of distribution, festivals are not without their contradictions but remain, both in the West and in Africa, the meccas where those who make African cinema meet their audience.

AIMING TRUE

Only those films which meet the quality criteria laid down by the international market can hope to make a profit in the Western marketplace. The success in France of such films as *Visages de femmes* (Désiré Ecaré, Ivory Coast, released 1985), *Yeelen* (Souleymane Cissé, Mali, 1987), *Bal Poussière* (Henri Duparc, Ivory Coast, 1988), *Yaaba* (Idrissa Ouedraogo, Burkina Faso, 1989) and *Tilaï* (Idrissa Ouedraogo, 1990), with total audience figures of between 120,000 and 340,000, hinted at a possible breakthrough to a mass audience, but this did not materialize.[1] *Samba Traoré* (Idrissa Ouedraogo, Burkina Faso, 1993) and *Hyenas/Ramatou* (Djibril Diop Mambety, Senegal, 1993) made their mark, but with box-office scores of 46,654 and 52,892 respectively for the whole of France, the audiences were disappointing. In 1997 the French audience figures were as follows: *Buud Yam* (Gaston Kaboré) 9,205; *Kini and Adams* (Idrissa Ouedraogo) 6,997; *Fools* (Ramadan Suleman) 4,369; *Keïta* (Dani Kouyaté) 3,544; *Macadam Tribu* (José Laplaine) 1,093; and *Clando* (Jean-Marie Teno) 486! The figures for 1999 were: *Mossane* (Safi Faye) 12,322; *Tableau Ferraille* (Moussa Sene Absa) 1,519; and *Watani* (Med Hondo) 772! The French audience figures for *Titanic* were 20,738,844, with video sales of 3,200,000. The fact that so few African films are actually produced means that all the more hope gets placed in an individual film. Now, for a film to make a profit, audience scores of 40,000–50,000 are required. For the purposes of comparison, in a survey carried out by *Le Film français* of 17 February 1995, examining forty American films whose production costs had already been amply covered by takings in the domestic market, the poorest performer had achieved a French audience of 30,000. Without state aid, 'different' forms of cinema are doomed.

The 'art cinema' audience, which tends in France to be centred in Paris and to be subject to fashion, has today turned towards Asian and American independent film. Consequently, African films now appear with very low-key publicity in a few little-known cinemas. How could it be otherwise, when the concentration of programming in the hands of a few large companies (Gaumont, Pathé, UGC) is constantly and increasingly squeezing alternative kinds of film (European as well as African) out of the domestic market? Yet there is no way of saving those kinds of film outside these official channels! When the head of Gaumont, Nicolas Seydoux, declares: 'Those who think you can convey a thousand ideas to someone through cinema ought to change their profession', it is not easy to see how current African films could fit into a circuit of huge multiplexes entirely orientated towards the success of American blockbusters.[2]

The problem has shifted, in this way, from distribution to exhibition, with many distributors no longer finding adequate cinemas to show their films in. Then the cruelty of competition kicks in with a vengeance: if the film does not come good in the first three weeks, it disappears for ever.

In this context, it is far from easy for the French programme of inter-departmental aid for little-shown film cultures to mitigate the shortcomings of the system. In pursuit of efficiency, that programme, which cannot impose draconian conditions on distributors, has recently attempted to break out of a culture based on hand-outs by demanding from the distributor a financial contribution to the promotion of the film, while at the same time doubling the overall funds available.[3]

Le Ballon d'or (Cheik Doukouré, Guinea, 1993), which was released in sixty cinemas, fifteen of them in Paris (followed by a further five in the second week), is an exception to this general state of affairs. It achieved an audience of 313,551 throughout France as a whole. With a popular theme (a young African becomes a football star), the film enjoyed the support of major backers who provided it with every opportunity to succeed, not least in international markets. 'I made it as a filmmaker subject to the demands of world cinema: the work is mine, but I worked the way any director the

Souleymane Cissé near Timbuktu on the set of *Waati* (Mali, 1995).
© Françoise Huguier.

world over works on a big production', says Cheik Doukouré.[4] The fact that
the film was able to reach a wide audience is also due to an efficient press
attaché; to a parallel poster campaign in Paris and the suburbs; to two weeks
of press showings; to presentations on all the television channels, and a large
number of radio stations; to a great effort on the part of the director to
present his film in a wide variety of places, particularly in the provinces; to
the commitment of professionals worldwide; to support from the Association française des cinémas d'art et d'essai (the French art film association),
which published a free leaflet presenting the film; and to the French Football Federation.

   Waati (Souleymane Cissé, Mali), which was presented in official competition at the Cannes Film Festival in 1995, was released shortly afterwards
by a large distributor in a sizeable number of cinemas with publicity that
combined a generous amount of advertising space with a generally favourable press. After viewing figures of 340,811 for *Yeelen*, throughout France as
a whole, *Waati*'s 54,722 was a disappointing score. Michel Brunet (cinema

office of the Ministry of Co-operation) and Jean-Pierre Garcia (Amiens Festival) concluded in an editorial in *Film Africain* that the film had been wrongly targeted: 'In spite of its "spectacular" qualities and the considerable resources deployed, *Waati* was and remains a film in the *auteur* tradition, and this implies a certain kind of distribution.'[5] A film which stands outside the dominant norms must, they argued, receive an enhanced form of distribution, including publicity exercises, presentation packs and special efforts to promote it in original ways. The two authors called for the formation of a network of motivated exhibitors capable of supporting film from the southern hemisphere in both France and Europe.

The way *Kini and Adams* (Idrissa Ouedraogo, 1997) flopped – the film was selected for the official competition at Cannes, and well received by the critics – seems to confirm their view. Although it was distributed with copious advertising by a major distributor, Polygram, it was seen by only 7,000 people in France over a six-week period.

Boosting distribution will increase the availability of access to the films, but will not create an audience for them: that requires people who are interested in Africa, in other countries. A society which conceals from itself the fact that it is a plural one will not take an interest in another culture, even if it rubs shoulders with it every day. A society which not so long ago believed that it had a civilizing mission in Africa, and which today regards that same mission as hopeless, will not go to see African films. The colonial past imposes a terrible burden. As Andrée Davanture says, 'Being French-speaking is a double-edged sword: if Africans didn't speak French, we'd be more conscious of their difference!'[6]

A LIMITED AUDIENCE

The 'art' film audience cannot simply be expanded at will. As with experimental literature, the hard core of dedicated, curious people who follow 'different' film is limited in number. There are not enough people to consume all the products aimed at them! Filmmakers are reduced to hoping to break into a market that is already too difficult (without exactly believing they are going to do this): they know they can hope, because some succeed; but they also know success is rare, and they do not, therefore, hope too much. All the same they do hope a little bit too much, because the ideology conveyed by the media is an ideology of mobility and success! In all this they are not so different from you or me, since we also hope 'a little bit too much' to climb the social ladder.[7] But breaking into the European market means meeting the quality standards defined by that particular audience. 'The general quality of African films is not high enough', says the producer Alain Rozanes. 'The fact that a film is African is not sufficient in itself to make someone go and see it.'[8] This opinion is confirmed by Alain Jalladeau, the director of the 'Trois Continents' film festival at Nantes: 'The public has undoubtedly fallen away on account of a number of mistakes, the release of certain films having left African cinema tarred with an image of poor quality.'[9] The 'short-comings' of the other films of the 'African cinema' genre thus determine too heavily the perception of an individual film, and this leads directors to want to be rid of this 'African filmmaker' label which they cannot throw off. They want to be allowed just to make films, like everyone else.

There is one cinema in Paris which has attempted to specialize in 'black' film (Black Africa and the African diaspora), without restricting itself wholly to that. The director of that cinema, Sanvi Panou, stresses that his screening policy is open to other films of quality which have difficulty being shown ('Why create ghettos when we are being pushed further into one every day?').[10] This concern to escape a reductive image does not mean that the team at *Images d'ailleurs* [Images from Elsewhere] do not set out to try to bring in an audience with a black cultural background: 'We have to go and find the audience where it is. We undertake concerted campaigns with the immigrant workers' associations to make the community aware of our presence.' Over time, the project has achieved results, with families coming in from the suburbs at weekends to afternoon showings. But a commercial company would not have had so long to find its audience: *Images d'ailleurs* operates as a non-profit-making association. In London, Kwesi Owusu runs a similar venture at the Electric Cinema Club in Portobello Road.

The filmmaker who ventures on to Western terrain is not a traitor to his country. He may be opening himself up to a new view of things: the confrontation with another culture may allow him to avoid being confined in an 'authenticity' verging on fundamentalism. The key is not to lose one's soul in the process. We shall come back to this point. Europe can spell catastrophe or salvation. Exploring a new place can validate one's experience and one's approach: one finds this repeatedly in all fields of artistic endeavour. 'In *Bako, l'autre rive* [Jacques Champreux, 1978]', says the Ivorian actor Sidiki Bakaba,

> I played an African who didn't know city life and who was discovering it for the first time, whereas I had already done that and the process had left its mark on me. I came to see that technique can precede the actual acting. It was as though I'd been a musician and I'd learned classical music before going back to the rhythm of the tom-tom, which is in me, to give a perfect performance in a village. I was living proof that it was wrong to say a French-trained actor was lost in Africa. In fact I had gained by my training: the West opened Africa up to me![11]

But the filmmaker takes a hard hit coming to Europe. The European audience's lack of interest is altogether too pronounced. Cineastes would really like to fall back on Africa, hoping 'a little bit too much' that the changes in that continent will speed up to the point where films really can be made there. How would it be, they wonder, if the African market were not so insignificant? But this would require a radical evolution. 'Our states have never understood that the crisis today is a cultural crisis. They merely see it as economic', declared Souleymane Cissé on Malian television in 1991. 'We shall never be able to develop until we develop our culture: that is where human health resides.'[12] This idea is growing on African governments, but even to describe the conversion as slow would be euphemistic.

PROMOTION THROUGH FESTIVALS

Since no satisfactory distribution system exists, the only solution is to create events. This is the aim of the various festivals which have sprung up around the world. They were born of a desire to show films which would never make it into Western cinemas, and they have gradually gained in importance, to the point where the relative merits of films are assessed there even before they are released in Africa. Since the disappearance of film clubs, festivals have been the place to meet and discuss film. Their budgets are sometimes large enough for them to bring in filmmakers from overseas, enticed by an airline ticket for one of the world's capital cities and the prospect of prizes from competitions, though, given the low level of annual production, these seem to bring the eternal return of the same old names. Some of the festivals, however, pleading the limitations of their budgets and the publicity they are supposed to be giving to the films, omit to pay the filmmakers for showing their work. In this way, the film finds its European audience, but does so without accruing any income.

After studying cinema, Fanta Nacro from Burkina Faso made a short entitled *Un certain matin* (1993) which attracted a lot of attention. Apart from its artistic qualities, the film had an amusing central idea: a peasant, who knows nothing about films and filming, injures an actor who is chasing a woman! 'I humped the film around to all the festivals to see which ones were worth the bother. I went round the world with it, from Dakar to Harare by way of the Canadian and US university circuits.'[13] Directors who become globetrotting stars can spend a couple of years doing nothing but presenting their films, only to ask in the end whether they were really supporting their work or not perhaps supporting the festivals themselves (and, consequently, the cities which subsidize them). Henri Duparc, for instance, says he is now going to confine himself to those festivals which help him to sell his films.[14] A difference consequently arises between the 'little' festivals, which are seen as exploitative, and the 'big international set pieces', which enable the film to be promoted effectively to the media and the profession.

However, the commitment of the teams responsible for some of the 'little' festivals gives them a warmth and a quality which are seldom found nowadays in cinema events. The conviviality of this kind of meeting with the public is essential to a filmmaker hungry for immediate feedback which is not merely from professionals in the sphere of public subsidy, analysis or sales. Here again, it is all a question of how one looks at things. Alongside festivals which are outstanding for the intelligence of their programming (retrospectives, seminars and cultural events), one also finds cases of a paternalism tinged with a sense of a guilty conscience which sends a chill down the spine. Presenting an African film sometimes becomes a humanitarian act – if not, indeed, the crucial plank in the humanitarian campaign. 'They talk to me sometimes as though I'm responsible for the situation in the country', says Pierre Yameogo, 'and as though I ought absolutely to support every action to aid Burkina Faso!'[15]

When it comes to deciding where to premiere those films which meet international criteria, there is an obvious choice between the big promotional festivals (Cannes, Berlin, Venice) and the pan-African festivals (Ouagadougou, Carthage and, since 1993, Harare, which is centred more on the English-speaking zone). Should one primarily seek recognition in Africa, or gamble on achieving international celebrity? There is, then, once again, a line of demarcation between two visions of cinema, reflecting different approaches to the audience. One can either prioritize the African audience or seek universality. In reality, it is essential to be at Cannes or Berlin if a film is to get into the Western market, which is, theoretically, the way it can hope to be profitable. Winning the 'Étalon de Yenenga', the main prize at the Ouagadougou Fespaco, does not give you an easier entrée to European cinemas. *Au nom du Christ* (Gnoan Roger M'Bala, Ivory Coast, 1993) and *Guimba* (Cheikh Oumar Sissoko, Mali, 1995) testify painfully to that fact.

However, both Fespaco, which was launched in 1969, and the Journées cinématographiques de Carthage, created in 1966, have contributed substantially to the awareness and promotion of African films. Every two years Fespaco – the main cultural event in Burkina Faso, and a great festival which fires the enthusiasm of the whole city – reminds a relatively uninterested Europe that black culture is teeming with original creative artists. In Africa it periodically revives the debate on the place of culture in development, and encourages states to focus on the economic issues raised by the film industry.

Without Fespaco, directors would find it difficult to negotiate financial aid from their ministries of culture, so positive is the effect of the films which win awards there on the image of their countries of origin. Going some way beyond the political and media festival (though not far enough, say the advocates of a more professional festival), Fespaco is orientated towards films selected for their quality, with a view to promoting them across the entire continent.

Various countries, such as Niger, Ivory Coast and Togo have their 'weeks' of African cinema, though none of these is as large as the 'Recidak' in Dakar. They all start out with the same aim: to show those African films that are 'forgotten' by the distributors. Increasing the number of these festivals, though it would allow an African audience to see the films made by their own directors, would probably lead to a contradiction similar to the one encountered in the West: Black African films would find it even more difficult to gain access to the traditional commercial distribution circuits, and would be seen only by a small audience of the initiated. Fespaco, by contrast, has the merit of being very popular with the inhabitants of Ouagadougou, who do not rush to see African films at other times. In just one week, swept along by the event, they devour an impressive number of what are sometimes difficult, subtitled films, projected in all the city's cinemas! This biennial orgy of cinema-going, which has something of the pilgrimage about it, is largely down to an assiduous promotion campaign. The city's main streets are adorned with big yellow banners proclaiming its slogans: 'Going to Fespaco means supporting African cinema', 'Fespaco, the pride of a continent', or 'Let's go to the pictures and stay young!'

NOTES

1. *Visages de femmes* had audience figures of 60,525 in Paris and its periphery over 16 weeks, and 130,105 for the whole of France. The figures for *Yeelen* were 138,866 in Paris (26 weeks) and 340,811 for France. For *Bal Poussière*, 104,373 in Paris (12 weeks) and 223,731 for France. For *Yaaba*, 52,838 in Paris (25 weeks) and 285,214 for France. For *Tilaï*, 53,885 in Paris (30 weeks) and 124,663 for France. (Source: CNC–Le Film Français.)

2. Quoted by Carlos Pardo, 'Le Cinéma français étouffé par Hollywood', *Le Monde diplomatique*, May 1996, p. 32. The original remark appeared in *Le Figaro magazine*, 23 December 1995.

3. The Centre national de la Cinématographie has signed an agreement with five Parisian art house cinemas by which they agree to keep on their programme for at least four weeks the films receiving support within the framework of this programme. The interdepartmental fund (the government departments involved are those of Culture, Co-operation and Foreign Affairs, each of which contributes

one million francs) supports a distributor with financial assistance up to a maximum of 200,000 francs, which enables that distributor to acquire the distribution rights to a film and to finance its subtitling. In return, the distributors commit themselves to investing an equivalent sum in the promotion costs required for releasing a film in Paris and the provinces.

4. Interview with Cheik Doukouré, Paris, 1996.
5. *Film Africain* 22, November 1995, p. 3.
6. Interview with Andrée Davanture, Paris, 1995.
7. This argument is developed by Jean Baudrillard in *For a Critique of the Political Economy of the Sign.* trans. Charles Levin, Telos Press, St Louis MO, 1981.
8. Interview with Alain Rozanes, producer of *Hyenas/Ramatou* (Djibril Diop Mambety, Senegal, 1991).
9. Interview with Alain Jalladeau, Paris, 1995.
10. Interview with Sanvi Panou, Paris, 1995.
11. Interview with Sidiki Bakaba, Paris, 1996.
12. The remark was made on the Malian television programme 'Cinétribune' on the occasion of Fespaco 1991.
13. Interview with Fanta Nacro, Paris, 1994.
14. Sambolgo Bangré, 'Le Cinéma africain dans la tempête des petits festivals', *Écrans d'Afrique* 7, 1994, p. 56.
15. Interview with Pierre Yameogo, Paris, 1994.

FIFTEEN

'WHEN YOU'VE GOT MEAT TO COOK, YOU GO AND FIND SOMEONE WITH FIRE': THE LOGICS OF WESTERN AID

Try to smile at the caiman when you have your finger in its mouth![1]

The successes of African films have left that cinema vulnerable. External influence on content is growing, and the policy of financial aid, which meets the Western need for images from the southern hemisphere, creates pressure for adaptation to international quality standards.

THE HEART AND THE HEAD

The successes registered by Black African film in the mid-1980s, together with the development of festivals, paradoxically rendered that cinema vulnerable: they increased the Western pressures on the content of films, and prompted a radical change in aid policy.

Filmmakers from French-speaking Africa were previously supported for their capacity to reflect an Africa breaking away from the West; their films held up a mirror to a quest for decolonization coupled with apprehension about modernity.[2] The French Ministry of International Co-operation was practically the sole partner for cineastes taking advantage of structures and financing which did not exist in their own countries. All are emphatically agreed that the Ministry did not intervene in the subject matter of the films. The philosophy of its support involved a constant trade-off between heart and head, described by Michel Brunet in his 1999 film *Le Coeur et la raison*. France's co-operation with its former colonies had its rationale in a solidarity which connected with a sound understanding of the nation's own interests. The moral duty to provide aid is also rational, because it opens up a market of potential consumers. In François Mitterrand's famous formulation, 'helping the Third World is helping oneself'.[3] When this is understood, support for the existence of an African film culture becomes one of the cultural dimensions of development aid.

And yet, several decades after the African countries achieved their independence, the failure is patent. The African states are submerged in a crisis that is both economic and sociocultural. The 1980s, characterized as they were by economic recession and the growing marginalization of Africa, have been declared 'lost' to development. In a distant echo of Raymond Cartier's famous call, first formulated in *Paris-Match* in 1956, to 'put the Corrèze before the Zambezi', there are voices advocating that aid to Africa should be dropped and France should, rather, concentrate on more potentially fruitful collaboration, for example with the new states of Eastern Europe. But at this point the heart comes to the aid of the head to ensure a surprising continuity in France's African policy.

French public opinion and France's political class subscribe to a policy which is so opaque as to flout all the rules of democratic openness. This is not a product of deception; it arises from the unease of a collective consciousness oscillating between shame and self-interest. No doubt the enabling mental structure goes back to childhood memories of the circus double-act in which the white clown (Monsieur Loyal), educated and rational, brings his knowledge and assistance to the black clown (Auguste), who gets more and more mixed up and does everything wrong.[4] The misunderstandings and buffoonery lead inevitably to failure, but this does not stop them trying again. Furthermore, as one sketch turns into another, an undeniable complementarity – if not, indeed, a complicity – develops between the two clowns, levelling out the initial imbalance. The black clown manages to bring the human factor to the fore, while the white loses some of his haughtiness.

GIVING AND AFTER

In the ambiguity of this duality, linking the bad conscience and 'burden' of civilized man to a fascination for what he is not, we can see the ambivalence of our attitude towards the Other, who is perceived at times as a threat and at times as an invitation to surpass oneself.[5] A consensus for a strategy of giving has been emerging, against a background of grand declarations on human rights from Brazzaville to Phnom Penh, and from Cancun to La Baule. Giving is a gamble on possible change, a quasi-spiritual investment in an enforced optimism – the profitability of the investment being promised by politicians only to sweeten the pill of a public opinion as concerned with morality as it is with the wise use of its money. The policy of international co-operation, which has too often been accused of dominating in order to exploit, asserts the primacy of giving. For example, the French Ministry of Co-operation has fought for the 'advance against takings' granted by the Fonds Sud (the umbrella organization for aid to feature films from the Co-operation, Culture and Foreign Affairs ministries) to become a true subsidy.[6] In this same vein, filmmakers have called for the Agence de la Francophonie (formerly the ACCT, the international body for promoting use of the French language overseas) to make its aid a genuine gift and not link it to the sale of screening rights to the television channel TV5.[7]

The Fonds Cinéma Sud (an interdepartmental fund providing selective financial assistance to film production in developing countries) grants subsidies ranging from 400,000 to 1,000,000 francs to feature films, up to a total of 12 million francs per year. These grants have to be spent in France on post-production operations, the purchase of film stock, wages for French technicians, the hire of filming equipment or subtitling in French. Here we find the same logic of heart and head: through generous support to the creative work of artists from the southern hemisphere, it is the French cinema industry which is being subsidized – on the pretext of monitoring that the funds are properly spent. Many voices have been raised against a policy which involves giving with one hand and taking back with the other. Cheikh Oumar Sissoko from Mali, for instance, believes that this arrangement minimizes the possibility of a cinema industry emerging in Africa.

Voices have been raised recently against the very principle of external aid. 'I don't see myself as a disabled person who couldn't be competitive and who has to be protected!' declares Cameroonian director Jean-Pierre Bekolo.

> In America there are lots of filmmakers who have nothing and that's when you can gauge their ability to reinvent something. It's when you face problems that you learn. What has this aid produced? It's time now to take stock. African cinema is too protected. This all prevents real thinking taking place. Let African cinema suffer, live and even die. Its survival, like that of Africa, does not depend on anyone.

Bekolo responded to a commission to produce the African entry for a series commemorating the centenary of cinema with *Aristotle's Plot* (1997), a disturbing, provocative film, which takes up this same argument: 'In my view this cinema is still-born. We have to bury it and cut off the drip-feed, or the rot will set in. It isn't connected to people. Rot and decay spread poison.'[8]

Since Marcel Mauss, anthropology has shown that any relationship of giving involves domination: to take advantage of the gift, the recipient, sometimes unwittingly, abandons his own understanding of reality and takes on the other party's perspective.[9] 'Can a cow suckle a goat?' asks a proverb repeated in Fadika Kramo-Lanciné's film *Djeli* (Ivory Coast, 1981). If aid to a foreign cinema is ambiguous, this is not because it makes it an 'assisted' cinema. All cinema is in this position – even Hollywood cinema.[10] The point is that it is aid to *something other* than itself. *La Haine* (Mathieu Kassovitz, France, 1995) did not receive an advance against takings from the Centre national de la cinématographie, but was able to find other backers from among the television channels who have certainly not regretted the move. African filmmakers do not have this possibility in their homelands. They sit uneasily between two wholly different economic and cultural systems, and this inevitably leads to contradictions and concessions.

THE INTERNATIONALIZATION OPTION

The 1980s vogue for Black African film occurred in the context of a profound re-examination of procedures and policies. Jacques Lang's arrival at the French Ministry of Culture brought a new relationship between money and culture, which now had to be, if not profitable, then at least managerially responsible for its own funding. The fact of receiving grant monies did not absolve the filmmakers from proper management of their funds. At the same time, the failure of 'development' led to its being re-examined as an imported notion, which could not be generally applied to the whole planet. It was seen, indeed, as a Western projection on to the Third World in the service of Western hegemony. The radical, culturalist critique of 'development' presented it as synonymous with Westernization. To escape this dilemma, and to take account of the historical fracture represented by the emergence of the South within Western societies, there was an appeal to a new consciousness of Humanity, in which respect for – and affirmation of – cultural diversity would make it possible to avoid a war between cultures.

It followed from this that Black African cinema cultures had to be brought out of their ghettos. The bodies which provided aid chose the market as the route to this end, and sought to integrate those cultures into the world cinema economy. The North needed images from the South: rather than grant 100 per cent subsidies to films which would never be seen outside the charmed circle of the specialized festivals, international aid policy aimed to create a 'quality' cinema, capable of finding its niche in the international marketplace and asserting the existence of African culture. To that end, African cinema had to be made profitable. 'It's not for us to dictate their subjects to the filmmakers', said Frédéric Bontems, head of the Media Office in the Ministry of International Co-operation, 'but to emphasize the risk of marginalization they run in terms of funding if they don't meet the expectations of their audiences more fully.'[11] Given the way distribution circuits have melted away in Africa, the audience referred to here is still the European one: 'Economically speaking, the only real market is currently that in the northern hemisphere.'

At a point when privately owned channels are eating into the audiences for the public ones, the only television stations which are really investing in Black African cinema (Channel 4 in Britain, ZDF and WDF in Germany) have considerably reduced their involvement. To finance their films, directors have barely any other choice than to knock on the doors of the various public funders, whether French or European, and the few, rare charitable foundations.[12] But this does not always produce results. 'Fonds Sud becomes problematic when it's the only place left', stresses producer Jacques Bidou. 'Filmmakers who have had 25–30 per cent of their finance for two years cannot find the rest.'[13] Funding is a battle fought on alien terrain, littered with unpleasant surprises and uncertainties. It is a terrain on which filmmakers may expend the best part of their energies and may come to wonder, in the end, whether they are in the right job!

The reality of the situation is not very encouraging, but this is the lot of all creators of cinema. It costs more and more to make a film and the amount of public funding available is not rising – and will not rise – because states everywhere are making draconian cutbacks in their overall budgets. In the face of the competition, private investors are gradually moving out of film, which is problematic in terms of both box-office receipts and television viewing figures. Given all this, the need to conform to Western requirements is presented as inevitable: 'If you want to make films', says Frédéric Bontems,

> don't you have to adapt to another audience? It would only be stoking up illusions to support African filmmakers in making big-budget films solely for African audiences since it would run counter to all market realities. The paradox lies not in the policy of a ministry, but in the harsh reality of this situation.

CONSOLIDATING PROFESSIONALIZATION

'To join the dance, you have to know how to dance', says a Cameroonian proverb. To take on this international market, and hence ensure the survival of this style of cinema, the objective that has been set is one of professionalization. The idea is that assistance with rewriting will attempt to offset weaknesses in the screenplays; using European producers will guarantee that budgets are kept to; legal back-up and close involvement in the production will attempt to minimize the dangers of filmmakers going down the wrong channels, failing to find the right contacts. This is not a new conception: the pursuit of a solid professionalism has been part and parcel of the action of

Set photographer leaning on a reflector during the filming of *Hyenas/Ramatou* (Djibril Diop Mambety, Senegal, 1993). © Félix von Muralt/Lookat.

the partners of Black African cinema from the beginning – starting with the Cinema Office of the Ministry of International Co-operation.

A debate has begun on the way aid is spread around. Since funds are limited, it seems better to focus them on tried and tested propositions. But such an intensification of selection might prevent new talent being uncovered. Filmmakers are not exempt from competition. 'We are all trying to draw from the same well', observes the Mauritanian director Abderrahmane Sissako, whom Pierre Yameogo from Burkina Faso is fond of quoting. 'We are all grey lizards on the same wall!' That is to say, we are all in the same boat, and it is shipping water. All on the same wall, like those fat lizards who bask in great numbers on the sides of African houses... and in the first shot of *Wendemi* (1993)! Fonds Sud subsidizes between five and seven feature film projects at a time, and its chairman, Frédéric Mitterrand, does not consider that the aid is being diluted.[14] Nor is this the impression of Robert Lombaerts at the Agence de la Francophonie, which tries to give 'the most it can to good projects'.[15] The trend, then, is towards greater selectivity, given that it is the dream underlying all efforts at internationalization to see another African film triumph at Cannes the way *Yeelen* did in 1987 – a triumph which would have positive knock-on effects for the whole of African cinema. Where there's life there's hope – and, indeed, the question of life and survival is paramount today. But if we accept that the judges at the big festivals reflect their times, the trend within the Western audience is not towards the appreciation of Black African cinema. That audience, which is giving up on the idea of progress, is undergoing an identity crisis deepening the gulf between it and other cultures. Rejecting the Other for his or her difference, or mythifying him or her on the grounds of that same difference amounts to denying the Other by refusing to recognize him/her in his/her diversity and diffuseness; in his/her uncertainty and tentative questings... Pierre-André Taguieff has shown that when anti-racism exalts difference, it becomes another form of racism.[16]

WRESTLING WITH THE BLANK PAGE

For African cineastes, submerged by a reifying market logic, the danger is clearly one of losing their souls. 'You see films twisting their message to reach a Western market', says producer Jacques Bidou. 'You come to see, in the end, that the industry dimension can't be given precedence over the creative: without creative artists there is no industry.' The creative artist's vision must be untrammelled by external constraints. 'It is precisely in so far as we work up stories which affect us, in a close relationship with our societies', says Malian director Cheikh Oumar Sissoko, 'that we have something to say to the rest of the world.'[17] Successful African creative work cannot be based on the expectations of the Western public, but pressure is applied from all sides, by everyone from critic to producer: 'This cinema has become vulnerable because they're beginning to tell it what it should be', says Gaston Kaboré, president of the Pan-African Federation of Filmmakers.

> It's being told, for example, that it has to get out of the villages or that it has to portray African dramas. Whereas African cinema is a cinema of urgency, which has true legitimacy only in so far as it profoundly explains today's reality. So, once again, the dominant Western way of thinking is foisting its ideas on Africa.[18]

We are verging here on the ultimate negation of the Other, which consists in thinking in his stead and for his own good. What African director hasn't had to fight with a producer to have the thrust of his film respected? 'Some producers I approached after *Laafi* was short-listed at Cannes', says Pierre Yameogo, 'sent me off to see *Black micmac* to show me the comedy I ought to make!'[19] Sembène Ousmane had to bring a legal action against his producer (who had been foisted on him so that he could get CNC aid) before he could get permission not to include erotic scenes in *Mandabi/The Money Order* (1968).[20] When the Kenyan director Wanjiru Kinyanjui wanted to make a film set on the Kenyan plateau, she presented the producers with photos of her locations. Many found the landscape too green, and advised her to shift the filming to the savannah. One producer even offered to provide her with round huts.[21]

However, whereas the demand for exoticism, eroticism or hedonism is easily identifiable, the danger for the filmmaker remains one of leaving the ground of his own reality and tailoring his judgement to someone else's. Ngangura Mweze tells of how, in local Zaïrean parlance, exclamations are routinely repeated. When Kourou (Papa Wemba) brings a second chicken in *La Vie est belle* (1987), the mother of the young heroine Kabibi exclaims: 'How happy I am! How happy I am!' 'We had a long argument with the editor', he says. 'She wanted to cut out the repetition, but it's normal in our part of the world to repeat the expression because she was happy!' In the end, a harmony has to be found, and this requires finesse and determination from the filmmaker. 'Intangible economic factors force you to yield to certain pressures', stresses Raymond Rajaonarivelo, 'but you have to go subtly so as not to wreck the story. The real battle is with the blank sheet of paper. You can see that something won't get through, and you have to say it another way so that it will.'

THE 'ÉCRANS DU SUD' EXPERIENCE

The concern to professionalize African film lay behind the creation in March 1992 of a new structure, Écrans du Sud, the aim of which was to put filmmakers from the South in contact with professionals from the North and to promote the emergence of an African cinema which could meet the demands of the hour. Écrans du Sud came out of a twofold realization: that the audiovisual sector is an essential vehicle of exchange between cultures and that acknowledged talent exists in the southern hemisphere which cannot find expression where the resources are inadequate. This realization, reached by those represented at the French-speaking countries' Summit of November 1991 [le Sommet de la Francophonie], is a good illustration of the factors which have played their part in the development of French thinking on overseas aid: the success of certain African films, which made it seem possible that other African films could find their niche in the international marketplace; the failure of development policies and the questioning of the notion of development; the need to develop intercultural exchange in response to the problems of the integration of immigrant communities, as shown by the French urban riots; and the need to bring in private funds to supplement public funding, the latter having failed to keep pace with the increased costs of filmmaking. Last but not least, the declared ultimate goal of Écrans du Sud was to see 'the emergence of genuine co-productions between countries in the southern hemisphere, the only sure way of creating local film industries'.[22]

Écrans du Sud helped filmmakers to find their way around the small Parisian cinema world so that films could be made in the best possible conditions, both artistic and financial.[23] The aim was to give southern-hemisphere filmmakers an instrument that was more independent, less bound up with the state and hence not so dependent on the political developments which might possibly constrain the various government departments. Consequently, the organization was to receive joint (public and private) funding. The experiment was short-lived. The Association was wound up in 1993, the official reason being that it had not found the requisite private funds. Filmmakers had appreciated the involvement of those professionals who had been moved to take part, the support from the network that had been set up, and the thinking which had gone into the venture.

In fact, the Écrans du Sud experience had an eye-opening effect, prompting fresh thinking and a shift within the whole sector towards greater openness: decisions on financial assistance were now taken by commissions of professionals, the various funders were better co-ordinated, and relationships were created between professionals so that filmmakers were not plunged into aid-dependency. We might ask whether the aim of becoming the sole provider of support and funding for African cinema was a desirable one, and also whether it was really necessary to subscribe to the obsession with 'speaking with one voice' which has characterized the debate on external aid since the 1930s. Might it not in fact be said that the existing scattered range of players in this field guarantees a plurality of points of view, and ensures that all interests are defended? France is the only Western country which does not have just one overseas aid and co-operation department, but a range of uncoordinated and often contradictory micro-policies.[24] But why should this be an issue? A varied raft of approaches is a guarantee of flexibility and creativity in responding to a wide range of requests for funding and maintaining the fecundity of those projects.

A KEY MINISTRY

Since the overall amount of aid could not increase, Écrans du Sud was financed by tapping into the budgets of the government departments concerned. In not renewing its support for Écrans du Sud, the French Ministry of Co-operation was undoubtedly wishing to preserve its direct aid, which enabled it to intervene independently. Direct aid might be said to be the cornerstone of the action of the Ministry of Co-operation. It is that direct relationship which enables it to support a screenplay, such as Pierre Yameogo's *Laafi* (1991), which might have been turned down by Fonds Sud, or to get around the condition imposed by that body which excludes films not mainly shot in the southern hemisphere, such as Med Hondo's *Lumière noire* (1994); or to enable a strong film like *Hyenas/Ramatou* (Djibril Diop Mambety, 1992) to be subtitled, to have a press secretary at Cannes, additional copies or a preview for the cinema distributors; or, alternatively, to make it possible for shorter-than-full-length fiction films, creative documentaries and an audiovisual production to exist, whereas Fonds Sud finances only full-length feature films; to set up training schemes or to help people in the cinema business to get together at the 'Cinémas du Sud' stand at Cannes.

With the disappearance of Écrans du Sud, and in the light of the persistent non-participation by African states, the Ministry of Co-operation has acquired a key role, through its direct aid and its historic significance, in choosing which proposals receive backing. Other bodies, such as the European Communities and the Agence de la Francophonie, often wait for a positive decision from the Ministry before making their own decisions, which means that filmmakers have no option but to take this route. Rejection by the Ministry can be a catastrophe for the filmmakers, whose hopes can go up in smoke in an instant. The Ministry does not like to have this pressure on it, even though the number of proposals it receives has in fact fallen.[25]

Although it is often accused of conservatism, it was the first body to opt to internationalize the sector. Its aim is not, however, to commit all African filmmakers to making universal cinema: it continues, with its schemes of direct aid, to subsidize films and audiovisual products which are aimed typically at African audiences. It asserts its difference by opposing the Fonds Sud criteria, which specify that a film must be made mainly in Africa. For filmmakers who have, in many cases, lived in Paris for a long time, this condition is very restrictive: it attests to an inability to consider a foreigner with his or her own culture as a full member of French society. Does anyone ask French directors to shoot in France before they can obtain an advance against takings? What is it but their own identity that excludes African filmmakers from receiving a subsidy for shooting in Europe? The African director is an irremediably non-integrable Other, as a consequence of his cultural difference; on the other hand, he is already part of French society and is helping to cross-fertilize it at a deep level. The effect of this is the almost total absence of films relating to the experience of the black community in Europe. The members of the commission of the Fonds Sud are also trying to take things forward: having had to reject Med Hondo's *Lumière noire* (1994), which depicts an investigation into the links between a crime and the expulsion of 101 Malians (the film is essentially a 'thriller' based on a novel by crime writer Didier Daeninckx), they granted the maximum support they are allowed to provide to Idrissa Ouedraogo's *Le Cri du coeur* (1994), a film shot largely in Lyon.

SURVIVING

Le Cri du Coeur was in the end granted an advance against takings separate from the Fonds Sud money. The 'advance against takings' arrangement – which provides a distinctly more attractive sum, but is in principle reserved for French and EU filmmakers – is also open to foreign residents or to production companies from countries which have signed co-production agreements with France.[26] By comparison, Fonds Sud, financed from the budgets of the three ministries involved in Third World aid, is part of a strategy of international co-operation. The aid it gives is friendly assistance for a different style of cinema, though its commitment is a relatively limited one. Yet its twelve million francs, set against a total of a hundred million paid out in advances against takings, is not negligible. As Frédéric Mitterrand stressed at Cannes in 1996, a number of foreign films shown at the festival have benefited from its support. The commission of industry professionals involved gives the films they select a validation and notoriety which are significant when they come to seek further funding. On the other hand, such films do run the risk of being labelled 'Third World Cinema', which is not generally an advantage.

Given the threats to the cultural sector which have been revealed in the debates around the renegotiation of the GATT agreement, it would seem reasonable for countries not to become isolated. It seems to be in the interest of French cinema to support the survival of national cinemas of whatever origin to ensure that a plurality of images is maintained in the face of the great Hollywood steamroller, and hence to ensure its own survival.[27] But this aid will become fully effective only if the films make their mark on the international level. The bilateral agreements signed between France and

Gaston Kaboré on the set of *Rabi* (Burkina Faso, 1992).
© Marc Salomon.

Burkina Faso, Ivory Coast, Cameroon, Senegal and Guinea have improved the conditions for Franco-African co-productions, providing them with an uncontested legal status which, among other things, gives them access to the 'advance against takings' arrangement and allows them to be shown on television channels as part of the European film quota.

During a period of infatuation with African film, this access to the French market would make it possible to offset the increase in production costs. Currently, however, box-office takings are insufficient either in France or in Africa to make up for that increase.[28] This is a major contradiction. Moving from craft production to a more industrial economy requires a situation in which there is a return on investment; otherwise there is a great risk of a failure that will harm the whole of the cinematography concerned. This is, in fact, how things stand today. Although no one is arguing against the need for professionalization, the aim of getting African film on to the international circuit is a controversial one. Will it bring an advance or a retreat? Every filmmaker wants to see his or her film find new audiences, but not on absolutely any terms, or by compromising on all fronts. Similarly, it might be argued that the northern hemisphere needed southern films to challenge its own perceptions, but what would be the point if the import of those films was denatured? No one would gain. 'All those who have made the painful attempt to meet Western criteria', points out the editor Andrée Davanture, 'have found it hard to put the necessary heart into it and have met with terribly scathing criticism.'[29] Adapting too much to those criteria brings with it the danger that future films will be compromised. If it is forced to make the concessions inherent in internationalization, African cinema runs the risk of losing both its soul and its chances of survival.

To meet the economic imperative of finding an audience, nimble footwork of a kind well understood in artistic circles is required. If artists seek merely to please, they lose their capacity to fly in the face of fashions and norms. Without a shock effect, there can be no art: to stimulate thinking, art must disconcert; it must be novel, break with the dominant forms, challenge the audience's ordinary ways of thinking, reveal to the public that it is in some way behind the times. When the order between creative work and the attendant economic contingencies is reversed, the work tends to be doomed to banality and oblivion – even if it achieves some fleeting success on the way.

Ultimately, sure progress would be achieved if access to the international market were combined with the emergence of African structures capable of developing South–South co-productions for a popular cinema rooted in local cultures, with an improvement in the distribution and exhibition of films. Unless African states commit funds to them, such structures cannot be set up, as the requisite investment exceeds the capacities of the few French ministries concerned. 'The current levels of funding mean that a certain level of filmmaking can be maintained', says Frédéric Bontems, 'but they are not sufficient to develop a genuine film industry in Africa.'

Initiatives of all kinds do, however, show that embryonic solutions can prepare the ground for a future cinema industry which will allow Africa to escape the eternal dialectic between heart and head. Overseas development support for the creation of the Institut africain d'éducation cinématographique (INAFEC) in Ouagadougou made a contribution to training the African technicians needed for such structures. Although INAFEC had in the end to close (when the funds promised by the other African partner states failed to materialize, the costs of the institute were too heavy to be borne by the university alone), training schemes are still organized today by the French Ministry of Co-operation and the Agence de la Francophonie. The Association des Trois Mondes also publishes detailed country-by-country lists of available technicians and equipment. A project undertaken by the various ministries concerned, based on the experience of the Consortium interafricain de distribution cinématographique (CIDC), is aiming to provide a less state-based support for film distribution through a partnership with a network of pilot cinemas. Proposals from the Fédération panafricaine des cinéastes (FEPACI), which would facilitate the production of advertising material, videos, documentaries and television programmes, enabling film-makers to make a living from their work, are also under consideration.

PLANET ATRIA

The Association technique de recherches et d'informations audiovisuelles (Atria) was the striking and heart-warming creation of a period in which some still believed in generosity. It was a centre seething with activity, a meeting place for all involved in African cinema and a place where film-makers from Africa could find support. There was a warm welcome to be had there, and no place for mistrust or suspicion. Atria, a non-governmental organization, grew out of a period when the future of French aid was in the balance. The audiovisual technical section of the French Ministry of Co-operation ceased functioning in 1980: the Ministry no longer wished to be the obligatory channel through which this fully developing cinema culture had to pass. The decision was a sudden one: there were films in post-production which were in danger of not being completed. Faced with this emergency, technicians and filmmakers mobilized to create an independent structure which was able to continue the project of professionalization that had been begun. This was to be not a grant-awarding body but a working unit, providing a welcome for filmmakers and liaison with professionals in the northern hemisphere, advice on pitching proposals and on costings, documentation and loans of films to festivals, training in editing and pro-duction, technical production with editing studios, and production manage-ment under the umbrella of the Atriascope co-operative. This was how Atria was born, with the aid of financial support from a Protestant charitable organization and, subsequently, help from the French Cultural Intervention Fund. Limited funding was subsequently granted almost every year by the Ministry of Co-operation and the CNC. Atria's small team of workers lost count of the hours of overtime they worked, though they remained opposed to the diktat of profitability. 'You can't look at building a heritage in terms of profitability', says general manager Andrée Davanture. 'Do they expect the state opera to make a profit? The key thing is that African cinema should exist!'[30]

Atria, as a small pocket of practitioners who were not particularly in-clined to be influenced by the developments within the French aid regime, fought, on a non-exclusive basis, for images in which Africans could see themselves reflected. Andrée Davanture asked:

> Why shouldn't I support soaps or popular TV films with just as much sympathy
> and commitment as any other project? Our philosophy is precisely to allow this
> kind of cinema to exist too! The most unpretentious African film will be better
> than most of the images served up to Africans!

Yet Atria, none the less, had a hand in a number of films which were short-
listed at the Cannes Film Festival, or won awards throughout the world.

The commitment of the team at Atria was impressive for the respect they
showed for all forms of expression. That commitment remained a complement to the action of other partners – most notably that of the Ministry of
Co-operation, which also offered forms of personalized back-up and helped
to support the emergence of certain forms of popular cinema, particularly
television films, aimed at African audiences. The commitment of both Atria
and the film bureau of the Ministry of Co-operation was gratefully appreciated by the entire profession. Without their activities, the fate of Black
African film would not have been what it is, and I would perhaps have had
little to write about here.

Atria did, however, have the merit of reminding us, despite all the difficulties, that Africa means diversity, and that you cannot impose a single logic
on a continent so skilled at turning its relations with the West into a history
of resistance or – often syncretic – misappropriation. 'A village with only a
single path to it is a bad village. Don't go there!' says a Fulani proverb.

Breaking with the idea that one is going to 'develop' the Other (without
giving in to the idealization of that Other) entails a new realism which
sidesteps the obsession with *a priori* coherence.[31] If we are genuinely prepared to believe that the Westernization of the world is not inevitable, we
cannot treat African artistic expression, characterized as it is by extraordinary
vitality and a fluid pluralism, in terms of the mere question of its survival.
Since the days when the African states gained their independence, Africa has
borrowed from modernity without ever being wholly contented with it. It is
neither an area of devastation nor a cultural reservation. It cannot be seen
merely as a drifting world, occupied solely with regaining its identity. If it
wishes, today, to be the engine of genuine cultural change, foreign aid must
take the richness and diversity of Africa into account. In other words, it
must reject all conceptual certainties, and accept uncertainty and doubt. It
is within a framework of this kind that giving can recover a less stifling
dynamic, and it will do so as soon as it throws off the logic of efficiency and
interest to accept the unknown and the uncertain, and to operate on trust.
Far from promoting irresponsibility or lapsing into indifference, it would in
this way come close to the dynamic of birth which, in all societies, represents *the* gift par excellence.

In 1999, the integration of the Ministry of Co-operation into the Ministry of Foreign Affairs cut the ground from under Atria, which had its subsidy withdrawn. To general consternation within the profession, Atria is dying and Andrée Davanture is trying to save the archives.

Although the disappearance of a ministry solely devoted to the former colonies gladdens the heart, since it might set relations between France and Africa on a clearer footing, the brutal cessation of aid to essential structures like Atria is scandalous. To cut its funding without any prior consultation amounts to showing contempt for twenty years of work and commitment. 'Up until 1987', Davanture explains, 'there was a genuine exchange between institutions on each of the projects we were backing. Since then, we've been tolerated rather than supported.'[32] And what was tolerated was precisely another vision of the relationship with Africa. In the 1990s the Ministry wanted to back only those films which were likely to 'find a French audience', to be shown at the European festivals, especially Cannes. This was an approach diametrically opposed to that of Andrée Davanture, with her concern to preserve the independence and freedom of a cinematography finding its way by diverse paths:

> African filmmakers are responsible for their works and their greatest desire is to find an African audience, even though success in France and elsewhere may enhance their reputations. I think I can say that this perspective has never been taken into account, and that has surely been detrimental to the development of African cinema.

The Ministry made no effort to create a dialogue:

> I called for consultations on several occasions, without success. I was even told one day that it wasn't necessary. Then, on one occasion, it was explained to me, in passing, in a corridor, that the politicians are transient, but the civil servants remain – which is a whole programme in itself.

Davanture condemns the failings of co-operation with Africa: 'We are often directive with the best intentions in the world, and this is horrendous: it amounts to thinking in the other party's stead. This tendency often shows up in the comments on screenplays.' But she throws back the charges of paternalism which have at times been laid at Atria's door: 'You can salve your conscience by helping with the funding of a film.... But if you don't shepherd the whole project through, if it's interrupted or the directing is second-rate, then it's money down the drain.'

NOTES

1. Proverb quoted in *Djeli* (Fadika Kramo-Lanciné, Ivory Coast, 1981).
2. Great Britain and Portugal never established any institutional support for film production in their former colonies. In France, this role falls to the Ministry of Co-operation, whereas the Foreign Affairs Ministry covers the other countries of the world. Fonds Sud is open to all countries from the southern hemisphere without distinction.
3. This directly echoes General de Gaulle's formula, at his press conference of 11 April 1961: 'It is a fact that decolonization is our interest and, as a consequence, our policy.'
4. Roland Louvel, *Quelle Afrique pour quelle coopération? Mythologie de l'aide française*, L'Harmattan, Paris, 1994, p. 33.
5. Ibid., p. 151.
6. For detailed information on this aid, see Jean-Pierre Garcia, *Sous l'arbre à palabres, guide pratique à l'usage des cinéastes africains*, published by Le Film Africain. This is an excellent guide, with a wealth of relevant addresses and views on the funding, production, distribution and technical aspects of African cinema.
7. The Tunisian filmmaker Ferid Boughedir spoke in this vein at the press conference held by Frédéric Mitterrand, president of Fonds Sud, at the 1996 Cannes Film Festival. Med Hondo and the African Filmmakers' Committee which he co-ordinates also wrote to the general secretary of ACCT in May 1993 that the acquisition of the audiovisual rights to a film (valid after three years), one of the conditions on which the agency gives aid, represented a low level of investment yet gave the agency the role of distributor, since African films sometimes have difficulty finding a distributor in Africa within that period. Ibrahima Signaté, *Med Hondo, un cinéaste rebelle*, Présence Africaine, Paris, 1994, p. 122.
8. Interview with Jean-Pierre Bekolo, Paris, 1997.
9. Serge Latouche, *L'Occidentalisation du monde: essai sur la signification, la portée et les limites de l'uniformisation planétaire*, La Découverte, Paris, 1989, p. 28.
10. In the sense that the action of the American government in the renegotiation of the GATT agreement for the free circulation of audiovisual programmes and films is also a way of assisting an industry which is already self-sufficient. See Joel Augros, *L'Argent d'Hollywood*, L'Harmattan, Paris, 1996, p. 12.
11. Interview with Frédéric Bontems, Paris, February 1996.
12. Apart from the three French ministries mentioned, the European Union (within the framework of the 'Cultural Co-operation' strand of the Lomé Agreements), the Agence de la Francophonie (the former ACCT), the Communauté française de Belgique and the Office fédéral de la culture suisse also subsidize southern-hemisphere cinema. Since 1989, the European Union has co-financed productions which present Africa in terms of its own images. The originality of its aid is that it is aimed, within the framework of the European Development Fund (EDF), at the African Caribbean and Pacific (ACP) countries, which determine how it is attributed. Since it forms part of the co-production contract between the director and the ACP country, it is considered as the matching funding element of the ACP country or the filmmaker in the funding plan. Where films are successful, the corresponding percentage of profit comes back to the ACP country. Another advantage is that a European production company is not imposed on the project as part of the funding arrangements. On the down side, however,

filmmakers do have to convince the authorities in their country to propose their project. There is now new European funding which does not need this official support: see 'Entretien avec Serge Kancel', in *Africultures* 29, 2000. The aim of the aid from the Agence de la Francophonie is essentially to co-finance films of quality with broad audience appeal which can provide material for the French-speaking TV5 satellite channel, which has an African subsidiary, TV5–Afrique. The maximum aid granted is 600,000 francs for a cinematic production and 500,000 francs for a television production. Aid is also provided for dubbing and subtitling into French up to a total amount of 100,000 francs. See 'Entretien avec Jean-Claude Crépeau (Agence de la Francophonie)', in *Africultures* 21, 1999.

Funding is also available from the Hubert Bals Foundation in Rotterdam, from the Centro Orientamento Educative (COE), which organizes the Milan Festival, from the Montecinemaverita Foundation of the Locarno Festival in Switzerland and from the Canadian 'Programme d'incitation à la coproduction Nord–Sud'.

13. Interview with Jacques Bidou, Ouagadougou, 1995.
14. Frédéric Mitterrand, reply to a question from the Tunisian producer Ahmed Attia (press conference, 1996 Cannes Festival).
15. Interview with Robert Lombaerts, Paris, 1995.
16. Pierre-André Taguieff, *La Force du préjugé: essai sur le racisme et ses doubles*, La Découverte, Paris, 1987.
17. Interview with Cheikh Oumar Sissoko on the Malian private radio station Kayira, quoted in *Écrans d'Afrique* 15, 1996, p. 54.
18. Interview with Gaston Kaboré, Ouagadougou, 1995.
19. 'Entretien de J.-P. Garcia et D. Aloïa avec Pierre Yameogo et René Sintzel', *Le Film Africain* 12, May 1993, p. 6.
20. Manthia Diawara, *African Cinema: Politics and Culture*, Indiana University Press, Bloomington and Indianapolis, 1992, p. 32.
21. Wanjiru Kinyanjui, 'Leinwandafrika', *Zoom – Zeitschrift für Film* (Zurich), November 1993, p. 9.
22. Press pack distributed on the launch of Écrans du Sud, January 1993.
23. Interview with Marc Silvera, former director of Écrans du Sud, Paris, 1995.
24. J. Adda and M.C. Smouts, *La France face au Sud: le miroir brisé*, Karthala, Paris, 1989, p. 253.
25. Interview with Michel Brunet, co-ordinator of the cinema office of the Ministry of Co-operation between 1990 and 1996, Paris, 1995.
26. In 1995, 45 films were granted an advance against receipts, representing a total amount of 99,550,000 francs – an average of aid of 2.2 million francs per film. The maximum possible grant was made to Bernard Giraudeau's *Les Caprices d'un fleuve*, a film set in Gambia during the French Revolution (CNC info. no. 261, May 1996).
27. Dominique Wallon, 'L'Afrique et le cinéma', in FEPACI, *L'Afrique et le centenaire du cinéma*, Présence Africaine, Paris, 1995, p. 385. Dominique Wallon was director of the Centre national de la cinématographie from 1988 to September 1995.
28. Interview with Dominique Wallon, Paris, June 1995.
29. Interview with Andrée Davanture, Paris, 1996.
30. Interview with Andrée Davanture, Paris 1996.
31. Marc Poncelet, *Une utopie post-tiermondiste: La dimension culturelle du développement*, L'Harmattan, Paris, 1994, p. 333.
32. Interview with Andrée Davanture, Paris, 1999, published in *Africultures* 19.

SIXTEEN

TELEVISUAL STRATEGIES

If you let go his tongue, the lion will eat you!
Hausa proverb

African television will survive only if it finds an original voice. Is this not an opportunity for filmmakers?

AFRICA CAN MAKE IT!

I am fortunate to live amid trees near a little provincial town with a two-auditorium cinema. Under the combined fire of satellite dishes and video-hire shops, that cinema was going to close. The local authority – falling victim in its turn, perhaps, to the double-act of heart and reason – reluctantly bought it up and handed it to a film buff to run, and he immediately scheduled a series of 'art' films. A miracle occurred: in the depths of Provence, cinema rediscovered an audience and became profitable again. It has been a close shave at times, but it is still there. Now, this will not necessarily work everywhere, and it would be strange if it were directly exportable to Africa. But the point is valid all the same: television does not necessarily kill off film. It may, indeed, provide an opportunity for a quality cinema to exist. As Serge Daney wrote, television addresses itself to adults in so far as they are capable of shutting it up – capable, that is, of rejecting infantilization and going and rediscovering their childhood – or something of it – in the cinema.[1]

Television is, admittedly, a deculturing force, in the sense that it endlessly offers a culture different from that of its audience. *Dallas, Dynasty, Santa Barbara, Falcon Crest* and *Baywatch* – not to mention Brazilian series such as *Dona Beija*, which African stations reschedule endlessly on account of their success – are all advertisements for an American lifestyle that is already being aped by the *nouveaux riches*. They produce fashions in hairstyles and dress which can have disastrous consequences – as, for example, when the women of Dakar go in for skin depigmentation in order to look whiter.

MTV is already present in Kenya, Nigeria and, particularly, in South Africa, thanks to a partnership arrangement with the South African Broadcasting Corporation (SABC), and there are plans for it to extend throughout Africa. That invasion, using a subtle mix of American video-clips and local bands carefully selected to fit the dominant cultural mould of the channel, will complete a much-criticized 'colonization' of screens and minds among young people – a colonization already begun with the various packages of channels available on satellite.[2]

Here again, however, we should be wary of catastrophism in an Africa which is always quick to mount resistance. If African television stations find that they have serious competition on their own patch, they may be led to react. The establishment of international radio stations such as Radio France Internationale (RFI) or Africa 1 FM in most African capitals led national radio stations to improve their schedules. They now top the ratings everywhere.[3] If they can keep abreast of what their viewers want, African television stations will be able to hold their own against the competition. To do that, they will have to purvey products which are 'made in Africa'. There are some very encouraging success stories: in Benin, the programme *Tour de vis* [Turn of the Screw] offers fortnightly debates, preceded by satirical sketches, on the topics of corruption, violence and democracy. In the Ivory Coast, *Comment ça va?* [How are things?] has had an audience for many years for a satirical treatment of the major problems of the day: infidelity, AIDS, and so on. African TV films are still rare in French-speaking Africa, but they do exist. Local, low-budget productions have a passionate following, as the public sees their own daily life portrayed in them, with its share of romantic troubles, misery, lost jobs and visits to the marabout.[4]

L'Auberge du Salut, a serial of twenty-four 26-minute episodes made by the major names of Gabonese cinema – Charles Mensah, Philippe Maury, Henri-Joseph Koumba, Paul Mouketa, and so forth – was watched with great relish by the people of Gabon, delighted to see its own social realities portrayed on the small screen. In Senegal, Mahama Johnson Traoré made *Fann Ocean* as a co-production with Belgium. This is a serial of six 52-minute episodes recounting the marital and familial misadventures of the rich Massaté Cissé, married to a woman twenty-five years his junior. The serial, which was widely trailed in the media, attracted a large audience. An epic biography of Lat Dior, hero of the resistance to French colonial rule, was also very well received.[5]

Senegalese television produces TV films of quality on topical subjects. *Wendeelu Billy Boy* (Boubacar Ba, 1996, with a screenplay by Cheick Yarack Fall), shot in the style of a detective film, denounces corruption and warns against the dangers of drug abuse. In Guinea there have been television series in the various national languages (Sussu, Malinke, Kissi, etc.) since 1986, and they have enjoyed great success, both in that country and in the bordering nations which share the same languages. As a result, there are plans for co-productions between these countries. The public, hungry for images in which their daily problems are portrayed, are not put off by the poor technical quality of these soap operas, which are acted by local theatre companies.[6] In Burkina Faso, an attempt to raise finance by subscription for Adama Traoré's *L'Épopée des Mossé* [The Epic of the Mossi] (the plan was for thirty-three 26-minute episodes) collapsed in the face of a heated debate triggered by the subject matter: recounting the epic story of the majority ethnic group was seen as potentially divisive. In the end, the state intervened to fund the filming of two pilot episodes.[7]

In English-speaking Africa, African TV films are more common. Ghana has long been committed to 'fighting cultural colonialism' (Jerry Rawlings's phrase): since 1972, *Osofo Dadzie* has devoted an hour of comedy every Sunday evening to attacking corruption, nepotism and profiteering. The programme, which provides a topic for discussion in the offices and marketplaces on Monday mornings, also brings in an income on video. In Nigeria, there is a long tradition of sponsorship of serials by breweries such as Star and Heineken, and by the banks. These are made in English or urban pidgin. *The Village Headmaster*, produced by the Nigerian Television Authority (NTA) of Lagos, ran for more than twenty years. With the advent of a sequel, *The New Village Headmaster*, it has acquired an air of timelessness. An independent production, *Basi and Company*, uses pidgin English to send up Nigerians themselves, who love to laugh at their own foibles. The characters in this series who combine Western influences with African traditions are set against those who totally mimic Western ways – speaking a cut-glass English, wearing suits and ties and worshipping American music, sports cars and money. *Basi and Company*, which is broadcast every Wednesday evening, has more than 30 million viewers.[8] All these series attack head on both the corruption and the general mentality of the *nouveaux riches* who are pocketing the wealth of an oil-producing country currently in deep political and economic crisis.

As for South Africa, it had scarcely emerged from apartheid when, in *Africa Dreamings*, it began to explore the African imagination on a continental scale with six directors being invited by SABC to make 26-minute films on love in the wider sense of the word. The films in this series, lucid visions of an inner Africa, all evoke intense emotion. *Mamlambo*, the South African film made by Palesa ka Letlaka-Nkosi, who trained with Spike Lee, is a fable which many black South African children heard at their mother's knee. It is the story of a magical and unexpected friendship between two children who are both trapped: the one by the secret destiny from which he is attempting to escape, the other by the slavery of forced prostitution.

It was in Maputo's biggest shantytown, Bairro Chamanculo, that Joao Ribeiro, a young Cuban-trained filmmaker, made the Mozambican contribution to the series, *The Gaze of the Stars*. This tells the story of a young war orphan in search of his origins. He lives with his Uncle Salomao, who explains to him that the stars in the sky are the eyes of those who have died of love... The – highly poetic – screenplay is by Mia Couto, a great name in Mozambican literature. The producer, Pedro Pimenta, had to have everything brought in from South Africa: the camera, the cars and the generator. At independence in 1976 the government had set up a National Cinema Institute on Cuban lines, but after eight years of euphoria it was ravaged by the civil war, and a fire in 1991 finished it off.

In Zimbabwe, Joel Phiri, who learned his trade on Idrissa Ouedraogo's *Kini and Adams*, produced the episode directed by Farai Sevenzo, *The Last Picture*, about a young photographer's obsessive desire to meet a woman with very different origins from his own. From Namibia came *Sophia's Homecoming*, directed by Richard Pakleppa, a story of love and sacrifice. It tells of the personal struggle of a woman who, after twelve years working in the town to meet the needs of her family, returns home, only to find that there is no longer any place for her there. The Mauritanian Abderrahmane Sissako filmed his contribution to the series, *Sabriya*, in Tunisia. It is set in a café lost in the sands, where the main preoccupation of the patrons is chess. Said and Rajeh, the close friends who jointly own the café, get on swimmingly there, with the changing seasons and the changing fortunes of their games as backdrop. One day, into their ordered world chance suddenly brings a young woman... *So be it*, by the Senegalese director Joe Gaye Ramaka, depicts a man and his lover in a village dispensary who are tearing each other apart, 'imprisoned' as they are in a lethal union. The man, idealistic and convinced that he can change what he finds around him, will not leave. She, the woman – life – tries to drag him away, but in vain...

There is a potential market for low-budget African soaps. All African television stations, both private and public, will have to compete to reach a public which wants to see its own images. But, given that the public takes the professionalism of foreign images as the norm, the quality of those products will have to improve. Only by meeting this condition will they be able to cross frontiers and become profitable in a continental – or even international – marketplace. South Africa is already playing a role here. The popular series *Generations*, directed by Mfundi Vundla, which is produced and broadcast by the SABC, has been sold to other English-speaking countries such as Kenya, despite the fact that half its dialogue is in Xhosa and Sotho. It is also to be dubbed into French. *Generations*, set in 1994 in a South Africa just emerging from apartheid, portrays the relationship between two families in their struggle to survive. After being moved in the 1950s from Sophiatown, a multiracial suburb in the west of Johannesburg, to Soweto, the Maroka family had thrived by providing a front for the activities of Whites who did not have the right to operate in Soweto, while the Mthembu family went downhill. Conflict between the two families is sparked off when a Mthembu girl comes to work in the only Black South African advertising agency, run by Paul Maroka.[9]

GETTING BEYOND THE PASSIVE 'WAITING GAME'

Given the decaying state of film distribution and exhibition in Africa, will television provide African cinema with a last chance of survival? Up to now, television stations have turned their backs on it, for lack of resources, but also for lack of political will. 'I remember', says Françoise Balogun,

> in the early seventies we had two hour-long documentaries which we thought would fit into a television slot. We were living in Ife, 250 kilometres from Lagos. We took advantage of a free weekend to go there, and had a meeting with the head of the TV station. He viewed the films and didn't even offer us enough to cover our travel expenses. When we protested, he said the Americans provided hours of programmes free of charge![10]

To be sure that their compatriots see their work, filmmakers are at times reduced to 'making a gift' of a cassette to the national television station. And why should that station feel embarrassed to take them when offices for the promotion of French- or English-language material graciously hand out enough to fill their schedules?

'The coming of Canal France International', notes Ivorian director Gnoan Roger M'Bala, 'has led the television stations to play a waiting game, simply taking up the free programmes which the public consumes without any adverse reaction.'[11] I shall never, in fact, forget a discussion I had in an Abidjan bar with Idriss Diabaté, director of such documentaries on Ivorian culture as *Vous avez dit... peinture*, or the 26-minute short on the djembe player Adama Drame, while the television at the back of the bar was showing the middle-of-the-road French comedy show *Dimanche Martin*. Jacques Martin's show is one of the CFI programmes which has the greatest take-

The dish for receiving Canal France International (CFI)
within the grounds of RTI, the Ivorian TV and radio station, Abidjan.

up in Africa! That channel – created in 1989, and financed by the French Co-operation and Foreign Affairs ministries – broadcasts by satellite twenty-four hours a day, throughout the world, a selection of programmes and films which local television stations can tape and broadcast as they wish. 'I could put my film under my arm and go and see all the TV stations', says Kitia Touré, 'but nobody would take it: they know I'm going to sell to CFI! Among the Senufo, there's a saying, "Why climb a tree to see a married woman's breasts?" You have only to wait.'[12]

As a 'satellite-borne instrument of co-operation' – to quote its director, Philippe Baudillon – CFI is in the ambivalent position of being a tool of French presence in the world but one which is nevertheless duty-bound to support the emancipation of national television stations. 'Our strategy is to maintain a competition which seems positive to us, all the more so since if we were to pull out we would soon be replaced by English-speaking, Arabic or South African programmes, etcetera', comments Frédéric Bontems pragmatically.[13] The Ministry of Co-operation provides support to national television stations through such measures as training schemes or financial assistance for the purchase of equipment, but it is also developing CFI as a kind of proto-market for African audiovisual products.

CFI can be received by individuals if they have the appropriate satellite dish: as such, it is in competition with local channels, broadcasting a programme akin to the French satellite channels TV5 or Canal Horizons. Competition is maintained, but national television stations are now able to tape programmes exclusively, since off-peak transmission periods are specially encrypted for this purpose. This also restricts the amount of piracy carried out by other broadcasters. The schedule is currently being Africanized, a measure made easier by the regionalization of CFI since 1995. It is, for example, now part of CFI–Afrique's brief to initiate co-productions with African television stations, and also to broadcast programmes made by them throughout Africa. The Africanization of CFI will complement that of TV5, which has been broadcasting an African evening since September 1995, in the wake of Canal Horizons, the 'African' subsidiary of Canal Plus. That station has long been an innovator in this field, regularly including African films in its schedules.[14]

The Ministry's objective has been to promote a dynamic for local production on the part of the national television stations, which must modify the charters under which they operate, acquire financial independence, become credible in their news broadcasting, have a strategy of local programming, and so on. By broadcasting such events as the African Nations Cup in football, CFI enables national television stations to gain an audience and also an advertising revenue which may lead to autonomous productions. The International Olympic Committee granted broadcasting rights for the Atlanta Olympics free of charge, and CFI planned a daily hour on African athletes in collaboration with South African television (SABC).

Can CFI be an instrument for the pan-Africanization of images on African screens, then, rather than simply a conduit for international pap?[15] Who could complain at such a development, except perhaps those who might regret that the initiative has once again come from outside? While the encrypted programmes broadcast by CFI still have nothing African about them, national television stations are none the less able to preserve their role as intermediaries between Western programmes and African viewers.[16] Why not extend exchanges such as those already organized in real time by African television stations for news reporting (Afrovision) to the whole of African programming? The ball is in the court of the African states, which, if they wish to maintain national television stations, will have to adopt a new policy for television.[17]

TAKING TELEVISION BY STORM

The idea that the 'digital revolution' will assist the distribution of African film is not one we can accept. Because the amounts involved are enormous, and investors want to see a return, an increase in the number of channels will not lead to an increase in the number of African films broadcast, but, as everywhere else, to a levelling down and a flood of American images. The filmmaker will remain the fly in the ointment! ('So long as you live, rebel', says a Toucouleur proverb). In a context of heightened competition, the filmmaker increasingly appears as a last-ditch resistance fighter, the proponent of a logic different from that of a television culture which has a great deal of difficulty coping with difference, since it spends its time trying to convince us that it alone is capable of comforting us in our solitude, and that we should be content with its limited approach.

It is not cinema which needs television, but television which needs cinema – needs this added dimension of individual poetic creativity, this cultural response which, as Serge Toubiana stresses, is cultural, and *hence* political. It is a question of 'fighting *for* a greater diversity of films, *against* the standardization imposed by the laws of the market'.[18]

Television presents cinema with a chance of survival only in so far as it provides it with work, broadcasts its films, and opens up to its initiatives. It is for cinema to use television for its own purposes. 'The culture of tomorrow will depend on the new media', says Sarah Maldoror from Guadeloupe. 'That is why, now, we must take television by storm!'[19]

Television is, in fact, an extraordinary instrument for developing consciousness when it opens up to the social field. The National Conferences, which were broadcast on the small screen, were watched with eagerness, as was the trial of former president Moussa Traoré in Mali and the 'gangs trial' in Conakry. In this latter case, daily broadcasts of the trial provided the population of Guinea with genuine lessons in the basic principles of law. In these cases, television-watching ceases to be entertainment and becomes a learning process. Filmmakers did not miss the point. In the commentaries on his film *Kiti* (1996) and the debates surrounding it, David Achkar shows how much the affirmation of the judicial system, showing that criminals have rights, was vital in avoiding chaos in a country like Guinea, where offenders were commonly lynched in the street. Gahité Fofana produced a profile of one of those condemned to death in *Mathias* (1996), a film which, using images from the trial, provides a sense of its impact on safeguarding democracy in the country.

In June 1976, the brand-new South African television station SABC –

which had not yet been muzzled, and broadcast for only two hours a day – provided extraordinary coverage of the Soweto riots, showing images of a previously unseen reality – images which had their impact on the radical political and cultural change which ensued, and on the re-emergence of black resistance.

If African filmmakers have some hopes of being seen on African screens, they are inured now to the reluctance to give them exposure in Europe. Fictional images from Africa are hardly ever seen. In France, the public television channels make occasional 'contributions', but each contribution has to be made to last a long time! As Senegalese director Joseph Gaye Ramaka says: 'A Martian who had watched French television would be amazed to see Blacks and North Africans in the street.'[20] And the person who is not on the screen does not exist – at the very moment when our society is crying out for images of Africa to communicate with its minorities and its ghettos! Canal Plus, on the other hand, is giving air time to African feature films produced by French companies, and is virtually the only station to buy short films from African directors, provided that they meet the 'watchability' criteria of the French audience.[21] And La Sept–Arte is an encouraging exception to the general rule, being outstanding in the openness of its schedules to productions from the countries of the South. In specifying his criteria for the selection of films, Georges Goldenstern, head of co-productions and acquisitions at La Sept–Arte, provides a magnificent definition of what a different style of television could be: 'When different cultures and sensibilities, different styles of reasoning can be brought out and put into a story, that's what we're looking for. This is the best way to understand and get to know one another, by trying to get inside other patterns of thinking and acting than one's own – to get inside different frames of mind.'[22]

NOTES

1. Serge Daney, *Le Salaire du zappeur*, POL, Paris, 1993, p. 189.
2. Yves Eudes, 'MTV: musique, télévision et profits planétaires', *Le Monde diplomatique* 497, August 1995, pp. 6–7.
3. Interview with Frédéric Bontems, Paris, February 1996.
4. Thierry Pernet, 'Pluies d'images sur les écrans africains', *Le Monde Diplomatique* 505, April 1996, p. 24.
5. Sambolgo Bangré, 'Les Anti-Dallas sénégalais', *Écrans d'Afrique* 11, 1995, p. 52.
6. Yaye Haby Barry, 'Des productions originales pour un public enthousiaste', *Écrans d'Afrique* 11, 1995, p. 55.
7. Zoumana Wonogo, 'L'Épopée des Mossé pour restaurer l'histoire burkinabè et... consommer africain', *Écrans d'Afrique* 11, 1995, p. 57.

8. Nwachukwu Frank Ukadike, *Black African Cinema*, University of California Press, Berkeley/Los Angeles/London, 1994, p. 117.
9. Russell Honeyman, 'Les Feuilletons sud-africains visent les marchés internationaux', *Écrans d'Afrique* 11, 1995, p. 64.
10. Interview with Françoise Balogun, Paris, 1994.
11. Gnoan Roger M'Bala and Timité Bassori interviewed on Channel 2 of RTI, Abidjan, 1995.
12. Interview with Kitia Touré, Abidjan, 1995.
13. Interview with Frédéric Bontems, director of the media office of the Ministry of Co-operation, February 1996.
14. CFI came closer to TV5 in July 1995, when it bought into that channel. This should avoid competition or duplication between the two. Whereas TV5 – which is financed mainly by ACCT, though it also receives funding from French ministries – remains a French-speaking channel, broadcasting a single schedule of programmes worldwide, CFI is not restricted to broadcasting in French, and is aiming to develop its foreign-language output, particularly in English and Arabic.
15. An intention expressed by its director, Philippe Baudillon, at his press conference at the 1995 Fespaco (Ouagadougou).
16. Abdoul Ba, *Télévisions, paraboles et démocraties en Afrique noire*, L'Harmattan, Paris, 1996.
17. Lams Yaro, 'Bretelles d'accès aux autoroutes électroniques', in FEPACI, *L'Afrique et le centenaire du cinéma,* Présence Africaine, Paris, 1995, p. 305.
18. Serge Toubiana, 'Question de langage', *Cahiers du Cinéma* 486, December 1994, p. 41.
19. 'Entretien de Jadot Sezirahiga avec Sarah Maldoror', *Écrans d'Afrique* 12, 1995, p. 10.
20. Interview with Joseph Gaye Ramaka, Paris, 1996.
21. Interview with Patrice Bauchy, Canal Plus, 1995.
22. Interview with Georges Goldenstern, Paris, 1995.

CONCLUSION

Men are two dirty hands. You can only wash the one with the other.
Fulani proverb

I have now come to the end of two years spent listening to the cinema cultures of Black Africa. It has been a worthwhile journey, yet I have had to make many a turn to right and left to pin down the attraction which Africa and its cinema have exerted on me. In the end, I have arrived, I believe, at a clearer vision, and a number of simple ideas have emerged, which speak to me of my part in our shared humanity.

One must beware of fascination! When the drama is taken out of our way of seeing Africa, and when that way of seeing is no longer mere compassion for a state of wretchedness we Westerners regard as Africa's inescapable fate, it often bears within it a taint of jealousy. The laughter, dancing and liveliness of African film leave our northern societies looking so sad. But I am jealous of the Other's freedom only so long as I remain unaware of the hardships she or he has to put up with – hardships and deficiencies which only the cross-fertilization of ideas, experiences and cultures can remedy. To mystify the Other by attributing what I do not have to him or her, without perceiving what she or he lacks, amounts to denying the Other: it means ceasing to envisage an exchange between two questing beings – or, in other words, a *solidarity*. Solidarity has two aspects to it. It is, first, being aware that we have something in common and, second, recognizing the part of the Other which cannot be integrated: his or her difference.

Why should we especially think of African cinema cultures in terms of their unrelenting quest for origins? They throw light on our own search for identity, in a world in which barbarism is becoming entrenched. Their references to founding myths are essential, since they take us back refreshingly to the sources of what we have in common: the movement of nature and of the order of the world. The films I have referred to here do not, however, get bogged down in origins. They express neither a state of innocence nor the eternal soul of a people. They are situated in a History which identity mysticism cannot encompass: a confrontation between social forces in which the heritage of the past comes up against cultural contributions from outside. It is not sufficient, then, merely to assert that cultures are plural. We have also to specify what issues are expressed within them.

There is a danger that the energy rediscovered in the perception of founding myths will lead to the illusion of a fixed definition of our identity. And yet we cannot avoid seeing the disturbing fragility of that identity. Rooted as they are in the questioning of social norms and behaviour, the cinema cultures of Black Africa help us to come to terms with that uncertainty by challenging our identity-based, nationalist assertions, so that we avoid falling, ultimately, into fundamentalism and stupidity. We perceive, as a result, that we have had to pass through the Other to become what we are, and that even today cross-fertilization is the forward-looking solution. Forging one's identity involves the ever-renewed integration of difference: the films of Africa can be seen today as casting a crucial light on the fate of the minority communities living on the outer fringes of our comforts and certainties. We must inevitably face the issue of a change of vision: it is a question of leaving behind our pretensions to a universal understanding, and opening ourselves up to differences which are already present all around us, in the very heart of our own societies. And a question, therefore, also of ceasing to destroy those differences, and at the same time ceasing to destroy ourselves, since in denying the Other we deny a part of ourselves.

We have to envisage a genuine inversion of our vision, which begins with the learning of respect. 'I wanted the film to be within everyone's reach, and at the same time I wanted it to go deep', says Souleymane Cissé of *Waati/ Time* (1995).

> A viewer who knows the cultures of the South will clearly understand what he is watching more quickly. Like that image of the little girl standing beside her dead mother, stroking her hair. That shot pays homage to a culture of nobility and of absolute respect for the Other – of everything which is other, including death.[1]

Respecting the Other will mean listening to what he or she says, and trying to establish to what extent I share in it. It will mean accepting the portion of mystery that is in symbols, and trusting in emotion; it will mean letting yourself be told stories to rediscover a part of your childhood without losing sight of what is at stake in fables; it will mean situating the rhythm of films in the paradoxical space where uncertainty and reason meet; it will mean embracing the African accent as part of the sound of a culture.

Respecting the Other will mean rejecting an intellectual monoculture to take on board his or her diversity; it will mean opening oneself up to the unknown, to uncertainty and to trust, to broaden out the logic of giving.

Respecting the Other will mean no longer regarding him or her as a fixed, external entity, but as a living resource to help us to look at and understand the world. This requires us to turn our ethnological gaze upon our own behaviour! Stanislas Adotevi went so far as to say that there can be no possible ethnology 'other than that which studies the cannibalistic behaviour of the white man!'[2] How could this be done, except by apprehending that Africa whose economic and political gravitational pull has become so weak that it can hope to exist only by dint of its images? The cinema cultures of Black Africa are a vital alternative to the reductive representations forced on the Western consciousness by the media coverage of the chaos in Somalia, Rwanda or Liberia. But the myth of the noble savage is still very much alive.

Moctar, the child in *Le Cri du coeur* (Idrissa Ouedraogo, 1994), sees a hyena where adults do not: it eludes them as the Other can elude the Westerner. 'If I have any advice to give to African... filmmakers', said another hyena-lover, Djibril Diop Mambety,

> I would say, above all, do not try to please, if you want to be universal... African filmmakers and African people both have their part to play at the great meeting of humanity.... Cinema addresses itself not only to the eyes and ears, but to the heart also.... Cinema has to be put in the service of self-knowledge, and that is an urgent matter.[3]

NOTES

1. 'Entretien de Jean-Marc Lalanne et Frédéric Strauss avec Souleymane Cissé', *Cahiers du Cinéma* 492, June 1995, p. 58.
2. Stanislas Adotevi, *Négritudes et négrologues*, UGE 10/18, 1972, p. 182.
3. June I. Givanni, interview with Djibril Diop Mambety, in *African Conversations*, British Film Institute/Screen Griots, 1995, p. 31.

BIBLIOGRAPHY

Achebe, Chinua, *Anthills of the Savannah*. Heinemann, London, 1988.

Adda, J. and Smouts, M.C., *La France face au Sud: le miroir brisé*. Karthala, Paris, 1989.

Adotevi, Stanislas, *Négritudes et négrologues*. UGE, Paris, 1972.

Akchoté, Noël, 'Ecoutons-voir ce cinéma qu'on n'entend pas', *Cahiers du Cinéma*, special number: 'Musiques au Cinéma', 1995.

Akesson, Birgit, *Le Masque des eaux vives: danses et chorégraphies traditionnelles d'Afrique noire*. L'Harmattan/UNESCO, Paris, 1994.

Alphandéry, Pierre, Bitoun, Pierre, and Dupont, Yves, *L'équivoque écologique*. La Découverte, Paris, 1991.

Amarger, Michel, 'Les cinéastes africains et la presse se mettent à table', *Écrans d'Afrique*, 12, second quarter, 1995.

Amin, Samir, *Maldevelopment: Anatomy of a Global Failure*. Zed Books, London, 1990.

Armah, Ayi Kwei, *L'Âge d'or n'est pas pour demain*. Présence Africaine, Paris, 1976. *The Beautyful Ones Are Not Yet Born*, Heinemann, London, 1992.

Attali, Jacques, *Noise: The Political Economy of Music* (Theory and History of Literature, volume 16). University of Minnesota Press, Minneapolis, 1985.

Augros, Joël, *L'Argent d'Hollywood*. L'Harmattan, Paris, 1996.

Ba, Abdoul, *Télévisions, paraboles et démocraties en Afrique noire*. L'Harmattan, Paris, 1996.

Bachy, Victor, *Le Cinéma en Côte d'Ivoire*. OCIC–L'Harmattan, Paris, 1983.

Bachy, Victor, *Pour une histoire du cinéma africain*. OCIC, Brussels, 1987.

Baecque, Antoine de, 'Cela s'appelle l'aurore', *Cahiers du Cinéma* 402, December 1987.

Baecque, Antoine de and Braunschweig, Stéphane, 'Pionnier en son pays', *Journal des Cahiers du Cinéma* 381, March 1986.

Bakaba, Sijiri, 'Devant, derrière la caméra', in Fédération Panafricaine des Cinéastes (FEPACI), *L'Afrique et le centenaire du cinéma*. Présence Africaine, Paris, 1995.

Bakari, Imruh, 'Le Facteur X du nouveau cinéma afro-américain', *Écrans d'Afrique* 4, second quarter, 1993.

Bakhtin, Mikhail, *Rabelais and His World*, trans. Helene Iswolsky. MIT Press, Cambridge MA, 1968.

Bakhtin, Mikhail, *Problems of Dostoevsky's Poetics*, trans. Caryl Emerson. University of Minnesota Press, Minneapolis, 1984.

Bakupa-Kanyinda, Balufu, 'De l'exception historique', in Fédération Panafricaine des Cinéastes (FEPACI), *L'Afrique et le centenaire du cinéma*. Présence Africaine, Paris, 1995.

Bakyono, Jean-Servais, 'L'Afrique des sages', *ID* 911, 24 July 1988, Abidjan, Ivory Coast.

Balandrin, Stéphane, 'Les Cinémas africains en résistance', *Cahiers du Cinéma* 492, June 1995.

Balogun, Françoise, *Le Cinéma au Nigeria*. OCIC–L'Harmattan, Paris, 1984.

Balogun, Françoise, *Cinéma et libertés*. Présence Africaine, Paris, 1993.

Bangré, Sambolgo, 'Le Cinéma africain dans la tempête des petits festivals', *Écrans d'Afrique* 7, first quarter, 1994.

Bangré, Sambolgo, 'Les Anti-Dallas sénégalais', *Écrans d'Afrique* 11, first quarter, 1995.

Barlet, Olivier, 'Cinémas d'Afrique noire: le nouveau malentendu', *Cinémathèque* 14, Autumn 1998, Cinémathèque française, Paris.

Bassan, Raphaël, 'Haïlé Gerima, l'Afro-américain', *Cinémaction* 46 ('Le Cinéma noir américain'), 1988.

Baudelaire, Charles, 'De l'essence du rire', in *Oeuvres complètes*. Éditions de la Pléiade, Paris, vol. III.

Baudrillard, Jean, *For a Critique of the Political Economy of the Sign*, trans. Charles Levin, Telos Press, St. Louis MO, 1981.

Bavuala Matanda, Tshishi, 'Discours filmique africain et communication traditionnelle', in Centre d'Étude sur la Communication en Afrique, *Camera nigra, le discours du film africain*. OCIC–L'Harmattan, Paris, undated.

Benasayag, Miguel and Charlton, Edith, *Critique du bonheur*. La Découverte, Paris, 1989.

Bender, Wolfgang, *Sweet Mother: Modern African Music*, trans. Wolfgang Freis, University of Chicago Press, Chicago and London, 1991.

Benghozi, Pierre-Jean, *Le Cinéma, entre l'art et l'argent*. L'Harmattan, Paris, 1989.

Bensmaïa, Reda, 'Jean Rouch ou le cinéma de la cruauté', in René Prédal, 'Jean Rouch, un griot gaulois', *Cinémaction* 17, 1982.

Bergala, Alain, *Jean-Luc Godard par Jean-Luc Godard*. Cahiers du Cinéma/Éditions de l'Étoile, Paris, 1985.

Bergson, Henri, *Laughter: An Essay on the Meaning of the Comic*, trans. Cloudesley Brereton and Fred Rothwell. Macmillan, London, 1911.

Biny Traoré, Jean-Claude, *Cinéma et histoire*. Mimeo, Direction de l'enseignement secondaire des Hauts-Bassins, Bobo-Dioulasso, Burkina Faso 1995.

Biro, Yvette, *Mythologie profane: cinéma et pensée sauvage*. L'Herminier, Paris, 1982.

Blachère, Jean-Claude, *Négritures, Les écrivains d'Afrique noire et la langue française*. L'Harmattan, Paris, 1993.

Boughedir, Ferid, *Le Cinéma africain de A à Z*. OCIC, Brussels, 1987.

Breton, André, *Anthologie de l'humour noir*. Livre de Poche/Biblio, Paris, 1986.

Browne, Françoise, 'Sony Labou Tansi: une écriture nostalgique d'unité', in Anny Winchank and Philippe-Joseph Salazar, *Afriques imaginaires, regards réciproques et discours littéraires, 17e–20e siècles*. L'Harmattan, Paris, 1995.

Bruyn, Olivier de, 'Hyène de vie', *Les Inrockuptibles* 4, 5–11 April 1995.

Cabral, Amilcar, *Unité et lutte*. Maspéro, Paris, 1980.

Césaire, Aimé, *Discourse on Colonialism*, trans. Joan Pinkham. Monthly Review Press, New York, 1972.

Cham, Mbye, 'Le passé, le présent et l'avenir', *Écrans d'Afrique* 4, second quarter, 1993.

Cheriaa, Tahar, 'La FEPACI et nous', in Fédération Panafricaine des Cinéastes (FEPACI), *L'Afrique et le centenaire du cinéma*. Présence Africaine, Paris, 1995.

Cheriaa, Tahar, 'Le Groupe et le héros', in Centre d'étude sur la communication en Afrique, *Camera nigra, le discours du film africain*. OCIC-L'Harmattan, Paris, undated.

Chevrier, Jacques, 'Sembène Ousmane, écrivain', *Cinémaction* 34, 1985.

Copans, Jean, 'Entre l'histoire et les mythes', *Cinémaction* 34, 1985.

Coquery-Vidrovitch, Catherine, *Afrique noire, permanences et ruptures.* L'Harmattan, Paris, 1992.

Coquery-Vidrovitch, Catherine, Hémery, Daniel and Piel, Jean, *Pour une histoire du développement: états, sociétés, développement.* L'Harmattan, Paris, 1988.

Daney, Serge, *La Rampe.* Cahiers du Cinéma/Gallimard, Paris, 1983.

Daney, Serge, 'Cissé très bien, qu'on se le dise', *Libération*, 9–10 May 1987.

Daney, Serge, *Le Salaire du zappeur.* POL, Paris, 1993.

Daney, Serge, *Persévérance – entretien avec Serge Toubania.* POL, Paris, 1994.

Davanture, Andrée, 'Une indépendance nécessaire', in Fédération Panafricaine des Cinéastes (FEPACI), *L'Afrique et le centenaire du cinéma.* Présence Africaine, Paris, 1995.

Debrix, Jean-René, 'Dix ans de coopération franco-africaine ont permis la naissance du jeune cinéma d'Afrique noire', *Sentiers* 1, 1970.

Deleuze, Gilles, *Cinema 2: The Time-Image*, trans. Hugh Tomlinson and Roberts Galeta. University of Minnesota Press, Minneapolis, 1989.

Depestre, René, *Bonjour et adieu à la négritude.* Seghers, Paris, 1989.

Devésa, Jean-Michel, *Sony Labou Tansi, écrivain de la honte et des rives magiques du Kongo.* L'Harmattan, Paris, 1996.

Diawara, Manthia, 'Oral Literature and African Film: Narratology in Wend Kuuni', in Jim Pines and Paul Willemen, *Questions of Third Cinema.* British Film Institute, London, 1989, pp. 199–211.

Diawara, Manthia, *Black American Cinema.* Routledge, New York and London, 1993.

Diawara, Manthia, *African Cinema: Politics and Culture.* Indiana University Press, Bloomington and Indianapolis, 1992.

Dieterlen, Germaine, 'A propos de Marcel Griaule et du cinéma ethnographique', in C.W. Thompson (ed.), *L'Autre et le sacré, surréalisme, cinéma, ethnologie.* L'Harmattan, Paris, 1995.

Diop, Cheikh Anta, *The African Origin of Civilization.* Lawrence Hill Books, New York, 1991.

Diop, Cheikh Anta, *Civilization or Barbarism: An Authentic Anthropology.* Lawrence Hill Books, New York, 1991.

Diop, David, *Coups de Pilon.* Présence Africaine, Paris, 1973.

Douchet, Jean, 'Rossellini ou l'évidence', *Cahiers du Cinéma* 427, January 1990.

Drame, Adama, and Senn-Borloz, Arlette, *Jeliya: être griot et musicien aujourd'hui.* L'Harmattan, Paris, 1992.

Eboussi-Boulaga, Fabien, *La Crise du Muntu.* Présence Africaine, Paris, 1977.

Ecaré, Désiré, 'Quelques reflexions sur cinema et liberté à propos de visages de femmes', in *Cinéma et libertés.* Présence Africaine, Paris, 1993.

Écrans de la liberté, *Afrique du Sud: Cinéma sous influence, cinéma de résistance.* La Cinémathèque française, Paris, 1990.

El Ftouh, Youssef, 'L'Afrique dans les images coloniales', *Écrans d'Afrique* 9–10, third and fourth quarters, 1994.

Ela, Jean-Marc, *The African Cry*, trans. Robert R. Barr. Orbis, London, 1986.

Eudes, Yves, 'MTV: musique, télévision et profits planétaires', *Le Monde diplomatique* 497, August 1995.

Faïk-Nzuji Madiya, Clémentine, 'Symbolisme et cinéma africain', in Centre d'Étude sur la Communication en Afrique, *Camera nigra, le discours du film africain.* OCIC–L'Harmattan, Paris, undated.

Faïk-Nzuji Madiya, Clémentine, *Symboles graphiques en Afrique noire*. Karthala, Paris, 1992.

Fainzang, Sylvie, and Journet, Odile, *La Femme de mon mari: anthropologie du mariage polygamique en Afrique et en France*. L'Harmattan, Paris, 1988.

Fanon, Frantz, *Black Skin, White Masks: The Experience of a Black Man in a White World*. Trans. Charles Lam Markmann. Granada (Paladin), London, 1970.

Garcia, Jean-Pierre, *Sous l'arbre à palabres, guide pratique à l'usage des cinéastes africains*. Le Film Africain, Festival du Film d'Amiens, 1996.

Gardies, André, *Cinéma d'Afrique noire francophone, l'espace miroir*. L'Harmattan, Paris, 1989.

Gardies, André, and Haffner, Pierre, *Regards sur le cinéma négro-africain*. OCIC, Brussels, 1987.

Genette, Gérard, *Palimpsestes, la littérature au second degré*. Le Seuil, Paris, 1982.

Genin, Bernard, 'Le Voyage du fils', *Télérama* 1977, 2 December 1987.

Giavarini, Laurence, 'Éloge du proche', *Cahiers du Cinéma* 465, March 1993.

Gibbal, Jean-Marie, 'Si jeunesse pouvait, si vieillesse savait...', *Positif* 264, February 1983.

Givanni, June, 'Cinéma et libertés: divergence ou dichotomies: entretien avec John Akomfrah', *Écrans d'Afrique* 7, first quarter, 1994.

Givanni, June, *African Conversations*. British Film Institute/Screen Griots, 1995.

Haby Barry, Yaye, 'Des productions originales pour un public enthousiaste', *Écrans d'Afrique* 11, first quarter, 1995.

Haffner, Pierre, 'L'Esthétique des films', *Cinémaction* 26 ('Cinémas noirs d'Afrique'), 1981.

Haffner, Pierre, 'Jean Rouch jugé par six cinéastes d'Afrique noire', *Cinémaction* 17, 1982.

Haffner, Pierre, 'Kino in Schwarzafrika', *Revue du CICIM*, Institut Français de Munich, Munich, 1989.

Haffner, Pierre, 'Stratégies du ciné-mobile, une note pour une histoire parallèle du cinéma et de l'Afrique noire', in Fédération Panafricaine des Cinéastes (FEPACI), *L'Afrique et le centenaire du cinéma*. Présence Africaine, Paris, 1995.

Haustrate, Gaston, *Le Guide du cinéma*, vol. 2. Syros, Paris, 1984.

Heinrichs, Hans-Jürgen, *'Sprich deine eigene Sprache, Afrika!': von der Négritude zur afrikanischen Literatur der Gegenwart*. Dietrich Reimer Verlag, Berlin, 1992.

Hennebelle, Guy, 'Sembène parle de ses films', in Fédération Panafricaine des Cinéastes (FEPACI), *L'Afrique et le centenaire du cinéma*. Présence Africaine, Paris, 1995.

Heymann, Danièle, 'Souleymane Cissé, L'Africain pluriel', *Le Monde*, 8 June 1995.

Hoffstadt, Stephan, *Black Cinema: Afroamerikanische Filmemacher der Gegenwart*. Hitzeroth, Marburg, 1995.

Honeyman, Russell, 'Les Feuilletons sud-africains visent les marchés internationaux', *Écrans d'Afrique* 11, first quarter, 1995,

Honke, Gudrun, *Als die Weissen kamen – Ruanda und die Deutschen, 1885–1919*. Peter Hammer Verlag, Wuppertal, 1990.

Hussein, Mahmoud, *Versant Sud de la liberté: essai sur l'émergence de l'individu dans le Tiers-Monde*. La Découverte, Paris, 1989.

Huston, Nancy, and Sebbar, Leïla, *Une enfance d'ailleurs, 17 écrivains racontent*. Belfond, Paris, 1993.

Ilboudo, Patrick G., *Le Fespaco 1969–1989: Les cinéastes africains et leurs oeuvres*. Editions La Mante, Burkina Faso, 1989.

Ismail, Richard T., 'Les Films africains en Afrique, une histoire d'ironies', *Écrans d'Afrique* 8, second quarter, 1994.

Issa, Maïzama, *Un regard du dedans: Oumarou Ganda, cinéaste nigérien.* Editions Enda, Dakar, 1991.

Kabiné Diabaté, Bemba, 'Exploitation et distribution au Mali: le chaos originel', *Écrans d'Afrique* 4, second quarter, 1993.

Kaboré, Gaston, 'Mon rapport au cinema', in Fédération Panafricaine des Cinéastes (FEPACI), *L'Afrique et le centenaire du cinéma.* Présence Africaine, Paris, 1995.

Kabou, Axelle, *Et si l'Afrique refusait le développement?* L'Harmattan, Paris, 1991.

Kacimi El Harani, Mohamed, 'Langue de Dieu et langue du Je', *Fractures*, 1994.

Kakou, Antoine, 'Les gris-gris d'un conteur', *Cinémaction* 34 ('Sembène Ousmane'), 1985.

Kariithi, Nixon K., 'Misreading Culture and Tradition: Western Critical Appreciation of African Films', in Fédération Panafricaine des Cinéastes (FEPACI), *L'Afrique et le centenaire du cinéma.* Présence Africaine, Paris, 1995.

Kaufmant, Yves and Anne-Marie, 'La Psychiatrie africaine, entretien avec Zirignon Grobli', *Synapses* 65, April 1990.

Kempf, Hervé, *La Baleine qui cache la forêt, enquêtes sur les pièges de l'écologie.* La Découverte, Paris, 1994.

Khayati, Khémais, 'La liberté de l'individu dans les cinémas arabes', in *Cinémas arabes: topographie d'une image éclatée.* L'Harmattan, Paris, 1996.

Kinyanjui, Wanjuri, 'Leinwandafrika', in *Zoom, Zeitschrift für Film*, Zurich, November 1993.

Kompaoré, Prosper, 'Le Spectateur africain et le spectacle cinématographique', *Revue du VIIème Fespaco*, Ouagadougou.

Konan, Yao, 'Cinéma et marginalité sociale: l'exemple des quartiers populaires', DEA thesis, Ethno-Sociology Institute of the Faculty of Letters, Arts and Human Sciences, University of Abidjan, 1990.

Koné, Amadou, *Des textes oraux au roman moderne, étude sur les avatars de la tradition orale dans le roman ouest-africain.* Verlag für Interkulturelle Kommunikation, Frankfurt-am-Main, 1993.

Kourouma, Ahmadou, *Les Soleils des indépendances.* Le Seuil, Paris, 1970.

Labou Tansi, Sony, *La Vie et demie.* Le Seuil, Paris, 1979.

Labou Tansi, Sony, *L'État honteux.* Le Seuil, Paris, 1981.

Labou Tansi, Sony, *Les Sept solitudes de Lorsa Lopes.* Le Seuil, Paris, 1985.

Lallemand, Suzanne, *L'Apprentissage de la sexualité dans les contes d'Afrique de l'Ouest.* L'Harmattan, Paris, 1985.

Larouche, Michel, 'Le Temps que l'on met à marcher', in Michel Larouche (ed.), *Films d'Afrique.* Guernica Press, Montreal, 1991.

Laryea Korley, Nii, 'Le boom des vidéos', *Écrans d'Afrique* 7, first quarter, 1994.

Latouche, Serge, *L'Occidentalisation du monde: essai sur la signification, la portée et les limites de l'uniformisation planétaire.* La Découverte, Paris, 1989.

Latouche, Serge, *La Planète des naufragés, essai sur l'après-développement.* La Découverte, Paris, 1991.

Lelieur, A.C., Peyrière, M.C., Bachollet, R. and Debost, J.B., *Negripub: l'image des Noirs dans la publicité*, revised edition. Éditions d'art L'Amateur Somogy, 1994.

Lévi-Strauss, Claude, *Tristes tropiques*, trans. John and Doreen Weightman, Penguin, Harmondsworth, 1976.

Liauzu, Claude, *Race et civilisation: L'autre dans la culture occidentale. Anthologie critique.* Syros, Paris, 1992.

Louvel, Roland, *Quelle Afrique pour quelle coopération? Mythologie de l'aide française.* L'Harmattan, Paris, 1994.

Louvel, Roland, *L'Afrique noire et la différence culturelle*, L'Harmattan, Paris, 1996

Lutz-Fuchs, Dominique, *Psychothérapies de femmes africaines*. L'Harmattan, Paris, 1994.

Magny, Joël, 'Le Sens des gestes', *Cahiers du Cinéma* 404, February 1988.

Malandrin, Stéphane, 'Les cinémas africains en résistance', *Cahiers du Cinéma* 492, June 1995.

Malkmus, Lizbeth, and Armes, Roy, *Arab and African Film Making*. Zed Books, London, 1991.

Mana, Kä, *L'Afrique va-t-elle mourir? Essai d'éthique politique*. Le Cerf, Paris, 1991 (republished Karthala, Paris, 1993).

Margot, Olivier, 'A Pietermaritzburg, l'actrice de *Waati* n'a pas voulu ramper', *L'Équipe*, 7 June 1995.

Marti, *Ome d'Oc*. Stock, Paris, 1977.

Martin-Granel, Nicolas, *Rires noirs, anthologie romancée de l'humour et du grotesque dans le roman africain*. Sépia/Centre culturel français de Libreville, Libreville, 1991.

Mbembe, Achille, *Afriques indociles: Christianisme, pouvoir et État en société postcoloniale*. Karthala, Paris, 1987.

Mbonimpa, Melchior, *Idéologies de l'indépendance africaine*. L'Harmattan, Paris, 1987.

Meda, Yrzoala Jean Claude, 'Le Cinéma colonial: les conditions de son développement', *Écrans d'Afrique* 9–10, third and fourth quarters, 1994.

Medeiros, François de, *L'Occident et l'Afrique (XIIIème–XVème siècle)*. Karthala, Paris, 1985.

Meillassoux, Claude, *L'esclavage en Afrique précoloniale*. Maspéro, Paris, 1960.

Metz, Christian, *The Imaginary Signifier: Psychoanalysis and the Cinema*, trans. Celia Britton, Annwyl Williams, Ben Brewster and Alfred Guzzetti. Indiana University Press, Bloomington, 1982.

Monga, Célestin, *Anthropologie de la colère: société civile et démocratie en Afrique noire*. L'Harmattan, Paris, 1994.

Morin, Edgar, *The Stars*. John Calder, London, 1960.

Mudimbe, Vumbi Yoka, *L'Odeur du Père. Essai sur les limites de la science et de la vie en Afrique noire*. Présence Africaine, Paris, 1982.

Mulenda, M'Pungu, 'Avec les spectateurs du Shaba', in Centre d'étude dur la Communication en Afrique, *Camera nigra – le discours du film africain*. OCIC–L'Harmattan, Paris, 1984.

N'Debeka, Maxime, *La Danse de N'Kumba ensorcelée*. Publisud, Paris, 1988.

N'Gakane, Lionel, 'En attendant avril 1994', *Écrans d'Afrique* 5–6, third and fourth quarters, 1993.

N'Gakane, Lionel, 'Developing Film Distribution and Exhibition in Region', in Fédération Panafricaine des Cinéastes (FEPACI), *L'Afrique et le centenaire du cinéma*. Présence Africaine, Paris, 1995.

N'Keury N'daw, Ali, 'Zalika: star des films nigériens', *Écrans d'Afrique* 5–6, third and fourth quarters, 1993.

Nathan, Tobie, *L'Influence qui guérit*. Éditions Odile Jacob, Paris, 1994.

Ngandu-Nkashama, Pius, *Écriture et discours littéraires. Études sur le roman africain*. L'Harmattan, Paris, 1989.

Niane, Tamsir, *Soundjata ou l'épopée mandingue*. Présence Africaine, Paris, 1966,

O'Grady, Betty, 'Le parler–écrit: l'exemple de Tchicaya U Tam'si', in Anny Wynchank and Philippe-Joseph Salazar (eds), *Afriques imaginaires: regards réciproques et discours littéraires, 17ème–20ème siècles*. L'Harmattan, Paris, 1995.

Obenga, Théophile, *Stèles pour l'avenir*. Présence Africaine, Paris, 1978.

Ouologuem, Yambo, *Bound to Violence*, trans. R. Manheim, Heinemann, London, 1971.

Oyono, Ferdinand, *The Old Man and the Medal*, trans. John Reed. Heinemann, London, 1982.

Pardo, Carlos, 'Le Cinéma français étouffé par Hollywood', *Le Monde diplomatique* 506, May 1996.

Partant, François, *La Ligne d'horizon: essai sur l'après-développement*. La Découverte, Paris, 1988.

Pernet, Thierry, 'Pluies d'images sur les écrans africains', *Le Monde diplomatique* 505, April 1996.

Petty, Sheila, 'Whose Nation is it Anyhow? The Politics of Reading African Cinema in the West', in Fédération Panafricaine des Cinéastes (FEPACI), *L'Afrique et le centenaire du cinéma*. Présence Africaine, Paris, 1995.

Pfaff, Françoise, 'Hollywood's Diehard Jungle Melodramas', in Fédération Panafricaine des Cinéastes (FEPACI), *L'Afrique et le centenaire du cinéma*. Présence Africaine, Paris, 1995.

Poncelet, Marc, *Une utopie post-tiermondiste: La dimension culturelle du développement*. L'Harmattan, Paris, 1994.

Prédal, René, '*La Noire de...*: premier long métrage africain', *Cinémaction* 34 ('Sembène Ousmane'), 1985.

Ramonet, Ignacio, '*Yeelen* ou la magie des contes', *Le Monde diplomatique*, December 1987.

Ricard, Alain, *Littératures d'Afrique noire, des langues aux livres*. Karthala–CNRS, Paris, 1995.

Riss, Marie-Denise, *Femmes africaines en milieu rural*. L'Harmattan, Paris, 1989.

Rouch, Jean, 'Cartes postales', *Cinémaction* 26 ('Cinémas noirs d'Afrique'), 1981.

Ruiz, Raoul, *Politique du cinéma*. Éditions Dis Voir, Paris, 1995.

Sama, Emmanuel, 'Le Film africain étranger sur son propre territoire', *Écrans d'Afrique*, 4, second quarter, 1993.

Sembène, Ousmane, *Black Docker*, trans. Ros Schwartz. Heinemann, London, 1987.

Sembène, Ousmane, *God's Bits of Wood*, trans Francis Price. Heinemann, London/ Ibadan/Nairobi/Lusaka, 1970.

Sembène, Ousmane, *Niiwam and Taaw*, trans. Catherine Glenn-Lougha. Heinemann, London, 1992.

Senghor, Léopold Sédar, *Oeuvre Poétique*. Le Seuil, Paris, 1990.

Serceau, Daniel, '*Emitaï*: L'échec d'une transposition dramatique', *Cinémaction* 34 ('Sembène Ousmane'), 1985.

Serceau, Michel, 'Le cinéma d'Afrique noire francophone, face au modèle occidental: la rançon du refus', in Nwachukwu Frank Ukadike (ed.), *Iris, revue franco-américaine de théorie de l'image et du son* 18 ('New Discourses of African Cinema'), Spring 1995.

Sibony, Daniel, *Entre-deux, l'origine en partage*. Le Seuil, Paris, 1991.

Signaté, Ibrahima, *Med Hondo, un cinéaste rebelle*. Présence Africaine, Paris, 1994.

Somé, Valère D., *Thomas Sankara, l'espoir assassiné*. L'Harmattan, Paris, 1990.

Speciale, Alessandra, 'La triple galère des femmes africaines actrices', *Écrans d'Afrique* 7, first quarter, 1994.

Stoller, Paul, 'Artaud, Rouch et le cinéma de la cruauté', in C.W. Thompson, *L'Autre et le sacré, surréalisme, cinéma, ethnologie*, L'Harmattan, Paris, 1995.

Stoneman, Rod, 'Axe Sud–Sud... pour un cinéma fait par, avec et pour les Africains', *Écrans d'Afrique* 5–6, third and fourth quarters, 1993.

Ströter-Bender, Jutta, *L'Art contemporain dans les pays du 'Tiers-Monde'*, trans. Olivier Barlet. L'Harmattan, Paris, 1995.

Taguieff, Pierre-André, *La Force du préjugé: essai sur le racisme et ses doubles*. La Découverte, Paris, 1987.

Tapsoba, Clément, 'De l'orientation de la critique du cinéma africain', in Fédération Panafricaine des Cinéastes (FEPACI), *L'Afrique et le centenaire du cinéma*. Présence Africaine, Paris, 1995.

Taylor, Clyde, 'Les Grands axes et les sources africaines du nouveau cinema noir', *Cinémaction* 46 ('Le Cinéma noir américain'), 1988.

Teno, Jean-Marie, 'Liberté, le pouvoir de dire non', in *Cinéma et libertés*. Présence Africaine, Paris, 1993.

Tesson, Charles, 'Genèse', *Cahiers du Cinéma* 397, June 1987.

Thomas, Louis-Vincent, and Luneau, René, *La Terre africaine et ses religions*. L'Harmattan, Paris, 1975 (revised edition 1995).

Tierou, Alphonse, 'Danses d'Afrique', *Revue noire* 14, September 1994.

Tomaselli, Keyan, 'Le Cinéma sud-africain est-il tombé sur la tête?', *Cinémaction* 39, 1986.

Tomaselli, Keyan, *The Cinema of Apartheid*. Routledge, London, 1989.

Toubiana, Serge, 'Question de langage', *Cahiers du Cinéma* 486, December 1994.

Touré, Kitia, 'Les structures des films', *Cinémaction* 26, ('Cinémas noirs d'Afrique'), 1981.

Tutuola, Amos, *The Palm-Wine Drunkard*. Faber & Faber, London, 1952.

Tutuola, Amos, *My Life in the Bush of Ghosts*. Faber & Faber, London, 1964.

U Tam'si, Tchicaya, *Ces fruits si doux de l'arbre à pain*. Seghers, Paris, 1988.

U Tam'si, Tchicaya, *Les Cancrelats*. Albin Michel, Paris, 1980.

U Tam'si, Tchicaya, *Le Ventre*. Présence Africaine, Paris, 1978.

U Tam'si, Tchicaya, *Les Méduses ou les orties de mer*. Albin Michel, Paris, 1982.

Ukadike, Nwachukwu Frank, *Black African Cinema*. University of California Press, Berkeley/Los Angeles/London, 1994.

Ukadike, Nwachukwu Frank (ed.), *Iris, revue franco–américaine de théorie de l'image et du son* 18 ('New Discourses of African Cinema'), Spring 1995.

Vieyra, Paulin Soumanou, 'La Critique, la critique africaine et la critique de la critique', in *Réflexions d'un cinéaste africain*. OCIC, Paris, 1990.

Vieyra, Paulin Soumanou, *Le Cinéma africain des origines à 1973*. Présence Africaine, Paris, 1975.

Vieyra, Paulin Soumanou, *Sembène Ousmane cinéaste*. Présence Africaine, Paris, 1972.

Wallon, Dominique, 'L'Afrique et le cinéma', in Fédération Panafricaine des Cinéastes (FEPACI), *L'Afrique et le centenaire du cinéma*. Présence Africaine, Paris, 1995.

Wonogo, Zoumana, 'L'Epopée des Mossé pour restaurer l'histoire burkinabé et... consommer africain', *Écrans d'Afrique* 11, first quarter, 1995.

Wynchank, Anny, and Salazar, Philippe-Joseph, *Afriques imaginaires: regards réciproques et discours littéraires, 17ème–20ème siècles*. L'Harmattan, Paris, 1995.

Yaro, Lams, 'Bretelles d'accès aux autoroutes électroniques', in Fédération Panafricaine des Cinéastes (FEPACI), *L'Afrique et le centenaire du cinéma*. Présence Africaine, Paris, 1995.

Zimmer, Christian, *Cinéma et politique*. Seghers, Paris, 1974.

Zyl, John van, 'Une expérience: le Centre du Cinéma Direct', *Cinémaction* 39 ('Le Cinéma sud-africain est-il tombé sur la tête?'), 1986.

APPENDIX

WHERE TO SEE BLACK AFRICAN FILMS

The festivals listed here are devoted either wholly or largely to African cinema. Many international festivals also include African films, though they do not specialize in them. See also list on www.africultures.com.

FESTIVALS

January

Rencontres cinéma de Manosque (Hautes Alpes, France). A convivial event, very receptive to African film.
Hôtel de Ville, 04100 Manosque. Tel. (33 4) 92 70 34 07. Fax (33 4) 92 70 34 24. Email manosque-rencontres-cinema@wanadoo.fr.

Rotterdam Festival (Netherlands). General festival including many African films. Competition since 1996.
PO Box 21 696 3001 AR, Rotterdam. Tel. (31) 10 411 80 80. Fax (31) 10 890 90 91.

February

FESPACO (Festival Panafricain du Cinéma et de la Télévision de Ouagadougou: Ouagadougou). For amateur and professional alike, this is the event not to be missed. Biennial since 1969. Films from all over Africa are shown in all the cinemas of Ouagadougou, which goes into festive mood for the event. Exhibitions, debates, press conferences, seminars, cultural events, African products market. Competition, many awards. Also includes the International Market of African Television and Cinema (MICA).
01 BP 2505, Ouagadougou 01, Burkina Faso. Tel. (226) 30 75 38. Fax (226) 31 25 09. Email sg@fespaco.bf.

Pan African Film Festival (Los Angeles). Founded in 1992. Runs over twelve days with some fifty films from Africa and the diaspora. Also debates and meetings with university and school students.
PO Box 2418, Beverly Hills CA 90213, USA. Tel. (1 213) 295 1706. Fax (1 213) 295 1952.

Black International Cinema (Berlin – and also in Chicago, New York and Los Angeles). Cinema and video, conferences, exhibitions, shows. Held since 1986 in Berlin, over a period from February to May.
Fountainhead Tanz Theater, Tempelhofer Damm 52, 12101 Berlin, Germany. Tel./Fax (49 30) 786 34 66.

Festival international du court métrage de Clermont-Ferrand (France). Major short-film festival, which every other year includes a programme entitled 'Regards d'Afrique' devoted specifically to the African short film. Competition for feature-length films and shorts.
26 rue des Jacobins, 63000 Clermont-Ferrand. Tel. (33 4) 73 91 65 73. Fax (33 4) 73 92 11 93. Email info@clermont-filmfest.com.

Rencontres de Loudun Cinémas d'Afrique (Vienne, France). Biennale showing recent films, retrospectives, workshops for school and university students.
86120 Roiffé. Tel. (33 5) 49 98 77 79. Fax (33 5) 49 98 12 88.

March

Festival del cinema africano (Milan). Held since 1991. Some eighty films from Africa and the Caribbean. Also includes a retrospective, a themed section and a video section, together with round-table discussions involving cinema professionals. Feature-length and short fiction and documentary competition. Organized by the 'COE', which co-publishes the revue *Écrans d'Afrique* and organizes African cinema weeks in several Italian cities.
COE, via Lazarroni 8, 20124 Milano, Tel. (39 02) 669 62 58. Fax (39 02) 667 143 38. Email coe@io.it.

Rencontres du cinéma africain de Khourigba (Morocco). A biennial festival created in 1977, including film showings, round-table discussions, lectures and debates. Competition.
Municipalité de la ville de Khourigba, Morocco. Tel. (212 3) 49 34 04. Fax (212 3) 49 26 23.

Semaine de l'image (Lomé, Togo). This festival, inaugurated in 1996 and including film showings and discussions, aims to promote the television and cinema production of Togo.
Association pour la promotion de la culture, des arts et des loisirs, 71 avenue de la Libération, BP 300, Lomé, Togo. Tel. (228) 21 17 61.

Filmwelt Afrika (Berlin). Organized by the 'House of World Cultures', this is an important biennial retrospective stretching over several months, showing, among other things, the films from the previous year's FESPACO.
Haus der Kulturen der Welt, John-Foster Allee 10, D – 10557 Berlin. Tel. (49 30) 397 870. Fax (49 30) 394 86 79. Email film@hkw.de.

Cinéma du Réel (Paris). Documentaries. Africa is often included. Competition for feature-length films and shorts.

Centre Georges Pompidou, 19 rue Beaubourg, 75197 Paris Cedex 04. Tel. (33 1) 42 77 12 33. Fax (33 1) 42 77 72 41.

Festival des films de Fribourg (Fribourg). More than a hundred films from Asia, Africa and Latin America, a retrospective and an overview of a filmmaker or country, and a video section. In existence since 1980, with a 'Films du Sud' circuit organized throughout Switzerland. Competition for feature-length films and shorts, both fiction and documentary.

8 rue de Locarno, CH 1700 Fribourg, Switzerland. Tel. (41 26) 322 22 32. Fax (41 26) 322 79 50. Email info@fiff.ch.

April

Vues d'Afrique (Montreal). Founded in 1985. A great many (cinema and television) films from Africa and the creole countries shown, together with international documentaries on those countries, exhibitions, concerts, shows, lectures etc. Competition, with many awards.

67 rue Ste. Catherine Ouest, Montréal, Québec H2X 1Z7, Canada. Tel. (1 514) 284 33 22. Fax (1 514) 845 06 31. Email infos@vuesdafrique.org.

New York African Film Festival (USA). Held in the Lincoln Center and at the Brooklyn Museum, New York, and also in six American cities. Continues until June with showings of African film and public debates.

Film Society of Lincoln Center, Walter Reade Theater, 70 Lincoln Center Plaza, New York, NY 10023-6595, USA. Tel. (1 212) 243 25 22. Email nwaf@erols.com.

Africa Live (Frankfurt): biennale organized around African cinema by some twenty organizations.

Kommunales Kino des deutschen Filmmuseums, Schaumainkai 41, 60359 Frankfurt/Main. Tel. (49 69) 212 388 30. Fax (49 69) 212 378 81.

Festival des films de culture noire (Paris). Organized since 1993 by *Images d'ailleurs*, including films, debates, an exhibition and concerts. A different theme each year: in 1995, forty years of black cinema and the memory of black music; in 1996, black peoples in short films.

Images d'ailleurs, 1 rue de la Clef, 75005 Paris. Tel. (33 1) 47 63 74 00.

May

Africa Film Festival (Hanover). Biennale created in 1996, running over two months and including showings, lectures, children's events, all-night showings.

Afrika Initiative Hannover, Lister Meile 4, 30161 Hanover, Germany. Tel. (49 511) 75 37 73.

Jenseits von Europa (Cologne). Healthy representation of African films since 1992.

FilmInitiativ Köln e.V., Vor den Siebenburgen 32, 50676 Cologne, Germany. Tel. (49 221) 31 00 962. Fax (49 221) 31 00 963.

Cinémas d'Afrique (Angers, France). Projections, debates, workshop for African professionals, courses and workshops for schoolchildren, many exhibitions and lectures, African market. Audience prizes for feature-length and short films.
44 boulevard Henri Arnauld, 49100 Angers, France. Tel. (33 2) 41 20 08 22. Fax (33 2) 41 20 08 27.

Rencontres Médias Nord-Sud (Geneva): since 1983, a meeting place for the public and professionals in the television and media world. Competitions for independent and television films on development problems and North–South relations. Exhibition and conferences, debates, meetings with students.
c/o Télévision suisse romande, 20 quai Ernest-Ansermet, CH 1211 Geneva 8. Tel. (41 22) 708 81 93. Fax (41 22) 328 94 10.

Afrika Filmfestival of Leuven (Belgium). Convivial event.
Leuvensebaan 323, 3220 Holsbeek, Belgium. Tel. (32 2) 242 4341. Fax (32 2) 245 8583. Email guido.huysmans@skynet.be.

Ecrans noirs du cinéma francophone de Yaoundé (Cameroon), also in Douala, Libreville and Bangui.
Tel. (237) 21 49 41. Fax (237) 21 49 42. Email ta@iccnet.cm.

June

Recidak (Dakar). Founded in 1990. Films from Africa, round table discussions, conference for industry professionals, debate between directors and the public.
BP 10402, Dakar, Senegal. Tel : (221) 827 17 20.

Cinémas d'Afrique (Brussels). Held since 1994. A week of African films and a professional conference. Fiction and documentary competitions (feature-length and shorts).
Diaspora Productions, 46 boulevard Charlemagne, 1040 Brussels, Belgium. Tel. (32 2) 230 58 58. Fax (32 2) 280 16 85.

Vues sur les Docs (Marseille). Documentaries, including African ones. Competition.
3, Square Stalingrad, 13001 Marseille. Tel. (33 4) 95 04 44 90. Fax (33 4) 91 84 38 34.

July

Images of Africa (Copenhagen, Denmark). Cultural event devoted to Africa (concerts, shows, exhibitions, fashion shows, meetings and seminars, workshops, etc.), in which cinema and video have a considerable part. Spread over twenty other Danish towns and cities.
Copenhagen International Theater, Verstergade 8, DK 1456 Copenhagen, Denmark. Tel. (45 33) 15 15 64. Fax (45 33) 32 81 82. Email info@kit.dk.

Festival de Locarno (Switzerland). Large international festival, including a large amount of southern hemisphere cinema. Competition.
via Luini 3a, CH-6601 Locarno. Tel. (41 91) 756 2121. Fax (41 91) 756 2149. Email info@pardo.ch.

Festival of the Dhow Countries – Zanzibar International Film Festival (ZIFF)
PO Box 3032, 1st Floor, Old Fort Zanzibar, Tanzania, East Africa. Tel. (255) 54 233 135. Fax (255) 54 233 135. Email ziff@zanzibar.org.

August

Africa at the Pictures (London). African cinema biennale at the National Film Theatre and the regional cinemas of the British Film Institute.
38 King Street, London WC2E 8JT. Tel. (020) 7836 1973. Fax (020) 7836 1975.

Rencontres cinéma de Gindou (Lot). A convivial, free, open-air festival in a village near Cahors in the southwest of France, given over to African film every fourth year (1999, 2003 etc.).
46250 Gindou. Tel. (33 5) 65 22 89 99. Fax (33 5) 65 22 88 89. Email gindou.cinema @wanadoo.fr.

September

Africa in the Picture (Amsterdam). Biennial event on Africa and its diaspora, first held in 1980, presenting some eighty films and many other events (theatre, music, education, arts, information). Rialto Theatre, Amsterdam, and other cities.
Stichting Notorious Film, PO Box 17456, 1001 Amsterdam. Tel. (31 20) 625 24 23. Fax (31 20) 620 52 33.

South African Film Festival (Johannesburg and Capetown). The festival, jointly organized by the Film Resource Unit and the Weekly Mail and Guardian newspaper, also includes a television and video market.
Film Resource Unit, PO Box 11065, Johannesburg. Tel. (27 11) 83 8 4280/1/2. Fax (27 11) 83 8 445 1. Email fru@wn.apc.org.

Toronto International Film Festival. Has a permanent section on films from Africa and the diaspora.
Toronto International Film Festival, 2 Carlton Street, Suite 1600, Toronto ON, Canada M5B 1J3. Tel. (1 416) 967 73 7 1. Fax (1 416) 967 94 77. Email tiff@cossette.com.

Films from the South (Film fra Sor) Festival (Oslo). Twenty-five films exclusively from Africa, Asia and Latin America, seminars and meetings.
Fredensborgveien 39, N-0177 Oslo, Norway. Tel. (47) 22 36 07 18. Fax (47) 22 36 22 80. Email paracho@c2i.net.

Project Black Cinema (Sarasota, Florida). Held since 1992. Films from black Africa and the diaspora.
Tel. (1 813) 957 79 44.

Festival international du Film francophone (Namur, Belgium). A large number of francophone films from forty-seven countries. Round-table discussion on African cinema. Feature-length and short competitions for both fiction and documentaries.
175 rue des Brasseurs, 5000 Namur. Tel. (32 81) 24 12 36. Fax (32 81) 24 11 64. Email fiff@skynet.be.

October

Journées cinématographiques de Carthage (Tunisia). African biennial, alternating with the FESPACO. Mainly Arabic films. International film market, retrospectives, overviews, conferences, seminars and lectures, project workshops. Competition, many awards.

2 rue du Kenya, 1002 Tunis. Tel. (216 1) 287 776 or 892 668. Fax (216 1) 786 336.

Southern African Film Festival (Harare). African biennial, including a competition, retrospectives and round-table discussions between industry professionals. With Ouagadougou and Carthage, the third Panafrican festival on the continent. Competition.

1st floor, Pax House, 89 Union Ave, PO Box CY724, Causeway, Harare, Zimbabwe. Tel. (263 4) 791 156. Fax (263 4) 704 227. Email saff@zimsurf.co.zw.

November

Contemporary African Diaspora Film Festival (New York). Held since 1993. Films from all over the independent African diaspora.

Artmattan Productions, 535 Cathedral Parkway, Ste 14B, New York, NY 10025. Tel. (1 212) 749 60 20.

Festival international du film d'Amiens (France). Created in 1980, showing some thirty African films, with 'homages', retrospectives and a film market. Feature-length and short competition. Since 1991, the festival has published the revue *Le Film Africain*.

c/o MCA, place Léon Gontier, 8000 Amiens. Tel. (33 3) 22 71 35 70. Email amiensfilmfestival @burotec.fr.

Festival des trois continents (Nantes). Founded in 1979. Exclusively devoted to southern cinema. Large audience. Retrospectives on a director or a country. Feature-length fiction competition.

BP 44033, Nantes Cedex 01, France. Tel. (33 2) 40 69 09 73. Fax (33 2) 40 73 55 22.

Black Movie (Geneva). Founded in 1990. A festival built around some fifty contemporary films from Africa, which also includes theatre, music and an exhibition.

5 rue du Temple, 1201 Geneva, Switzerland. Tel./Fax (41 22) 738 1450. Email blackmovie @ssg.ch.

Cinemafrica (Zurich). Biennial since 1987. Film showings centred on an individual theme. Complemented by concerts, literary evenings, lectures and meetings.

Filmpodium de la ville de Zurich, Postfach 8022, Zurich, Switzerland. Tel. (41 1) 383 04 08. Fax (41 1) 451 43 66.

Au Sud du Sud (Marseille). Platform for African arts, in which cinema has had a growing presence.

Association Sarev, 13 rue des trois mages, 13001 Marseille, France. Tel. (33 4) 91 42 20 50. Fax (33 4) 91 42 16 18. Email sarev@easynet.fr.

Rencontres cinématographiques de Lille. Organized by the literacy festival Fest'Africa.
Arts et médias d'Afrique, 9/2 petite rue de l'Alma, résidence Alma Jacquet, 59800 Lille, France. Tel. (33 3) 20 06 21 59. Email festafrica@nordnet.fr.

Southern African International Film and Television Market (Sithengi, South Africa). Meeting of professionals and screening of films in competition.
Tel. (27 21) 430 8204. Fax (27 21) 430 8186. Email md@sithengi.co.za.

December

Festival Noir tout couleur (Guadeloupe).
Tel. (33 5) 90 94 02 97. Fax (33 5) 90 94 13 83.

OTHER RESOURCES

In Paris, take a good look at the programme of the **Images d'ailleurs** cinema (1 rue de la Clef, 75005 Paris. Tel. (33 1) 45 87 18 09. The events organized by this cinema and its general programme are mainly orientated towards black film.

Videos can be bought and hired from the **Médiathèque des trois mondes** (63 bis, rue du Cardinal Lemoine, 75005 Paris. Tel. (33 1) 43 54 33 38. Fax (33 1) 46 34 70 19. Catalogue on demand.

French associations and sociocultural organizations can borrow 16 and 35 mm films or videos from **Audecam**, the mediatheque of the Ministry of Co-operation (Les Patios St Jacques, 6 rue Ferrus, 75683 Paris Cedex 14. Tel. (33 1) 43 13 11 15. Fax (33 1) 43 13 11 16. This has a stock of some 500 films from French- and Portuguese-speaking African countries. Catalogue on demand.

The 'Cinémathèque africaine' of Ouagadougou, first opened in 1995, aims to ensure the permanent availability of African cinema. It is committed to the collection, conservation and distribution of films, documents and archives produced in Africa or relating to African production.

Lastly, the *Dictionnaire Les Cinémas d'Afrique* produced by the Association des Trois Mondes (Karthala, Paris, 2000) is an excellent resource listing the names of all distributors of African film.

INDEX

paradox, use of, 175–8
Parks, Gordon, *Solomon Northrup's Odyssey*
    (1980), 56
parody in film, 138–41
Partant, François, 94
Pathé company, 252
Pathé-Actualités, 25
Patry, Lucien, 25, 72, 242
Peck, Raoul: *Lumumba, la mort d'un prophéte*
    (1992), 13; *Lumumba, retour au Congo*, 13
Van Peebles, Melvin, 113; *Sweet Sweetback's
    Badass Song* (1971), 112
Petty, Sheila, 212
Peyrière, Marie-Christine, 68
Pfaff, Françoise, 210
Phiri, Joel, 243–4, 281
Pimenta, Pedro, 281
piracy of film, 284; restraining of, 239
Pohland, Hans Jürgen, *Bullfrog in the Sun*, 24
Pollack, Sidney, *Out of Africa* (1985), 54
polygamy, 101, 103, 135, 175, 222
Polygram company, 254
Popular Movement for the Liberation of
    Angola (MPLA), 20
pornography, 246
Portuguese colonialism, 19
post-production, costs of, 226
poverty in Africa, 14
practical problems of filming in Africa, 223
privatization of cinemas, 237
production, tribulations of, 229–30
professionalization, 264–6, 271
professionals, Northern, 267
proverbs, 37, 47–71 *passim*, 85, 264, 274, 283,
    285
pygmies, 161

race, concept of, development of, 4
Radio France Internationale (RFI), 279
Raeburn, Michael, 184
Ragosin, Lionel, *Come Back Africa* (1959), 110
Rajaonarivelo, Raymond, 121, 153, 159, 200,
    267; *Tabataba* (1987), 85, 159
Ramaka, Joseph Gaye, 8–9, 83, 118, 123, 137,
    286; *So be it*, 281; *Le Train bleu*, 193–4
Rampolokeng, Lesego, 111
rape, 75
Rappenau, Jean-Paul *Le Hussard sur le toit*, 227
Rawlings, Jerry, 280
realism, 213
Recidak festival, 258
recolonization, proposition of, 49
Resnais, Alain, 153; *Les Statues meurent aussi*
    (1955), 22, 153
Revue noire, 77
Ribeiro, Joao, *The Gaze of the Stars*, 281
Richard, Christian, *Gandaogo/Le Courage des*

autres (1987), 57
Rossellini, Roberto, 123, 143
Rouch, Jean, 6–8, 23, 28, 138; *Les Maîtres fous*
    (1958), 8; *Moi, un Noir* (1957), 7, 36; *Petit à
    petit* (1968), 117
Rozanes, Alain, 255
Rundle, Donne, *My Vote is My Secret* (1994), 29
Russia, 121, 122
Rwanda, 4, 57; genocide in, 9

Sabela, Simon, *U-Deliwe* (1975), 110
Sabriya series (Tunisia), 281
sacrifices, 157, 158
Samb Makharam, Ababacar, 27, 158, 164, 171,
    178; *Et la neige n'était plus* (1965), 228; *Jom ou
    l'histoire d'un peuple* (1981), 14–15, 164, 228;
    Kodou (1971), 75–6, 87, 158, 228
Sanga, Fatima, 173
Sankara, Thomas, 14, 98, 227
Sankofa, 48
Sankofa collective (London), 116
Sanogo, Niamanto, 100
Sarr, Ismaïla, 222
de Saussure, Ferdinand, 154
Savané, Naky Sy, 68, 206, 207
Schelling, Flora M'Bugu, *These Hands* (1992),
    192
Schmitz, Oliver: *Johannesburg Stories* (1997), 111;
    Mapantsula (1988), 110
Schweitzer, Albert, 48–9
self, revolt of, 42
Sembène Ousmane, 8, 21, 27, 39, 43, 58, 62,
    72–3, 97, 156, 158, 164, 165, 166, 172, 176,
    177, 188, 199, 212; *Black Girl* (1996), 45,
    156, 166; *Borom Sarret*, 72–3, 164, 166; *Camp
    de Thiaroye* (1988), 49; *Ceddo* (1977), 176; *Le
    Docker noir*, 16; *Emitaï* (1971), 158, 172–3;
    God's Bits of Wood, 16, 37; *Guelwaar* (1991),
    73; *Mandabi/The Money Order* (1968), 15, 21,
    267; *Niaye*, 34, 37–8; *Xala* (1974), 16–17, 37,
    200
Senegal, 16, 49, 137, 233, 237, 271, 279;
    cinemas closed, 238
Senghor, Léopold Sédar, 3, 183, 184, 197
La Sept-Arte, 286
Sept-Cinéma, 226
Serceau, Daniel, 214
Serceau, Michel, 213
Seven Songs for Malcolm X (1992), 115
Sevenzo, Farai, *The Last Picture*, 281
sexuality, 104, 105, 113
Seydoux, Nicolas, 252
Shabazz, Menelik, *Burning an Illusion* (1981),
    116
Shelen, Brendan, *Kulba na Barna*, 225
Sibony, Daniel, 97, 120
Sinclair, Ingrid, *Flame* (1996), 53, 225

Franklin Pierce College Library

00132432

DATE DUE

GAYLORD

PRINTED IN U.S.A.